Full Color on Every Page!

Microsoft®

Excel 97

Simplified™

IDG's 3-D Visual™ Series

IDG BOOKS

From maranGraphics™

IDG Books Worldwide, Inc.
An International Data Group Company
Foster City, CA • Indianapolis • Chicago • Dallas

Microsoft® Excel 97 Simplified™

Published by
IDG Books Worldwide, Inc.
An International Data Group Company
919 E. Hillsdale Blvd., Suite 400
Foster City, CA 94404

Library of Congress Catalog Card No.:
ISBN: 0-7645-6022-0

Printed in the United States of America
10 9 8 7

XX/XX/XX/XX/XX

Distributed in the United States by IDG Books Worldwide, Inc.

Distributed by Transworld Publishers Limited in the United Kingdom and Europe; by WoodsLane Pty. Ltd. for Australia; by WoodsLane Enterprises Ltd. for New Zealand; by Longman Singapore Publishers Ltd. for Singapore, Malaysia, Thailand, and Indonesia; by Simron Pty. Ltd. for South Africa; by Toppan Company Ltd. for Japan; by Distribuidora Cuspide for Argentina; by Livraria Cultura for Brazil; by Ediciencia S.A. for Ecuador; by Addison-Wesley Publishing Company for Korea; by Ediciones ZETA S.C.R. Ltda. for Peru; by WS Computer Publishing Company, Inc., for the Philippines; by Unalis Corporation for Taiwan; by Contemporanea de Ediciones for Venezuela. Authorized Sales Agent: Anthony Rudkin Associates for the Middle East and North Africa.

For general information on IDG Books Worldwide's books in the U.S., please call our Consumer Customer Service department at 800-762-2974. For reseller information, including discounts and premium sales, please call our Reseller Customer Service department at 800-434-3422.

For information on where to purchase IDG Books Worldwide's books outside the U.S., please contact our International Sales department at 415-655-3023 or fax 415-655-3299.

For information on foreign language translations, please contact our Foreign & Subsidiary Rights department at 415-655-3021 or fax 415-655-3281.

For sales inquiries and special prices for bulk quantities, please contact our Sales department at 415-655-3200 or write to the address above.

For information on using IDG Books Worldwide's books in the classroom or for ordering examination copies, please contact our Educational Sales department at 800-434-2086 or fax 817-251-8174.

For press review copies, author interviews, or other publicity information, please contact our Public Relations department at 415-655-3000 or fax 415-655-3299.

For authorization to photocopy items for corporate, personal, or educational use, please contact Copyright Clearance Center, 222 Rosewood Drive, Danvers, MA 01923, or fax 508-750-4470.

Trademark Acknowledgments

The animated characters are the copyright of maranGraphics, Inc.

U.S. Corporate Sales
Contact maranGraphics at (800) 469-6616 or Fax (905) 890-9434.

U.S. Trade Sales
Contact IDG Books at (800) 434-3422 or (415) 655-3000.

Welcome to the world of IDG Books Worldwide.

IDG Books Worldwide, Inc., is a subsidiary of International Data Group, the world's largest publisher of computer-related information and the leading global provider of information services on information technology. IDG was founded more than 25 years ago and now employs more than 8,500 people worldwide. IDG publishes more than 270 computer publications in over 75 countries (see listing below). More than 90 million people read one or more IDG publications each month.

Launched in 1990, IDG Books Worldwide is today the #1 publisher of best-selling computer books in the United States. We are proud to have received eight awards from the Computer Press Association in recognition of editorial excellence and three from Computer Currents' First Annual Readers' Choice Awards. Our best-selling ...For Dummies® series has more than 25 million copies in print with translations in 30 languages. IDG Books Worldwide, through a joint venture with IDG's Hi-Tech Beijing, became the first U.S. publisher to publish a computer book in the People's Republic of China. In record time, IDG Books Worldwide has become the first choice for millions of readers around the world who want to learn how to better manage their businesses.

Our mission is simple: Every one of our books is designed to bring extra value and skill-building instructions to the reader. Our books are written by experts who understand and care about our readers. The knowledge base of our editorial staff comes from years of experience in publishing, education, and journalism - experience which we use to produce books for the '90s. In short, we care about books, so we attract the best people. We devote special attention to details such as audience, interior design, use of icons, and illustrations. And because we use an efficient process of authoring, editing, and desktop publishing our books electronically, we can spend more time ensuring superior content and spend less time on the technicalities of making books.

You can count on our commitment to deliver high-quality books at competitive prices on topics you want to read about. At IDG Books Worldwide, we continue in the IDG tradition of delivering quality for more than 25 years. You'll find no better book on a subject than one from IDG Books Worldwide.

John Kilcullen
President and CEO
IDG Books Worldwide, Inc.

IDG Books Worldwide, Inc., is a subsidiary of International Data Group, the world's largest publisher of computer-related information and the leading global provider of information services on information technology. International Data Group publishes over 276 computer publications in over 75 countries. Ninety million people read one or more International Data Group publications each month. International Data Group's publications include: Argentina: Annuario de Informatica, Computerworld Argentina, PC World Argentina; Australia: Australian Macworld, Client/Server Journal, Computer Living, Computerworld, Computerworld 100, Digital News, IT Casebook, Network World, On-line World Australia, PC World, Publishing Essentials, Reseller, WebMaster; Austria: Computerwelt Osterreich, Networks Austria, PC Tip; Belarus: PC World Belarus; Belgium: Data News; Brazil: Annuário de Informática, Computerworld Brazil, Connections, Super Game Power, Macworld, PC Player, PC World Brazil, Publish Brazil, Reseller News; Bulgaria: Computerworld Bulgaria, Networkworld/Bulgaria, PC & MacWorld Bulgaria; Canada: CIO Canada, Client/Server World, ComputerWorld Canada, InfoCanada, Network World Canada; Chile: Computerworld Chile, PC World Chile; Colombia: Computerworld Colombia, PC World Colombia; Costa Rica: PC World Centro America; The Czech and Slovak Republics: Computerworld Czechoslovakia, Elektronika Czechoslovakia, Macworld Czech Republic, PC World Czechoslovakia; Denmark: Communications World, Computerworld Danmark, Macworld Danmark, PC Privat Danmark, PC World Danmark, PC World Danmark Supplements, TECH World; Dominican Republic: PC World Republica Dominicana; Ecuador: PC World Ecuador; Egypt: Computerworld Middle East, PC World Middle East; El Salvador: PC World Centro America; Finland: MikroPC, Tietoverkko, Tietoviikko; France: Distributique, Golden, Hebdo-Distributique, Info PC, Le Guide du Monde Informatique, Le Monde Informatique, Reseaux & Telecoms; Germany: Computer Partner, Computerwoche, Computerwoche Extra, Computerwoche Focus, I/M Information Management, Macwelt, PC Welt; Greece: GamePro, Multimedia World; Guatemala: PC World Centro America; Honduras: PC World Centro America; Hong Kong: Computerworld Hong Kong, PCWorld Hong Kong, Publish in Asia; Hungary: ABCD CD-ROM, Computerworld Szamitastechnika, PC & Mac World Hungary, PC-X Magazine; Iceland: Tolvuheimur/PC World Island; India: Information Systems Computerworld, PC World India, Publish in Asia; Indonesia: InfoKomputer PC World, Komputek Computerworld, Publish in Asia; Ireland: ComputerScope, PC Live!; Israel: People & Computers; Italy: Computerworld Italia, Computerworld Italia Special Editions, Macworld Italia, Networking Italia, PC Shopping, PC World Italia, PC World/Walt Disney; Japan: DTP World, HP Open World Japan, Macworld Japan, Nikkei Personal Computing, Open World Japan, OS/2 World Japan, SunWorld Japan, Windows World Japan; Kenya: East African Computer News; Korea: Hi-Tech Information/Computerworld, Macworld Korea, PC World Korea; Macedonia: PC World Macedonia; Malaysia: Computerworld Malaysia, PC World Malaysia, Publish in Asia; Mexico: Computerworld Mexico, Macworld, PC World Mexico; Myanmar: PC World Myanmar; Netherlands: Computer! Totaal, LAN Magazine, LanWorld Buyers Guide, Macworld, Net Magazine, Totaal! Beurskrant; New Zealand: Absolute Beginner's Guide, Computer Buyer, Computer Industry Directory, Computerworld New Zealand, MTB, Network World, PC World New Zealand; Nicaragua: PC World Centro America; Nigeria: PC World Nigeria; Norway: Computerworld Norge, Computerworld Privat (Datamagasinet), CW Rapport Norge, IDG's KURSGUIDE, Macworld Norge, Multimediaworld, PC World Ekspress, PC World Nettverk, PC World Norge, PC World's Produktguide, Windows World Spesial; Pakistan: Computerworld Pakistan, PC World Pakistan; Panama: PC World Panama; P. R. of China: China Computer Users, China Computerworld, China Infoworld, China Telecom World Weekly, Computer & Communication, Electronic Design China, Electronics Today, Electronics Weekly, Game Camp, Game Soft, Network World China, PC World China, Popular Computer Weekly, Software Weekly, Software World, Telecom World; Peru: Computerworld Peru, PC World Profesional Peru, PC World Peru; Poland: Computerworld Poland, Computerworld Special Report, Macworld, Networld, PC World Komputer; Philippines: Computerworld Philippines, PC World Philippines, Publish in Asia; Portugal: Cerebro/PC World, Computerworld/Correio Informático, Dealer World Portugal, Mac*In/PC*In, Multimedia World Portugal; Puerto Rico: PC World Puerto Rico; Romania: Computerworld Romania, PC World Romania, Telecom Romania; Russia: Computerworld Russia, Mir PK, Sety; Singapore: Computerworld Singapore, PC World Singapore, Publish in Asia; Slovenia: MONITOR; South Africa: Computing S.A., InfoWorld S.A., Network World S.A., Software World; Spain: Computerworld Espa-a, COMUNICACIONES WORLD, Dealer World, Macworld Espa-a, PC World Espa-a; Sweden: CAP&Design, Computer Sweden, Corporate Computing, MacWorld, Maxi Data, MikroDatorn, Nätverk & Kommunikation, PC/Aktiv, PC World, Windows World; Switzerland: Computerworld Schweiz, Macworld Schweiz, PCtip; Taiwan: Computerworld Taiwan, Macworld Taiwan, PC World Taiwan, Publish Taiwan, Windows World; Thailand: Thai Computerworld, Publish in Asia; Turkey: Computerworld Turkiye, MACWORLD Turkiye, PC WORLD Turkiye; Ukraine: Computerworld Kiev, Computers & Software, Multimedia World Ukraine, PC World Ukraine; United Kingdom: Acorn User, Amiga Action, Amiga Computing, Appletalk, Computing, GamePro, Macworld, Network News, Parents and Computers, PC Advisor, PC Home, PSX Pro UK, The WEB; United States: Cable in the Classroom, CD Review, CIO Magazine, Computerworld, Computerworld Client/Server Journal, Digital Video Magazine, DOS World, Federal Computer Week, GamePro, InfoWorld, I-Way, JavaWorld, Macworld, Multimedia World, Netscape World Online, Network World, PC Entertainment, PC World, Publish, SunWorld Online, SWATPro Magazine, Video Event, WebMaster; Uruguay: PC World Uruguay; Venezuela: Computerworld Venezuela, PC World Venezuela; and Vietnam: PC World Vietnam.

Every maranGraphics book represents the extraordinary vision and commitment of a unique family: the Maran family of Toronto, Canada.

Back Row (from left to right): *Sherry Maran, Rob Maran, Richard Maran, Maxine Maran, Jill Maran.*
Front Row (from left to right): *Judy Maran, Ruth Maran.*

Richard Maran is the company founder and its inspirational leader. He developed maranGraphics' proprietary communication technology called "visual grammar." This book is built on that technology—empowering readers with the easiest and quickest way to learn about computers.

Ruth Maran is the Author and Architect—a role Richard established that now bears Ruth's distinctive touch. She creates the words and visual structure that are the basis for the books.

Judy Maran is the Project Coordinator. She works with Ruth, Richard and the highly talented maranGraphics illustrators, designers and editors to transform Ruth's material into its final form.

Rob Maran is the Technical and Production Specialist. He makes sure the state-of-the-art technology used to create these books always performs as it should.

Sherry Maran manages the Reception, Order Desk and any number of areas that require immediate attention and a helping hand.

Jill Maran is a jack-of-all-trades and dynamo who fills in anywhere she's needed anytime she's back from university.

Maxine Maran is the Business Manager and family sage. She maintains order in the business and family—and keeps everything running smoothly.

Oh, and three other family members are seated on the sofa. These graphic disk characters help make it fun and easy to learn about computers. They're part of the extended maranGraphics family.

Credits

Author & Architect:
Ruth Maran

Copy Development & Screen Captures:
Brad Hilderley
Alison MacAlpine

Project Coordinator:
Judy Maran

Proofreaders:
Wanda Lawrie
Peter Lejcar
Tina Veltri
Carol Barclay

Layout Designers:
Christie Van Duin
Tamara Poliquin

Illustrations & Screens:
Chris K.C. Leung
Russell Marini
Ben Lee
Jeff Jones

Indexer:
Kelleigh Wing

Post Production:
Robert Maran

Acknowledgments

Thanks to the dedicated staff of maranGraphics, including Carol Barclay, Jamie Bell, Francisco Ferreira, Brad Hilderley, Jeff Jones, Wanda Lawrie, Ben Lee, Peter Lejcar, Chris K.C. Leung, Alison MacAlpine, Michael W. MacDonald, Jill Maran, Judy Maran, Maxine Maran, Robert Maran, Sherry Maran, Russ Marini, Tamara Poliquin, Christie Van Duin, Tina Veltri, Paul Whitehead and Kelleigh Wing.

Finally, to Richard Maran who originated the easy-to-use graphic format of this guide. Thank you for your inspiration and guidance.

TABLE OF CONTENTS

CHAPTER 1

Getting Started

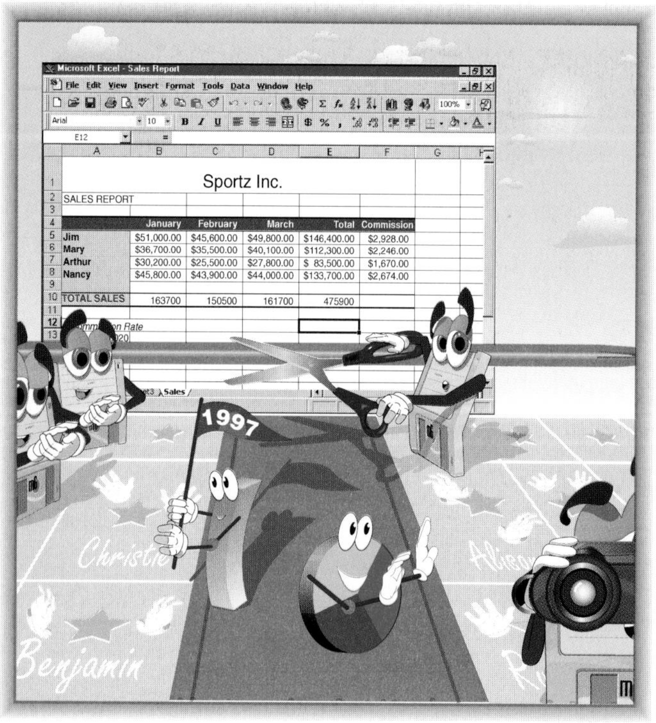

CHAPTER 2

Save and Open Your Workbooks

CHAPTER 3

Edit Your Worksheets

CHAPTER 4

Work with Formulas and Functions

TABLE OF CONTENTS

CHAPTER 5

Change Your Screen Display

CHAPTER 6

Format Your Worksheets

CHAPTER 7

Print Your Worksheets

CHAPTER 8

Work with Multiple Worksheets

TABLE OF CONTENTS

CHAPTER 9

Work with Charts

CHAPTER 10

Work with Graphics

CHAPTER 11

Manage Data in a List

CHAPTER 12

Excel and the Internet

Microsoft Excel - Sales Report
File Edit View Insert Format Tools Data Window Help
Arial
10
100%
E12
Sportz Inc.
SALES REPORT
January February March Total Commission
Jim $51,000.00 $45,600.00 $49,800.00 $146,400.00 $2,928.00
Mary $36,700.00 $35,500.00 $40,100.00 $112,300.00 $2,246.00
Arthur $30,200.00 $25,500.00 $27,800.00 $ 83,500.00 $1,670.00
Nancy $45,800.00 $43,900.00 $44,000.00 $133,700.00 $2,674.00
TOTAL SALES 163700 150500 161700 475900
Sales
1997
Christie
Benjamin

CHAPTER 1

GETTING STARTED

Are you ready to begin using Microsoft Excel 97? This chapter will help you get started.

INTRODUCTION

Editing

Excel lets you efficiently enter and edit data in your worksheets.

Formatting

There are many features in Excel that help you enhance the appearance of your worksheets.

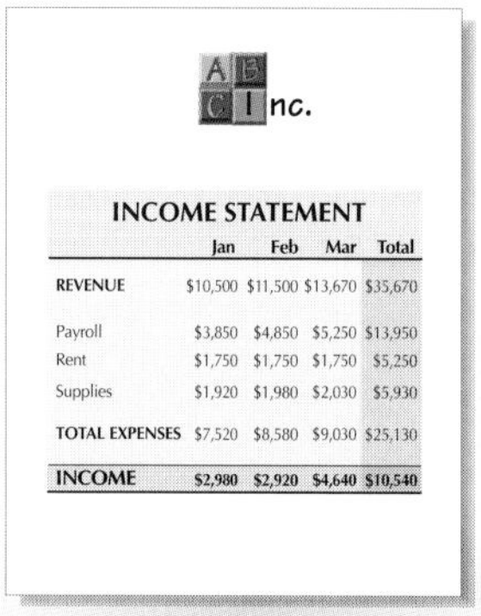

ABC Inc.

INCOME STATEMENT

	Jan	Feb	Mar	Total
REVENUE	$10,500	$11,500	$13,670	$35,670
Payroll	$3,850	$4,850	$5,250	$13,950
Rent	$1,750	$1,750	$1,750	$5,250
Supplies	$1,920	$1,980	$2,030	$5,930
TOTAL EXPENSES	$7,520	$8,580	$9,030	$25,130
INCOME	$2,980	$2,920	$4,640	$10,540

Formulas and Functions

Excel provides powerful tools to calculate and analyze data in your worksheets.

Charts

Excel helps you create colorful charts from your worksheet data.

Graphics

Excel comes with many types of graphics that you can use to enhance the appearance of your worksheets and charts.

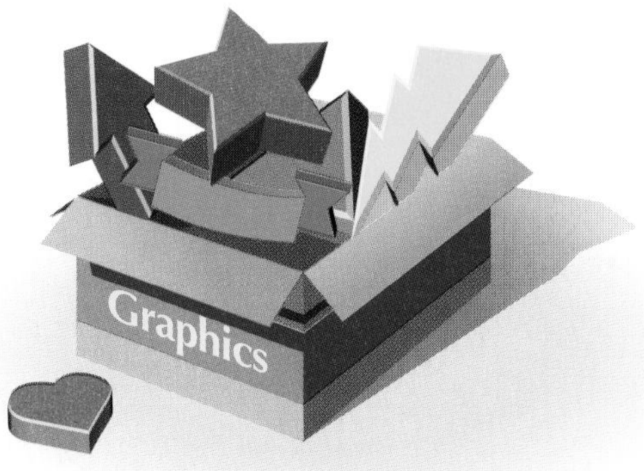

Managing Data in a List

Excel provides powerful tools that allow you to easily manage and analyze a large collection of information.

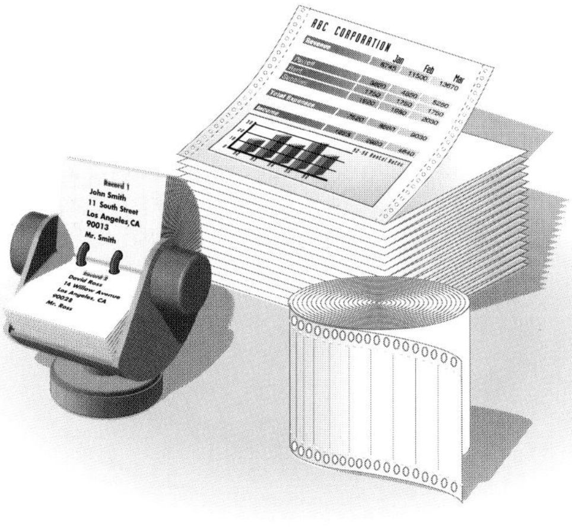

The Internet

Excel offers features that help you take advantage of the Internet. You can make worksheets you create available on your company's intranet or the Web.

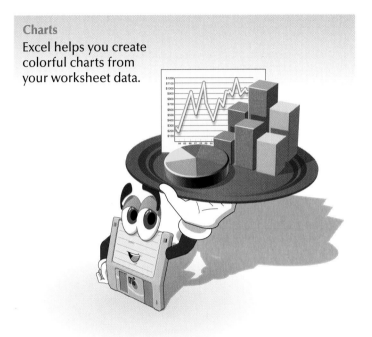

USING THE MOUSE

A mouse is a hand-held device that lets you select and move items on your screen.

Holding the Mouse

Resting your hand on the mouse, use your thumb and two rightmost fingers to move the mouse on your desk. Use your two remaining fingers to press the mouse buttons.

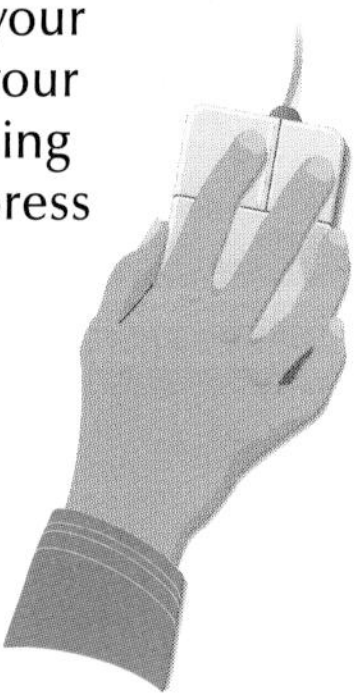

Moving the Mouse

When you move the mouse on your desk, the mouse pointer on your screen moves in the same direction.

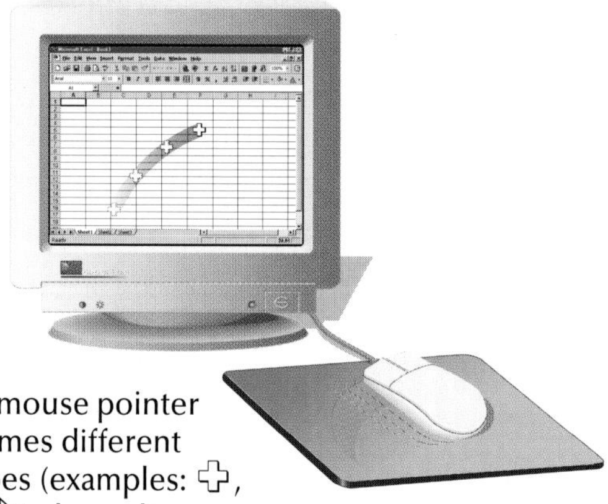

The mouse pointer assumes different shapes (examples: ✥, I or ↖), depending on its location on your screen and the task you are performing.

Cleaning the Mouse

A ball under the mouse senses movement. You should occasionally remove and clean this ball to ensure smooth motion of the mouse.

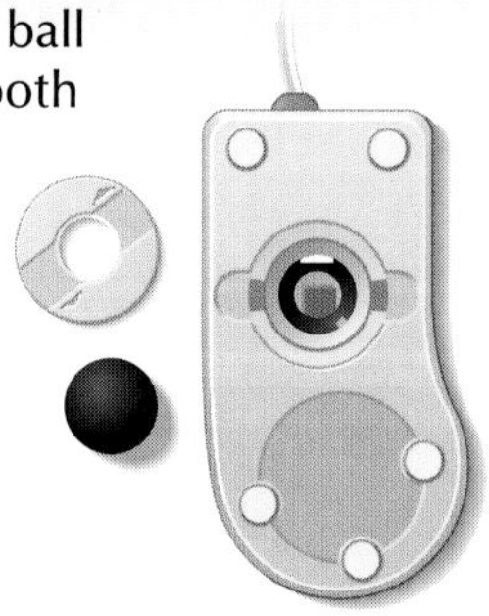

MOUSE ACTIONS

Click

Press and release the left mouse button.

Double-Click

Quickly press and release the left mouse button twice.

Drag and Drop

Move the mouse pointer ( ) over an object on your screen and then press and hold down the left mouse button. Still holding down the mouse button, move the mouse to where you want to place the object and then release the mouse button.

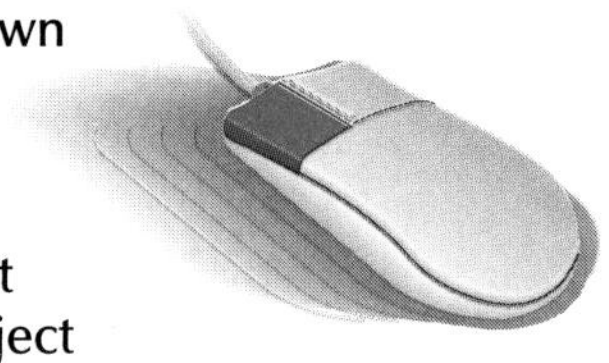

MICROSOFT INTELLIMOUSE

The new Microsoft IntelliMouse has a wheel between the left and right mouse buttons. Moving this wheel lets you quickly scroll through information on your screen.

You can also zoom in or out with the Microsoft IntelliMouse by holding down Ctrl on your keyboard as you move the wheel.

START EXCEL

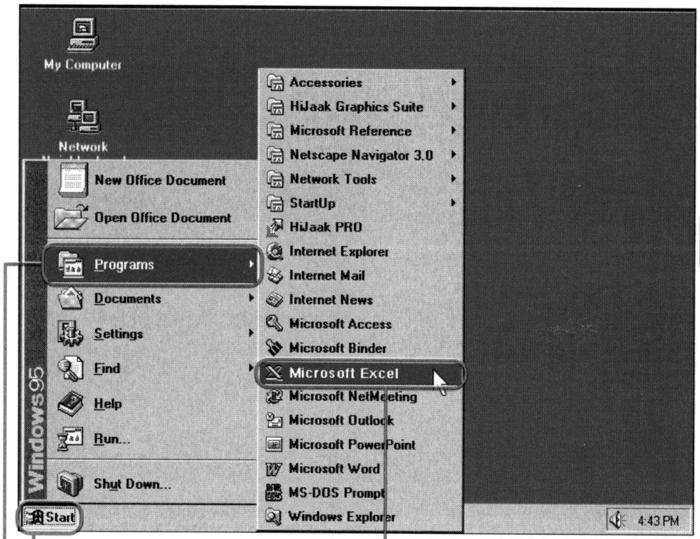

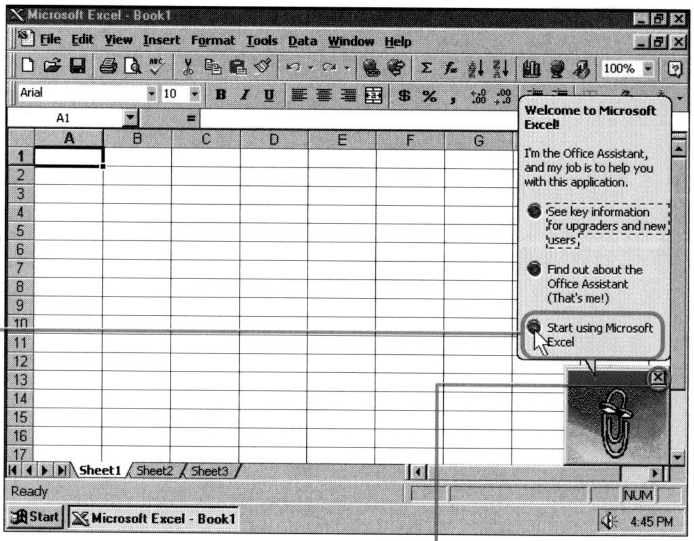

1 Move the mouse over **Start** and then press the left mouse button.

2 Move the mouse over **Programs**.

3 Move the mouse over **Microsoft Excel** and then press the left mouse button.

■ The **Microsoft Excel** window appears, displaying a blank worksheet.

■ If you are starting Excel for the first time, the Office Assistant welcome appears.

4 To start using Excel, move the mouse over this option and then press the left mouse button.

■ To hide the Office Assistant, move the mouse over ☒ and then press the left mouse button.

Note: For more information on the Office Assistant, refer to page 20.

THE EXCEL SCREEN

Menu Bar
Contains commands that let you perform tasks.

Toolbars
Contain buttons to help you quickly select common commands.

Formula Bar
Displays the cell reference and contents of the active cell.

Status Bar
Displays information about the task you are performing.

Worksheet Tabs
An Excel file is called a workbook. Each workbook is divided into several worksheets. Excel displays a tab for each worksheet.

A workbook is similar to a three-ring binder that contains several sheets of paper.

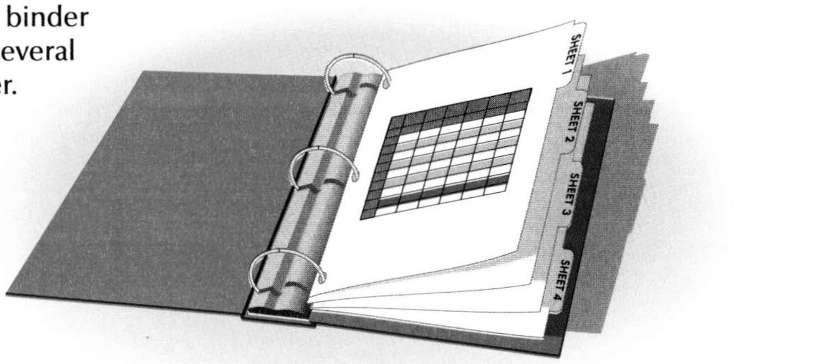

WORKSHEET BASICS

A worksheet consists of rows, columns and cells.
COLUMN
CELL
ROW

ROWS, COLUMNS AND CELLS

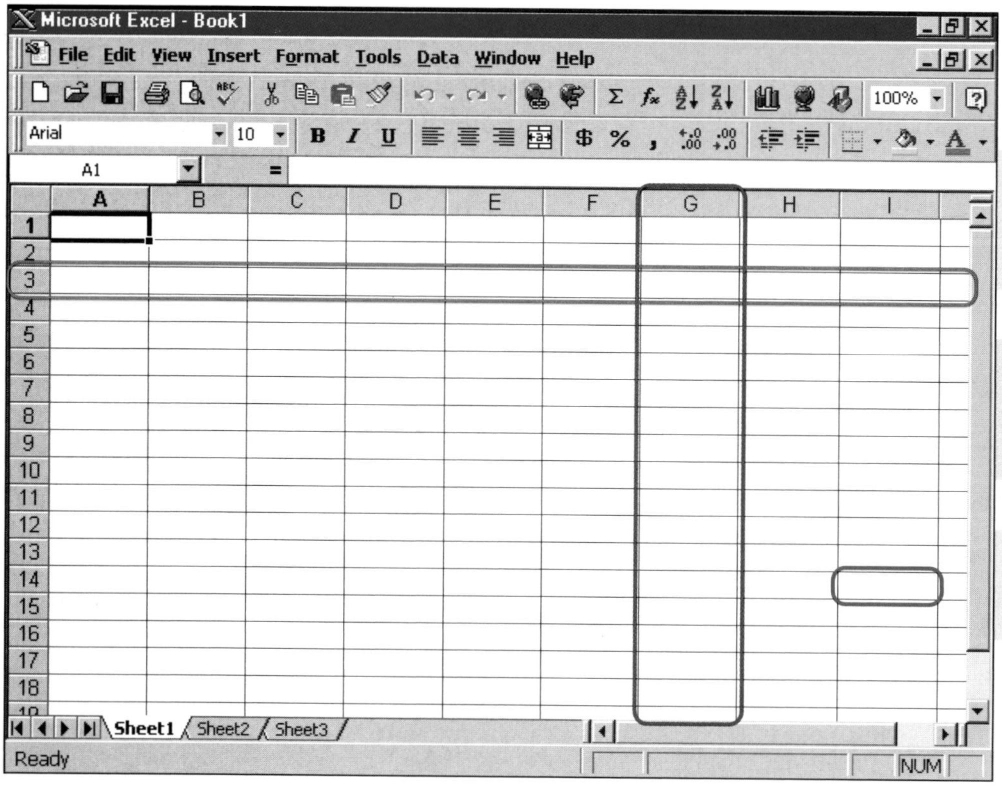

Row

A horizontal line of boxes. A number identifies each row.

Column

A vertical line of boxes. A letter identifies each column.

Cell

One box in a worksheet.

You enter information into the active cell in your worksheet.

THE ACTIVE CELL

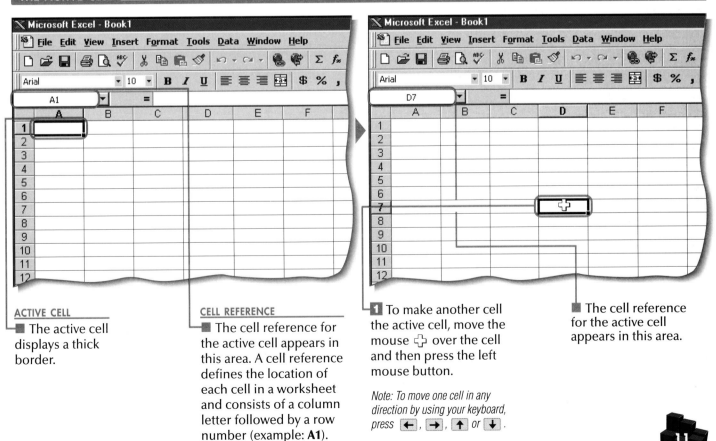

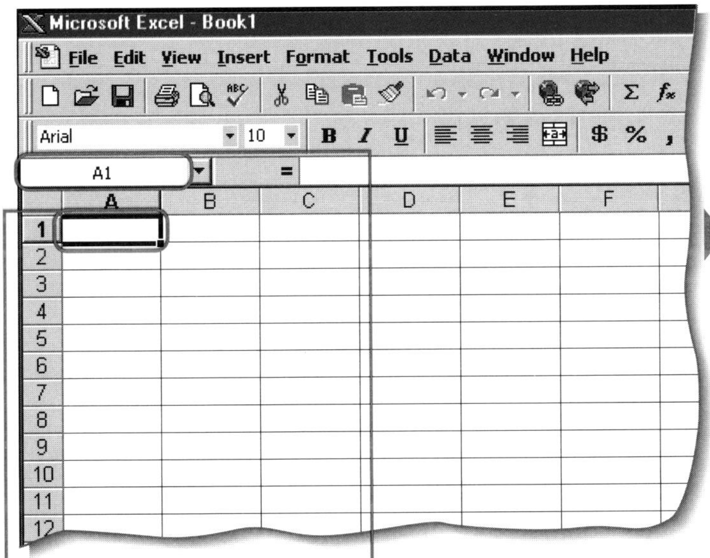

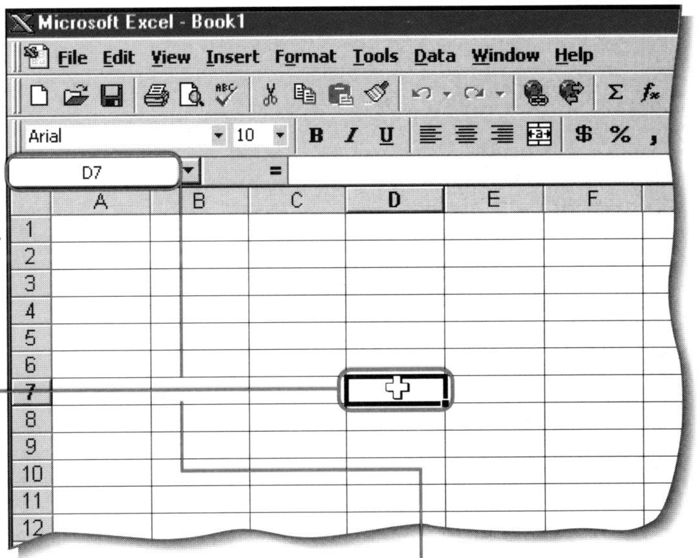

ACTIVE CELL

■ The active cell displays a thick border.

CELL REFERENCE

■ The cell reference for the active cell appears in this area. A cell reference defines the location of each cell in a worksheet and consists of a column letter followed by a row number (example: **A1**).

1 To make another cell the active cell, move the mouse ✥ over the cell and then press the left mouse button.

Note: To move one cell in any direction by using your keyboard, press ←, →, ↑ or ↓.

■ The cell reference for the active cell appears in this area.

ENTER DATA

You can enter data into your worksheet quickly and easily.

ENTER DATA

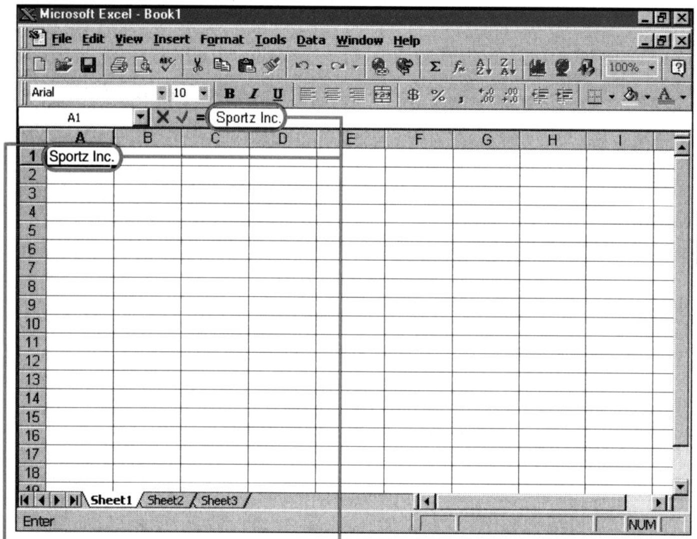

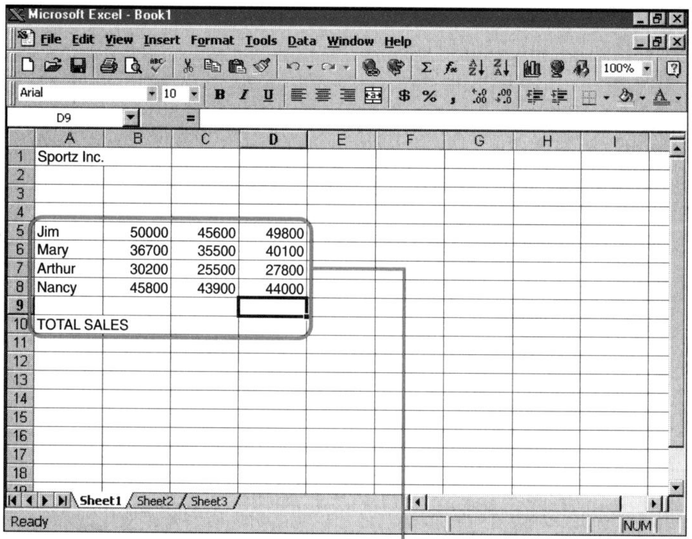

1 Move the mouse ✥ over the cell where you want to enter data and then press the left mouse button. Then type the data.

■ If you make a typing mistake, press **Backspace** on your keyboard to remove the incorrect data and then type the correct data.

■ The data you type appears in the active cell and in the formula bar.

2 To enter the data and move down one cell, press **Enter** on your keyboard.

Note: To enter the data and move one cell in any direction, press **↑**, **↓**, **←** *or* **→** *on your keyboard.*

3 Repeat steps 1 and 2 until you finish entering all the data.

How do I use the number keys on the right side of my keyboard?

When **NUM** appears at the bottom of your screen, you can use the number keys on the right side of your keyboard to enter numbers.

■ To turn the display of **NUM** on or off, press **Num Lock** on your keyboard.

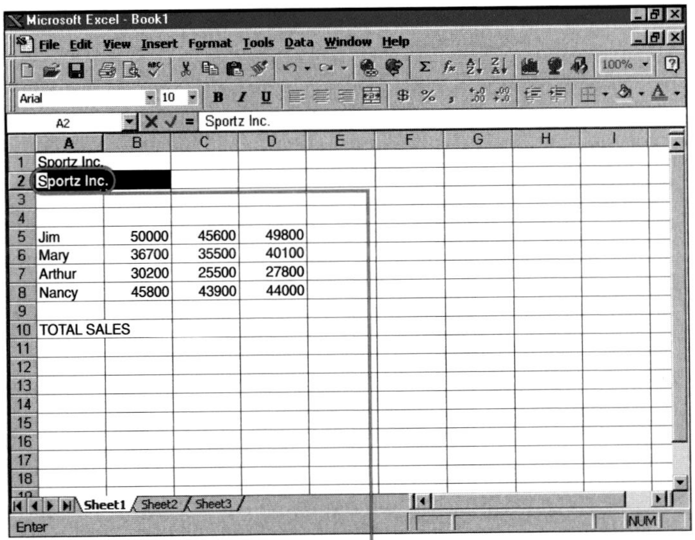

AUTOCOMPLETE

If the first few letters you type match another cell in the column, Excel will complete the text for you.

■ To keep the text Excel provides, press **Enter** on your keyboard.

■ To enter different text, continue typing.

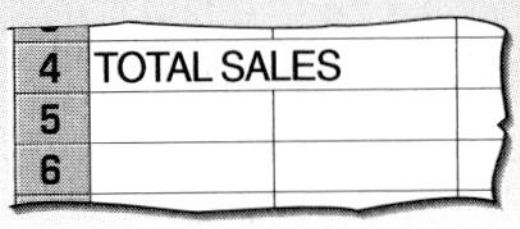

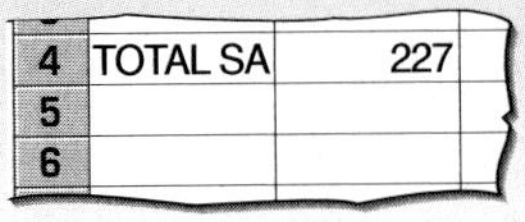

Long Words

If text is too long to fit in a cell, the text will spill into the neighboring cell.

If the neighboring cell contains data, Excel will display as much of the text as the column width will allow. To change the column width, refer to page 90.

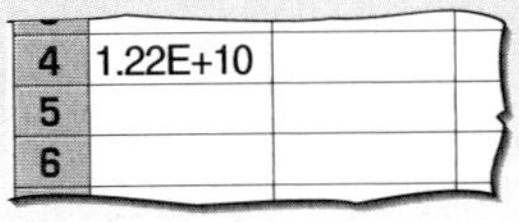

Long Numbers

If a number is too long to fit in a cell, Excel will display the number in scientific form or as number signs (#). To change the column width, refer to page 90.

COMPLETE A SERIES

Excel can save you time by completing a text or number series for you.

COMPLETE A SERIES

Text Series

Mon	Tue	Wed	Thu
Product 1	Product 2	Product 3	Product 4
1st Quarter	2nd Quarter	3rd Quarter	4th Quarter

■ Excel completes a text series based on the text in the first cell.

Number Series

1995	1996	1997	1998
5	10	15	20
202	204	206	208

■ Excel completes a number series based on the numbers in the first two cells.

These numbers tell Excel how much to add to each number to complete the series.

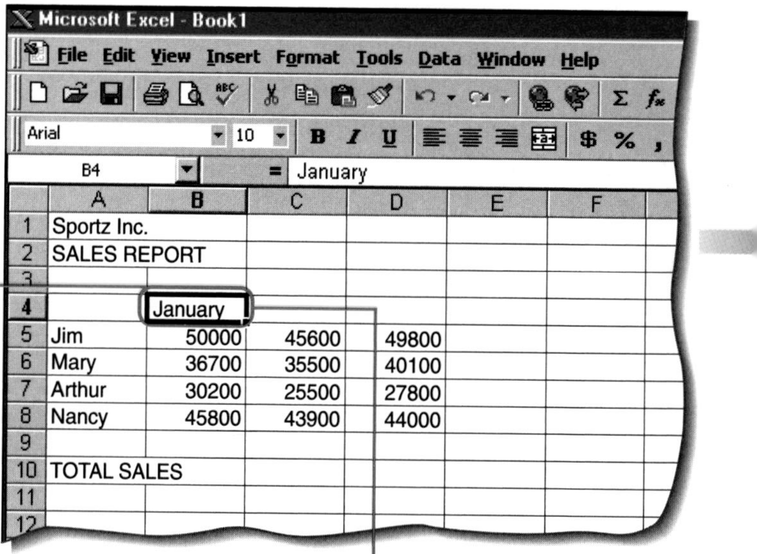

1 Enter the text or the first two numbers you want to start the series.

2 Select the cell(s) containing the text or numbers you entered. To select cells, refer to page 16.

Can I change the color of data in my worksheet?

You can easily change the color of data to make your worksheet more attractive. To do so, refer to page 111.

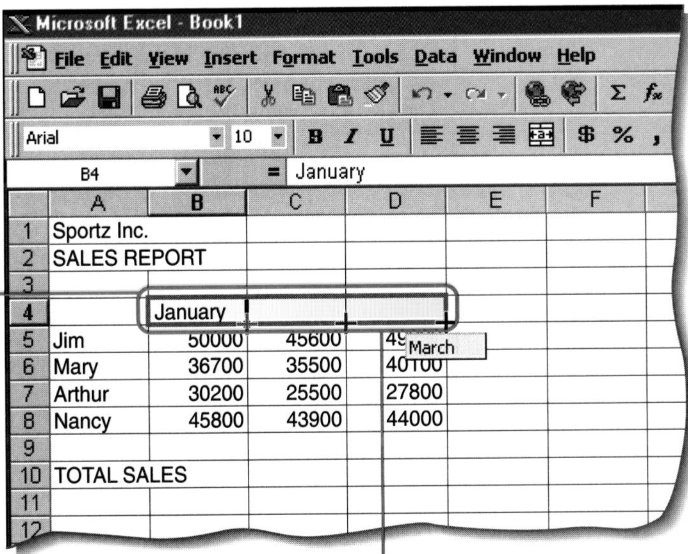

3 Move the mouse ✥ over the bottom right corner of the cell(s) (✥ changes to **+**).

4 Press and hold down the left mouse button as you move the mouse **+** over the cells you want to include in the series. Then release the mouse button.

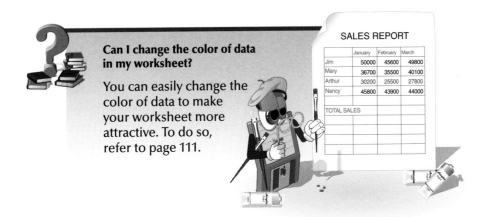

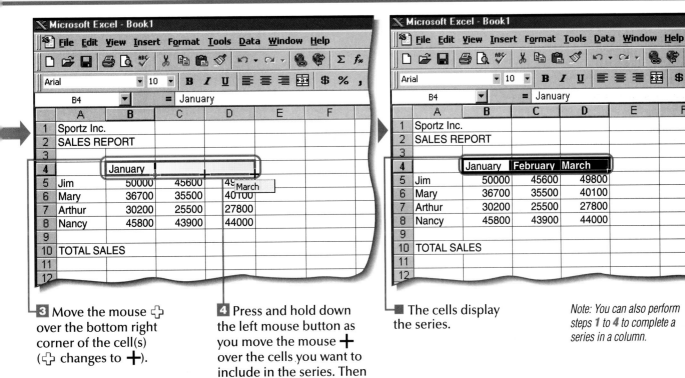

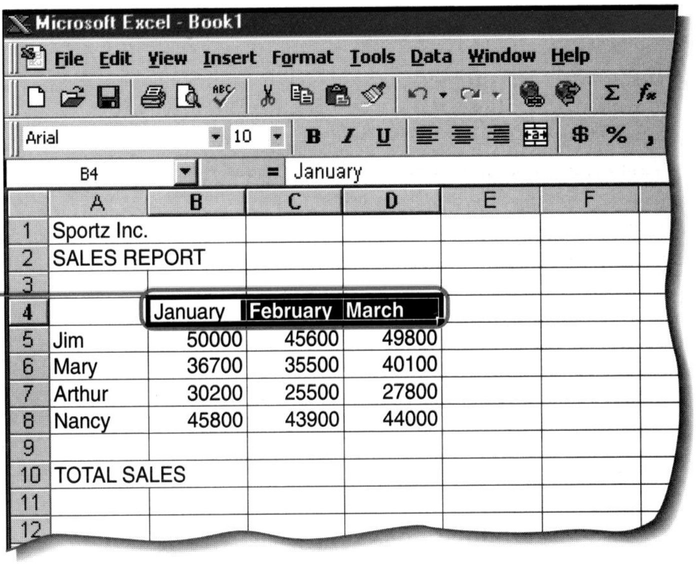

■ The cells display the series.

*Note: You can also perform steps **1** to **4** to complete a series in a column.*

SELECT CELLS

Before performing many tasks in Excel, you must select the cells you want to work with. Selected cells appear highlighted on your screen.

SELECT ONE CELL

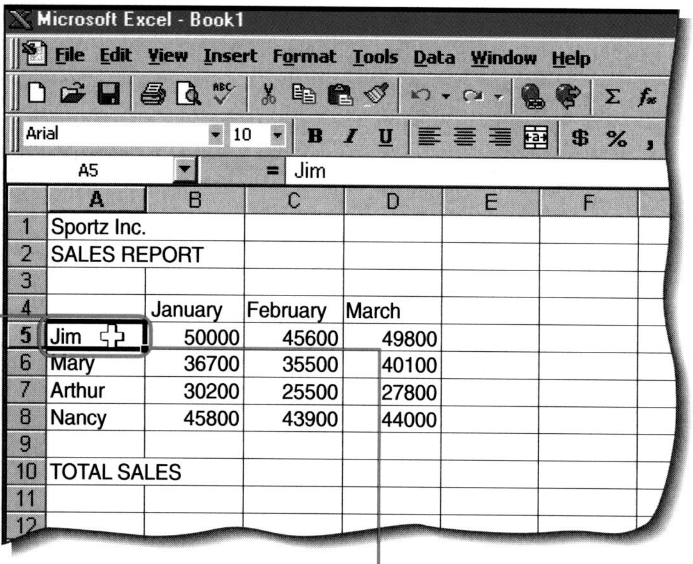

1 Move the mouse ✥ over the cell you want to select and then press the left mouse button.

■ The cell becomes the active cell and displays a thick border.

SELECT GROUPS OF CELLS

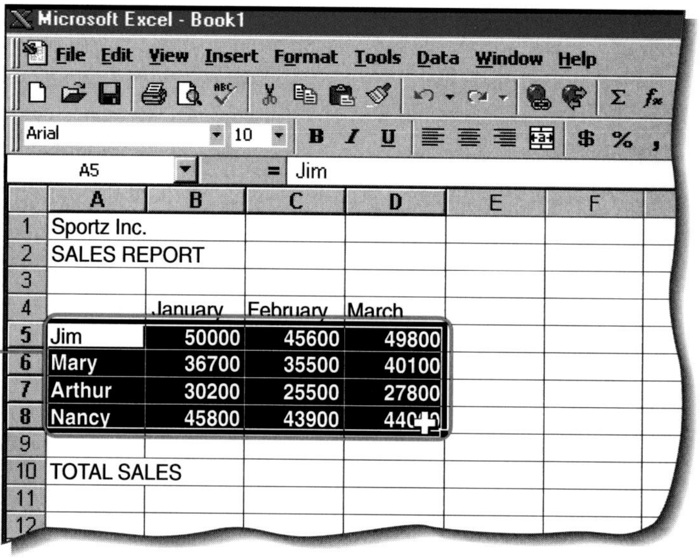

1 Move the mouse ✥ over the first cell you want to select.

2 Press and hold down the left mouse button as you move the mouse ✥ to highlight all the cells you want to select. Then release the mouse button.

■ To select multiple groups of cells, press and hold down **Ctrl** on your keyboard as you repeat steps 1 and 2 for each group.

■ To deselect cells, move the mouse ✥ over any cell and then press the left mouse button.

How do I select all the cells in my worksheet?

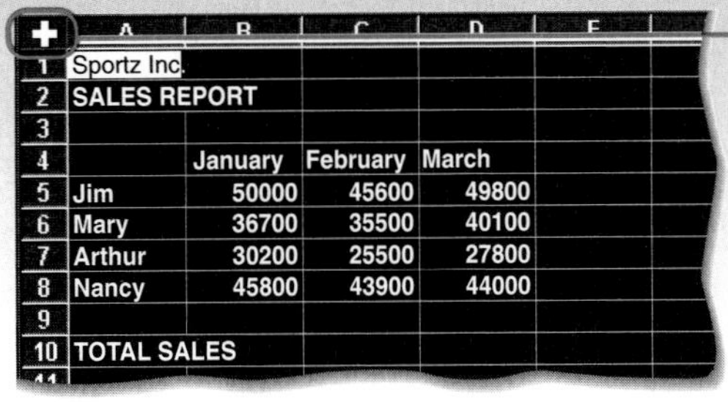

■ To select all the cells in your worksheet, move the mouse ✥ over the area where the row and column headings meet and then press the left mouse button.

SELECT A ROW

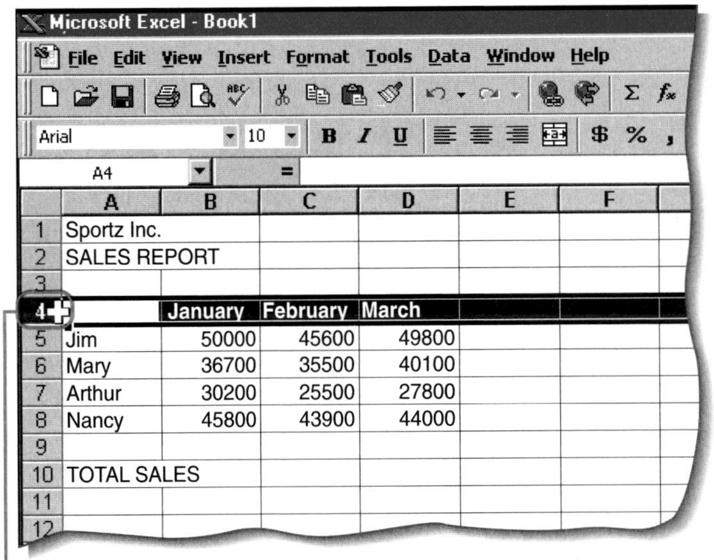

1 Move the mouse ✥ over the number of the row you want to select and then press the left mouse button.

SELECT A COLUMN

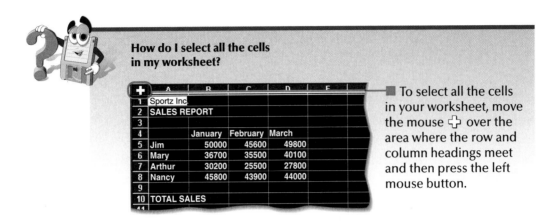

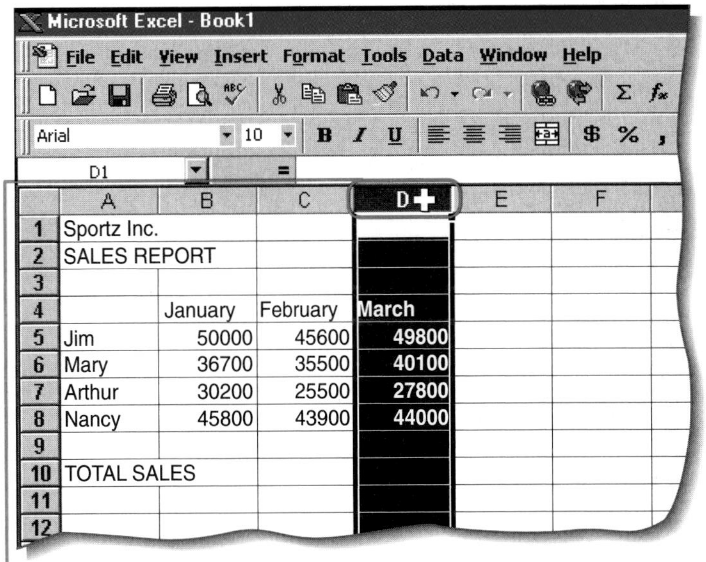

1 Move the mouse ✥ over the letter of the column you want to select and then press the left mouse button.

SCROLL THROUGH A WORKSHEET

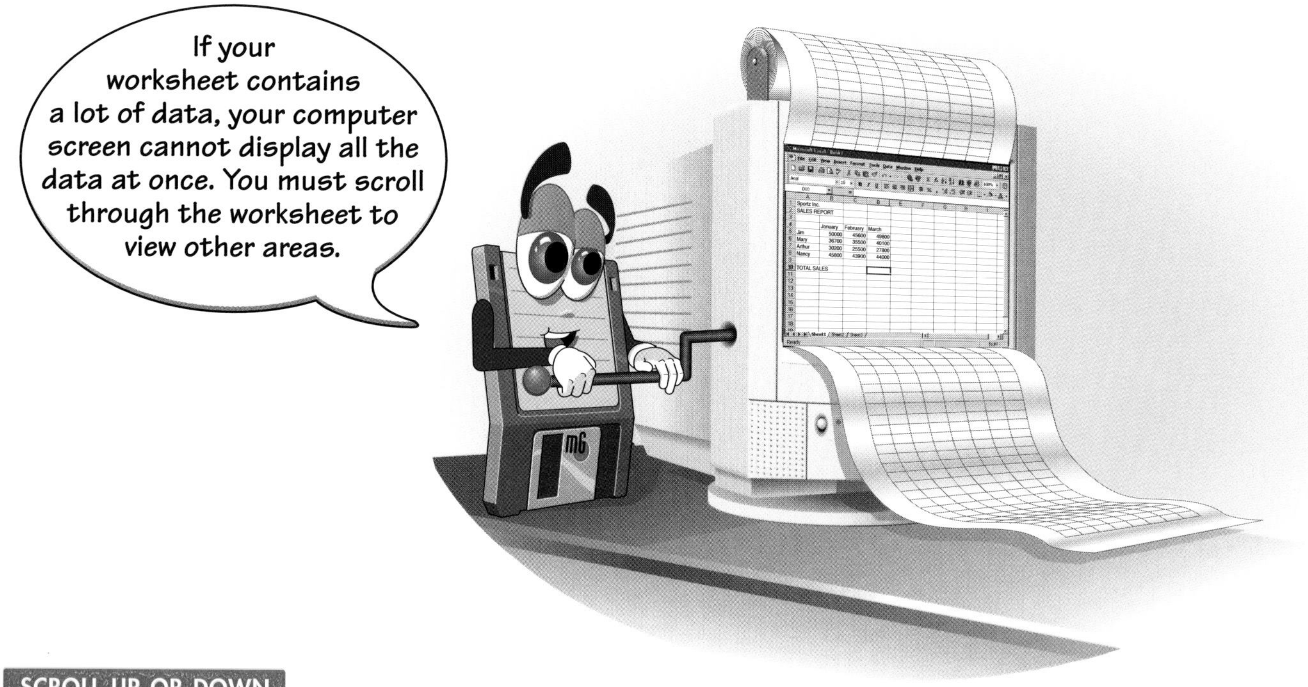

If your worksheet contains a lot of data, your computer screen cannot display all the data at once. You must scroll through the worksheet to view other areas.

SCROLL UP OR DOWN

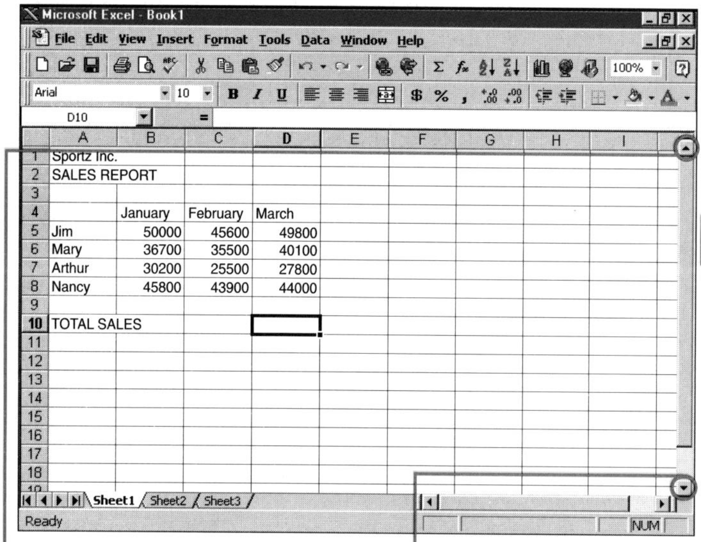

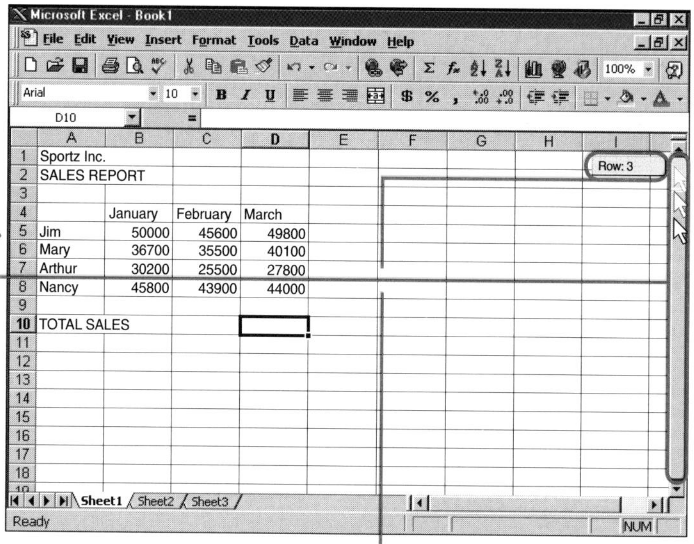

■ To scroll up one row, move the mouse over ▲ and then press the left mouse button.

■ To scroll down one row, move the mouse over ▼ and then press the left mouse button.

QUICKLY SCROLL

1 To quickly scroll to any row in your worksheet, move the mouse over the scroll box.

2 Press and hold down the left mouse button as you move the mouse up or down the scroll bar.

3 When this box displays the number of the row you want to view, release the mouse button.

How do I use the new Microsoft IntelliMouse to scroll through a worksheet?

The Microsoft IntelliMouse has a wheel between the left and right mouse buttons. Moving this wheel lets you quickly scroll up and down through a worksheet.

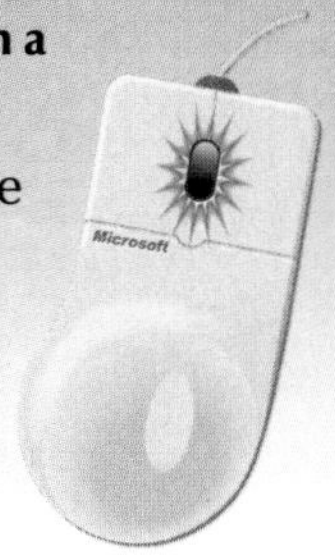

SCROLL LEFT OR RIGHT

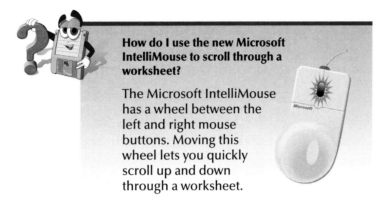

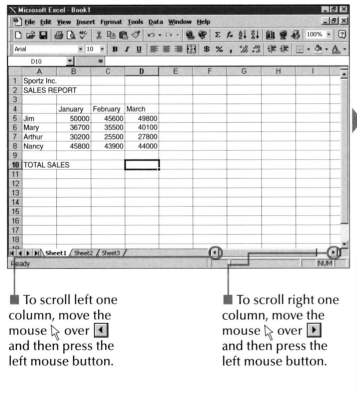

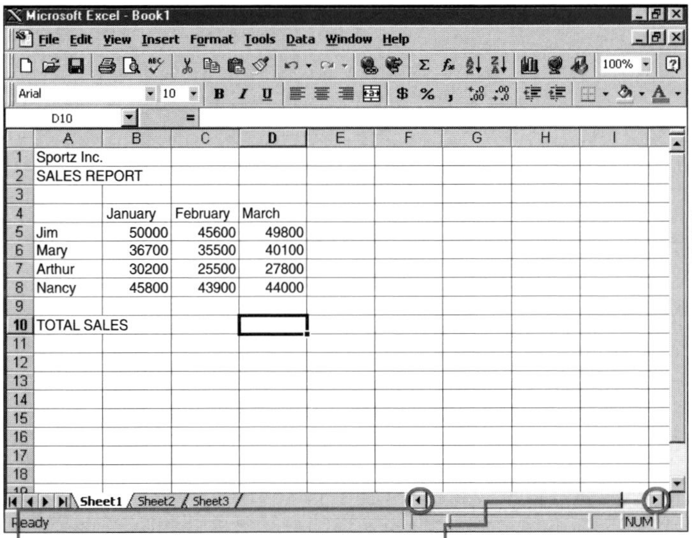

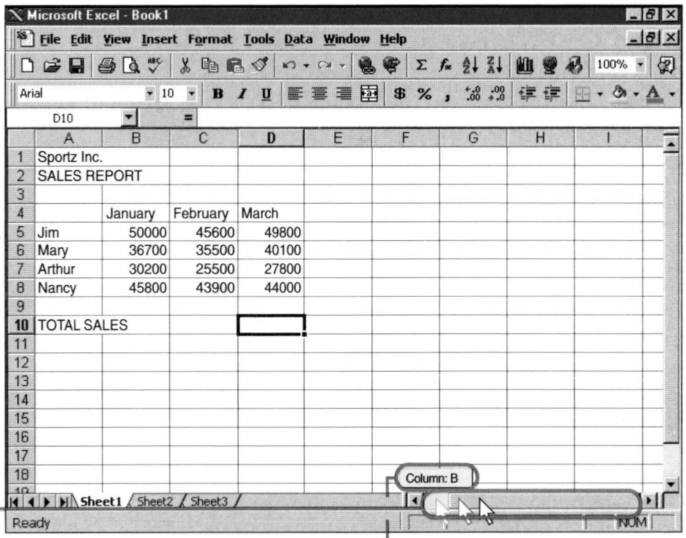

■ To scroll left one column, move the mouse ↖ over ◀ and then press the left mouse button.

■ To scroll right one column, move the mouse ↖ over ▶ and then press the left mouse button.

QUICKLY SCROLL

1 To quickly scroll to any column in your worksheet, move the mouse ↖ over the scroll box.

2 Press and hold down the left mouse button as you move the mouse ↖ left or right along the scroll bar.

3 When this box displays the letter of the column you want to view, release the mouse button.

GETTING HELP

If you do not know how to perform a task you can ask the Office Assistant for help.

GETTING HELP

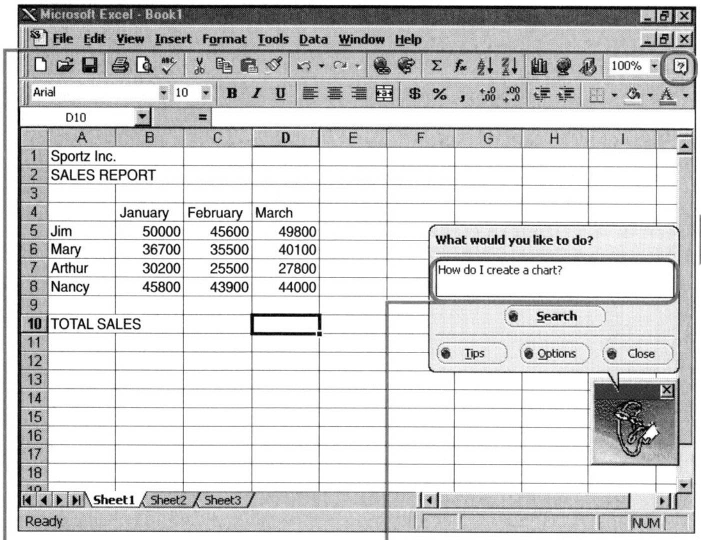

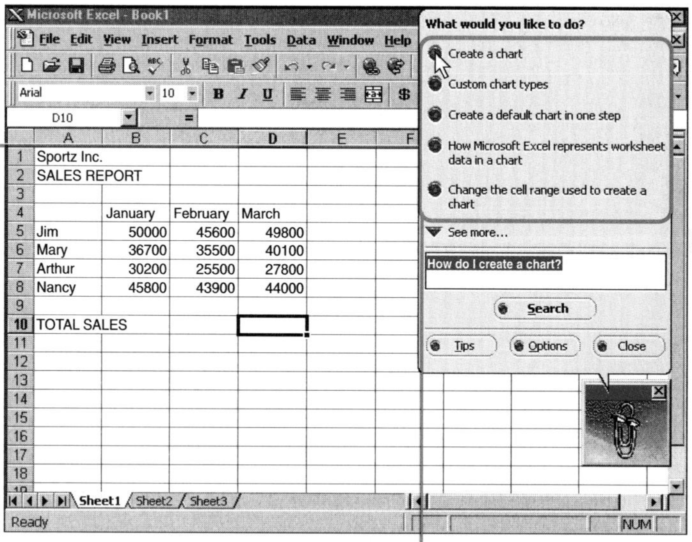

1 To display the Office Assistant, move the mouse over the Office Assistant button and then press the left mouse button.

2 Type the question you want to ask and then press **Enter** on your keyboard.

■ The Office Assistant displays a list of help topics that relate to the question you asked.

Note: If you do not see a help topic of interest, try rephrasing your question. Type the new question and then press **Enter** *on your keyboard.*

3 Move the mouse over the help topic you want information on and then press the left mouse button.

How do I display the name of each toolbar button?

To display the name of a toolbar button, move the mouse ↖ over the button. After a few seconds, the name of the button appears.

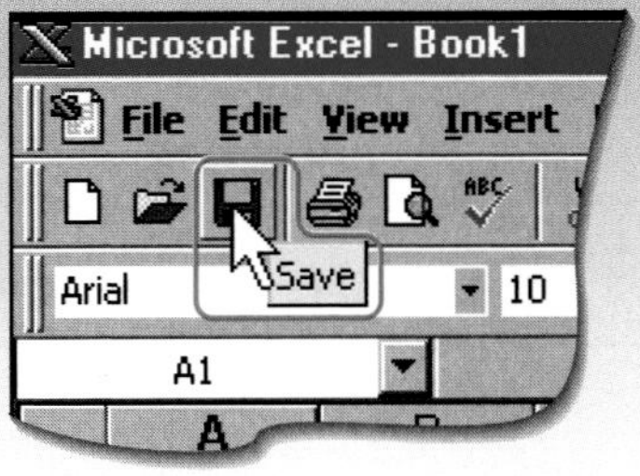

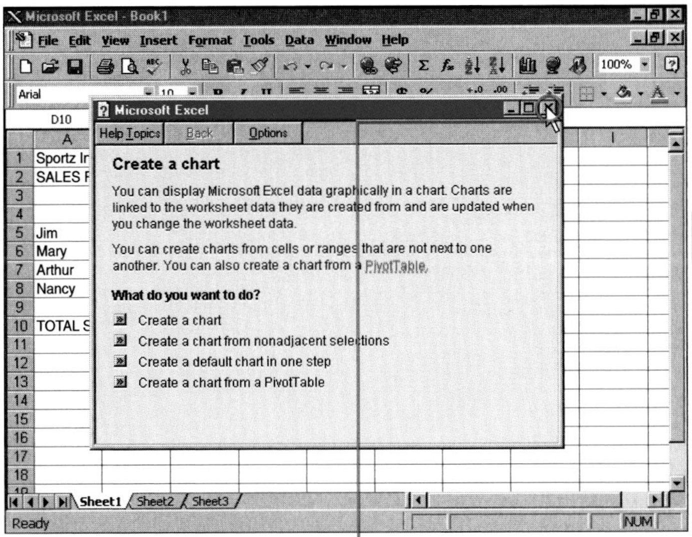

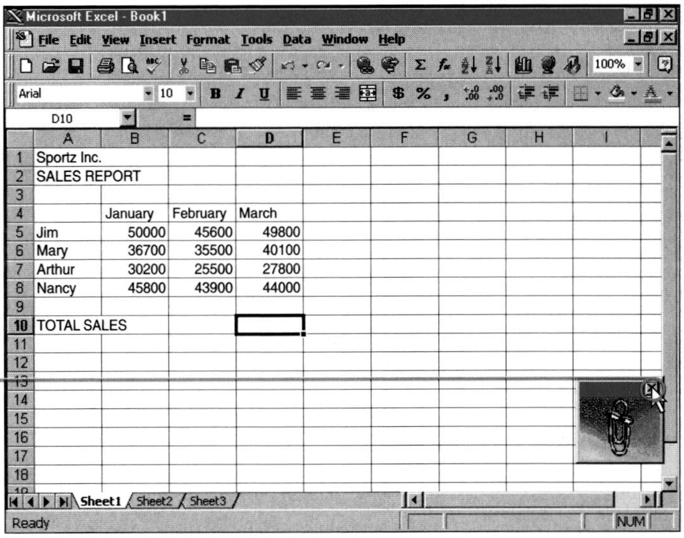

■ A window appears, displaying information about the topic you selected.

4 When you finish reading the information, move the mouse ↖ over ☒ and then press the left mouse button to close the window.

5 To hide the Office Assistant, move the mouse ↖ over ☒ and then press the left mouse button.

mG'S WORKBOOKS

CHAPTER 2

SAVE AND OPEN YOUR WORKBOOKS

Are you wondering how to save, close and open an Excel workbook? Do you want to create a new workbook? Learn how in this chapter.

You should save your workbook to store it for future use. This lets you later review and make changes to the workbook.

SAVE A WORKBOOK

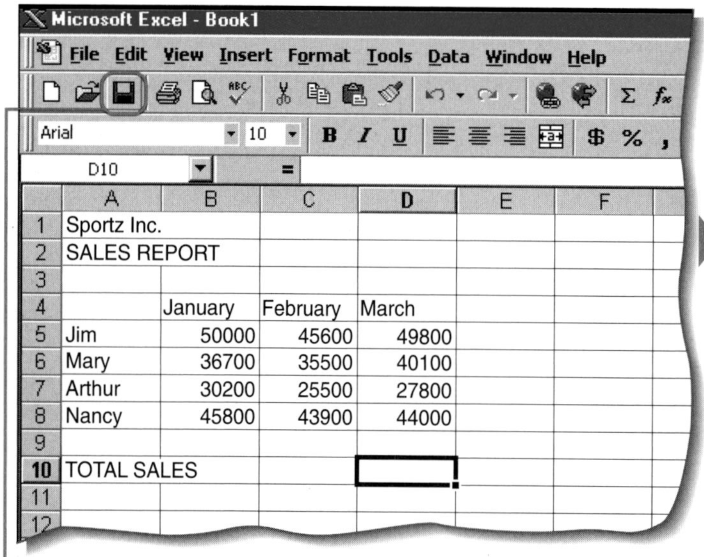

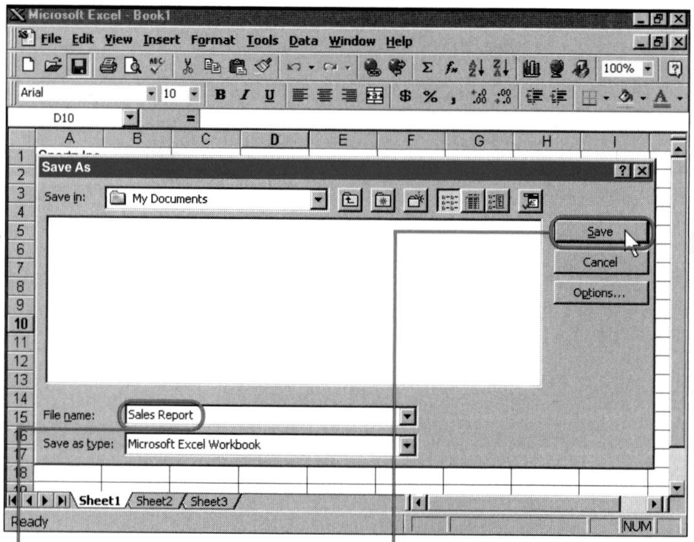

1 Move the mouse over 💾 and then press the left mouse button.

■ The **Save As** dialog box appears.

*Note: If you previously saved your workbook, the **Save As** dialog box will not appear since you have already named the workbook.*

2 Type a name for your workbook.

Note: You can use up to 218 characters, including spaces, to name a workbook.

3 Move the mouse over **Save** and then press the left mouse button.

What is the difference between a workbook and a worksheet?

An Excel file is called a workbook. Each workbook is divided into several worksheets. A workbook is similar to a three-ring binder that contains several sheets of paper.

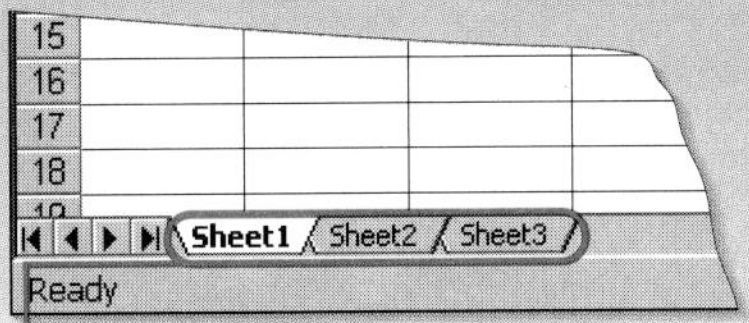

■ Excel displays a tab for each worksheet in your workbook.

Note: To use multiple worksheets in a workbook, refer to pages 140 to 149.

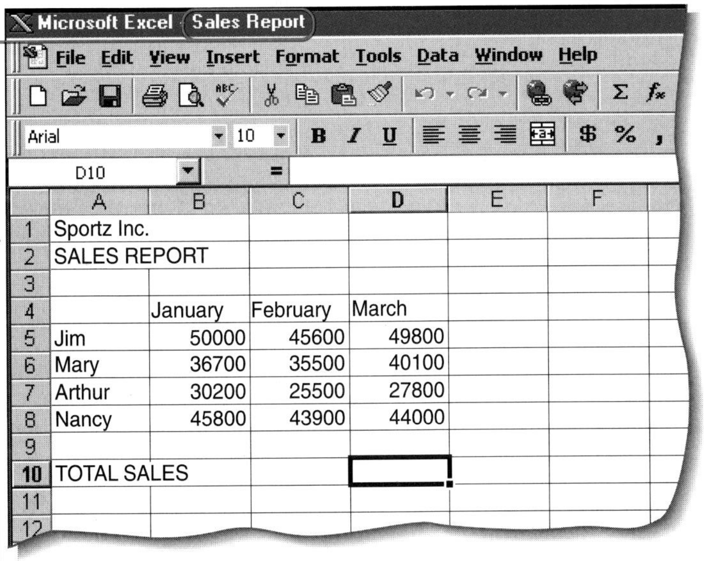

■ Excel saves your workbook and displays the name at the top of your screen.

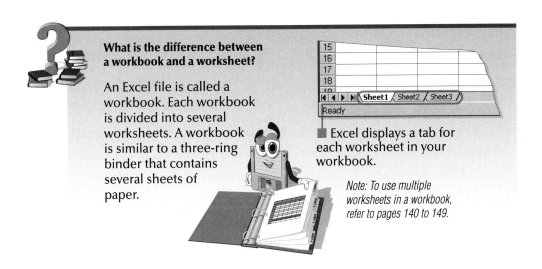

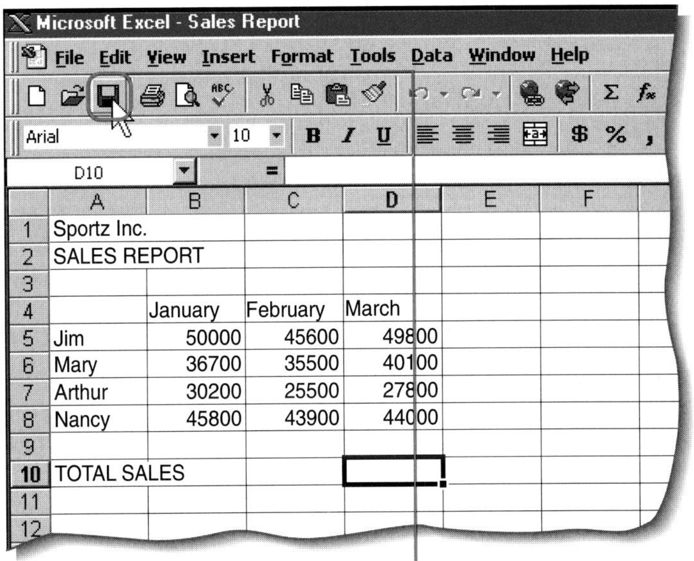

SAVE CHANGES

To avoid losing your work, you should regularly save changes you make to a workbook.

1 Move the mouse ⬚ over 🔲 and then press the left mouse button.

CREATE A NEW WORKBOOK

You can easily create another workbook to store new data.
Workbook

CREATE A NEW WORKBOOK

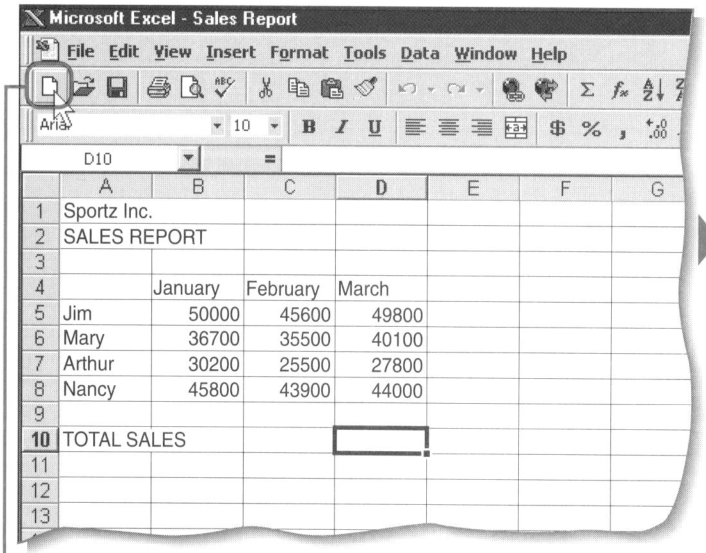

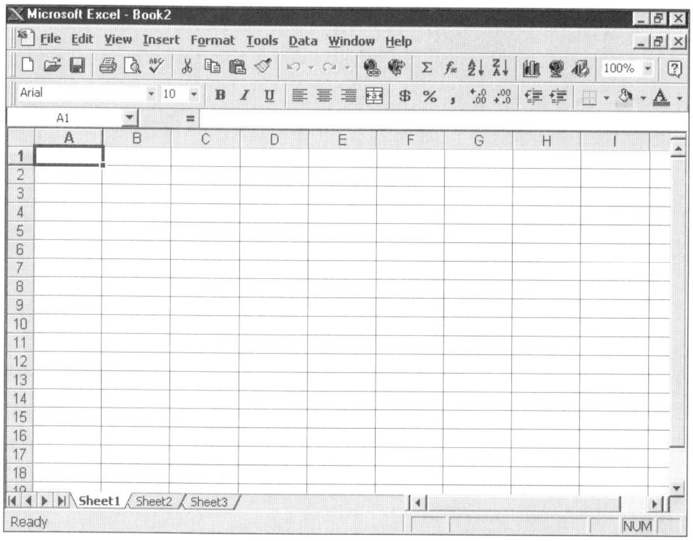

1 Move the mouse over ▢ and then press the left mouse button.

■ A new workbook appears. The previous workbook is now hidden behind the new workbook.

SWITCH BETWEEN WORKBOOKS

SWITCH BETWEEN WORKBOOKS

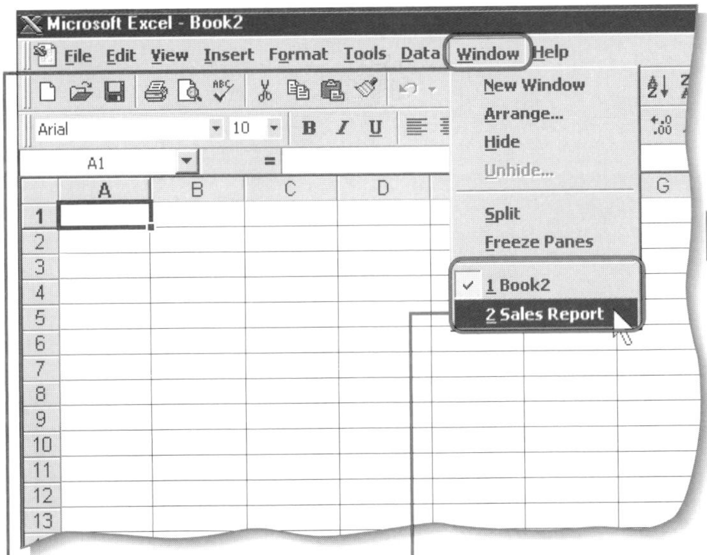

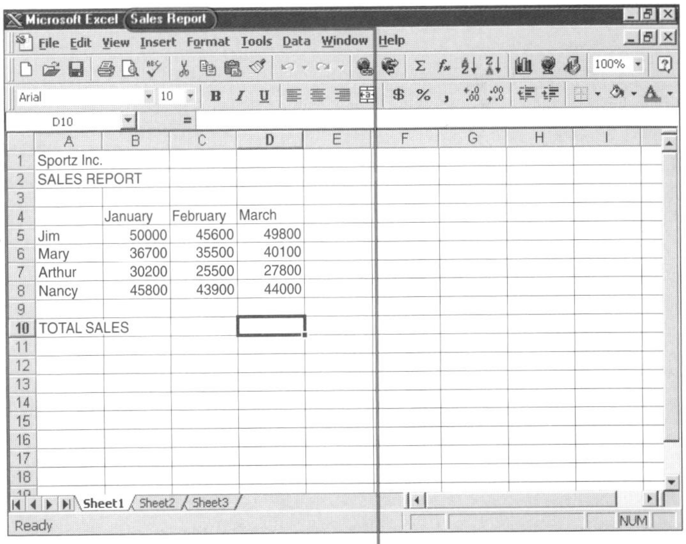

1 To display a list of all open workbooks, move the mouse over **Window** and then press the left mouse button.

2 Move the mouse over the workbook you want to display and then press the left mouse button.

■ The workbook appears.

■ Excel displays the name of the workbook at the top of your screen.

VIEW ALL OPEN WORKBOOKS

VIEW ALL OPEN WORKBOOKS

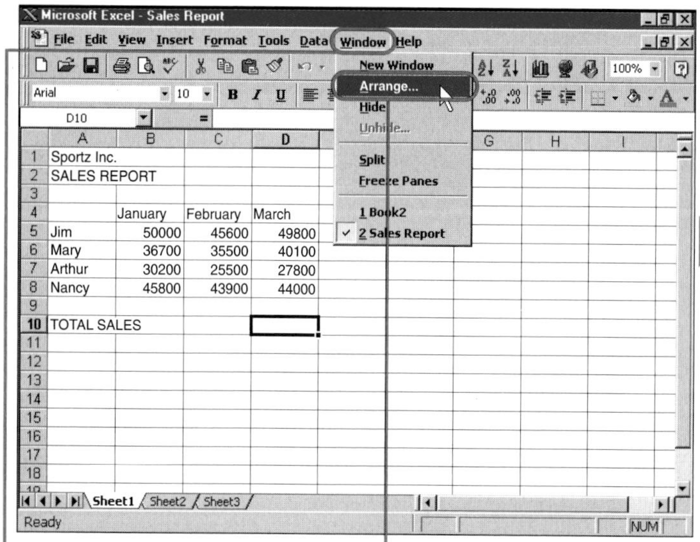

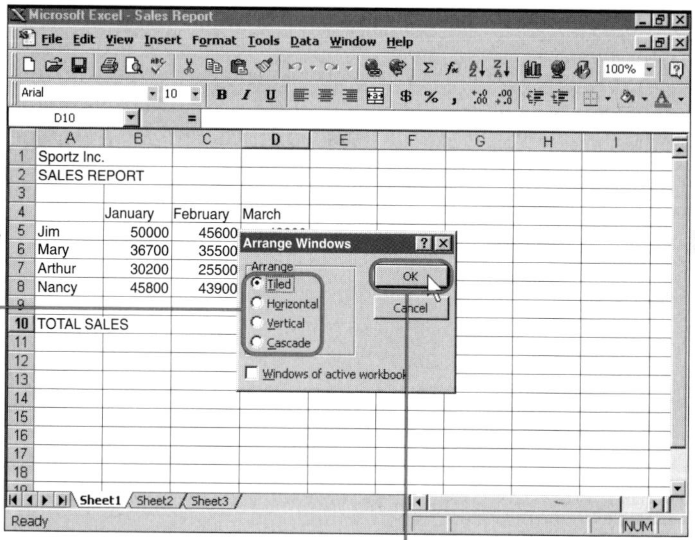

1 Move the mouse over **Window** and then press the left mouse button.

2 Move the mouse over **Arrange** and then press the left mouse button.

■ The **Arrange Windows** dialog box appears.

3 Move the mouse over the way you want to arrange all your open workbooks and then press the left mouse button (○ changes to ◉).

4 Move the mouse over **OK** and then press the left mouse button.

How can I arrange my open workbooks?

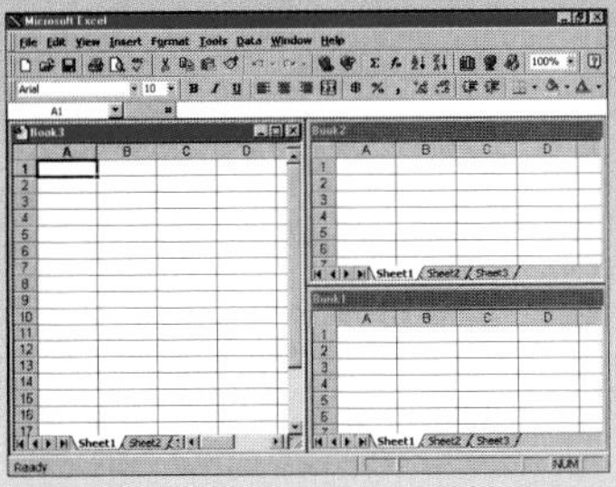

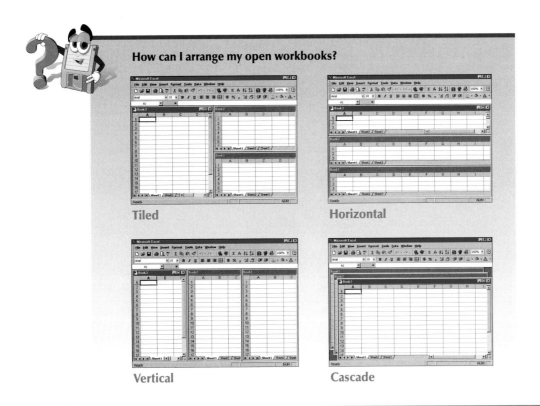

Tiled

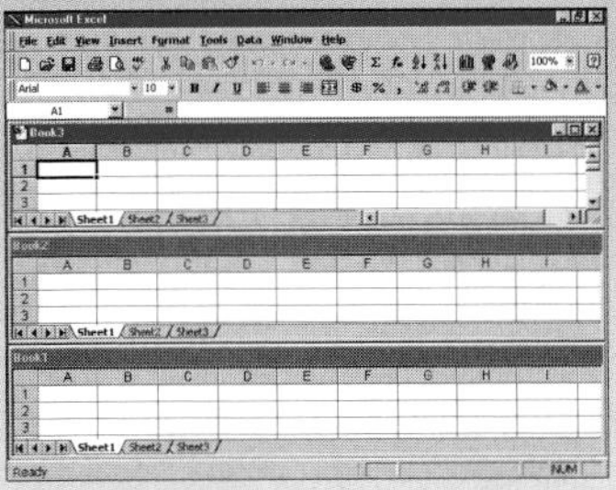

Horizontal

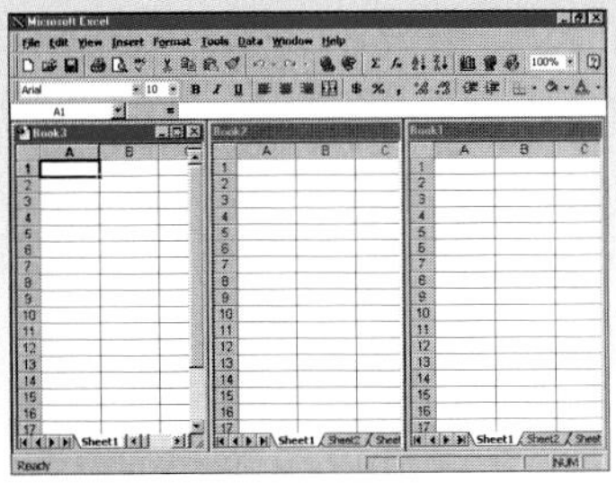

Vertical

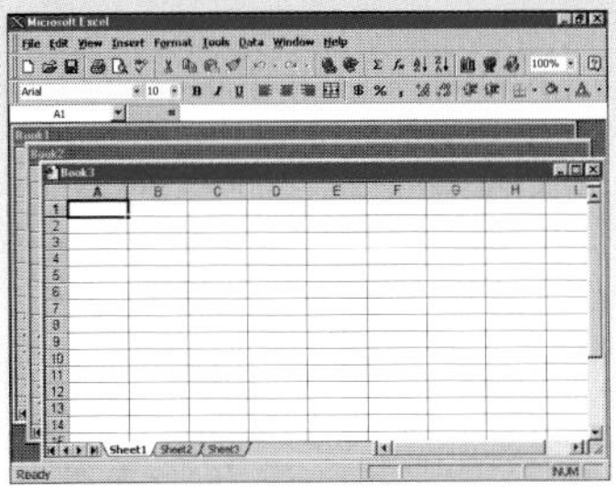

Cascade

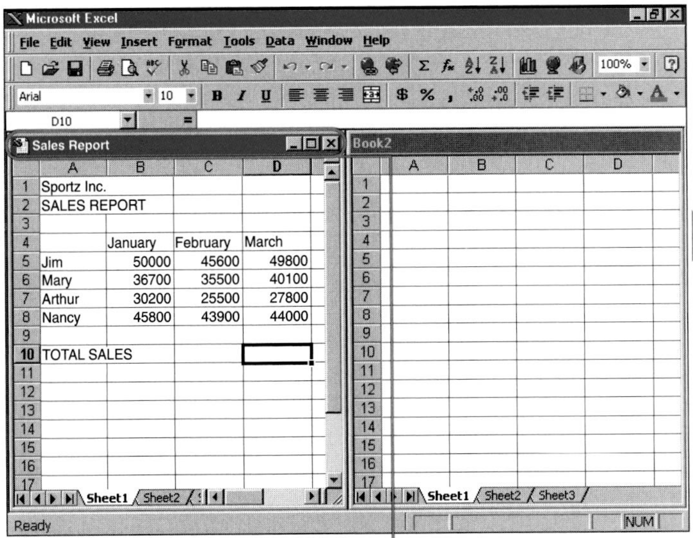

■ You can now view the contents of all your open workbooks.

■ You can only work in the current workbook, which displays a highlighted title bar.

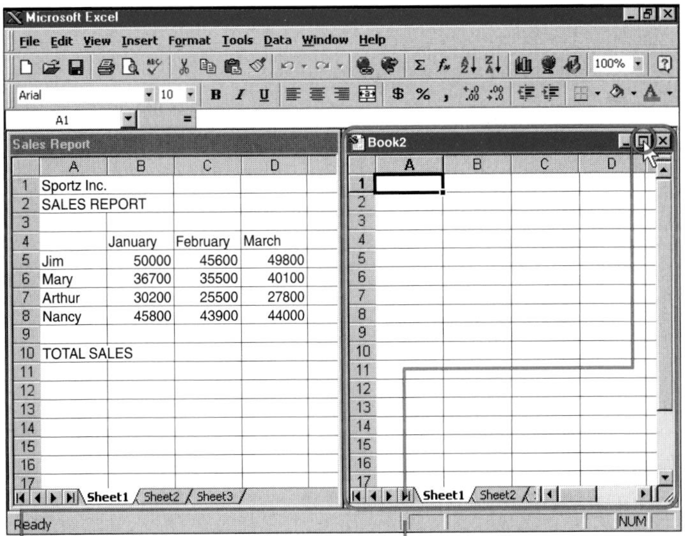

5 To make another workbook current, move the mouse anywhere over the workbook and then press the left mouse button.

■ To enlarge the current workbook to fill your screen, move the mouse over ▢ and then press the left mouse button.

CLOSE A WORKBOOK

When you finish using a workbook, you can close the workbook to remove it from your screen.
Workbook
Sheet 1
Sheet 2
Sheet 3

When you close a workbook, you do not exit the Excel program. You can continue to work with other workbooks.

CLOSE A WORKBOOK

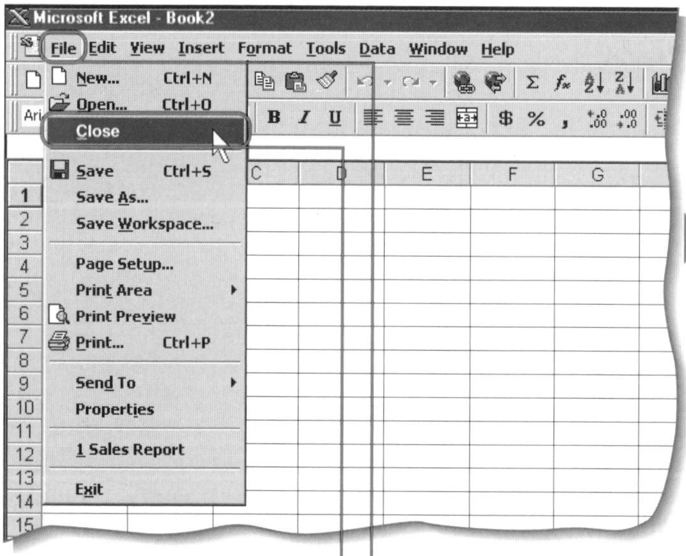

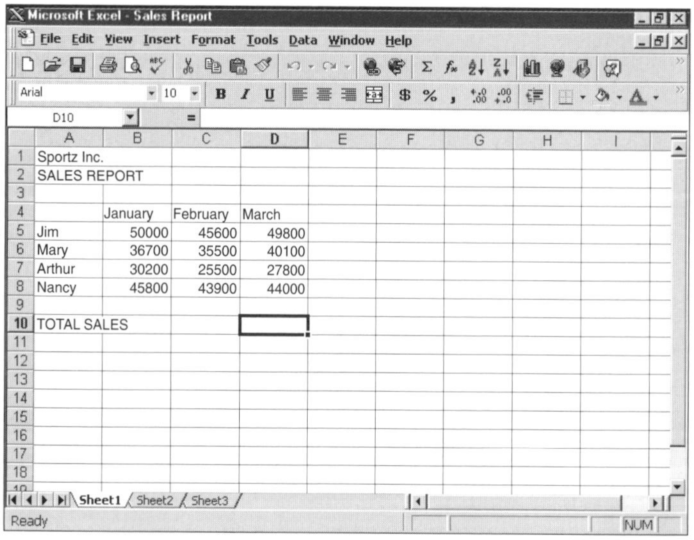

■ To save the workbook before closing, refer to page 24.

1 To close the workbook, move the mouse over **File** and then press the left mouse button.

2 Move the mouse over **Close** and then press the left mouse button.

■ Excel removes the workbook from your screen.

■ If you had more than one workbook open, the second last workbook you worked with appears on your screen.

EXIT EXCEL

When you finish using Excel, you can exit the program.
EXIT

You should exit all programs before turning off your computer.

EXIT EXCEL

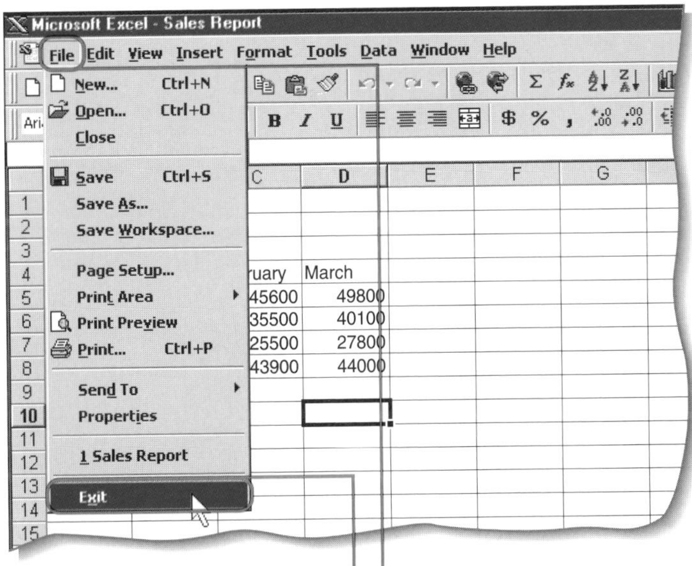

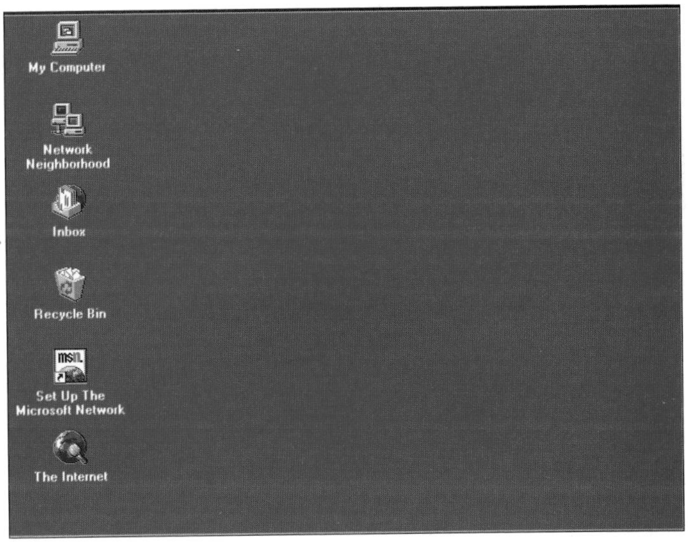

■ Save all open workbooks before exiting Excel. To save a workbook, refer to page 24.

1 Move the mouse over **File** and then press the left mouse button.

2 Move the mouse over **Exit** and then press the left mouse button.

■ The Excel window disappears from your screen.

Note: To restart Excel, refer to page 8.

OPEN A WORKBOOK

OPEN A WORKBOOK

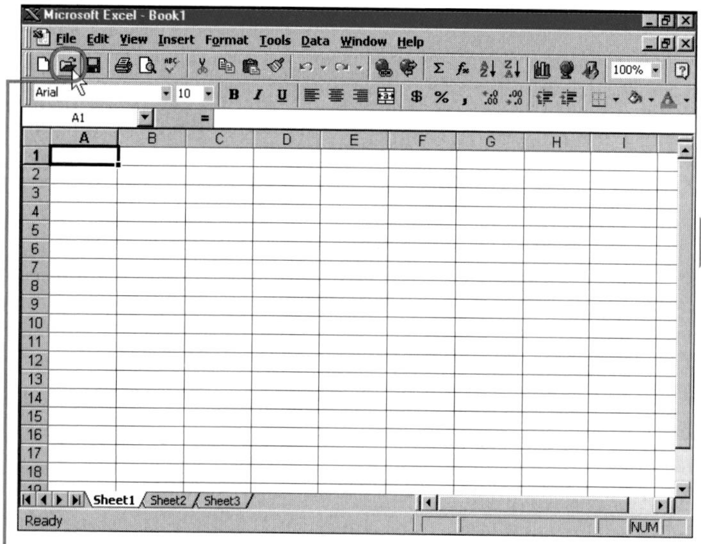

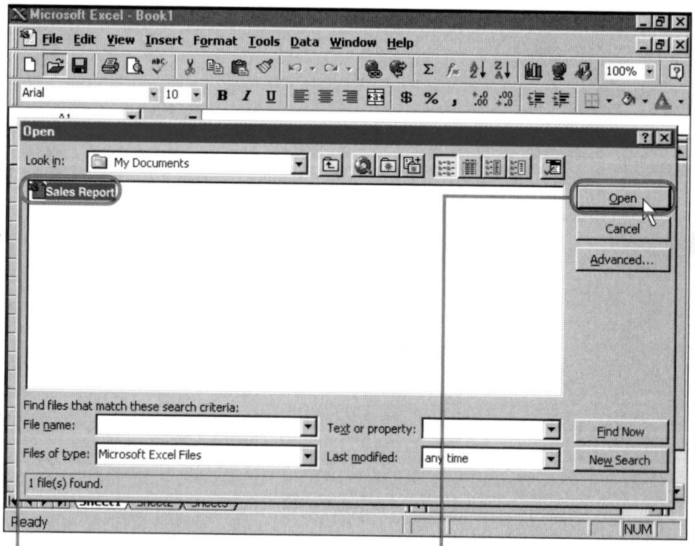

1 Move the mouse over and then press the left mouse button.

■ The **Open** dialog box appears.

2 Move the mouse over the name of the workbook you want to open and then press the left mouse button.

3 To open the workbook, move the mouse over **Open** and then press the left mouse button.

Excel remembers the names of the last four workbooks you opened. You can quickly open any of these workbooks.
Income

QUICKLY OPEN A WORKBOOK

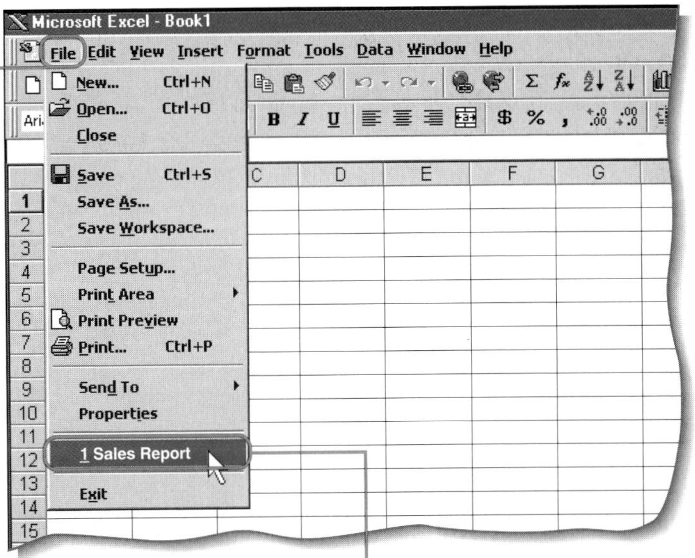

1 Move the mouse over **File** and then press the left mouse button.

2 Move the mouse over the name of the workbook you want to open and then press the left mouse button.

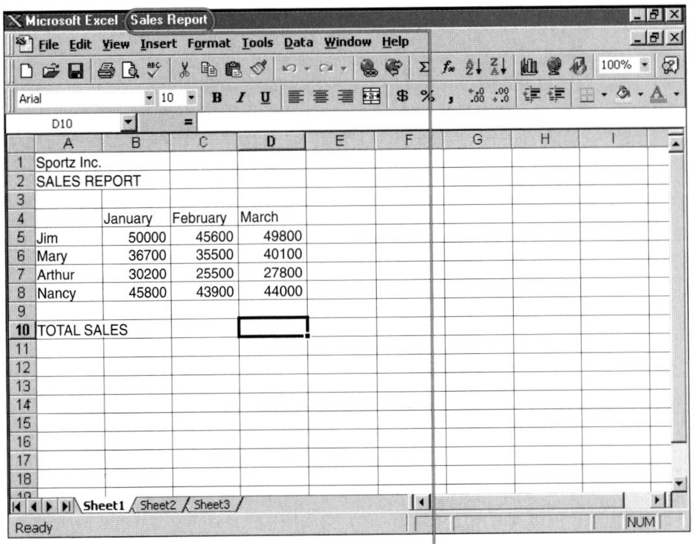

■ Excel opens the workbook and displays it on your screen. You can now review and make changes to the workbook.

■ The name of the workbook appears at the top of your screen.

FIND A WORKBOOK

If you cannot remember the name or location of a workbook you want to open, you can search for the workbook.

FIND A WORKBOOK

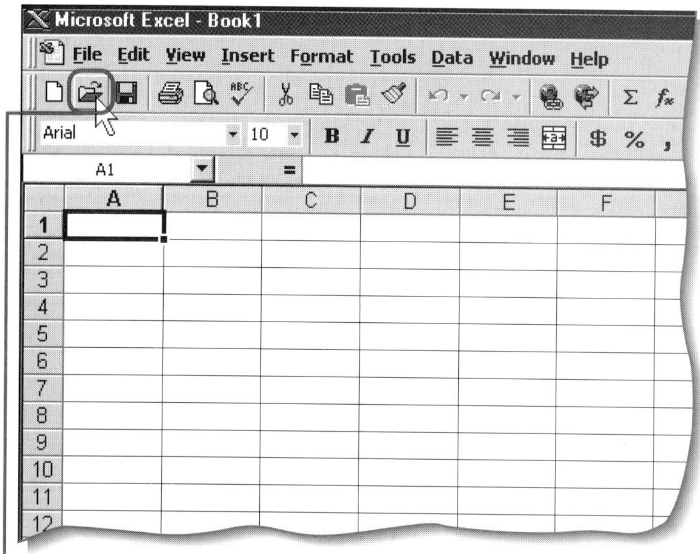

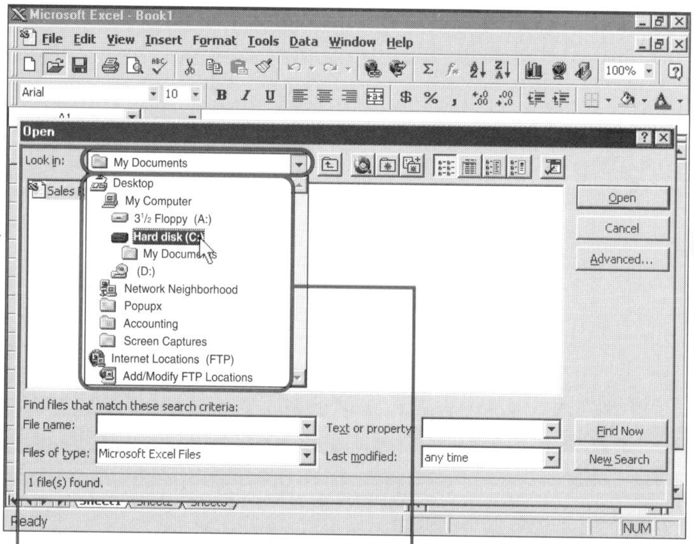

1 Move the mouse over the open button and then press the left mouse button.

■ The **Open** dialog box appears.

2 To specify where you want to search for the workbook, move the mouse over this area and then press the left mouse button.

3 Move the mouse over the location you want to search and then press the left mouse button.

Can Excel find a workbook if I know only part of the workbook name?

Excel will find all the workbooks with names containing the text you specify. For example, searching for **Income** will find **1997 Income**, **Income Statement** and **Mike's Income**.

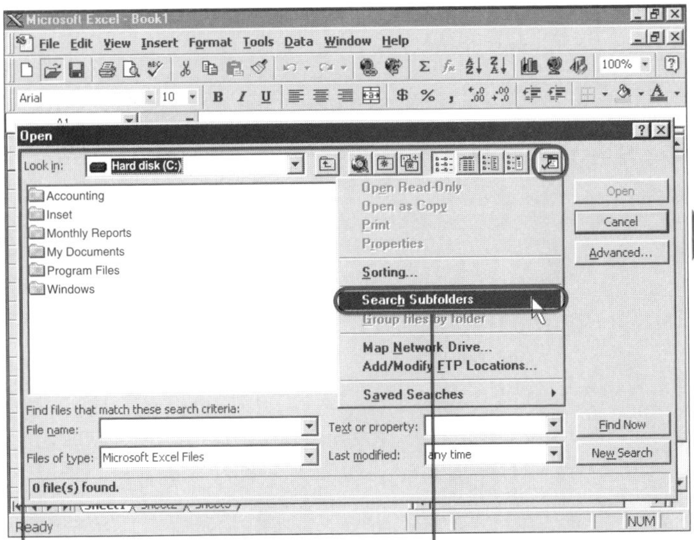

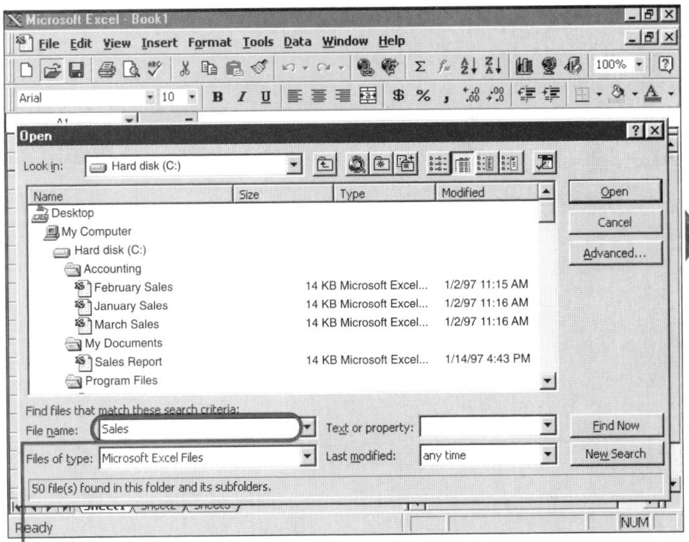

4 To search the contents of all the folders in the location you selected, move the mouse over the button and then press the left mouse button.

5 Move the mouse over **Search Subfolders** and then press the left mouse button.

6 If you know part or all of the name of the workbook you want to find, move the mouse over this area and then press the left mouse button. Then type the name.

CONTINUED

FIND A WORKBOOK

FIND A WORKBOOK (CONTINUED)

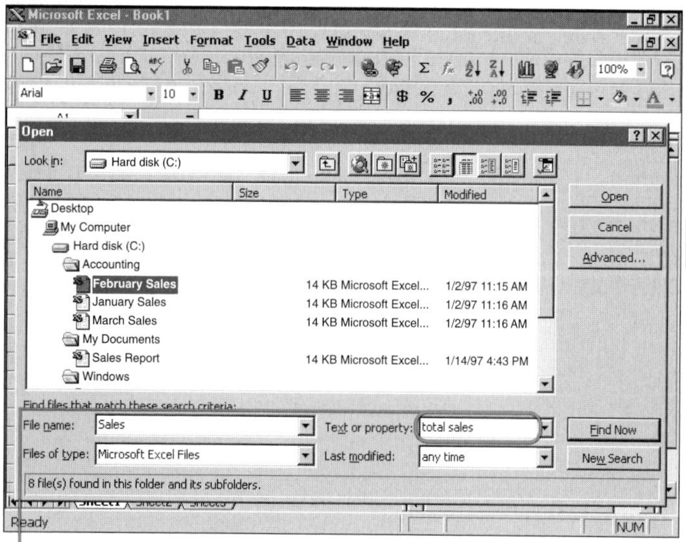

7 If you know a word or phrase in the workbook you want to find, move the mouse I over this area and then press the left mouse button. Then type the word or phrase.

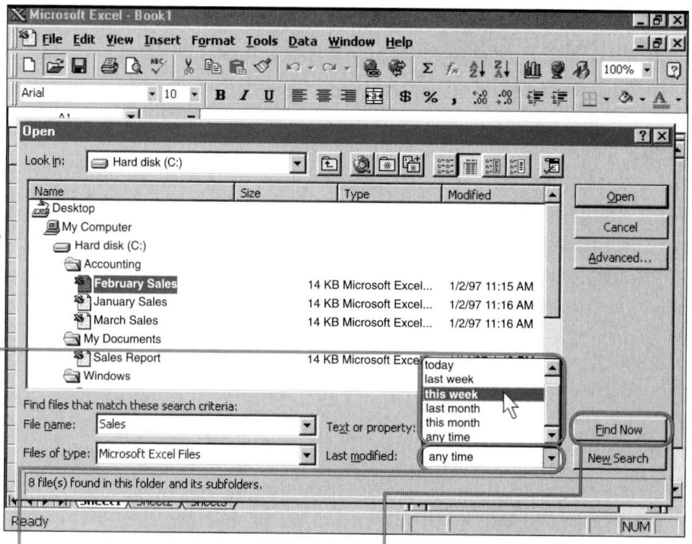

8 If you know when you last saved the workbook you want to find, move the mouse over this area and then press the left mouse button.

9 Move the mouse over the appropriate time period and then press the left mouse button.

10 To complete the search, move the mouse over **Find Now** and then press the left mouse button.

How can Excel help me find a workbook?

There are many ways you can search for a workbook.

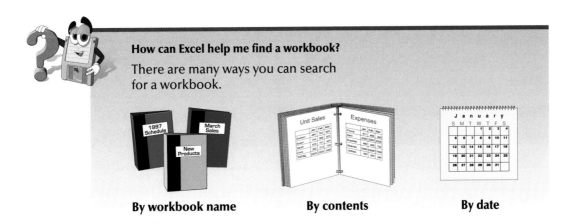

By workbook name

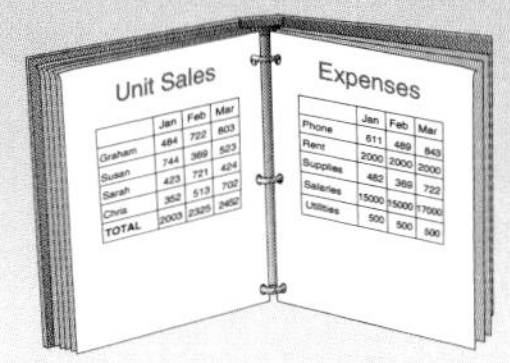

By contents

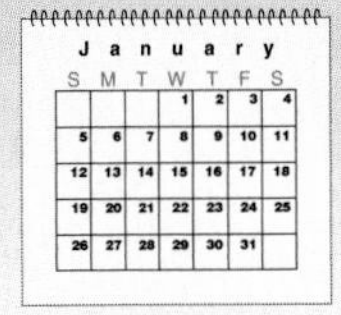

By date

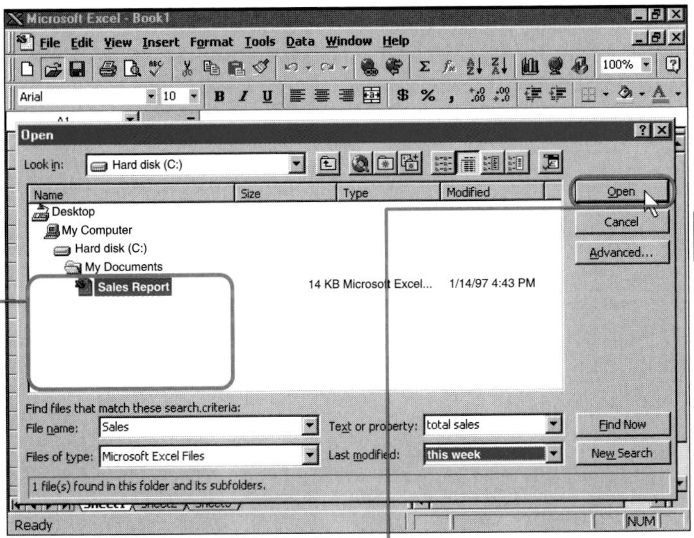

■ This area displays the names of the workbooks Excel found.

11 To open a workbook, move the mouse ↖ over the name of the workbook and then press the left mouse button.

12 Move the mouse ↖ over **Open** and then press the left mouse button.

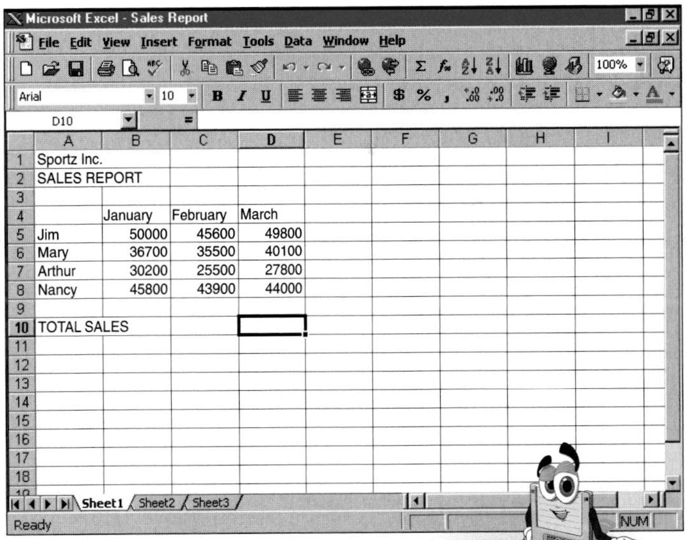

■ Excel opens the workbook and displays it on your screen. You can now review and make changes to the workbook.

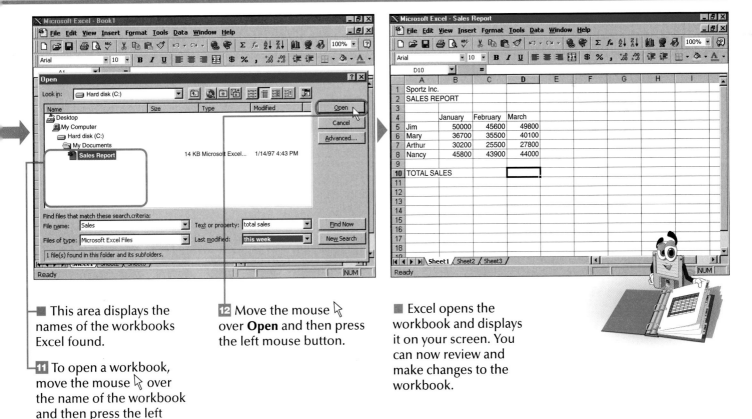

127

CHAPTER 3

EDIT YOUR WORKSHEETS

Do you want to edit the data in your worksheet? Are you wondering how to check for spelling errors? This chapter teaches you how.

EDIT DATA

EDIT DATA

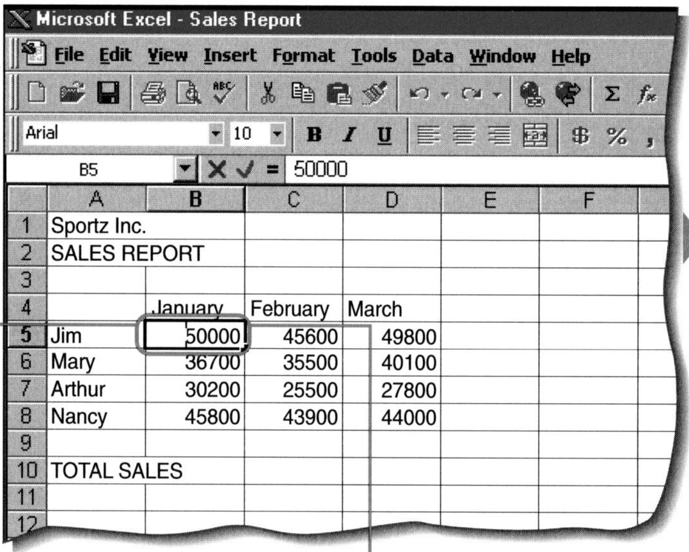

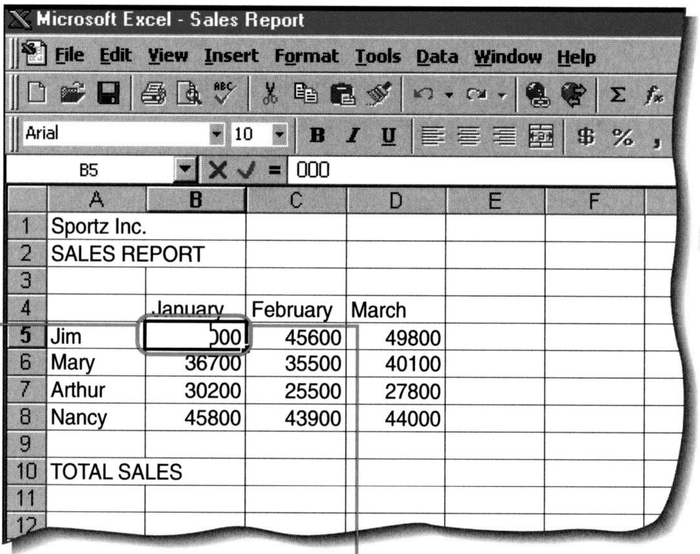

1 Move the mouse ✥ over the cell containing the data you want to edit and then quickly press the left mouse button twice.

■ A flashing insertion point appears in the cell.

2 Press ← or → on your keyboard to move the insertion point to where you want to add or remove characters.

3 To remove the character to the left of the insertion point, press Backspace on your keyboard.

How often should I save my workbook?

You should save your workbook every 5 to 10 minutes to avoid losing your editing changes. To save a workbook, refer to page 24.

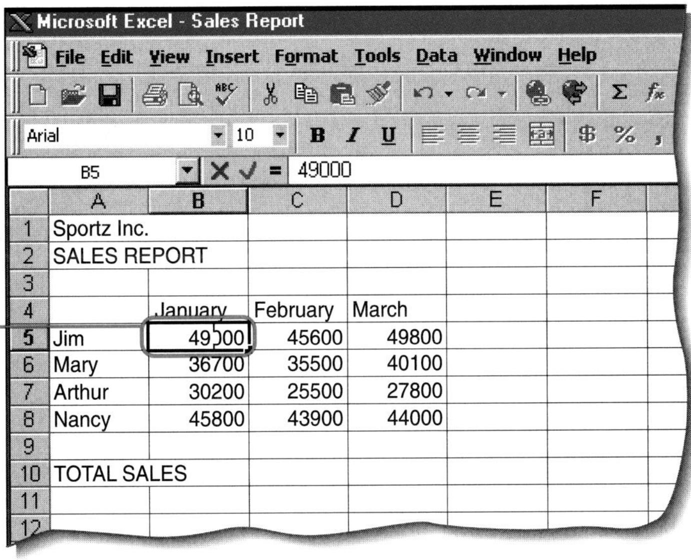

4 To insert data where the insertion point flashes on your screen, type the data.

5 When you finish making changes to the data, press Enter on your keyboard.

REPLACE ALL DATA IN A CELL

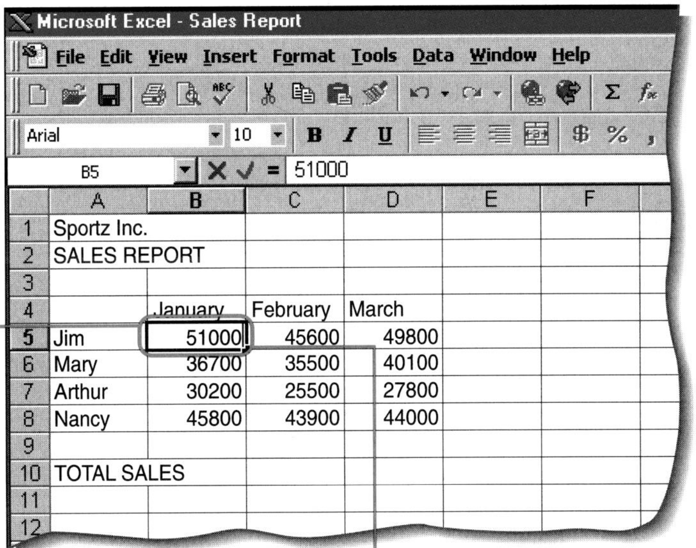

1 Move the mouse ✥ over the cell containing the data you want to replace with new data and then press the left mouse button.

2 Type the new data and then press Enter on your keyboard.

DELETE DATA

You can easily remove data you no longer need from cells in your worksheet.

DELETE DATA

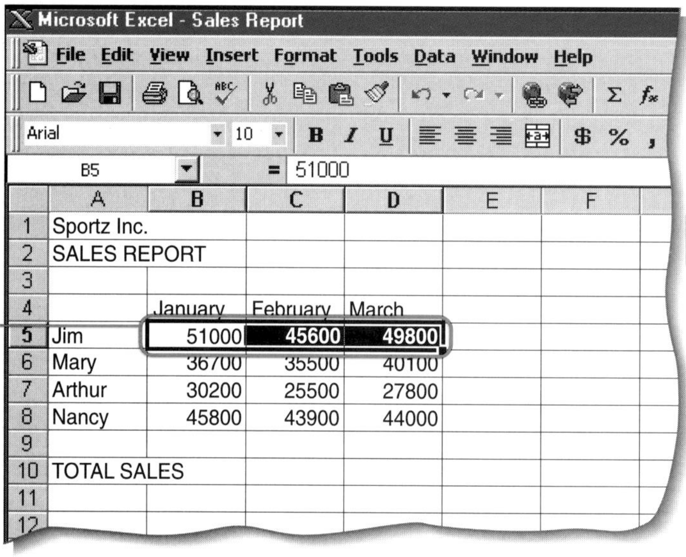

1 Select the cell(s) containing the data you want to delete. To select cells, refer to page 16.

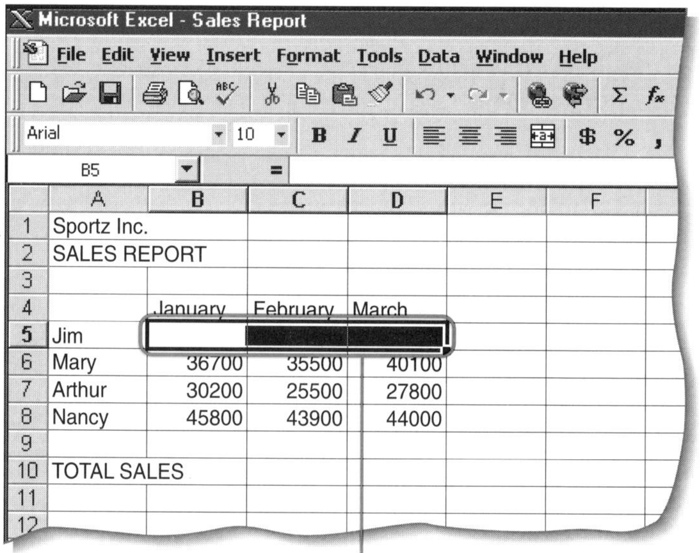

2 Press Delete on your keyboard.

■ The data in the cell(s) you selected disappears.

UNDO LAST CHANGE

UNDO LAST CHANGE

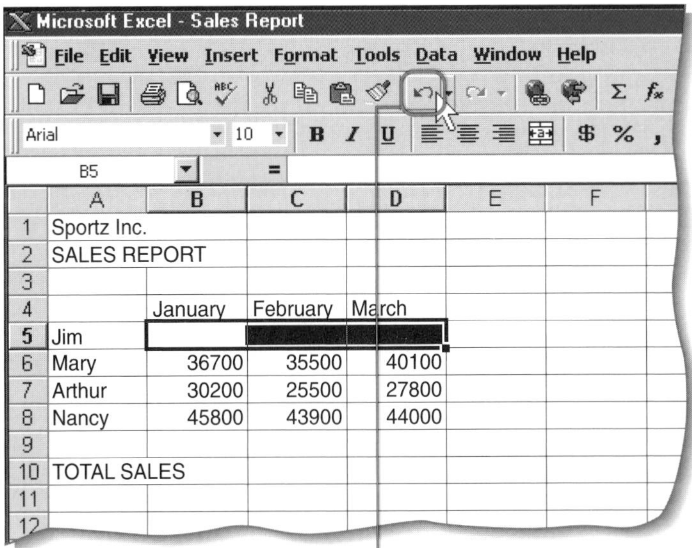

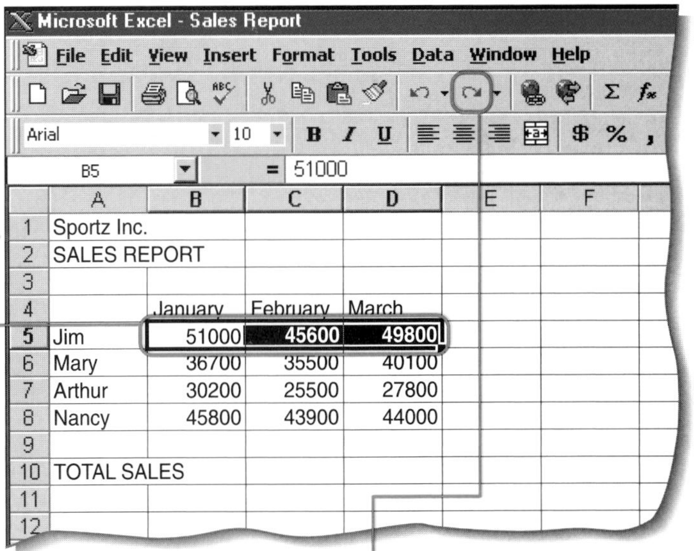

The Undo feature can cancel your last editing and formatting changes.

1 To undo your last change, move the mouse over the Undo button and then press the left mouse button.

■ Excel cancels the last change you made to your worksheet.

■ You can repeat step 1 to cancel previous changes you made.

■ To reverse the results of using the Undo feature, move the mouse over the Redo button and then press the left mouse button.

MOVE DATA

MOVE DATA

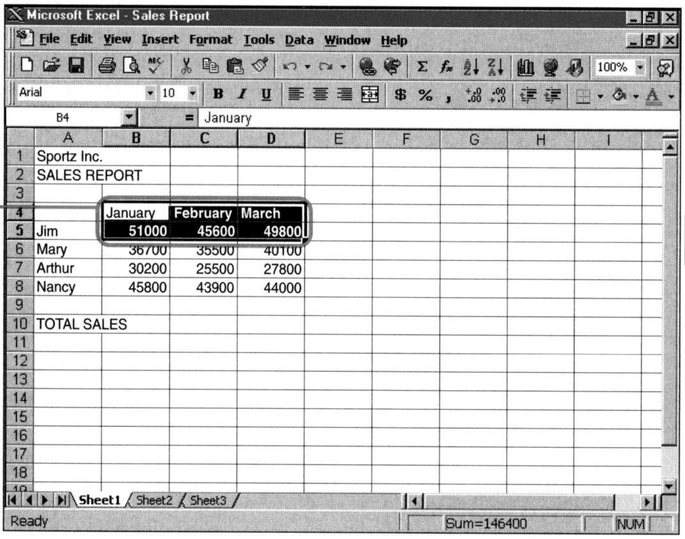

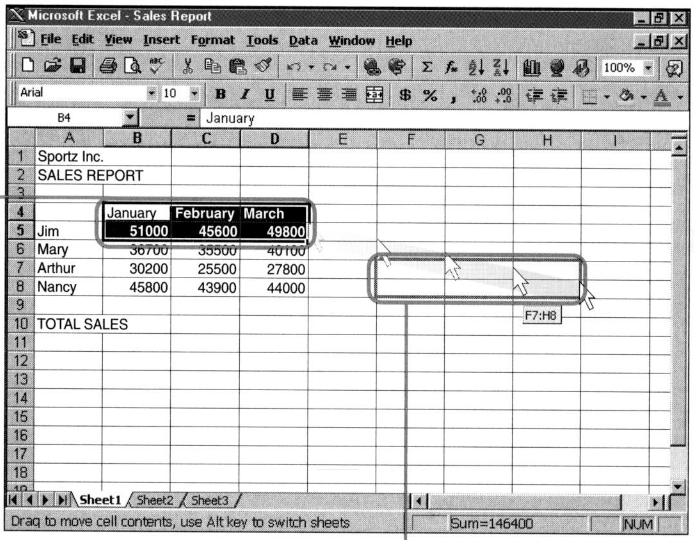

1 Select the cells containing the data you want to move. To select cells, refer to page 16.

2 Move the mouse ✥ over a border of the selected cells (✥ changes to ↖).

3 Press and hold down the left mouse button as you move the mouse ↖ to where you want to place the data.

Why does this message appear when I try to move data?

This message may appear when you try to move data to a location that already contains data.

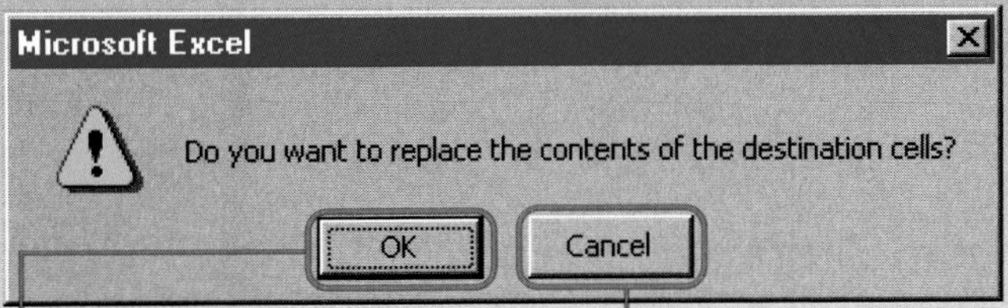

■ If you want Excel to replace the existing data with the data you are moving, move the mouse over **OK** and then press the left mouse button.

■ To cancel the move, move the mouse over **Cancel** and then press the left mouse button.

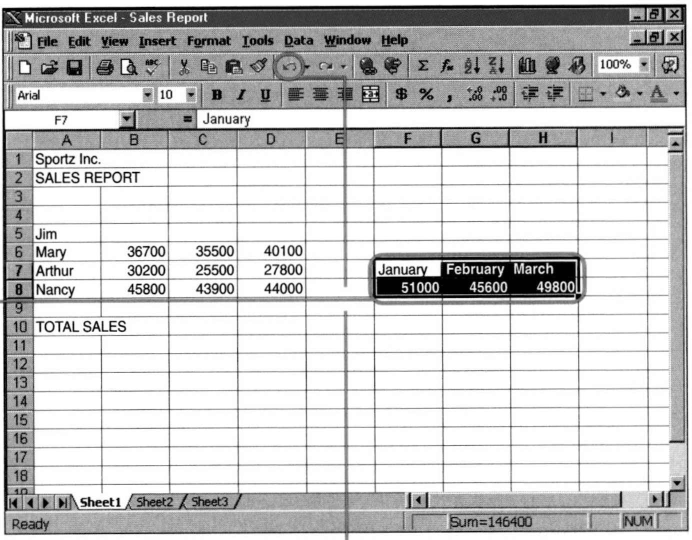

4 Release the mouse button and the data moves to the new location.

UNDO THE MOVE

■ To immediately move the data back, move the mouse over and then press the left mouse button.

MOVE DATA USING TOOLBAR BUTTONS

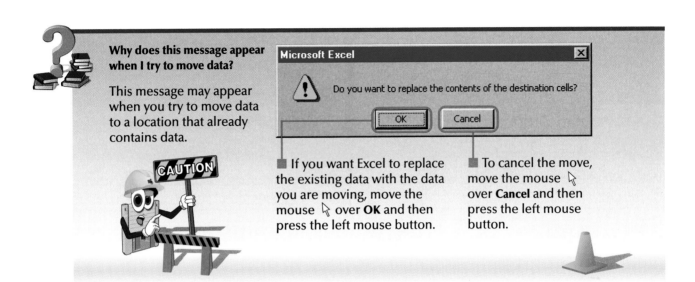

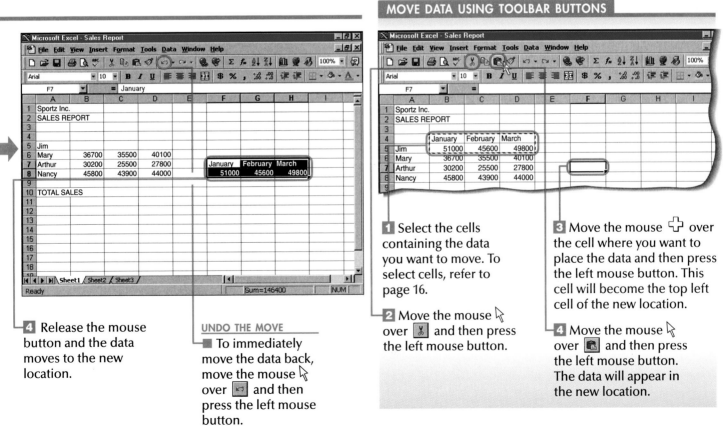

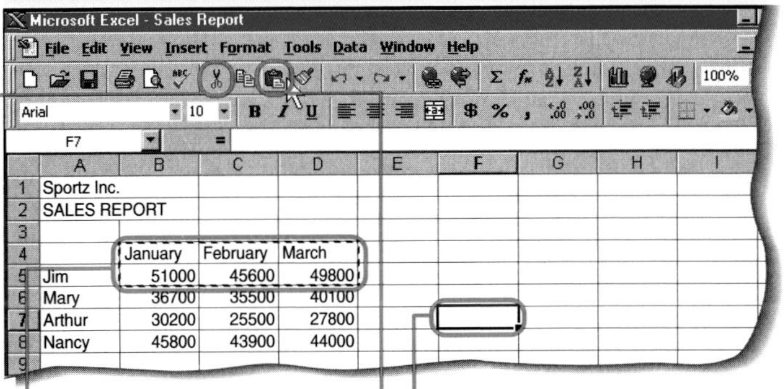

1 Select the cells containing the data you want to move. To select cells, refer to page 16.

2 Move the mouse over and then press the left mouse button.

3 Move the mouse over the cell where you want to place the data and then press the left mouse button. This cell will become the top left cell of the new location.

4 Move the mouse over and then press the left mouse button. The data will appear in the new location.

COPY DATA

You can place a copy of data in a different location in your worksheet. This will save you time since you do not have to retype the data.

COPY DATA

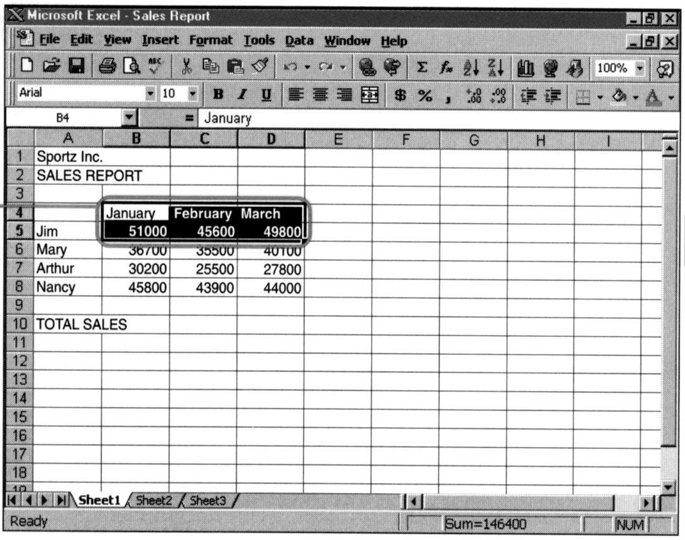

1 Select the cells containing the data you want to copy. To select cells, refer to page 16.

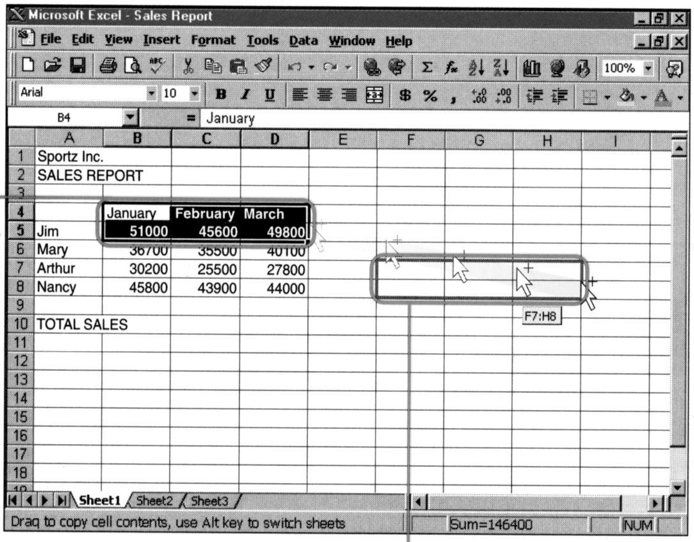

2 Move the mouse ✥ over a border of the selected cells (✥ changes to ↖).

3 Press and hold down **Ctrl** on your keyboard.

4 Still holding down **Ctrl**, press and hold down the left mouse button as you move the mouse ↖+ to where you want to place the copy.

How can I quickly copy data to the active cell?

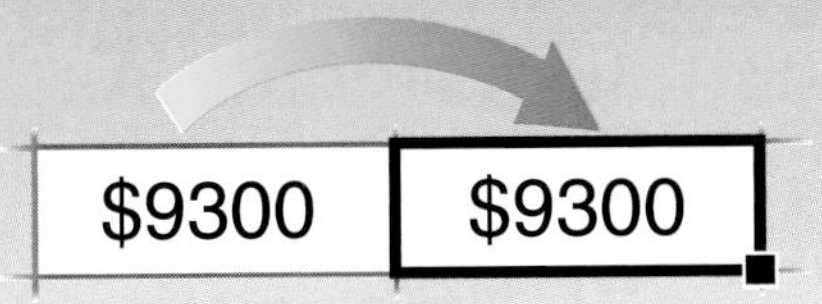

■ To quickly copy the contents of the cell on the left of the active cell, press and hold down Ctrl as you press R on your keyboard.

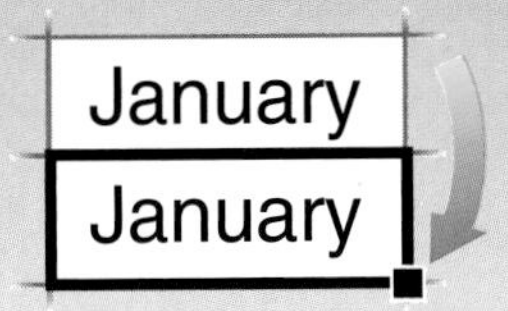

■ To quickly copy the contents of the cell above the active cell, press and hold down Ctrl as you press D on your keyboard.

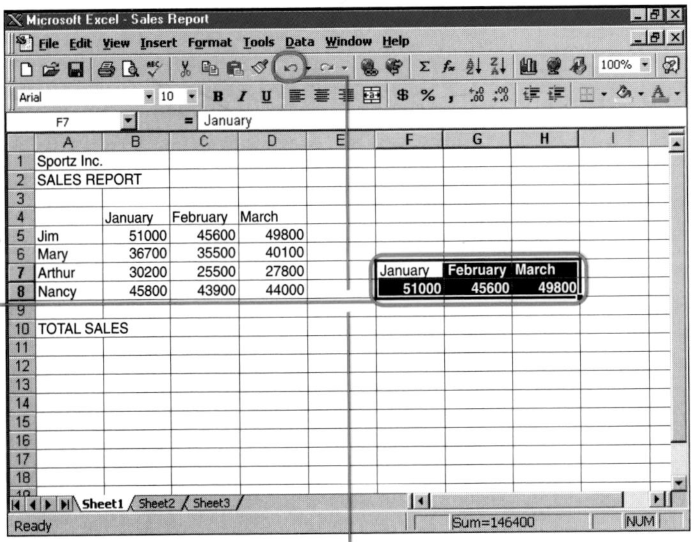

5 Release the mouse button and then release Ctrl.

■ A copy of the data appears in the new location.

UNDO THE COPY

■ To immediately remove the copy, move the mouse over the Undo button and then press the left mouse button.

COPY DATA USING TOOLBAR BUTTONS

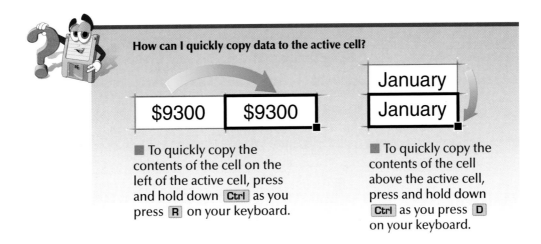

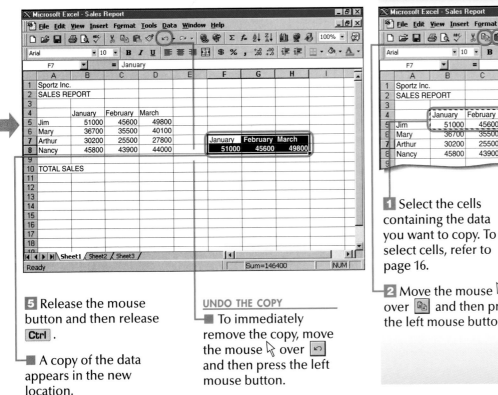

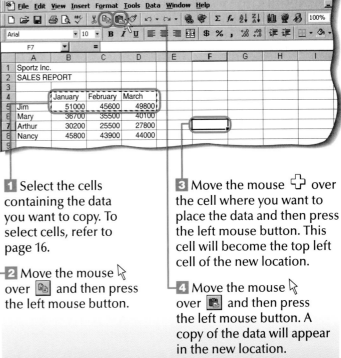

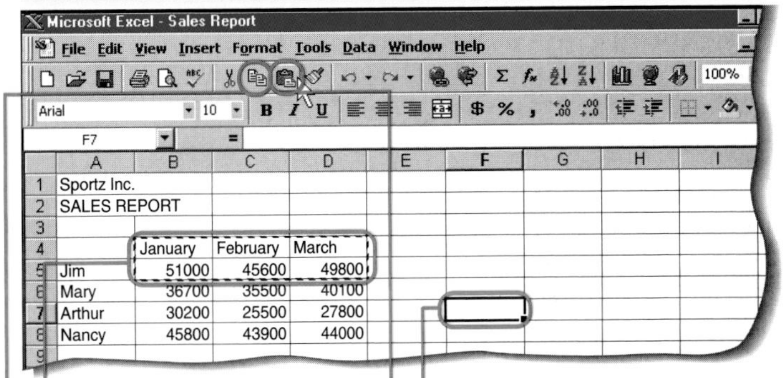

1 Select the cells containing the data you want to copy. To select cells, refer to page 16.

2 Move the mouse over the Copy button and then press the left mouse button.

3 Move the mouse over the cell where you want to place the data and then press the left mouse button. This cell will become the top left cell of the new location.

4 Move the mouse over the Paste button and then press the left mouse button. A copy of the data will appear in the new location.

CHECK SPELLING

Excel compares every word in your worksheet to words in its dictionary. If a word does not exist in the dictionary, Excel considers it misspelled.

CHECK SPELLING

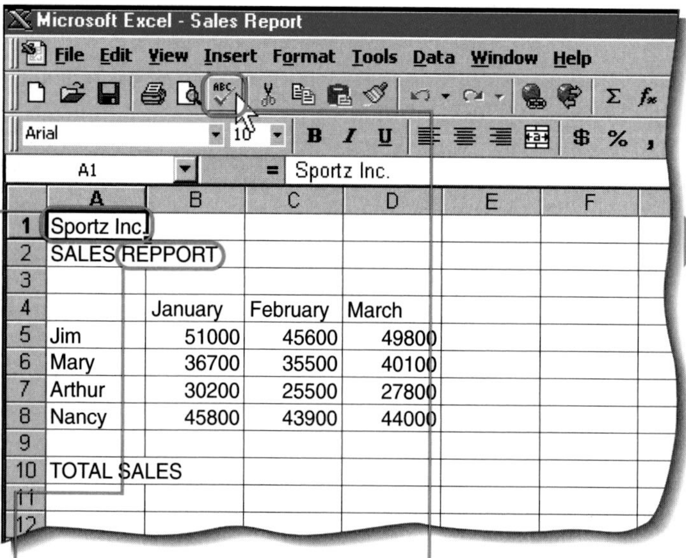

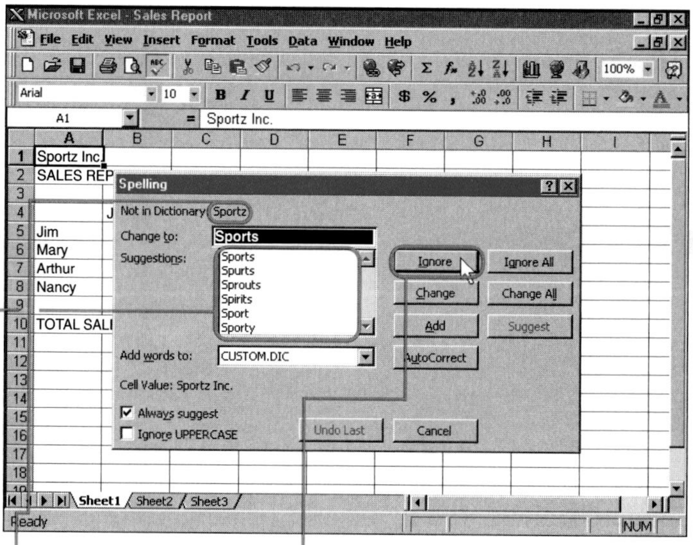

■ In this example, the spelling of **REPORT** was changed to **REPPORT**.

1 To start the spell check at the beginning of your worksheet, move the mouse over cell **A1** and then press the left mouse button.

2 To start the spell check, move the mouse over and then press the left mouse button.

■ The **Spelling** dialog box appears if Excel finds a misspelled word.

■ This area displays the first misspelled word.

■ This area displays suggestions to correct the word.

IGNORE AN ERROR

3 To ignore an error and continue checking your worksheet, move the mouse over **Ignore** and then press the left mouse button.

*Note: To ignore an error and all occurrences of the error in the worksheet, move the mouse over **Ignore All** and then press the left mouse button.*

Can Excel automatically correct my typing mistakes?

Excel automatically corrects common spelling errors as you type.

adn	and
alot	a lot
comittee	committee
statment	statement
nwe	new
occurence	occurrence
recieve	receive
seperate	separate
teh	the

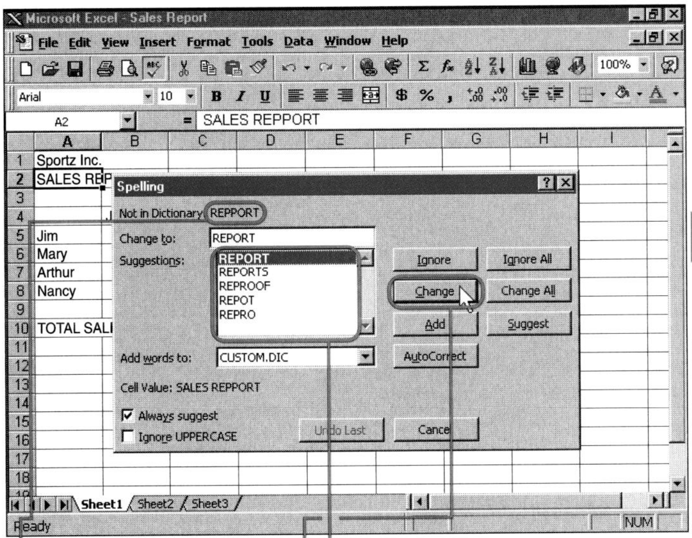

■ This area displays the next misspelled word.

CORRECT AN ERROR

4 To correct an error, move the mouse over the correct spelling and then press the left mouse button.

5 Move the mouse over **Change** and then press the left mouse button.

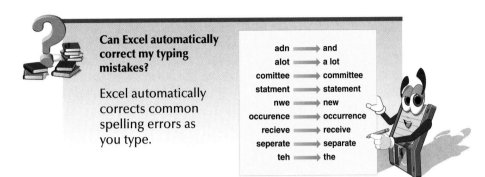

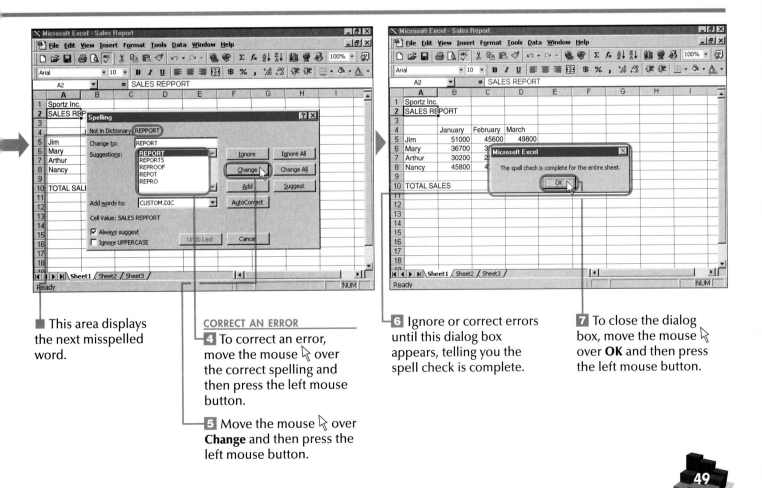

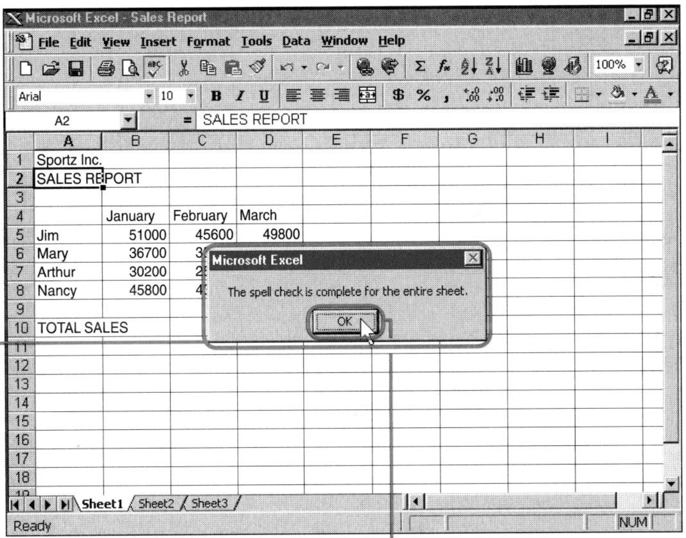

6 Ignore or correct errors until this dialog box appears, telling you the spell check is complete.

7 To close the dialog box, move the mouse over **OK** and then press the left mouse button.

FIND DATA

Excel will find the data even if it is part of a larger word or number. For example, searching for 105 will find 105, 2105 and 1056.

FIND DATA

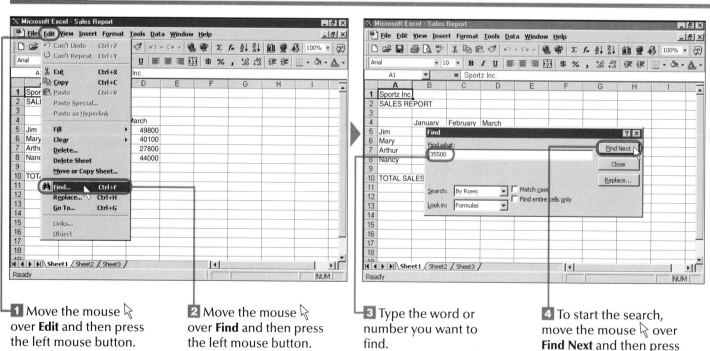

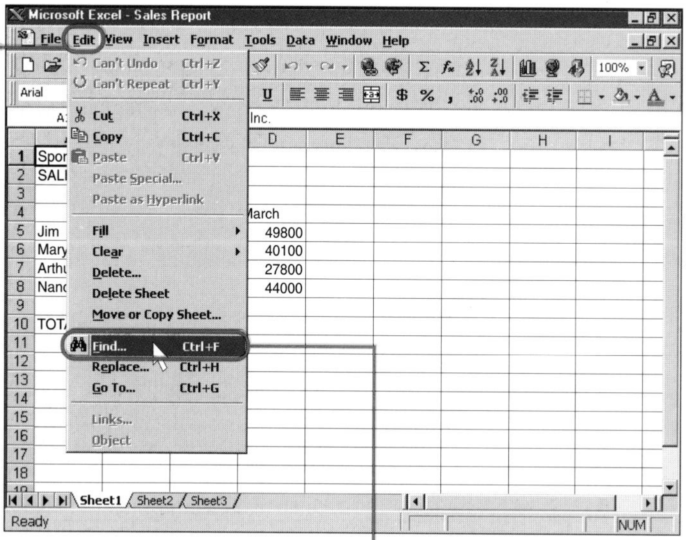

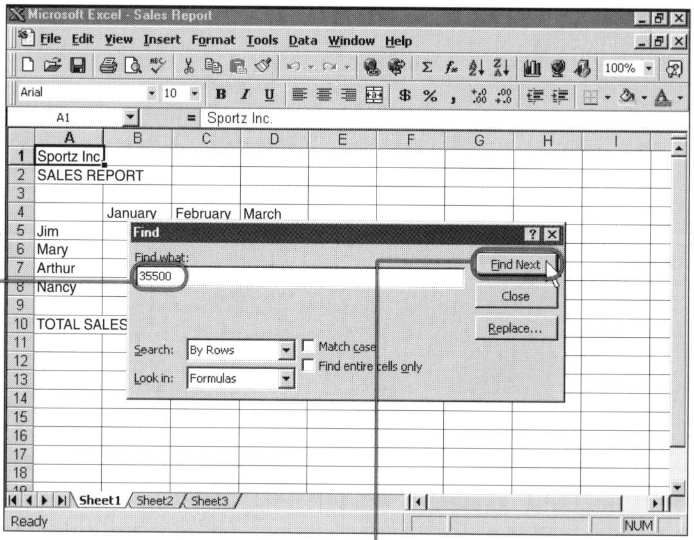

1 Move the mouse over **Edit** and then press the left mouse button.

2 Move the mouse over **Find** and then press the left mouse button.

- The **Find** dialog box appears.

3 Type the word or number you want to find.

4 To start the search, move the mouse over **Find Next** and then press the left mouse button.

What happens if Excel cannot find the word or number I am searching for?

If Excel cannot find the word or number you specified, a dialog box appears.

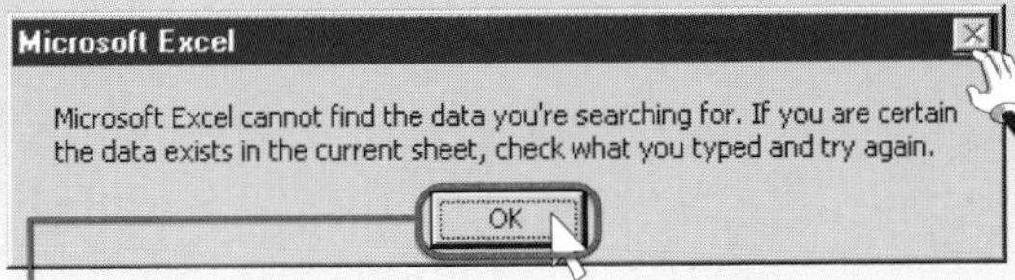

Microsoft Excel
Microsoft Excel cannot find the data you're searching for. If you are certain the data exists in the current sheet, check what you typed and try again.
OK

■ To close the dialog box, move the mouse over **OK** and then press the left mouse button.

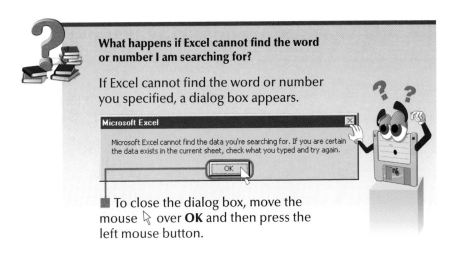

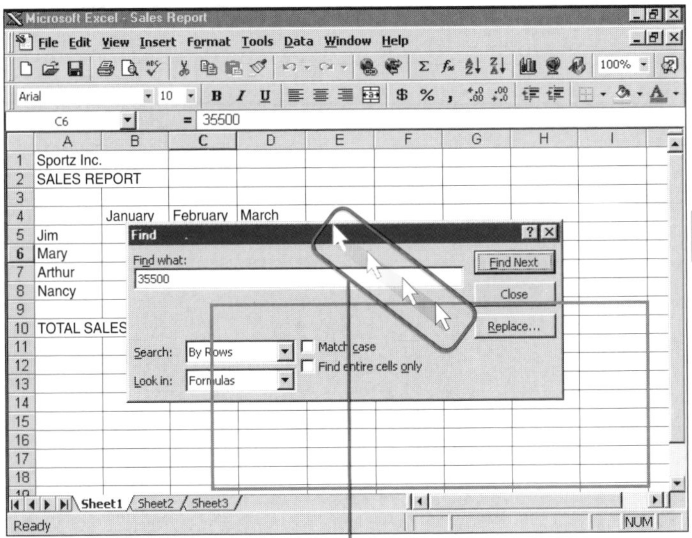

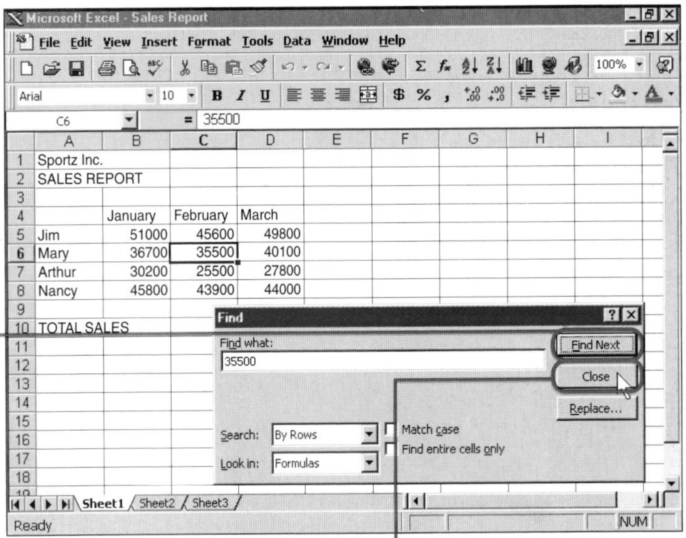

■ Excel highlights the first cell containing the word or number.

■ If the highlighted cell is hidden behind the **Find** dialog box, you can move the dialog box.

5 To move the **Find** dialog box, move the mouse over the title bar.

6 Press and hold down the left mouse button as you move the dialog box to a new location. Then release the mouse button.

7 To find the next matching word or number, move the mouse over **Find Next** and then press the left mouse button.

8 To close the dialog box, move the mouse over **Close** and then press the left mouse button.

INSERT A ROW OR COLUMN

INSERT A ROW

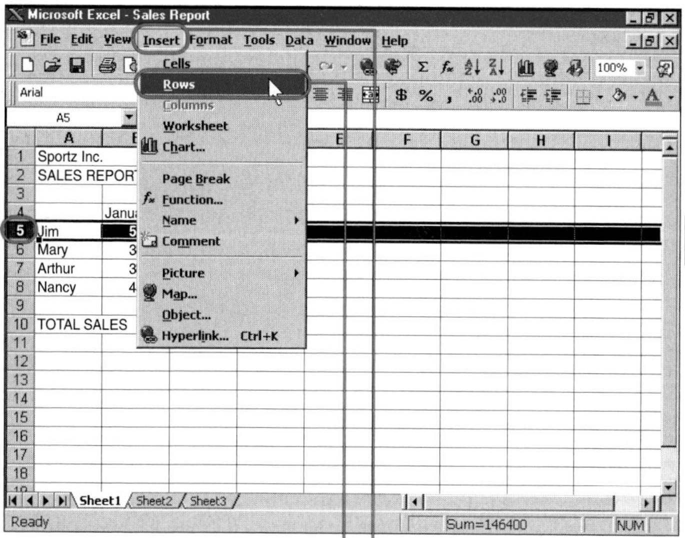

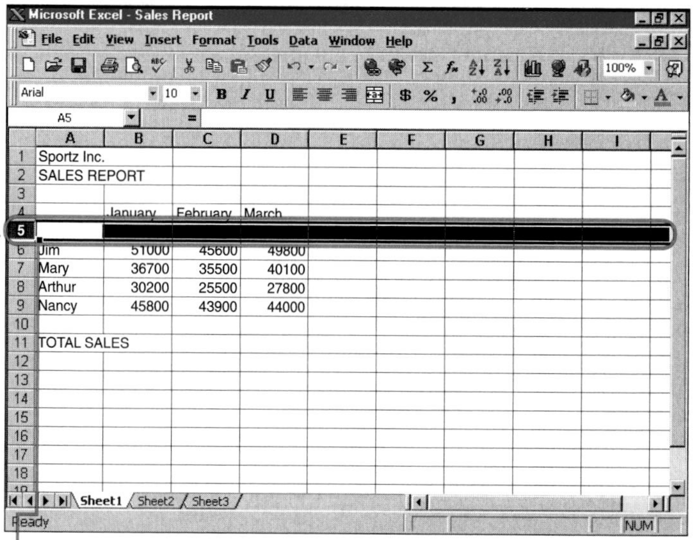

Excel will insert a row above the row you select.

1 To select a row, move the mouse ✚ over the row number and then press the left mouse button.

2 Move the mouse ↖ over **Insert** and then press the left mouse button.

3 Move the mouse ↖ over **Rows** and then press the left mouse button.

■ The new row appears and all the rows that follow shift downward.

Do I need to adjust my formulas when I insert a row or column?

When you insert a row or column, Excel updates any formulas affected by the insertion.

Note: For information on formulas, refer to page 58.

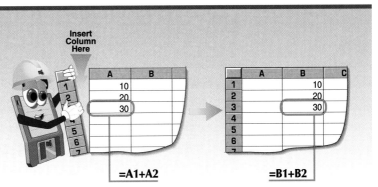

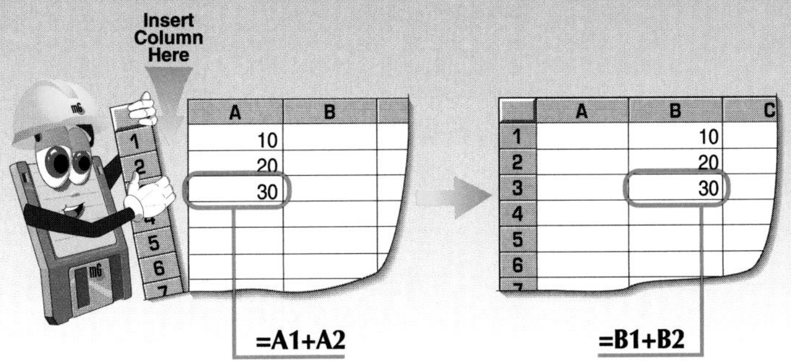

INSERT A COLUMN

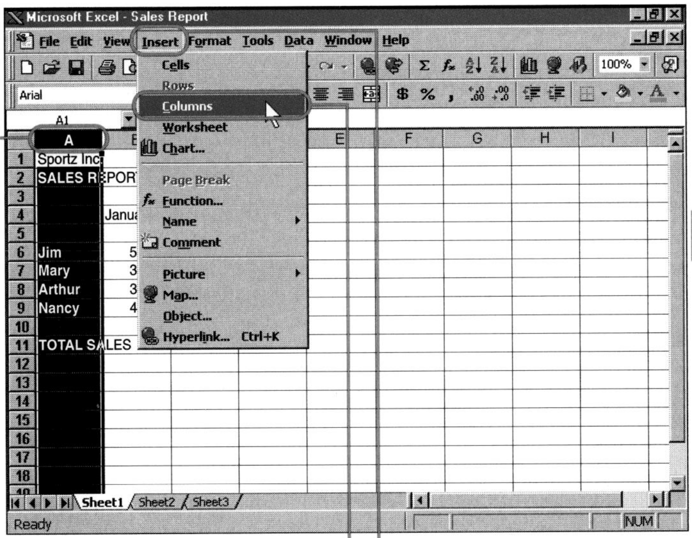

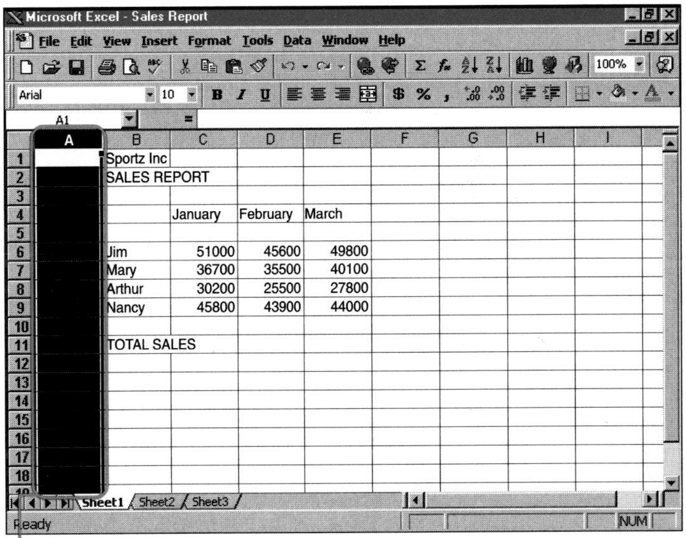

Excel will insert a column to the left of the column you select.

1 To select a column, move the mouse ✣ over the column letter and then press the left mouse button.

2 Move the mouse ↖ over **Insert** and then press the left mouse button.

3 Move the mouse ↖ over **Columns** and then press the left mouse button.

■ The new column appears and all the columns that follow shift to the right.

DELETE A ROW OR COLUMN

You can delete a row or column from your worksheet to remove cells you no longer need.

DELETE A ROW

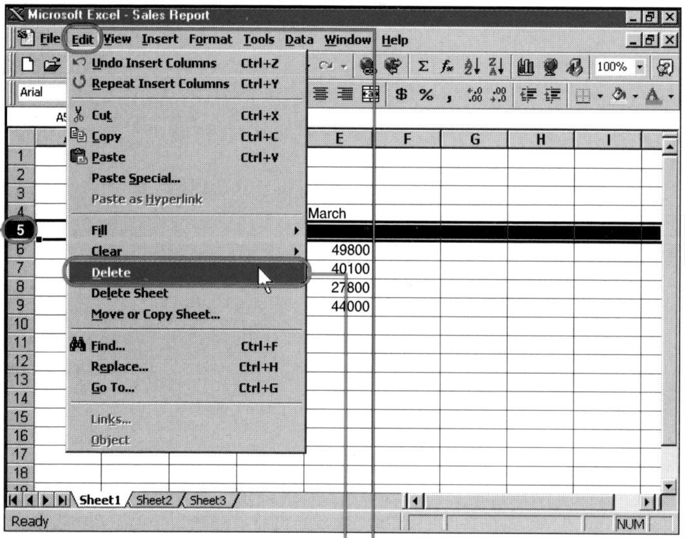

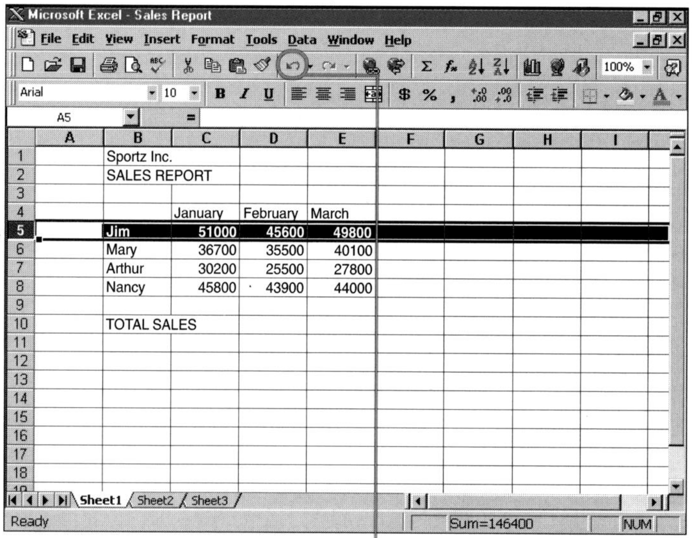

1 To select the row you want to delete, move the mouse over the row number and then press the left mouse button.

2 Move the mouse over **Edit** and then press the left mouse button.

3 Move the mouse over **Delete** and then press the left mouse button.

■ The row disappears and all the rows that follow shift upward.

■ To immediately return the row to your worksheet, move the mouse over the Undo button and then press the left mouse button.

Why did #REF! appear in a cell after I deleted a row or column?

If **#REF!** appears in a cell in your worksheet, you deleted data needed to calculate a formula.

Note: For information on formulas, refer to page 58.

DELETE A COLUMN

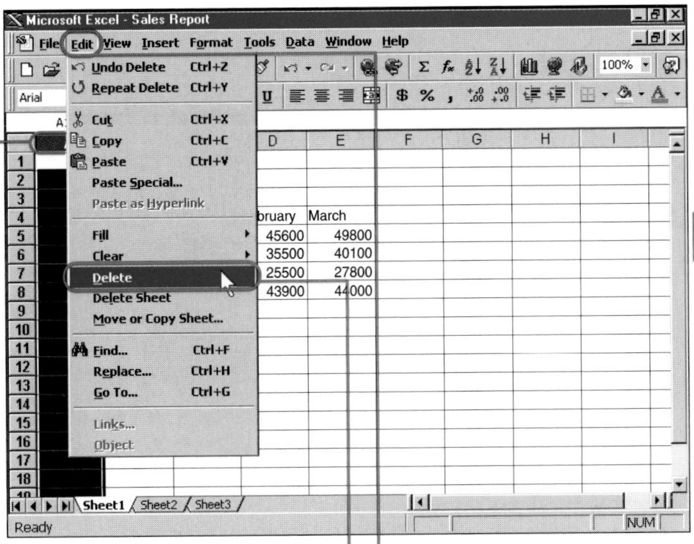

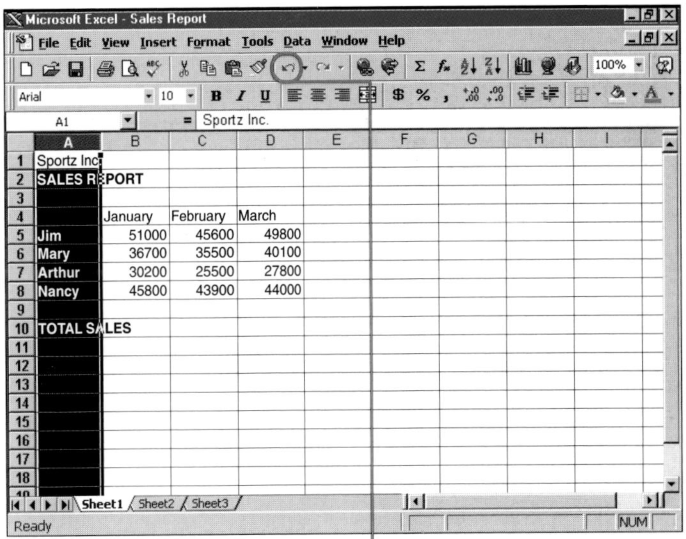

1 To select the column you want to delete, move the mouse ✥ over the column letter and then press the left mouse button.

2 Move the mouse ↖ over **Edit** and then press the left mouse button.

3 Move the mouse ↖ over **Delete** and then press the left mouse button.

■ The column disappears and all the columns that follow shift to the left.

■ To immediately return the column to your worksheet, move the mouse ↖ over ↶ and then press the left mouse button.

=AVERAG
=(A1+A2+
=(10+20+3
=25

CHAPTER 4

WORK WITH FORMULAS AND FUNCTIONS

Are you ready to perform calculations on the data in your worksheet? This chapter teaches you how to work with formulas and functions.

ENTER A FORMULA

A formula always begins with an equal sign (=).

INTRODUCTION TO FORMULAS

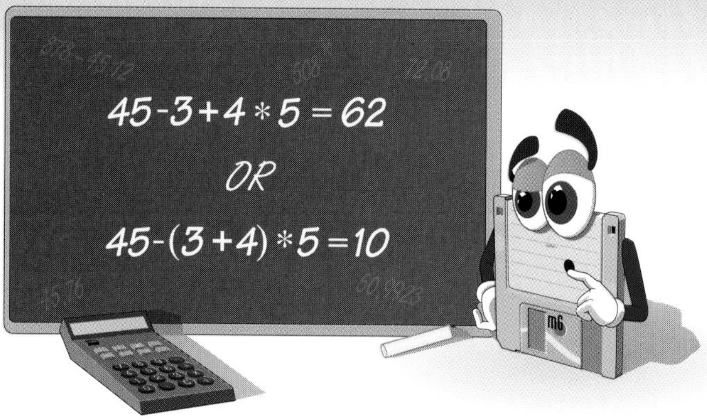

Order of Calculations

Excel performs calculations in the following order:

1 Exponents (^)
2 Multiplication (*) and Division (/)
3 Addition (+) and Subtraction (-)

You can use parentheses ( ) to change the order in which Excel performs calculations. Excel will calculate the data inside the parentheses first.

Cell References

When entering formulas, use cell references (example: **=A1+A2**) instead of actual data (example: **=10+30**) whenever possible. When you use cell references and you change a number used in a formula, Excel will automatically redo the calculations for you.

EXAMPLES OF FORMULAS

	A	B
1	10	
2	20	
3	30	
4	40	
5		
6	1230	

■ This cell contains the formula:

=A1+A2+A3*A4

=10+20+30*40

=1230

	A	B
1	10	
2	20	
3	30	
4	40	
5		
6	2010	

■ This cell contains the formula:

=A1+(A2+A3)*A4

=10+(20+30)*40

=2010

	A	B
1	10	
2	20	
3	30	
4	40	
5		
6	320	

■ This cell contains the formula:

=A1*A3-A2+A4

=10*30-20+40

=320

	A	B
1	10	
2	20	
3	30	
4	40	
5		
6	140	

■ This cell contains the formula:

=A1*(A3-A2)+A4

=10*(30-20)+40

=140

	A	B
1	10	
2	20	
3	30	
4	40	
5		
6	63	

■ This cell contains the formula:

=A3/A1+A2+A4

=30/10+20+40

=63

	A	B
1	10	
2	20	
3	30	
4	40	
5		
6	41	

■ This cell contains the formula:

=A3/(A1+A2)+A4

=30/(10+20)+40

=41

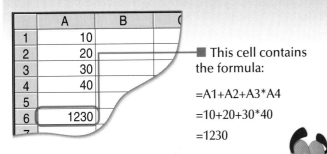

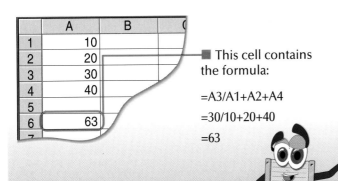

ENTER A FORMULA

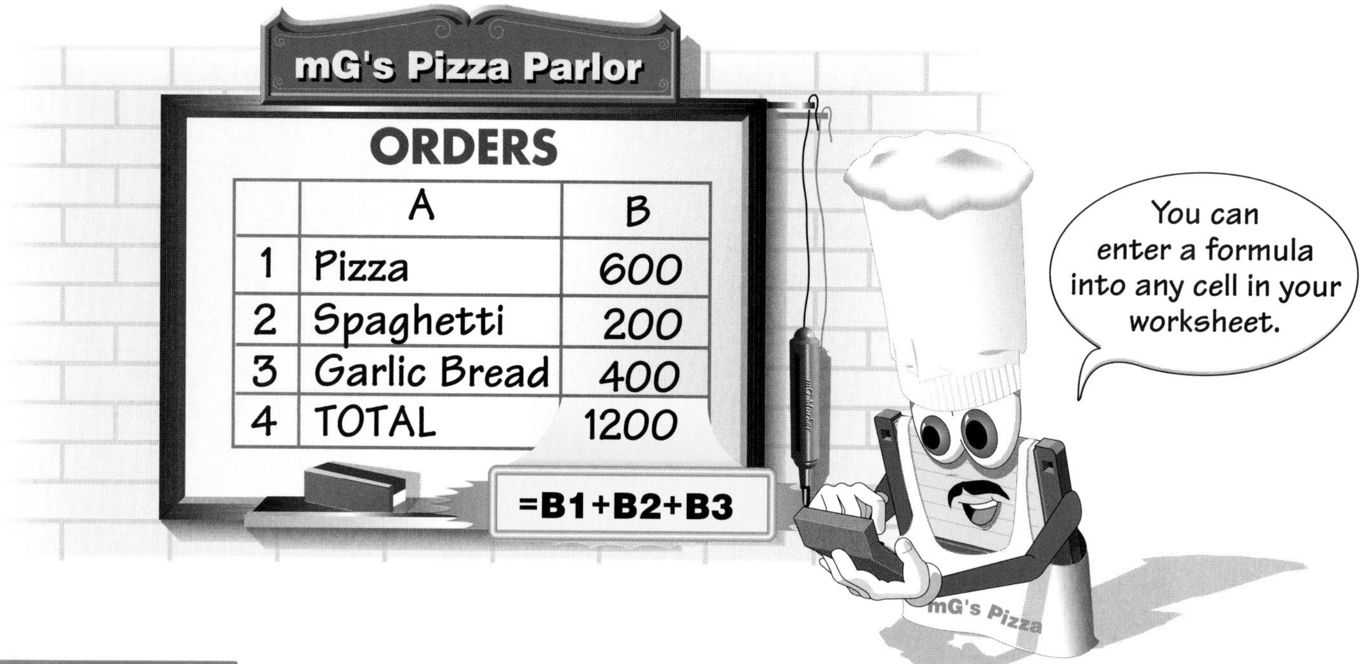

mG's Pizza Parlor
ORDERS
A B
1 Pizza 600
2 Spaghetti 200
3 Garlic Bread 400
4 TOTAL 1200
=B1+B2+B3
mG's Pizza
You can enter a formula into any cell in your worksheet.

ENTER A FORMULA

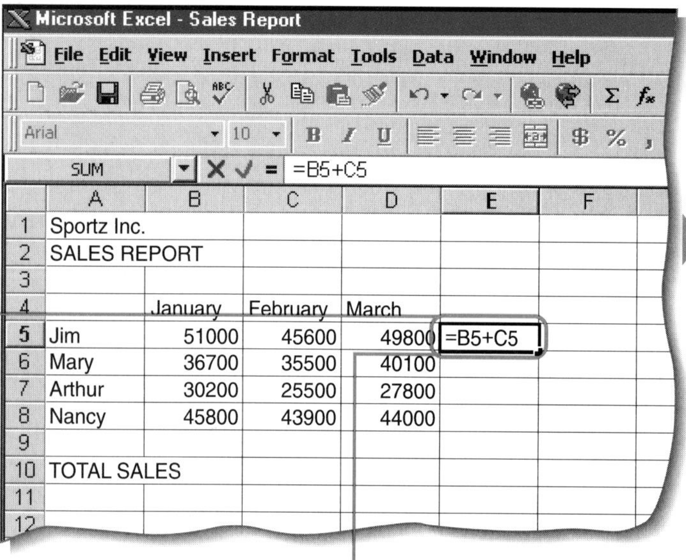

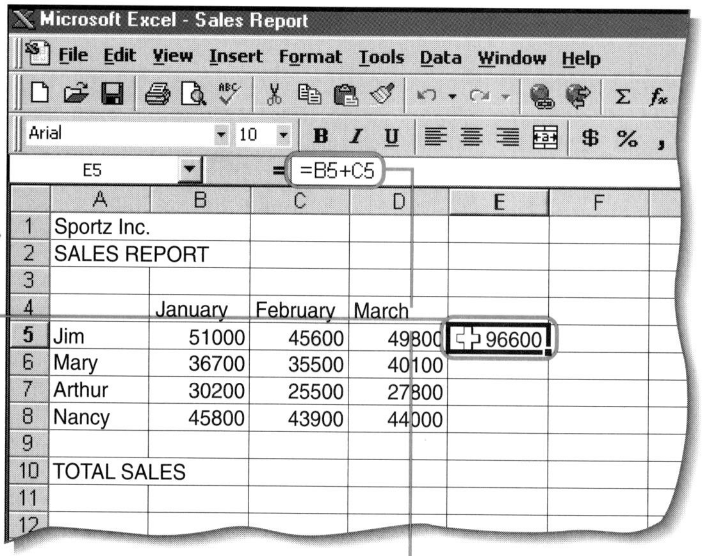

1 Move the mouse ✜ over the cell where you want to enter a formula and then press the left mouse button.

2 Type an equal sign (=) to begin the formula.

3 Type the formula and then press Enter on your keyboard.

■ The result of the calculation appears in the cell.

4 To view the formula you entered, move the mouse ✜ over the cell containing the formula and then press the left mouse button.

■ The formula for the cell appears in the formula bar.

What happens if I change a number used in a formula?

If you change a number used in a formula, Excel will automatically calculate a new result.

EDIT A FORMULA

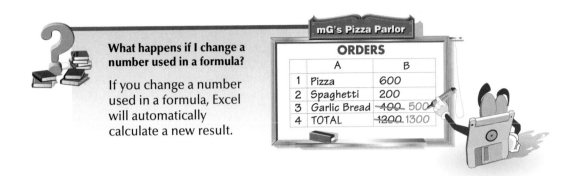

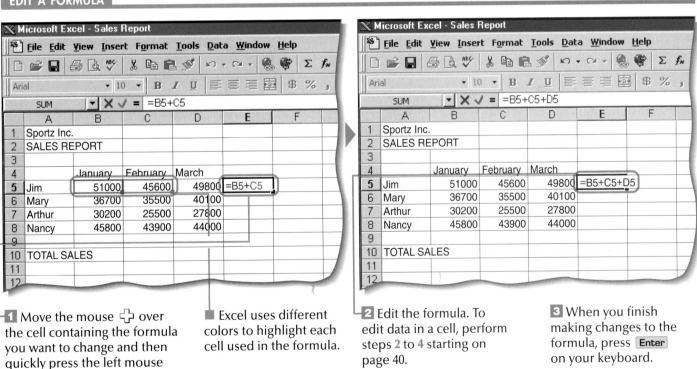

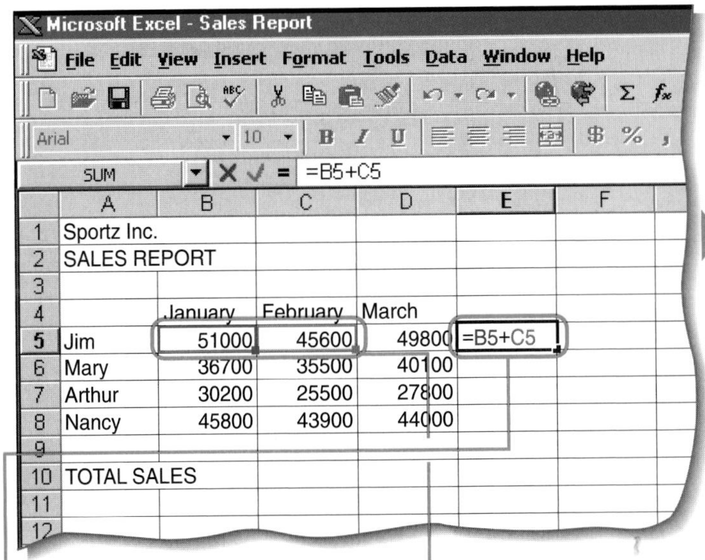

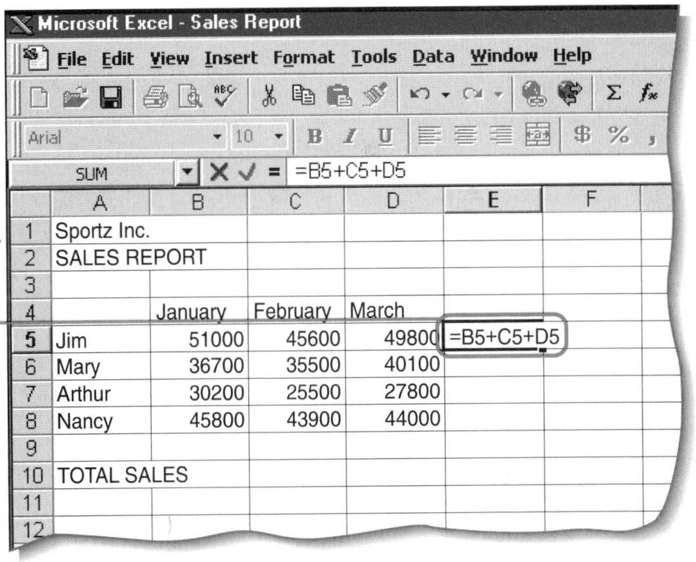

1 Move the mouse ✣ over the cell containing the formula you want to change and then quickly press the left mouse button twice.

■ The formula appears in the cell.

■ Excel uses different colors to highlight each cell used in the formula.

2 Edit the formula. To edit data in a cell, perform steps 2 to 4 starting on page 40.

3 When you finish making changes to the formula, press Enter on your keyboard.

ENTER A FUNCTION

A function is a ready-to-use formula that performs a specialized calculation on your worksheet data.
ROUND
SUM
MAX
AVERAGE
FUNCTIONS
Ready to use right out of the box!
FUNCTIONS

INTRODUCTION TO FUNCTIONS

■ A function always begins with an equal sign (=).

■ The data Excel will use to calculate a function is enclosed in parentheses ( ).

```
=SUM(A1,A2,A3)
=AVERAGE(C1,C2,C3)
=MAX(B7,C7,D7,E7)
=COUNT(D12,D13,D14)
```

Specify Individual Cells

When there is a comma (,) between cell references in a function, Excel uses each cell to perform the calculation.

For example, =SUM(A1,A2,A3) is the same as the formula =A1+A2+A3.

```
=SUM(A1:A3)
=AVERAGE(C1:C3)
=MAX(B7:E7)
=COUNT(D12:D14)
```

Specify Group of Cells

When there is a colon (:) THRU between cell references in a function, Excel uses the specified cells and all cells between them to perform the calculation.

For example, =SUM(A1:A3) is the same as the formula =A1+A2+A3.

COMMON FUNCTIONS

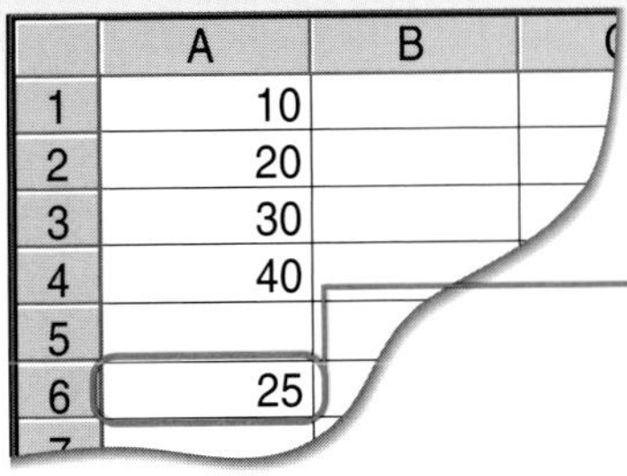

Average

Calculates the average value of a list of numbers.

■ This cell contains the function:

=AVERAGE(A1:A4)

=(A1+A2+A3+A4)/4

=(10+20+30+40)/4

=25

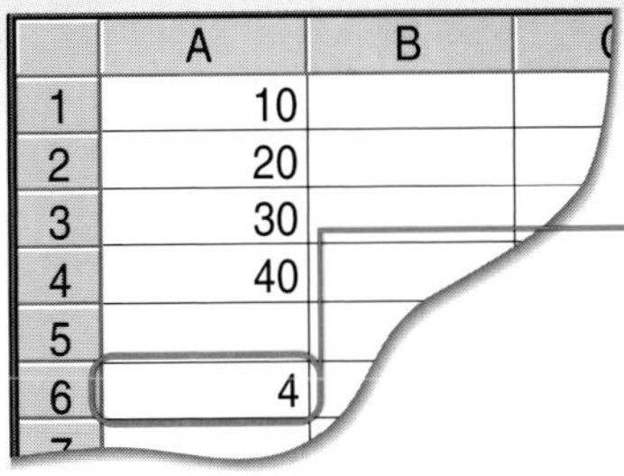

Count

Calculates the number of values in a list.

■ This cell contains the function:

=COUNT(A1:A4)

=4

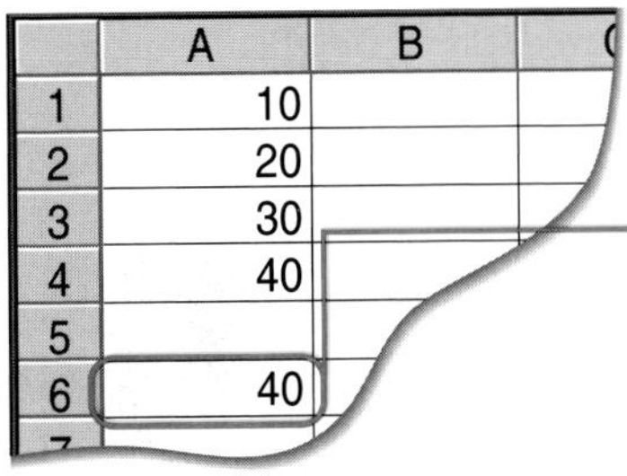

Max

Finds the largest value in a list of numbers.

■ This cell contains the function:

=MAX(A1:A4)

=40

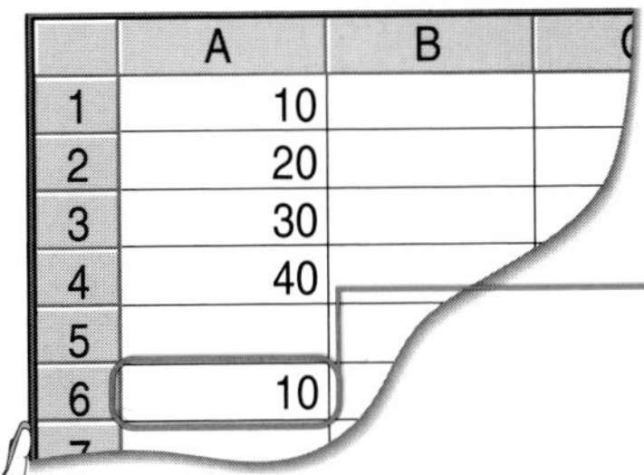

Min

Finds the smallest value in a list of numbers.

■ This cell contains the function:

=MIN(A1:A4)

=10

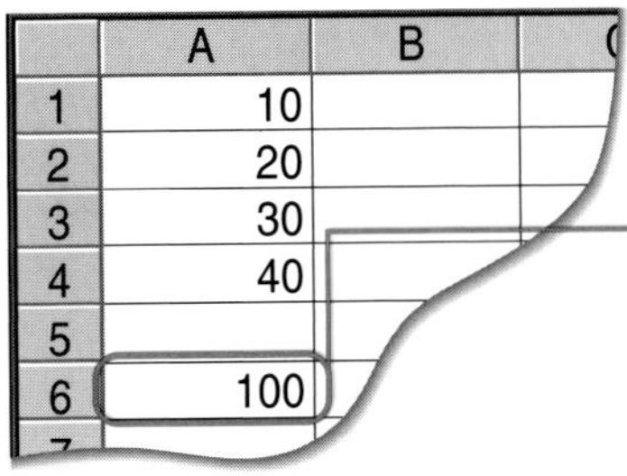

Sum

Adds a list of numbers.

■ This cell contains the function:

=SUM(A1:A4)

=A1+A2+A3+A4

=10+20+30+40

=100

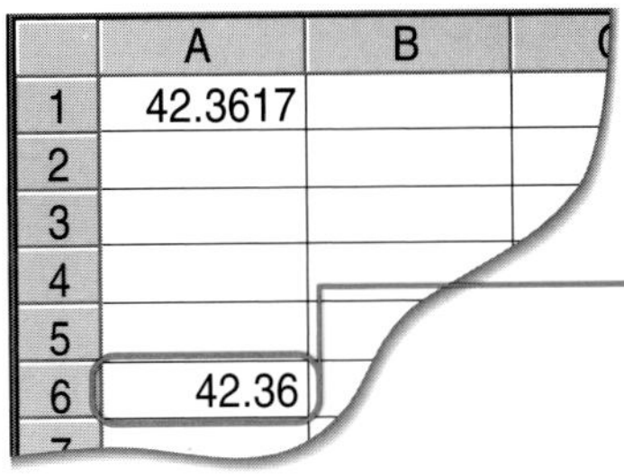

Round

Rounds a value to a specific number of digits.

■ This cell contains the function:

=ROUND(A1,2)

=42.36

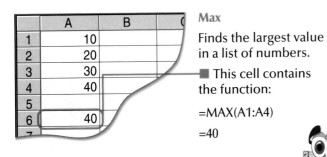

ENTER A FUNCTION

ENTER A FUNCTION

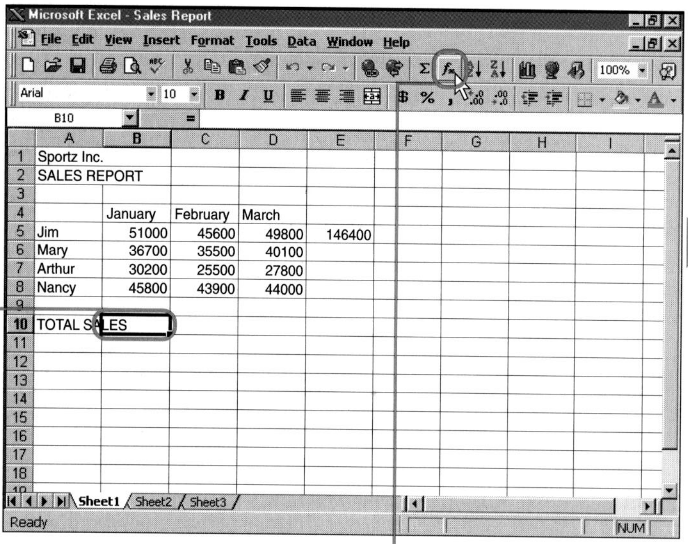

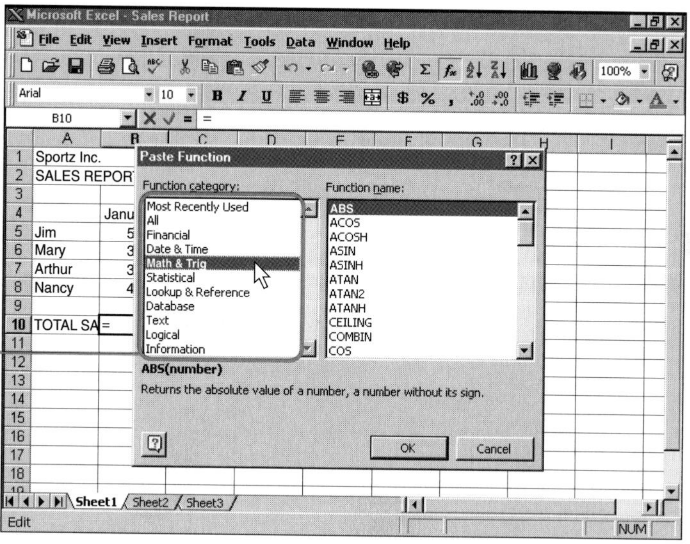

1 Move the mouse ✥ over the cell where you want to enter a function and then press the left mouse button.

2 Move the mouse ↖ over *fx* and then press the left mouse button.

■ The **Paste Function** dialog box appears.

3 Move the mouse ↖ over the category that contains the function you want to use and then press the left mouse button.

*Note: If you do not know which category contains the function you want to use, select **All** to display a list of all the functions.*

How many functions does Excel offer?

Excel offers over 200 functions to help you analyze data in your worksheet. There are financial functions, math and trigonometry functions, date and time functions, statistical functions and many more.

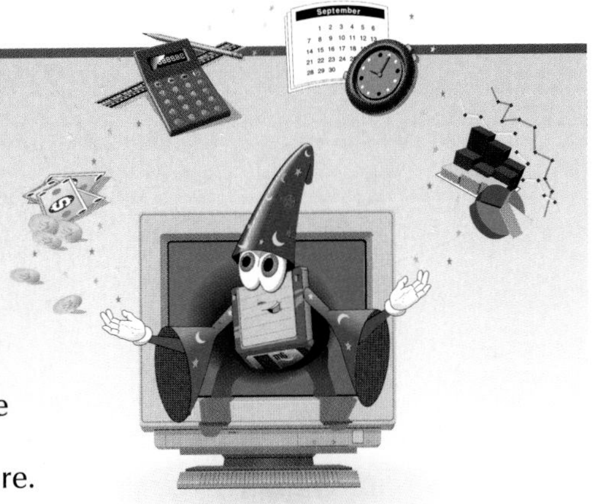

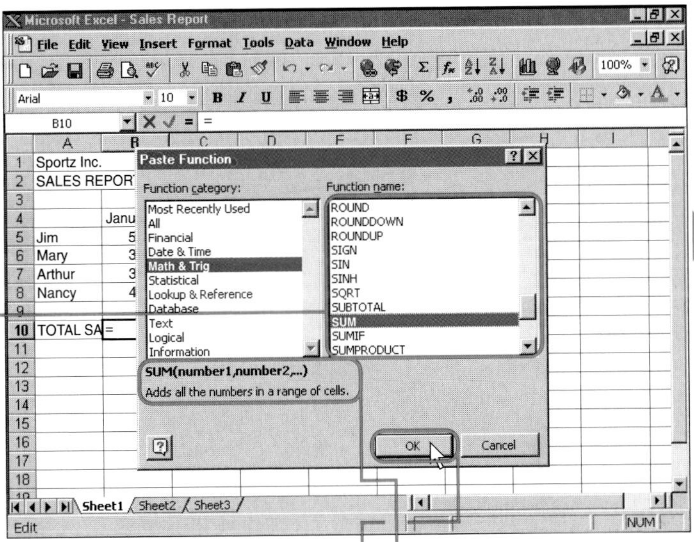

■ This area displays the functions in the category you selected.

4 Move the mouse over a function of interest and then press the left mouse button.

■ This area describes the function you selected.

5 To enter the function in your worksheet, move the mouse over **OK** and then press the left mouse button.

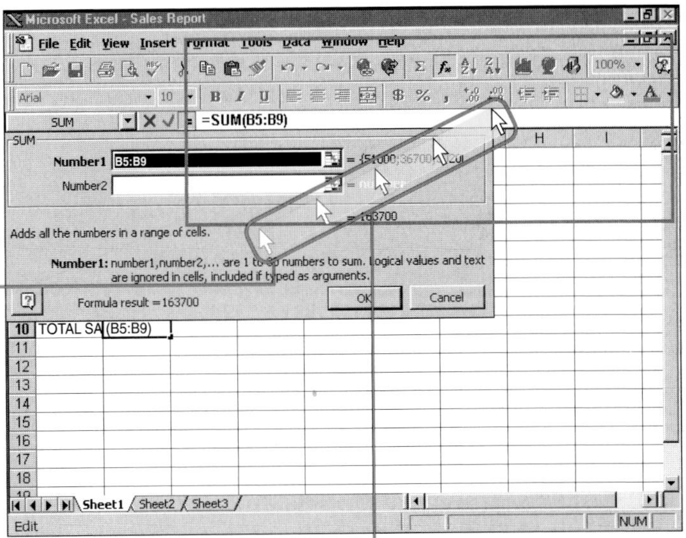

■ A dialog box appears. If the dialog box covers data you want to use in the calculation, you can move it to a new location.

6 To move the dialog box, move the mouse over a blank area in the dialog box.

7 Press and hold down the left mouse button as you move the dialog box to a new location. Then release the mouse button.

CONTINUED

ENTER A FUNCTION

ENTER A FUNCTION (CONTINUED)

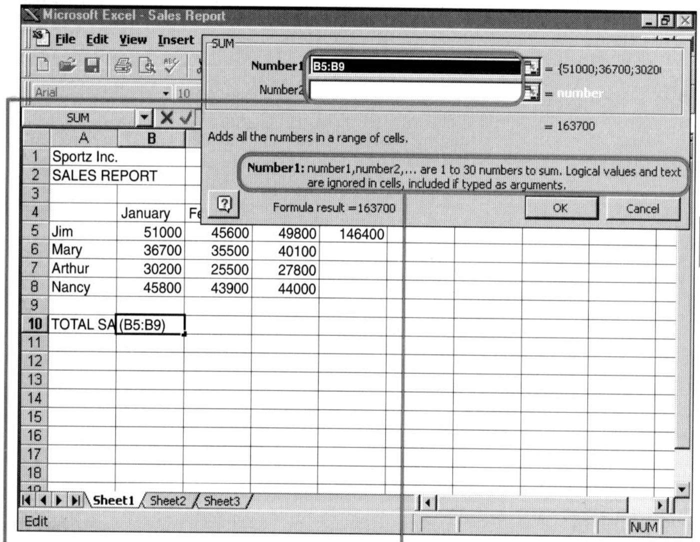

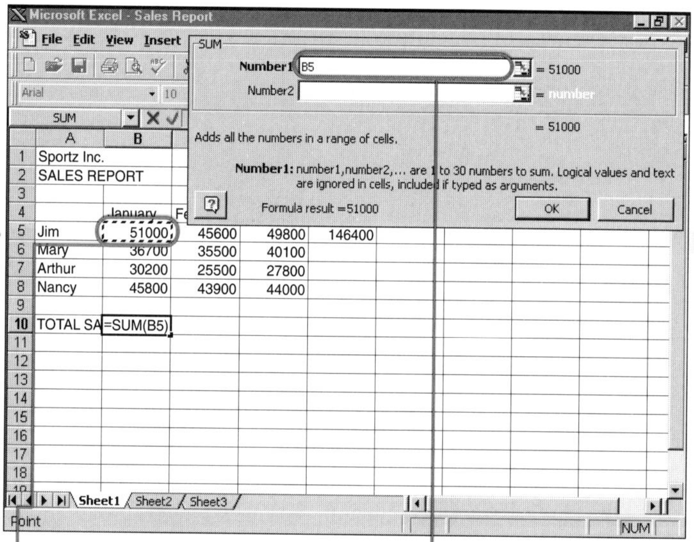

■ This area displays boxes where you enter the numbers you want to use in the calculation.

■ This area describes the number you need to enter.

8 To enter a number, move the mouse ✥ over the cell in your worksheet containing the number and then press the left mouse button.

Note: If the number you want to enter does not appear in the worksheet, type the number.

■ This area now displays the cell you selected.

Can I enter a function by myself?

You can easily enter a function yourself by typing the entire function into a cell.

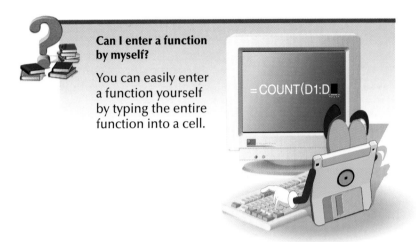

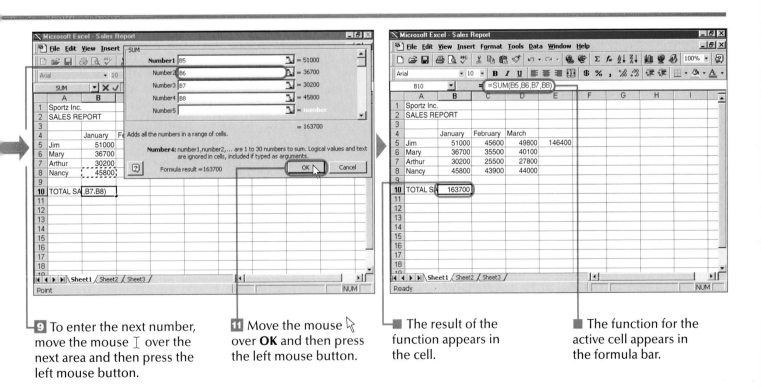

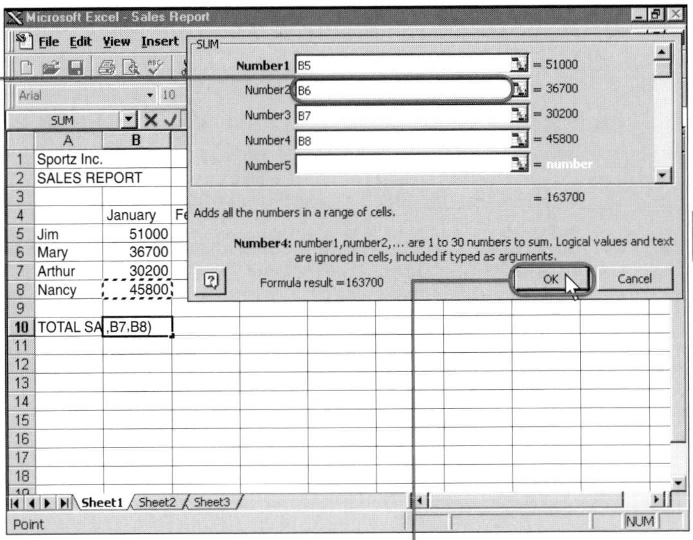

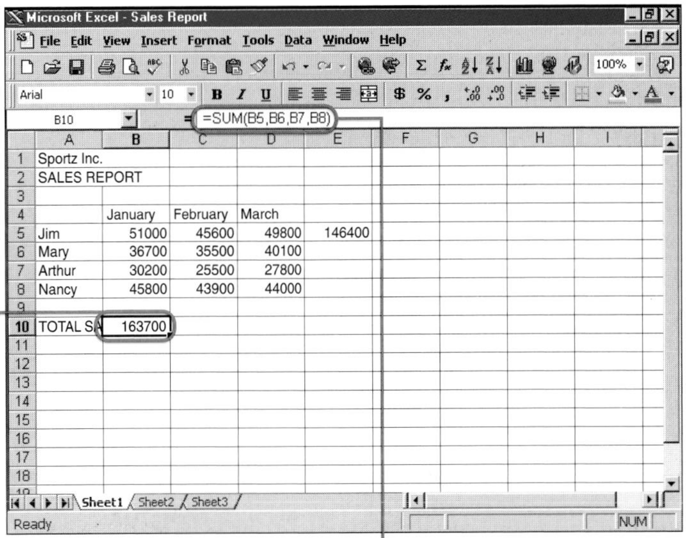

9 To enter the next number, move the mouse I over the next area and then press the left mouse button.

10 Repeat steps 8 and 9 until you have entered all the numbers you want to use in the calculation.

11 Move the mouse over **OK** and then press the left mouse button.

■ The result of the function appears in the cell.

■ The function for the active cell appears in the formula bar.

USING AUTOCALCULATE

USING AUTOCALCULATE

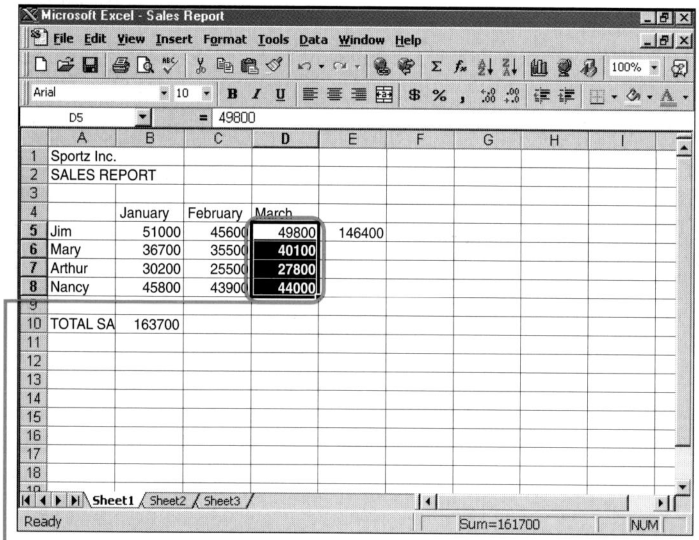

1 Select the cells you want to include in the calculation. To select cells, refer to page 16.

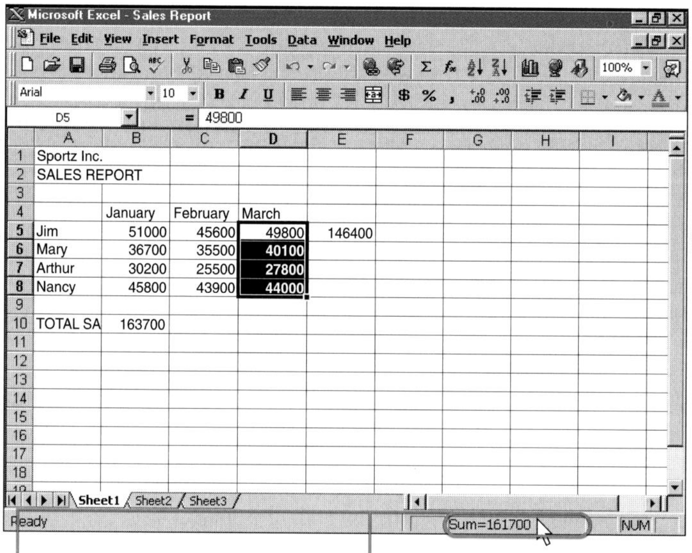

■ This area displays the sum of the cells you selected.

2 To display the result for a different calculation, move the mouse over this area and then press the **right** mouse button.

What calculations can AutoCalculate perform?

Average
Calculates the average value of a list of numbers.

Count
Calculates the number of items in a list, including text.

Count Nums
Calculates the number of values in a list.

Max
Finds the largest value in a list.

Min
Finds the smallest value in a list.

Sum
Adds a list of numbers.

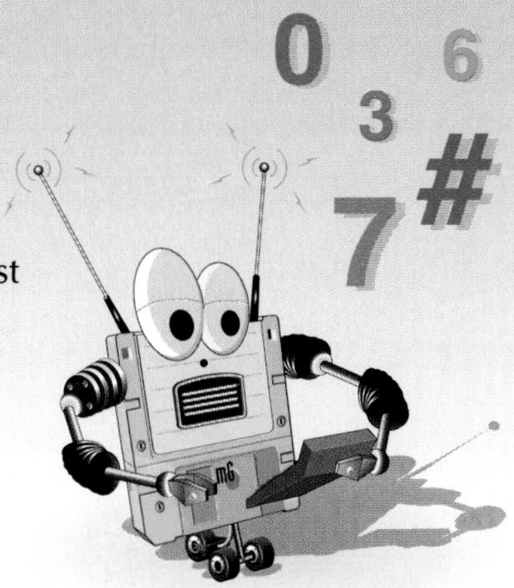

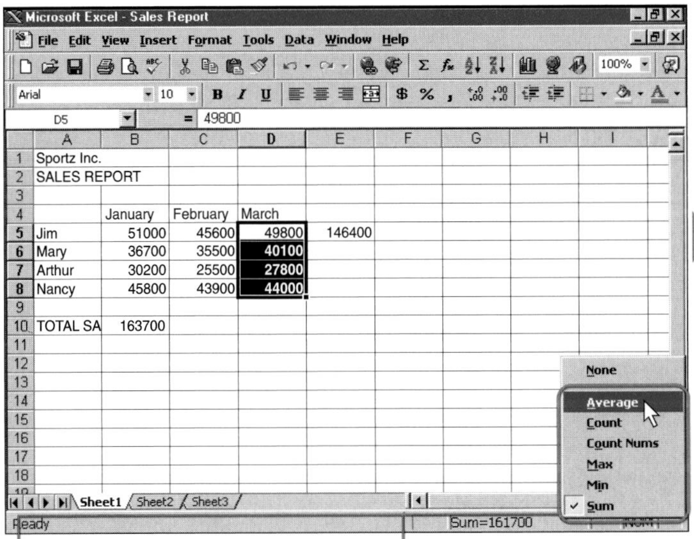

■ A list appears, displaying the calculations you can perform.

3 Move the mouse over the calculation you want to perform and then press the left mouse button.

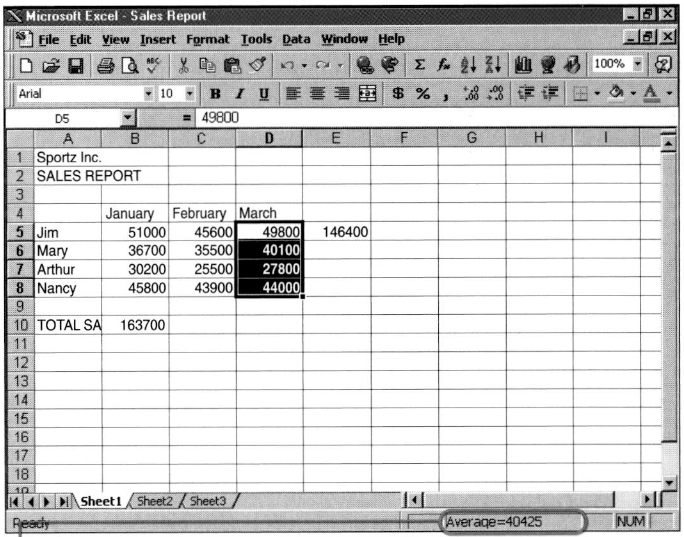

■ This area displays the result for the new calculation.

ADD NUMBERS

ADD NUMBERS

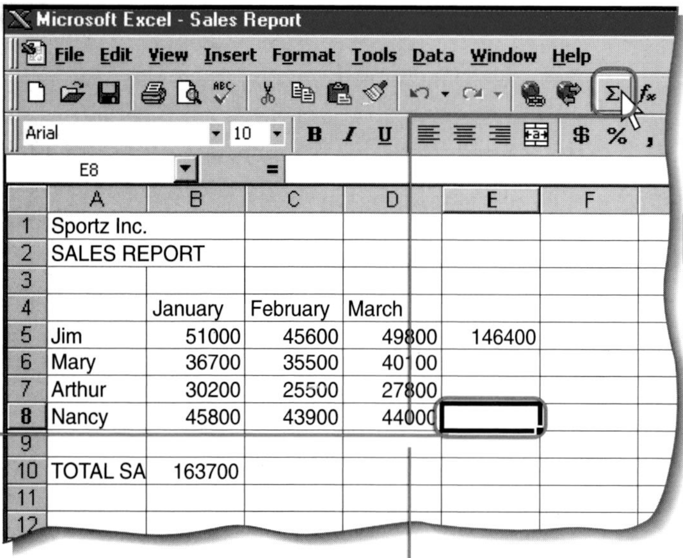

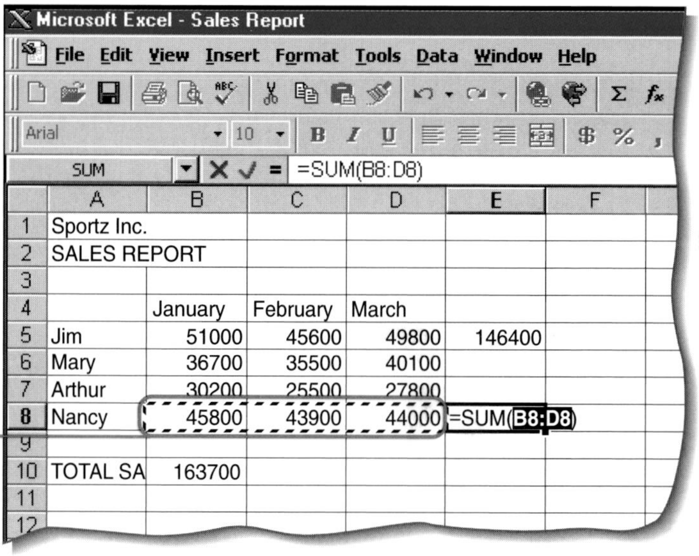

1 Move the mouse ✥ over the cell below or to the right of the cells you want to add and then press the left mouse button.

2 Move the mouse ↖ over Σ and then press the left mouse button.

■ Excel outlines the cells it will use in the calculation with a dotted line.

■ If Excel does not outline the correct cells, select the cells containing the numbers you want to add. To select cells, refer to page 16.

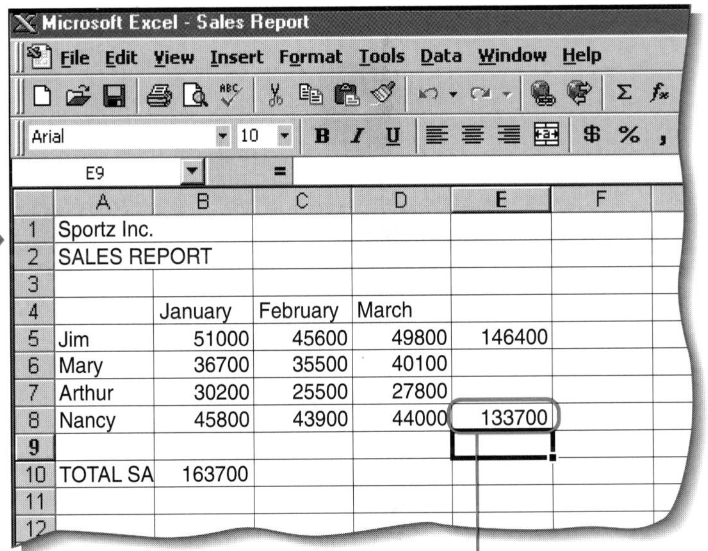

3 Press Enter on your keyboard to perform the calculation.

■ The result of the calculation appears.

CALCULATE A GRAND TOTAL

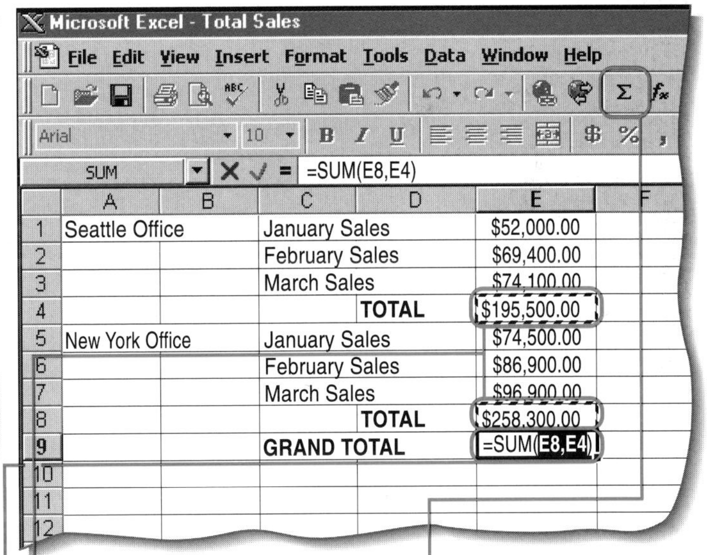

■ These cells contain subtotals.

1 Move the mouse ✚ over the cell below or to the right of the cells containing the subtotals and then press the left mouse button.

2 Move the mouse ↖ over Σ and then press the left mouse button.

3 Press Enter on your keyboard.

ERRORS IN FORMULAS

An error message appears when Excel cannot properly calculate a formula.
ERROR
ERROR

Errors in formulas are often the result of typing mistakes. You can correct an error by editing the cell containing the error. To edit data in a cell, refer to page 40.

#####

The column is too narrow to display the result of the calculation. To display the result, refer to page 90 to change the column width.

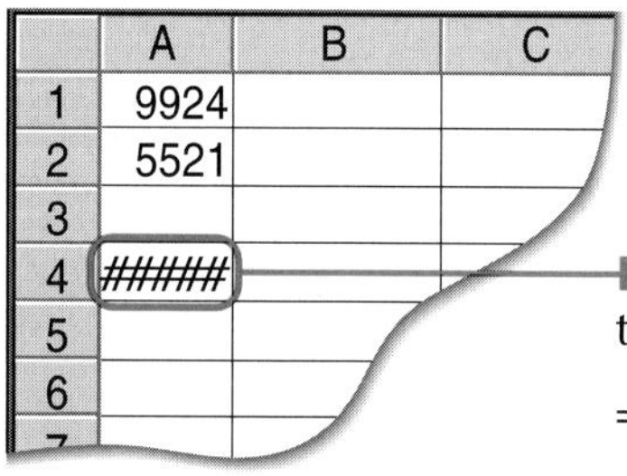

■ This cell contains the formula:

=A1*A2

#DIV/0!

The formula divides a number by zero (0). Excel considers a blank cell to contain a value of zero.

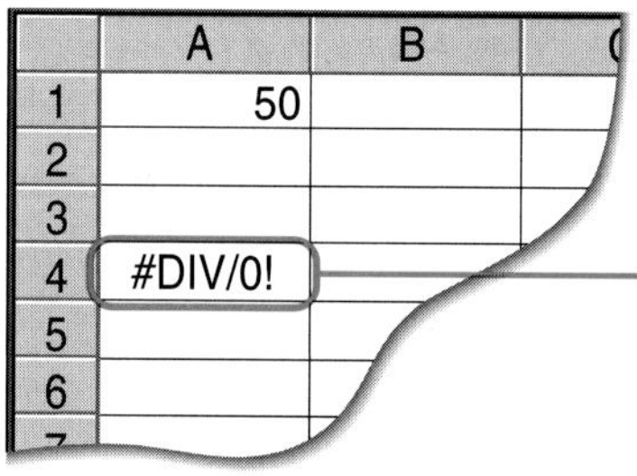

■ This cell contains the formula:

=A1/A2

=50/0

#NAME?

The formula contains a function name or cell reference Excel does not recognize.

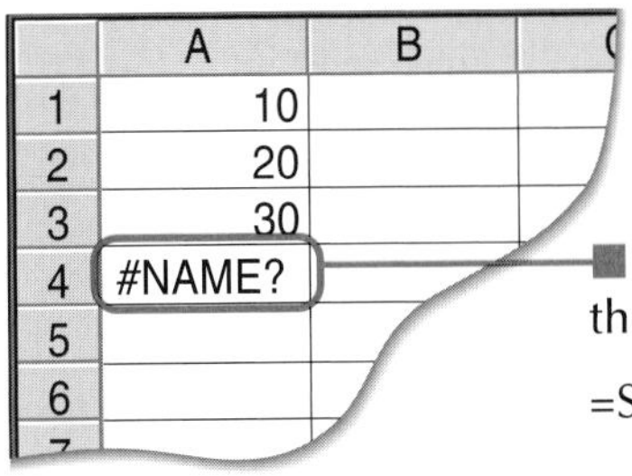
A
B
1 10
2 20
3 30
4 #NAME?
5
6

■ This cell contains the formula:

=SUMM(A1:A3)

In this example, the name of the SUM function was misspelled.

#REF!

The formula refers to a cell that is not valid.

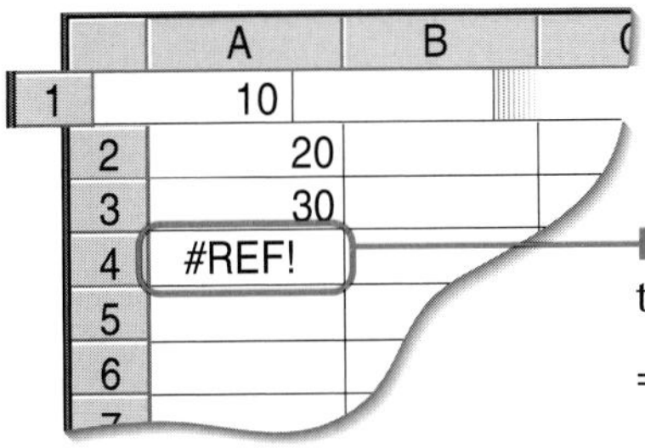
A
B
1 10
2 20
3 30
4 #REF!
5
6

■ This cell contains the formula:

=A1+A2+A3

In this example, a row containing a cell used in the formula was deleted.

#VALUE!

The formula refers to a cell that Excel cannot use in a calculation.

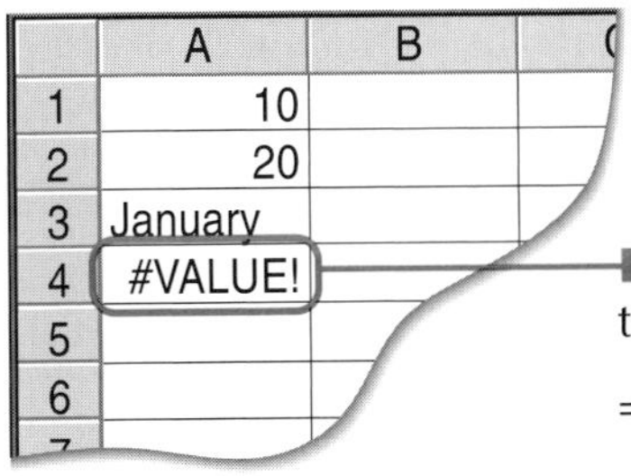
A
B
1 10
2 20
3 January
4 #VALUE!
5
6

■ This cell contains the formula:

=A1+A2+A3

In this example, a cell used in the formula contains text.

Circular Reference

A warning message appears when a formula refers to the cell containing the formula. This is called a circular reference.

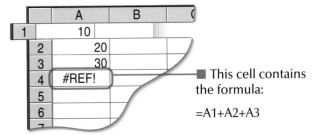

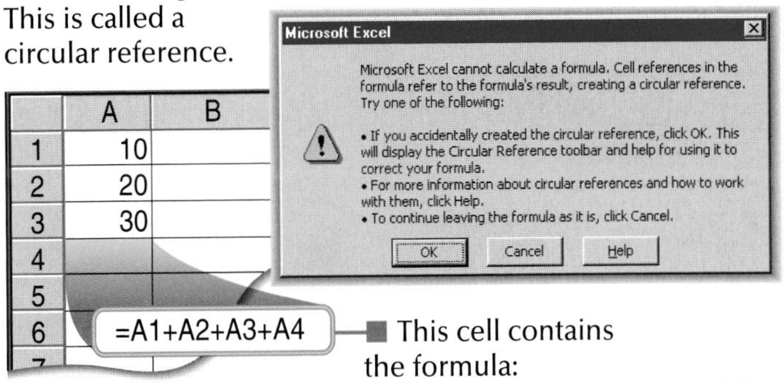
Microsoft Excel
Microsoft Excel cannot calculate a formula. Cell references in the formula refer to the formula's result, creating a circular reference. Try one of the following:
• If you accidentally created the circular reference, click OK. This will display the Circular Reference toolbar and help for using it to correct your formula.
• For more information about circular references and how to work with them, click Help.
• To continue leaving the formula as it is, click Cancel.
OK
Cancel
Help
A
B
1 10
2 20
3 30
4
5
6 =A1+A2+A3+A4

■ This cell contains the formula:

=A1+A2+A3+A4

COPY A FORMULA

COPY A FORMULA—USING RELATIVE REFERENCES

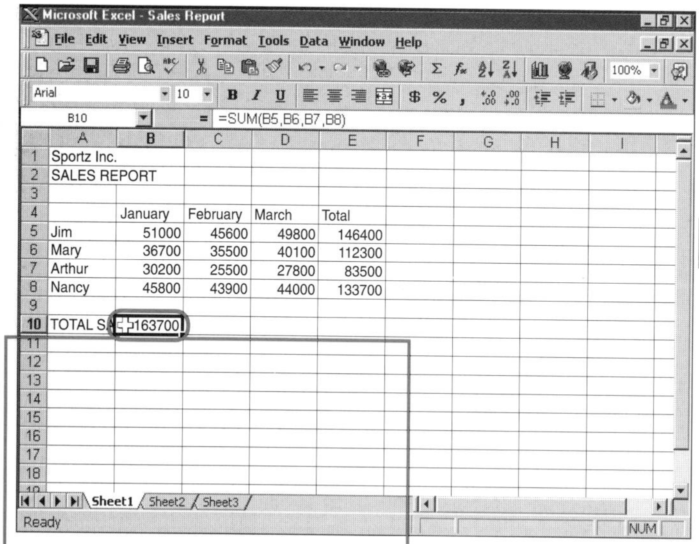

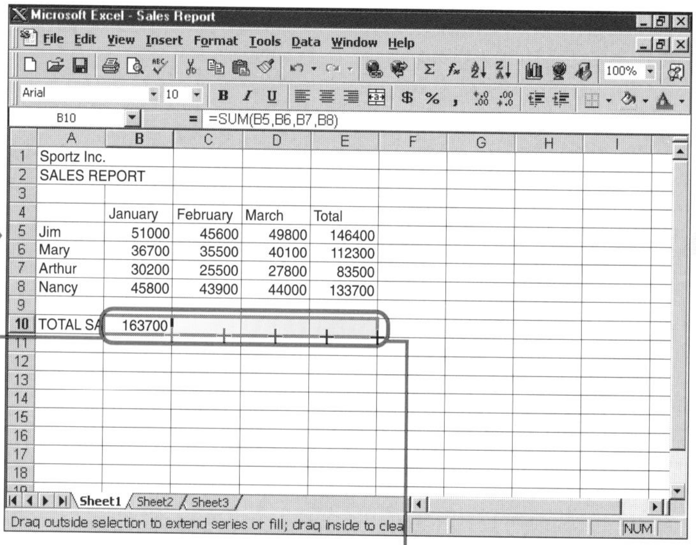

1 Enter the formula you want to copy to other cells.

■ In this example, cell **B10** contains the function **=SUM(B5,B6,B7,B8)**. A function is a ready-to-use formula.

2 Move the mouse ✥ over the cell containing the formula you want to copy and then press the left mouse button.

3 Move the mouse ✥ over the bottom right corner of the cell (✥ changes to +).

4 Press and hold down the left mouse button as you move the mouse + over the cells you want to receive a copy of the formula. Then release the mouse button.

What is a relative reference?

A relative reference changes when you copy a formula.

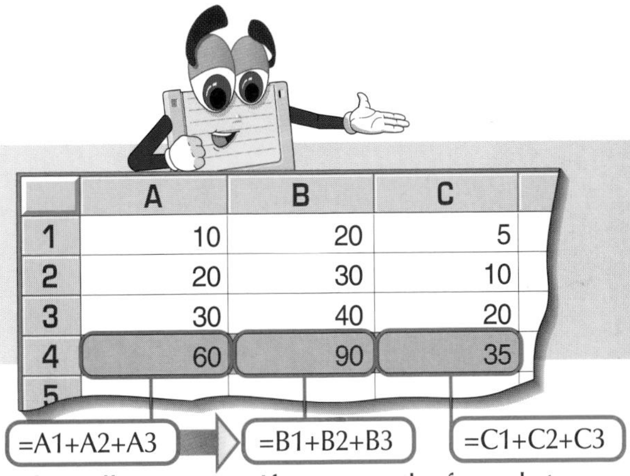

A
B
C
1 10 20 5
2 20 30 10
3 30 40 20
4 60 90 35
5
=A1+A2+A3
=B1+B2+B3
=C1+C2+C3

This cell contains the formula =A1+A2+A3.

If you copy the formula to other cells in your worksheet, Excel automatically changes the cell references in the new formulas.

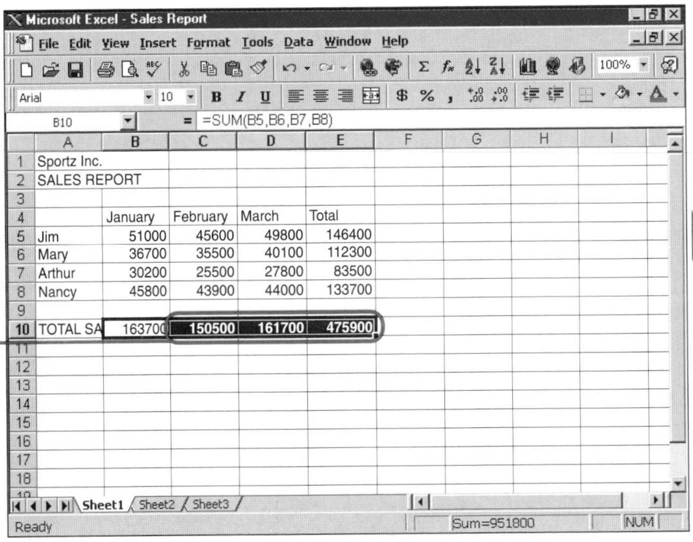

■ The results of the formulas appear.

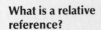

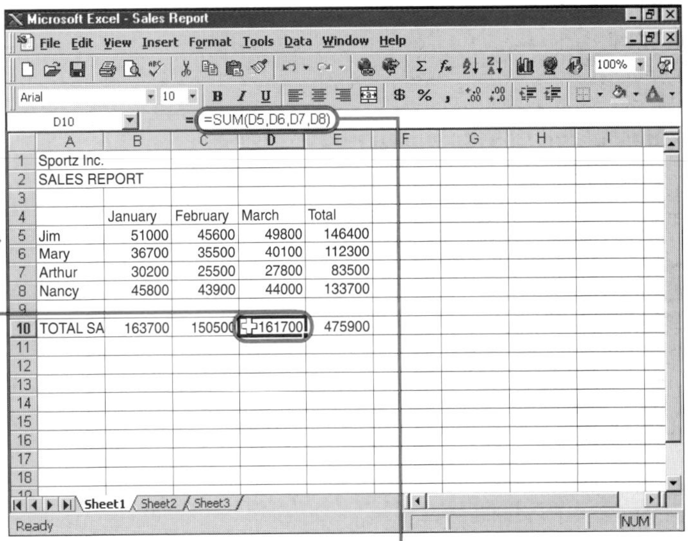

5 To see one of the new formulas, move the mouse ✚ over a cell that received a copy of the formula and then press the left mouse button.

■ The formula bar displays the formula with the new cell references.

COPY A FORMULA

You can copy a formula to other cells in your worksheet to save time. If you do not want Excel to change a cell reference when you copy a formula, you can use an absolute reference.

COPY A FORMULA—USING ABSOLUTE REFERENCES

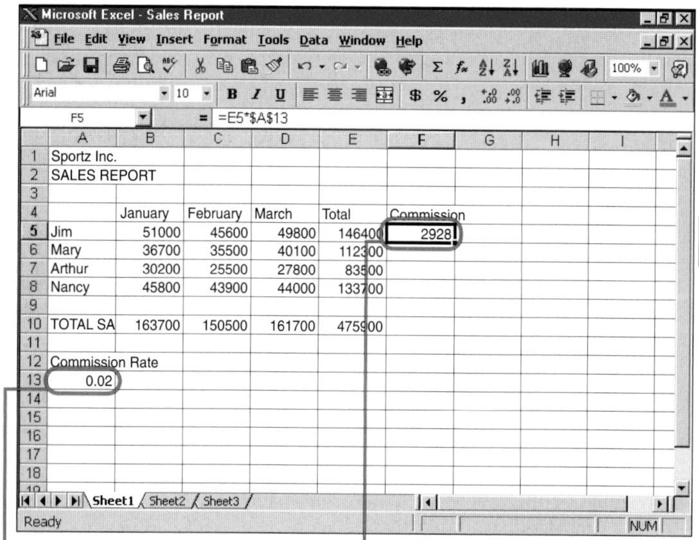

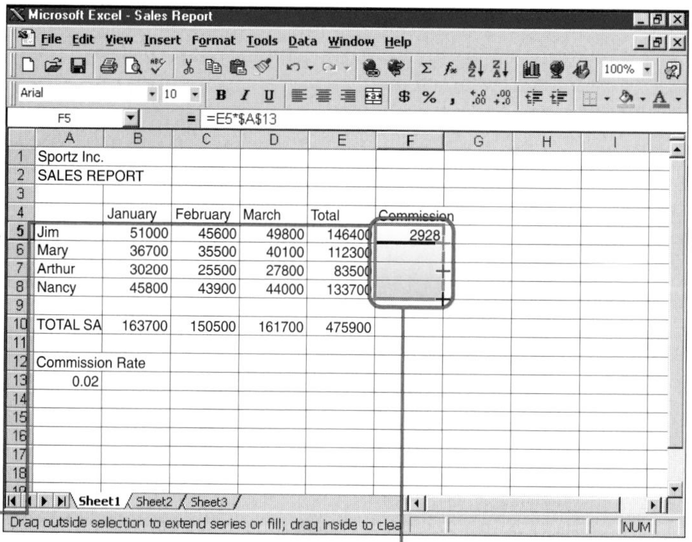

1 Enter the data you want to remain the same in all the formulas.

2 Enter the formula containing the absolute reference you want to copy to other cells. For information on absolute references, refer to the top of page 77.

■ In this example, cell **F5** contains the formula **=E5*A13**.

3 Move the mouse ✥ over the cell containing the formula you want to copy and then press the left mouse button.

4 Move the mouse ✥ over the bottom right corner of the cell (✥ changes to +).

5 Press and hold down the left mouse button as you move the mouse + over the cells you want to receive a copy of the formula. Then release the mouse button.

What is an absolute reference?

An absolute reference does not change when you copy a formula. To make a cell reference absolute, type a dollar sign ($) before both the column letter and row number (example: **A7**).

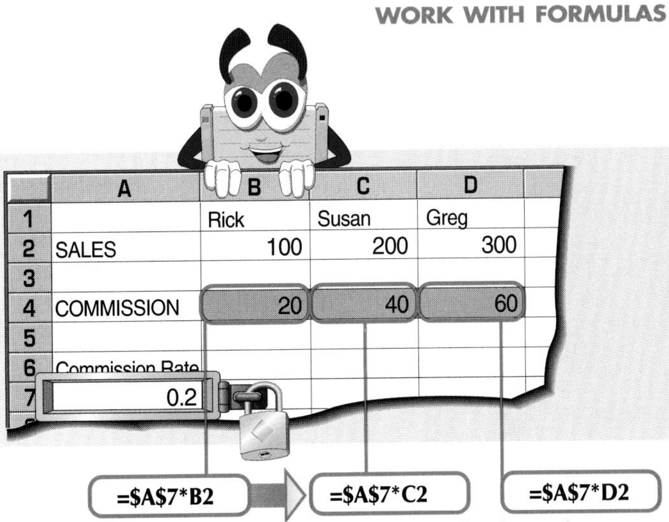

This cell contains the formula =A7*B2.

If you copy the formula to other cells in your worksheet, Excel does not change the absolute reference in the new formulas.

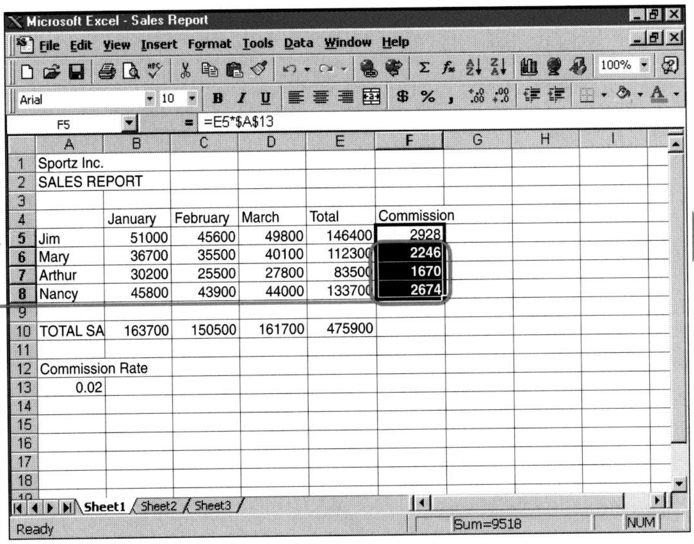

■ The results of the formulas appear.

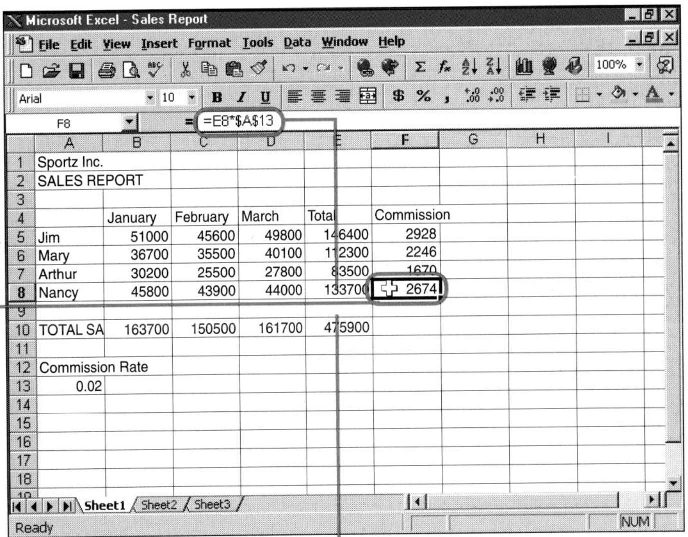

6 To see one of the new formulas, move the mouse ✚ over a cell that received a copy of the formula and then press the left mouse button.

■ The absolute reference (example: **A13**) in the formula did not change.

■ The relative reference (example: **E8**) in the formula did change.

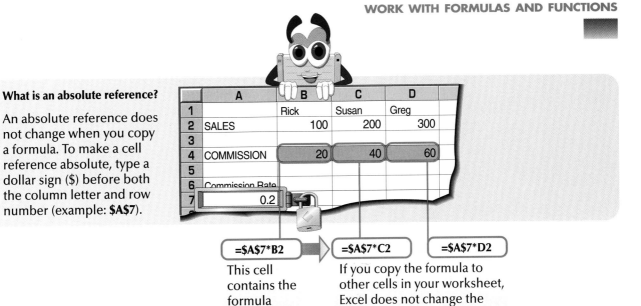

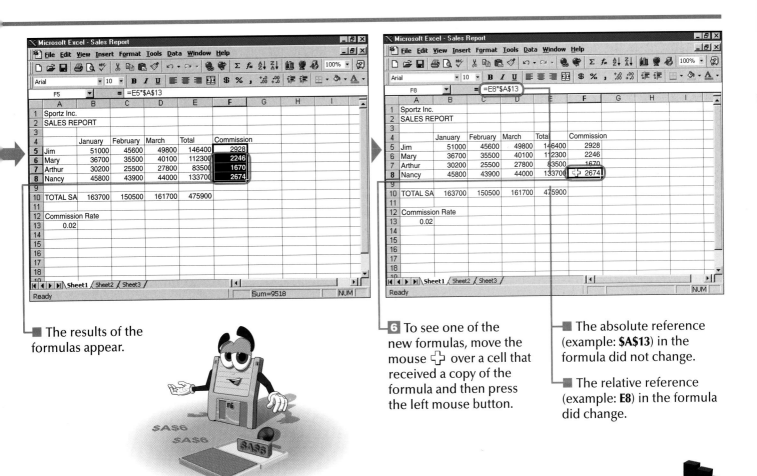

CHAPTER 5

CHANGE YOUR SCREEN DISPLAY

Are you interested in changing the way your worksheet appears on your screen? In this chapter you will learn how to display or hide a toolbar, zoom in or out and more.

ZOOM IN OR OUT

Changing the zoom setting will not affect the way data appears on a printed page.

ZOOM IN OR OUT

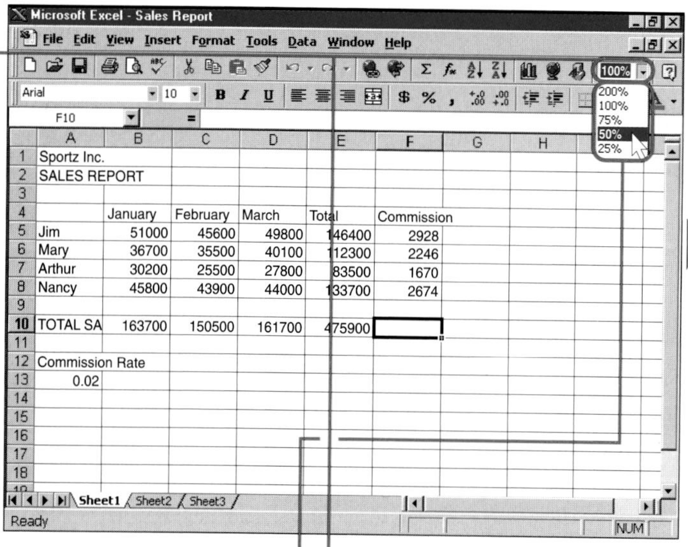

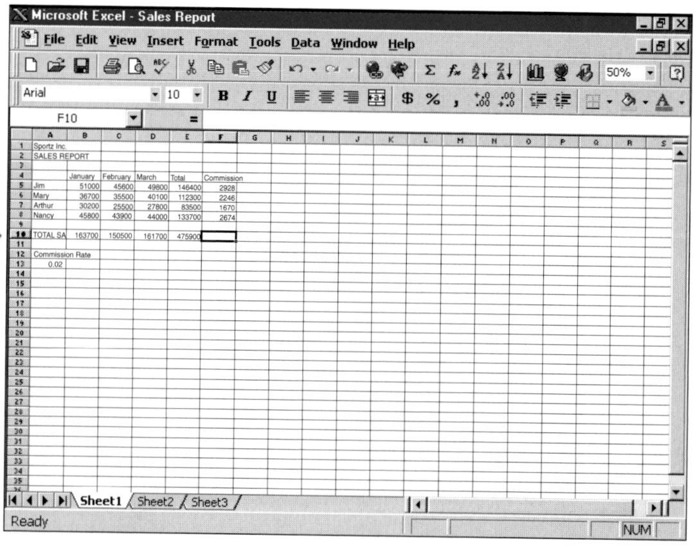

■ When you first start Excel, your worksheet appears in the 100% zoom setting.

1 To display a list of zoom settings, move the mouse over ▾ in this area and then press the left mouse button.

2 Move the mouse over the zoom setting you want to use and then press the left mouse button.

■ Your worksheet appears in the new zoom setting. You can edit your worksheet as usual.

■ To return to the normal zoom setting, repeat steps **1** and **2**, selecting **100%** in step **2**.

DISPLAY FULL SCREEN

You can display a larger working area by hiding parts of the Excel screen.

DISPLAY FULL SCREEN

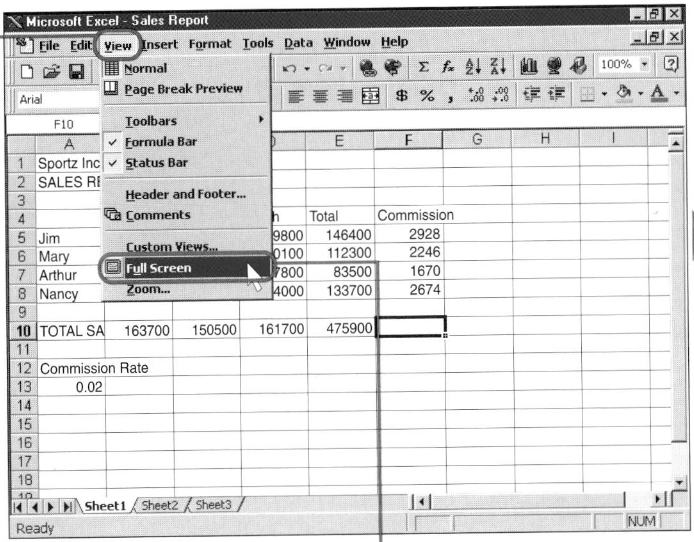

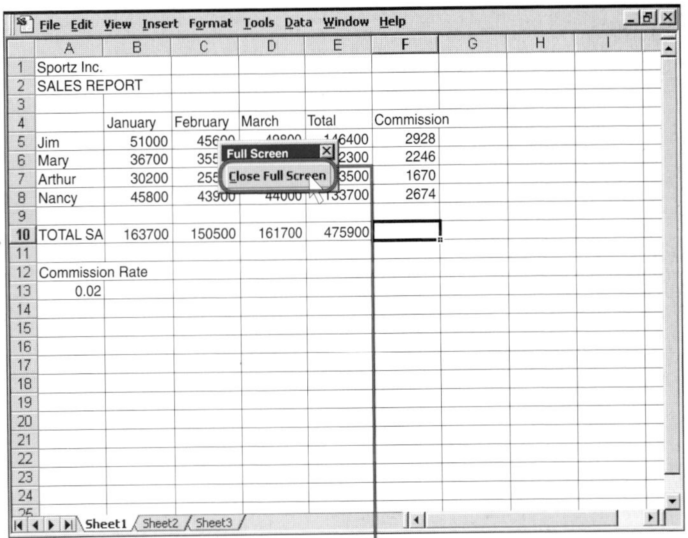

1 Move the mouse over **View** and then press the left mouse button.

2 Move the mouse over **Full Screen** and then press the left mouse button.

■ Excel hides parts of the screen to display a larger working area.

■ To once again display the hidden parts of the screen, move the mouse over **Close Full Screen** and then press the left mouse button.

DISPLAY OR HIDE A TOOLBAR

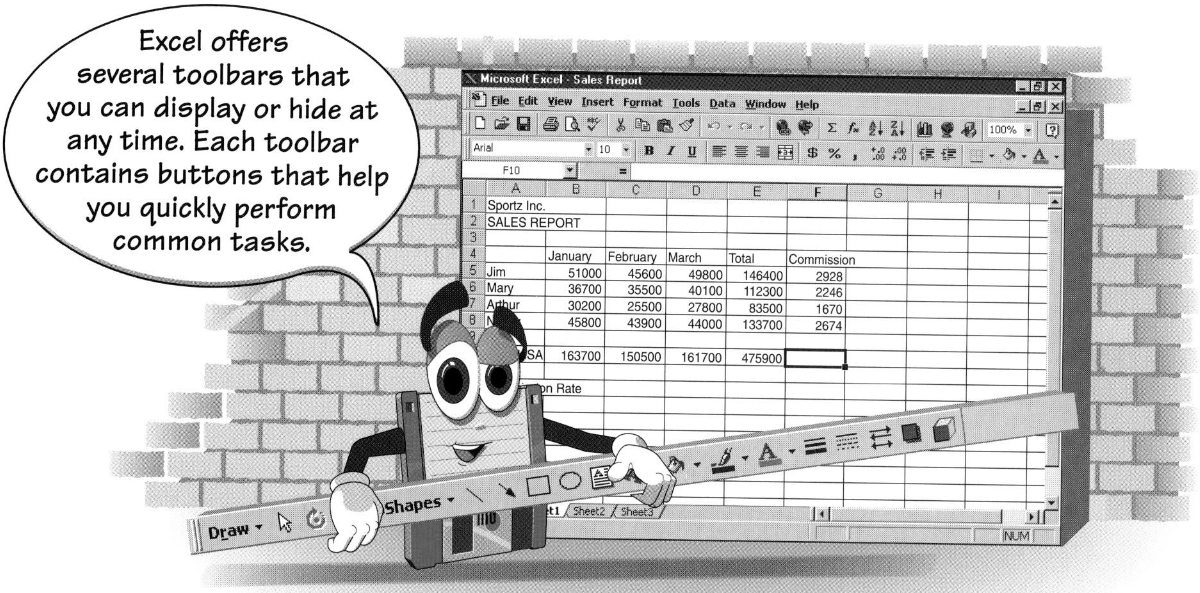

Excel offers several toolbars that you can display or hide at any time. Each toolbar contains buttons that help you quickly perform common tasks.
Microsoft Excel - Sales Report
Draw
Shapes

DISPLAY OR HIDE A TOOLBAR

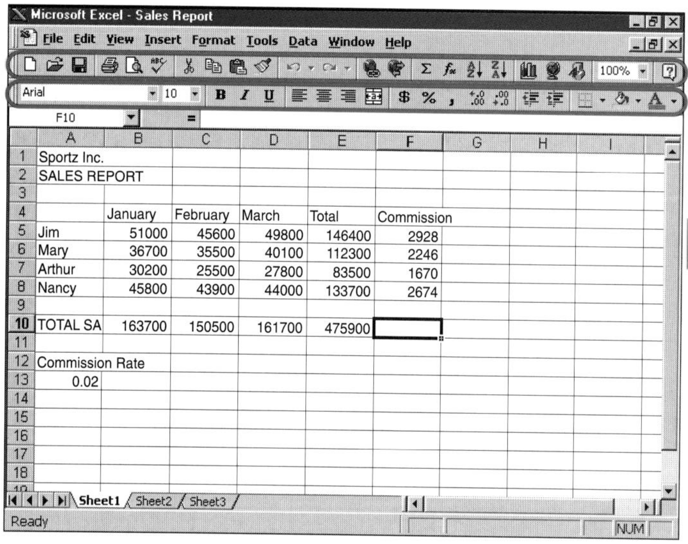

When you first start Excel, the Standard and Formatting toolbars appear on your screen.

Standard toolbar

Formatting toolbar

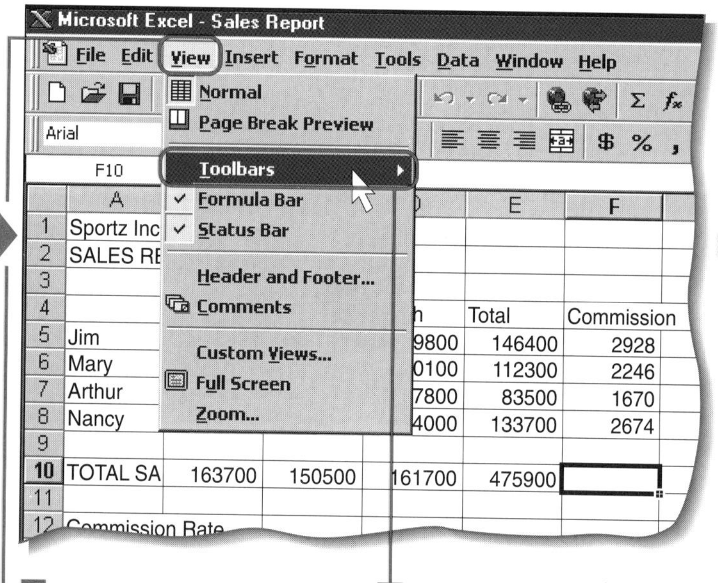

1 To display or hide a toolbar, move the mouse over **View** and then press the left mouse button.

2 Move the mouse over **Toolbars**.

Why would I hide a toolbar?

A screen displaying fewer toolbars provides a larger and less cluttered working area.

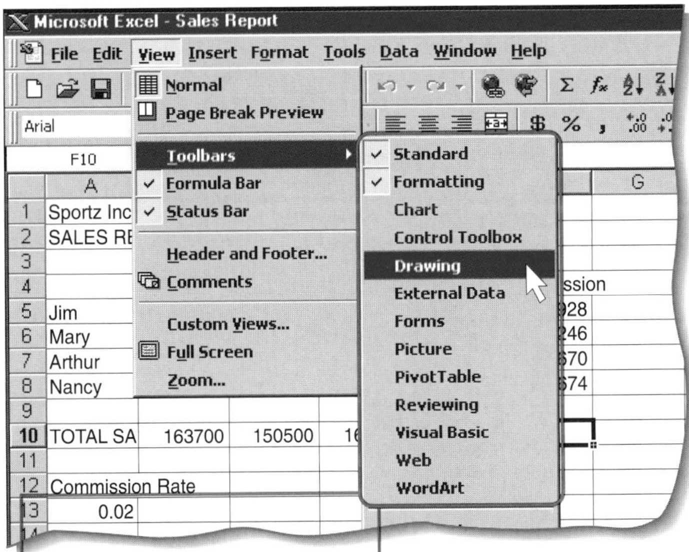

■ A list of toolbars appears. A check mark (✓) appears beside the name of each toolbar that is currently displayed.

3 Move the mouse over the name of the toolbar you want to display or hide and then press the left mouse button.

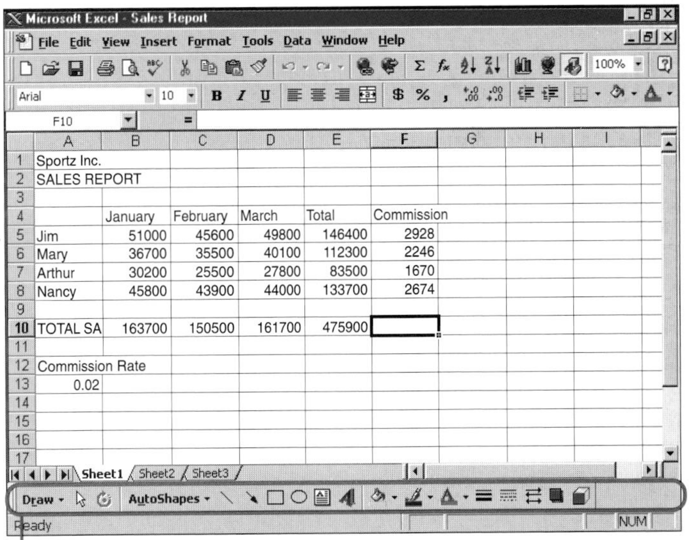

■ Excel displays or hides the toolbar you selected.

FREEZE ROWS AND COLUMNS

You can freeze rows and columns in your worksheet so they will not move. This lets you keep headings on your screen as you move through a large worksheet.

FREEZE ROWS AND COLUMNS

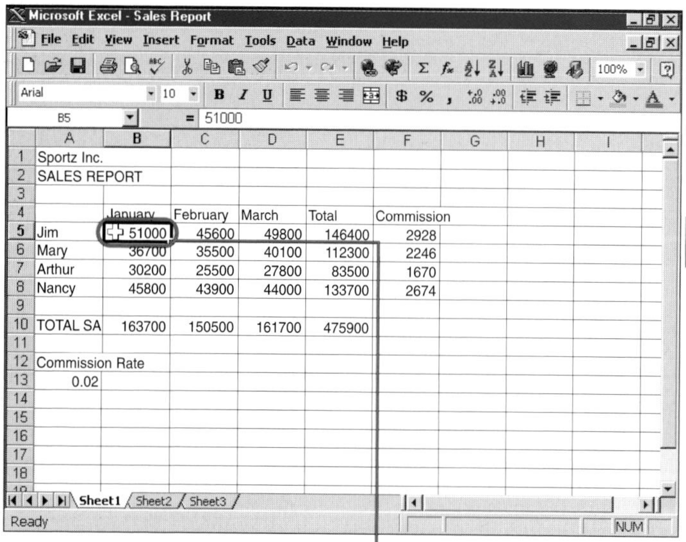

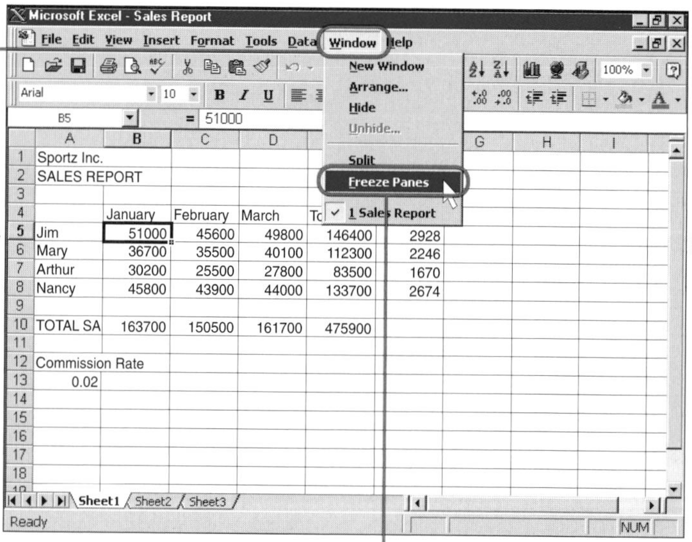

Excel will freeze the rows above and the columns to the left of the cell you select.

1 To select a cell, move the mouse ✚ over the cell and then press the left mouse button.

2 Move the mouse over **Window** and then press the left mouse button.

3 Move the mouse over **Freeze Panes** and then press the left mouse button.

How do I unfreeze rows and columns in my worksheet?

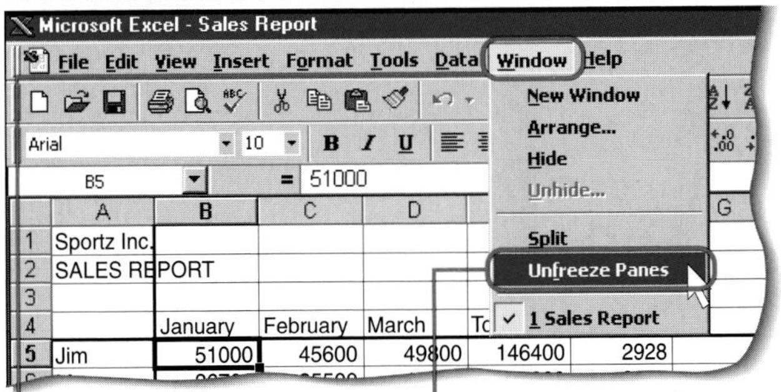

1 Move the mouse over **Window** and then press the left mouse button.

2 Move the mouse over **Unfreeze Panes** and then press the left mouse button.

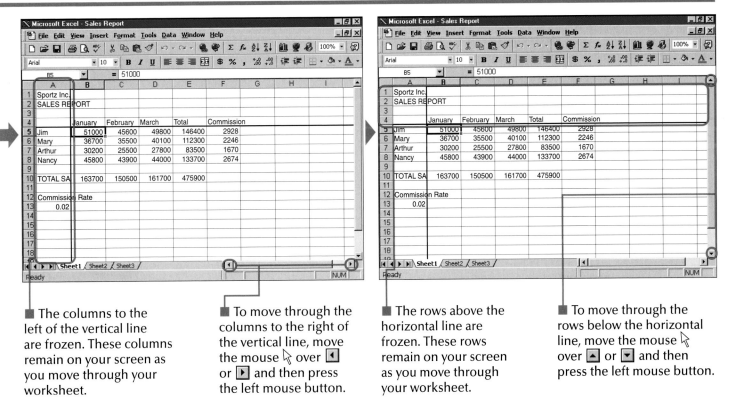

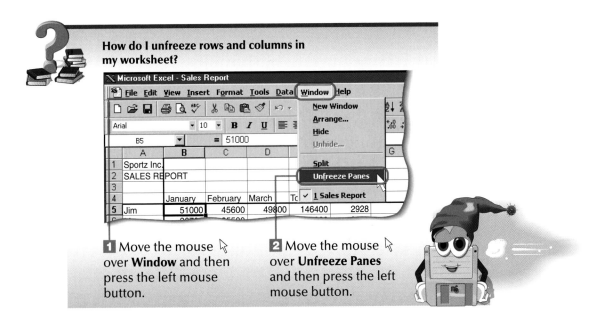

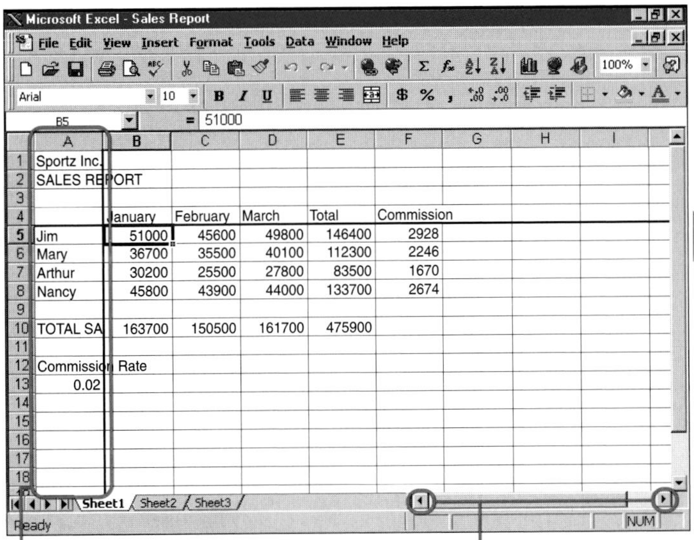

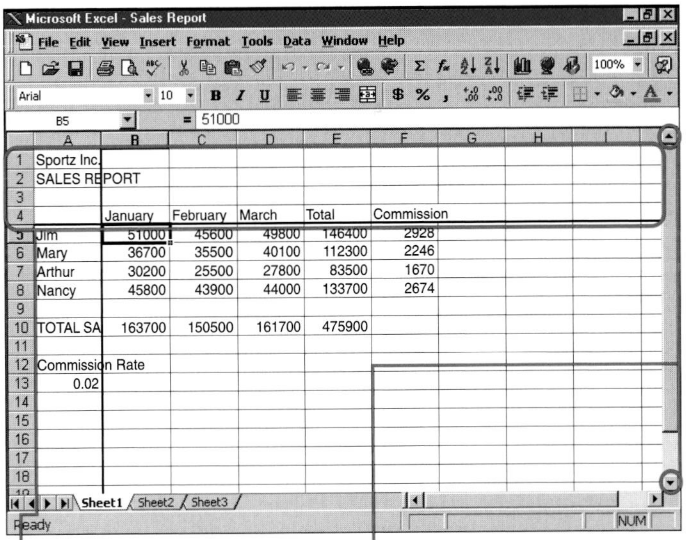

■ The columns to the left of the vertical line are frozen. These columns remain on your screen as you move through your worksheet.

■ To move through the columns to the right of the vertical line, move the mouse over ◄ or ► and then press the left mouse button.

■ The rows above the horizontal line are frozen. These rows remain on your screen as you move through your worksheet.

■ To move through the rows below the horizontal line, move the mouse over ▲ or ▼ and then press the left mouse button.

SPLIT A WORKSHEET

You can split your worksheet into separate sections. This lets you view different areas of a large worksheet at the same time.

SPLIT A WORKSHEET VERTICALLY

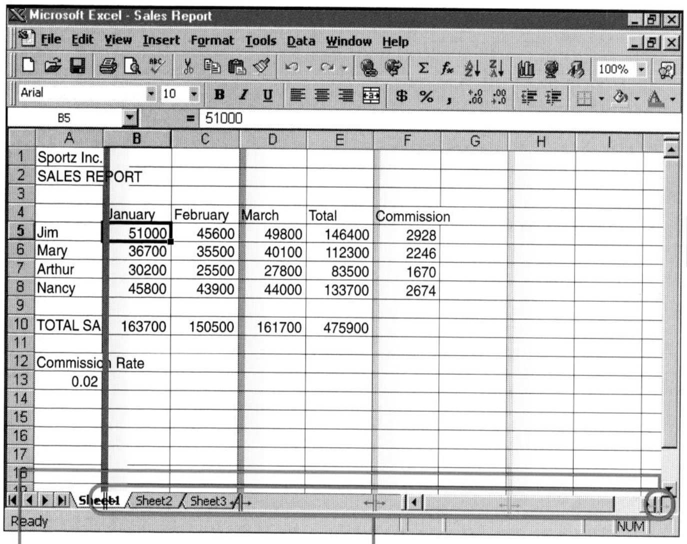

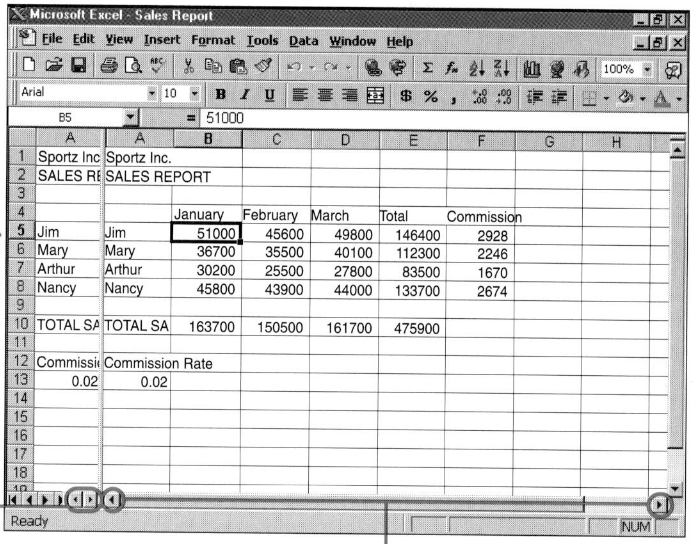

1 Move the mouse ⇖ over this area (⇖ changes to ⫲).

2 Press and hold down the left mouse button as you move the mouse ⫲ to where you want to split your worksheet. Then release the mouse button.

■ Your worksheet splits vertically into two sections.

■ To move through the columns to the left of the dividing line, move the mouse ⇖ over ◀ or ▶ and then press the left mouse button.

■ To move through the columns to the right of the dividing line, move the mouse ⇖ over ◀ or ▶ and then press the left mouse button.

How do I remove a split from my worksheet?

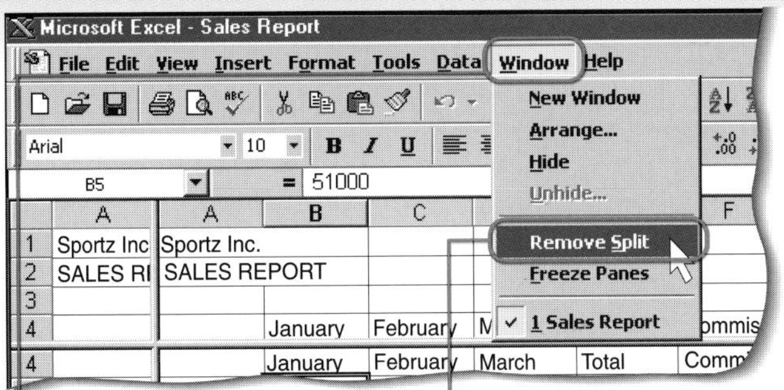

1 Move the mouse over **Window** and then press the left mouse button.

2 Move the mouse over **Remove Split** and then press the left mouse button.

SPLIT A WORKSHEET HORIZONTALLY

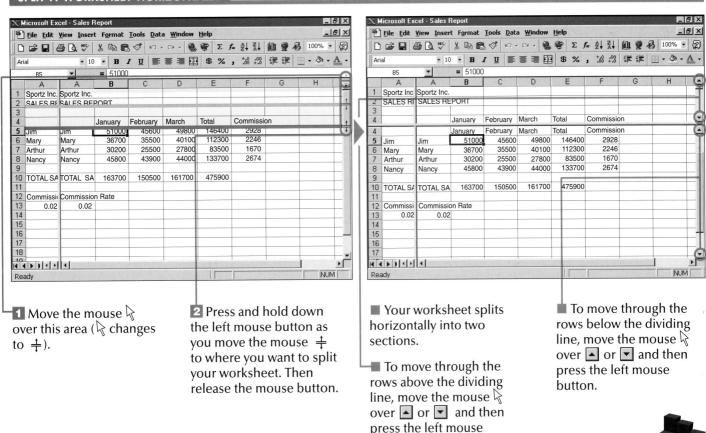

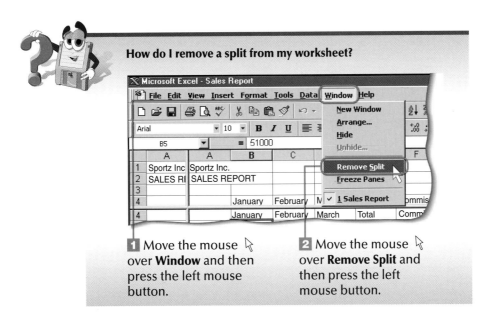

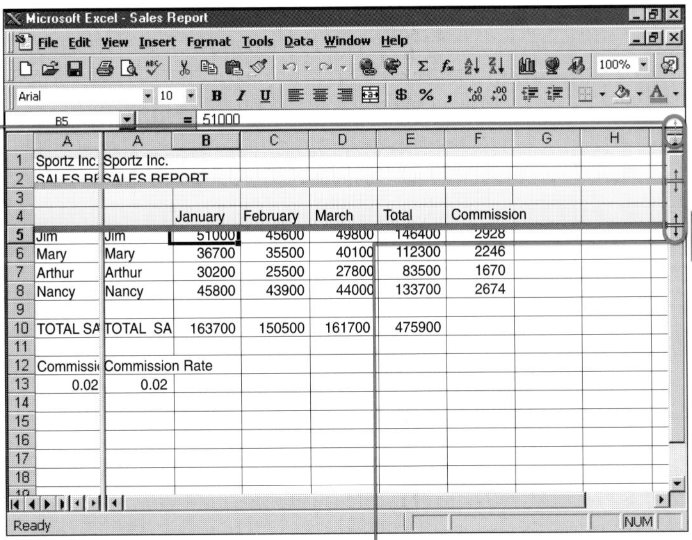

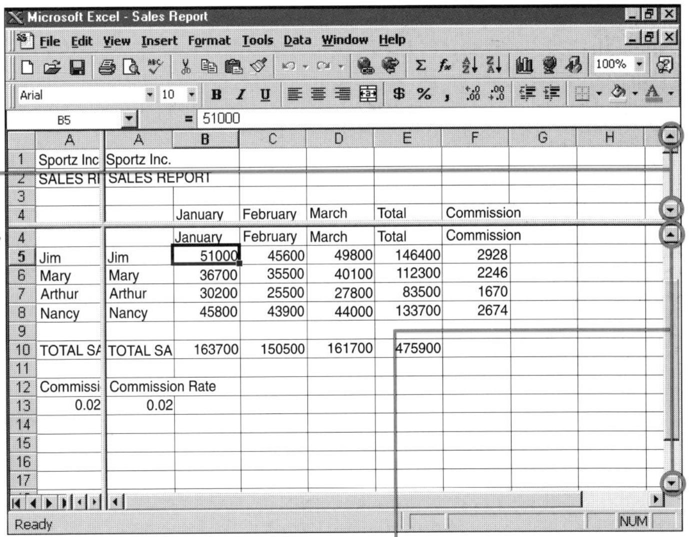

1 Move the mouse over this area (changes to ╪).

2 Press and hold down the left mouse button as you move the mouse ╪ to where you want to split your worksheet. Then release the mouse button.

■ Your worksheet splits horizontally into two sections.

■ To move through the rows above the dividing line, move the mouse over ▲ or ▼ and then press the left mouse button.

■ To move through the rows below the dividing line, move the mouse over ▲ or ▼ and then press the left mouse button.

Jan Feb Mar Total
East 7 7 5 19
West 6 4 7 17
South 8 7 9 24
Total 21 18 21 60
Jan Feb Mar Total
East 7 7 5 19
West 6 4 7 17
South 8 7 9 24
Total 21 18 21 60
Jan Feb
East $ 7 $ 7
West 6 4
South 8 7
Total $ 21 $ 18
Jan Feb Mar Total
East 7 7 5 19
West 6 4 7 17
South 8 7 9 24
Total 21 18 21 60
mG
mG
Acrylic Paint
color

CHAPTER 6

FORMAT YOUR WORKSHEETS

Are you wondering how to improve the appearance of your worksheet? This chapter shows you how to change fonts, align data, change cell and data colors, and much more.

CHANGE COLUMN WIDTH

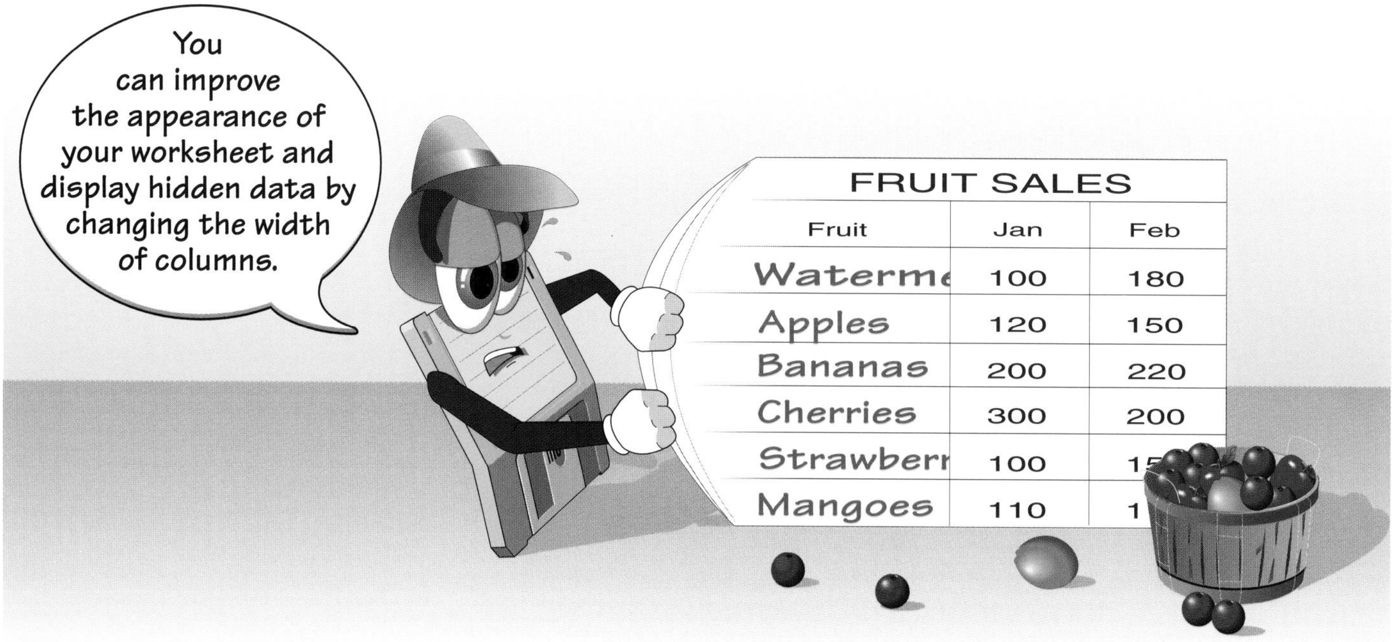

You can improve the appearance of your worksheet and display hidden data by changing the width of columns.
FRUIT SALES
Fruit
Jan
Feb
Waterme
100
180
Apples
120
150
Bananas
200
220
Cherries
300
200
Strawberr
100
Mangoes
110

CHANGE COLUMN WIDTH

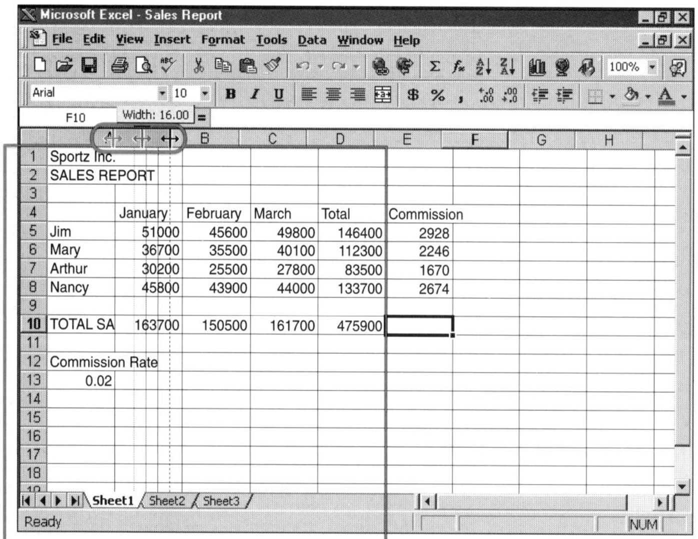

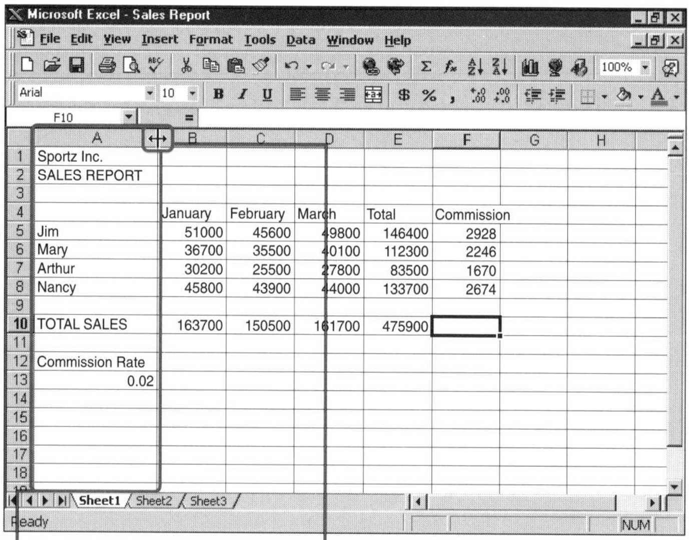

1 To change the width of a column, move the mouse ✥ over the right edge of the column heading (✥ changes to ↔).

2 Press and hold down the left mouse button as you move the column edge until the dotted line displays the column width you want. Then release the mouse button.

■ The column displays the new width.

FIT LONGEST ITEM

You can have Excel change a column width to fit the longest item in the column.

■ Move the mouse ✥ over the right edge of the column heading (✥ changes to ↔) and then quickly press the left mouse button twice.

CHANGE ROW HEIGHT

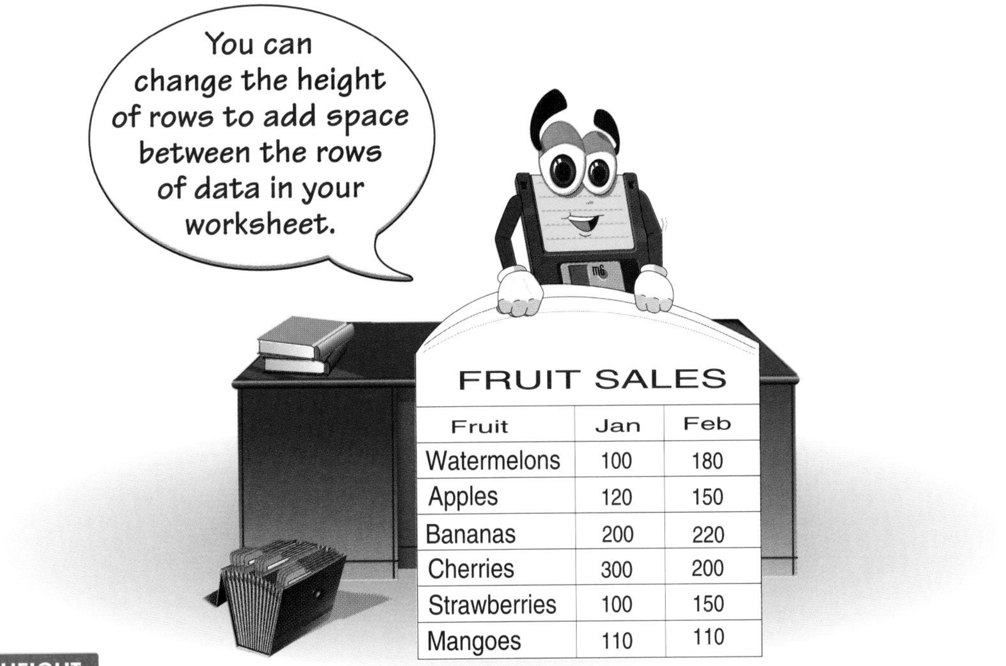

You can change the height of rows to add space between the rows of data in your worksheet.
FRUIT SALES
Fruit Jan Feb
Watermelons 100 180
Apples 120 150
Bananas 200 220
Cherries 300 200
Strawberries 100 150
Mangoes 110 110

CHANGE ROW HEIGHT

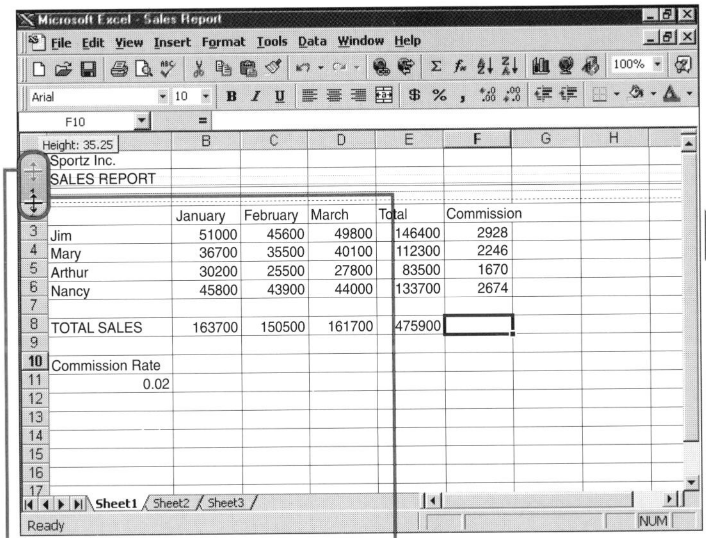

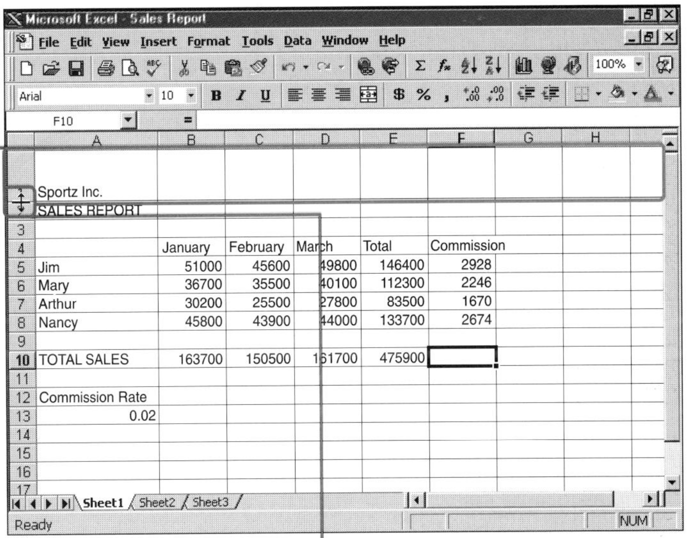

1 To change the height of a row, move the mouse ✥ over the bottom edge of the row heading (✥ changes to ✛).

2 Press and hold down the left mouse button as you move the row edge until the dotted line displays the row height you want. Then release the mouse button.

■ The row displays the new height.

FIT TALLEST ITEM

You can have Excel change a row height to fit the tallest item in the row.

■ Move the mouse ✥ over the bottom edge of the row heading (✥ changes to ✛) and then quickly press the left mouse button twice.

BOLD, ITALIC AND UNDERLINE

BOLD, ITALIC AND UNDERLINE

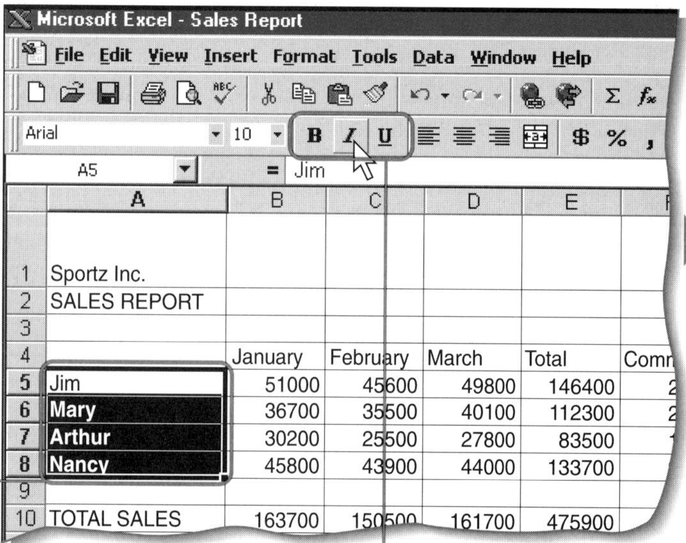

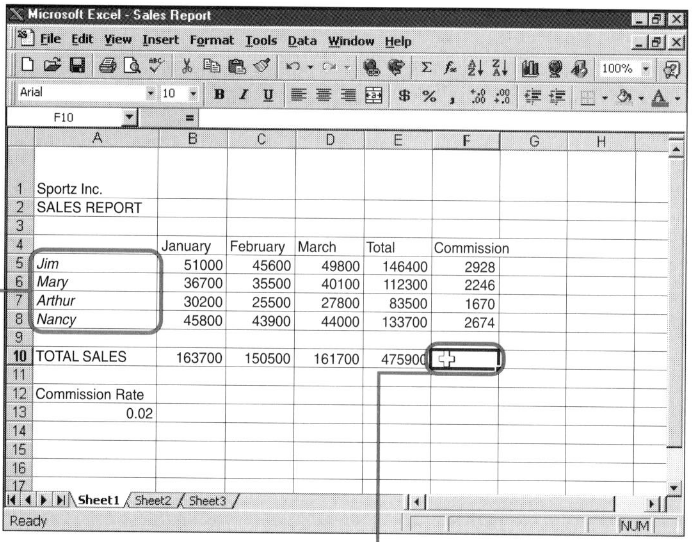

1 Select the cells containing the data you want to emphasize. To select cells, refer to page 16.

2 Move the mouse over one of the following options and then press the left mouse button.

- **B** Bold
- *I* Italic
- U Underline

■ The data displays the style you selected.

■ To deselect cells, move the mouse over any cell and then press the left mouse button.

■ To remove a bold, italic or underline style, repeat steps **1** and **2**.

CHANGE ALIGNMENT OF DATA

CHANGE ALIGNMENT OF DATA

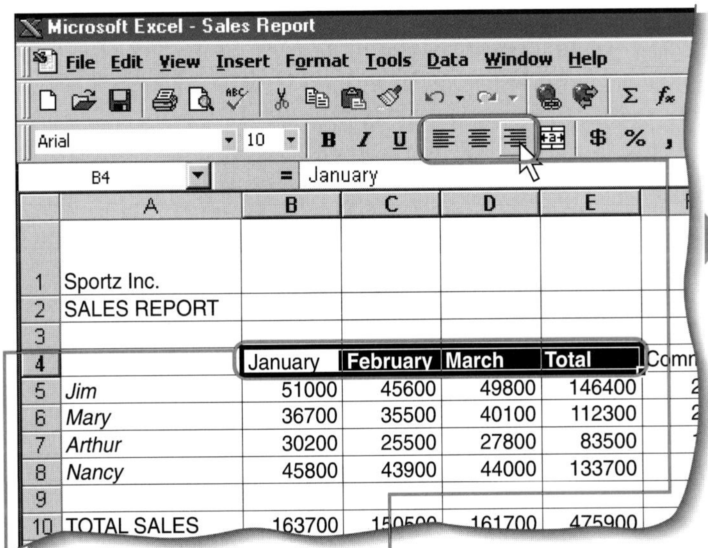

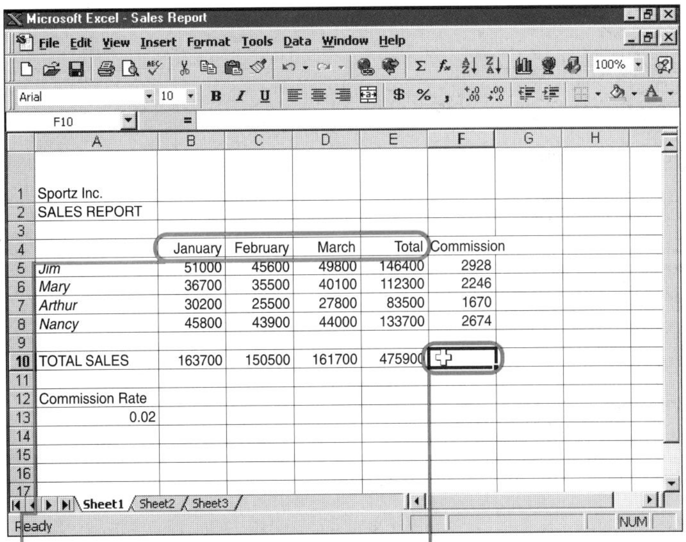

1 Select the cells containing the data you want to align differently. To select cells, refer to page 16.

2 Move the mouse over one of the following options and then press the left mouse button.

- Left align
- Center
- Right align

■ Excel aligns the data.

■ To deselect cells, move the mouse over any cell and then press the left mouse button.

CHANGE APPEARANCE OF NUMBERS

When you change the appearance of numbers, you do not change the value of the numbers.

CHANGE THE NUMBER STYLE

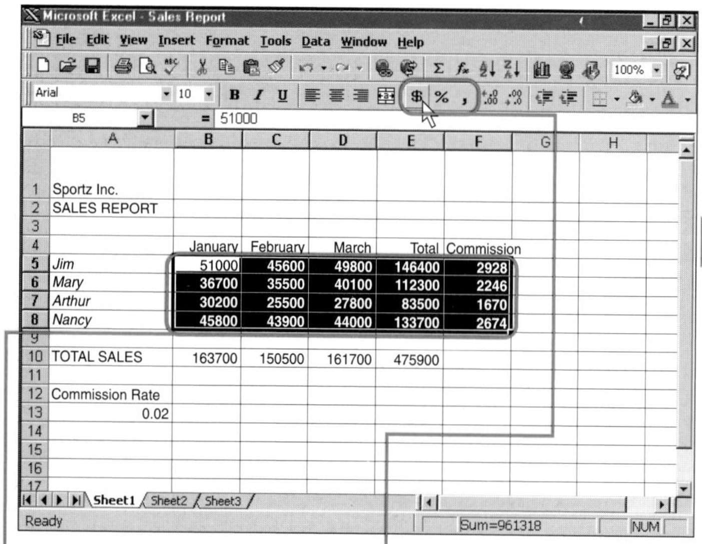

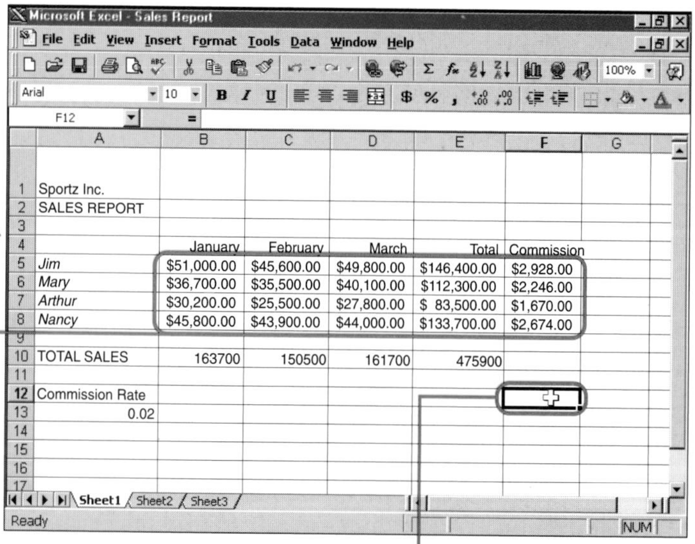

1 Select the cells containing the numbers you want to display in a different style. To select cells, refer to page 16.

2 Move the mouse over one of the following options and then press the left mouse button.

- **$** Currency style
- **%** Percent style
- **,** Comma style

■ The numbers display the style you selected.

■ To deselect cells, move the mouse over any cell and then press the left mouse button.

What changes can I make to the appearance of numbers in my worksheet?

Option	Example
Change to dollar value	10 → $10.00
Change to percentage	0.15 → 15%
Add comma and display two decimal places	1000 → 1,000.00
Add decimal place	10.19 → 10.190
Remove decimal place	10.19 → 10.2

ADD OR REMOVE A DECIMAL PLACE

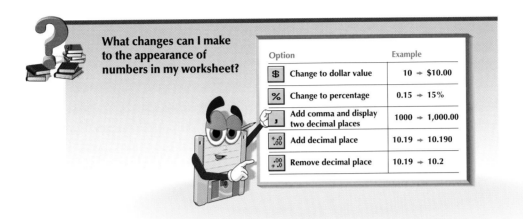

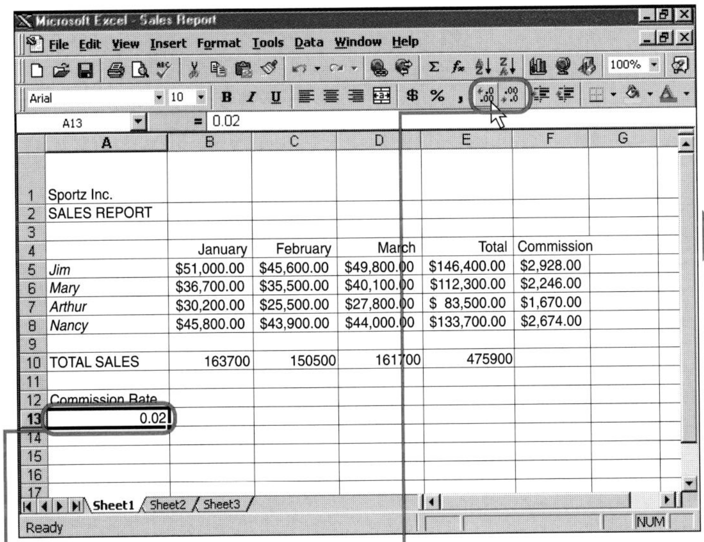

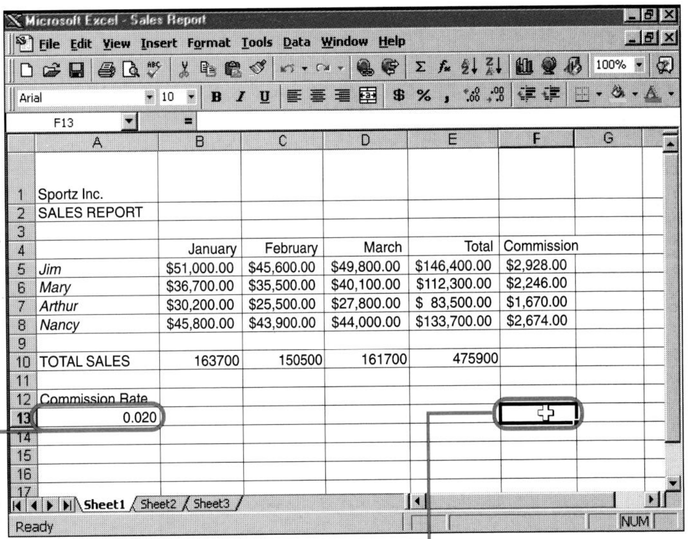

1 Select the cells containing the numbers you want to change. To select cells, refer to page 16.

2 Move the mouse over one of the following options and then press the left mouse button.

Add decimal place

Remove decimal place

■ The numbers display the number of decimal places you selected.

■ To deselect cells, move the mouse over any cell and then press the left mouse button.

CHANGE APPEARANCE OF NUMBERS

When you change the appearance of numbers, you do not change the value of the numbers.

CHANGE APPEARANCE OF NUMBERS

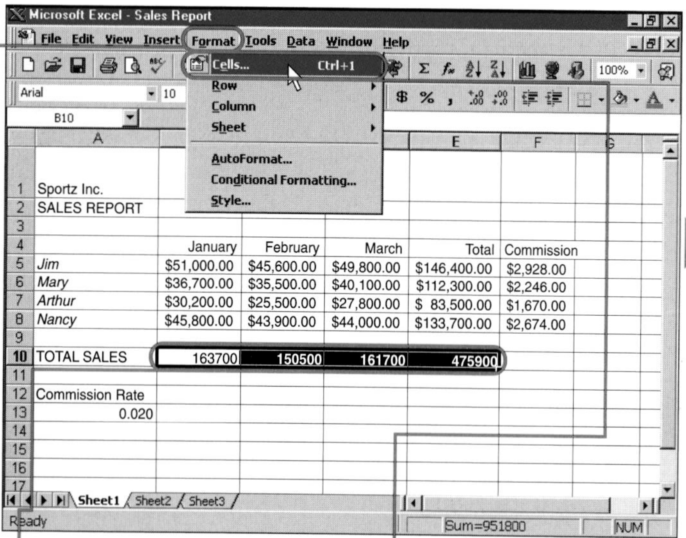

1 Select the cells containing the numbers you want to display differently. To select cells, refer to page 16.

2 Move the mouse over **Format** and then press the left mouse button.

3 Move the mouse over **Cells** and then press the left mouse button.

■ The **Format Cells** dialog box appears.

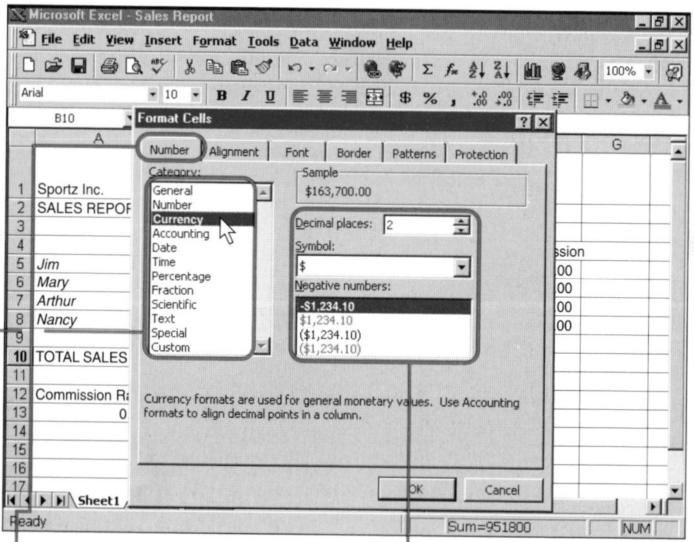

4 Move the mouse over the **Number** tab and then press the left mouse button.

5 Move the mouse over the category that identifies the numbers in your worksheet and then press the left mouse button.

■ This area displays all the options for the category you selected. Each category displays a different set of options.

Why did number signs (#) appear in a cell after I changed the appearance of numbers?

If number signs (#) appear in a cell, the column is not wide enough to display the entire number. To change the column width, refer to page 90.

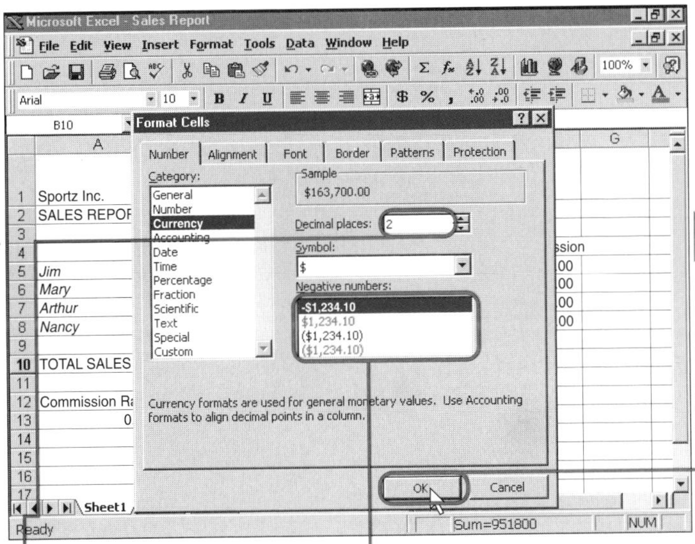

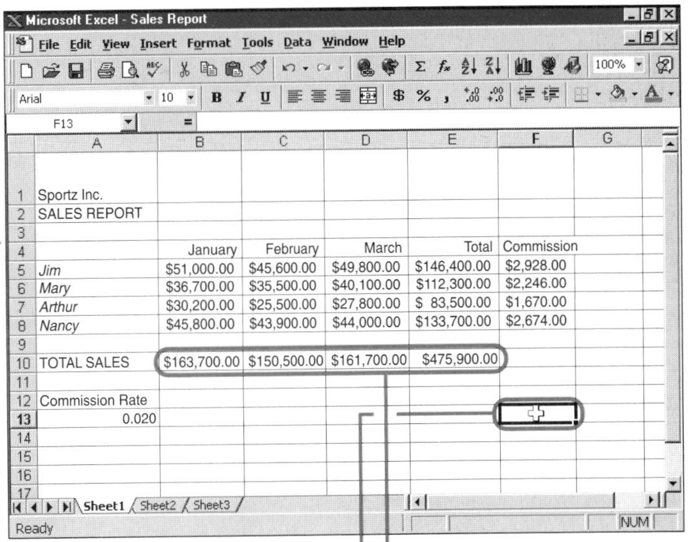

6 To select the number of decimal places you want the numbers to display, move the mouse I over this area and then quickly press the left mouse button twice. Then type the number of decimal places.

7 To select the way you want negative numbers to appear, move the mouse over one of the available styles and then press the left mouse button.

8 To apply the changes, move the mouse over **OK** and then press the left mouse button.

■ The numbers display the changes.

■ To deselect cells, move the mouse over any cell and then press the left mouse button.

CHANGE FONT OF DATA

CHANGE FONT OF DATA

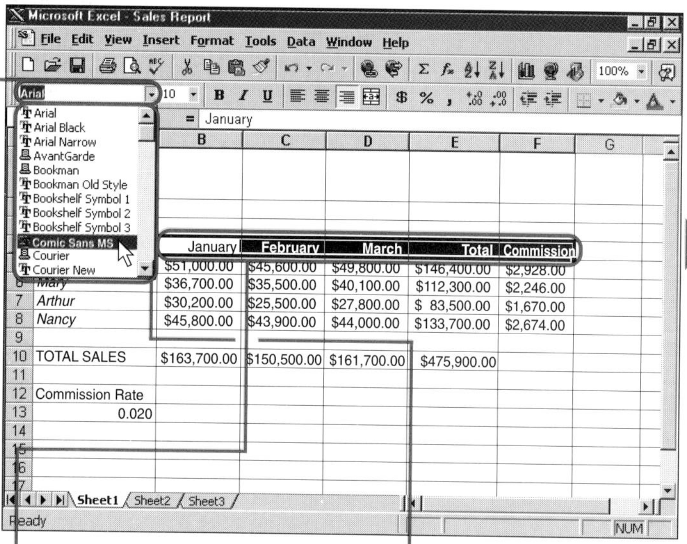

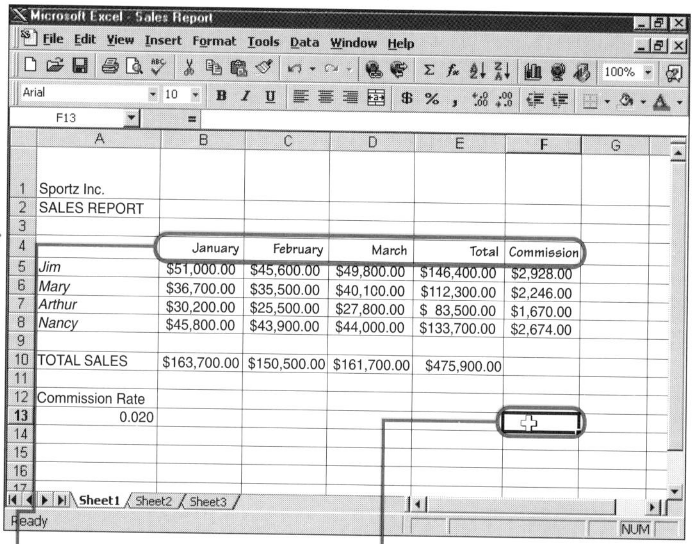

1 Select the cells containing the data you want to change to a new font. To select cells, refer to page 16.

2 To display a list of the available fonts, move the mouse ⇖ over ▾ in this area and then press the left mouse button.

3 Move the mouse ⇖ over the font you want to use and then press the left mouse button.

■ The data displays the font you selected.

■ To deselect cells, move the mouse ✥ over any cell and then press the left mouse button.

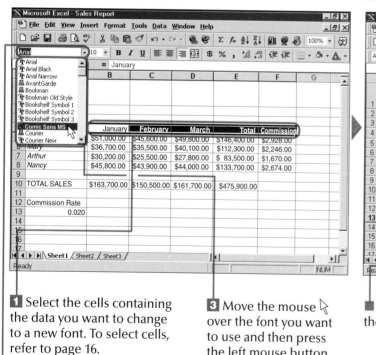

CHANGE SIZE OF DATA

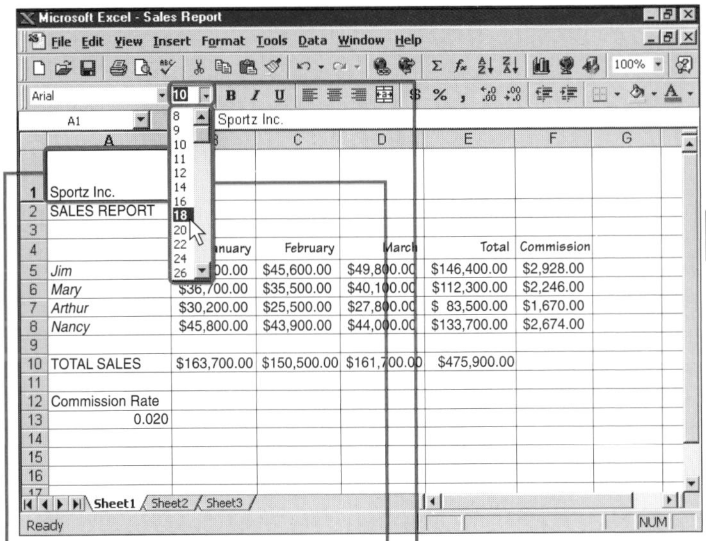

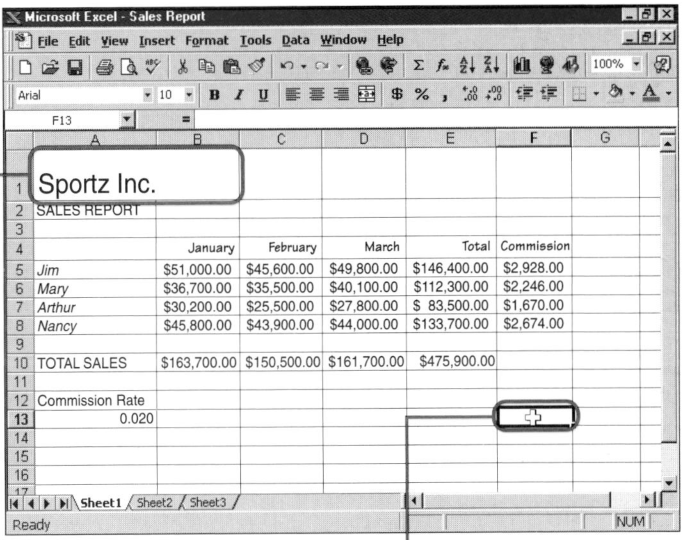

1 Select the cells containing the data you want to change to a new size. To select cells, refer to page 16.

2 To display a list of the available sizes, move the mouse over ▾ in this area and then press the left mouse button.

3 Move the mouse over the size you want to use and then press the left mouse button.

■ The data displays the size you selected.

■ To deselect cells, move the mouse over any cell and then press the left mouse button.

CHANGE FONT OF DATA

You can change the design, style and size of data in your worksheet at the same time.

CHANGE FONT OF DATA

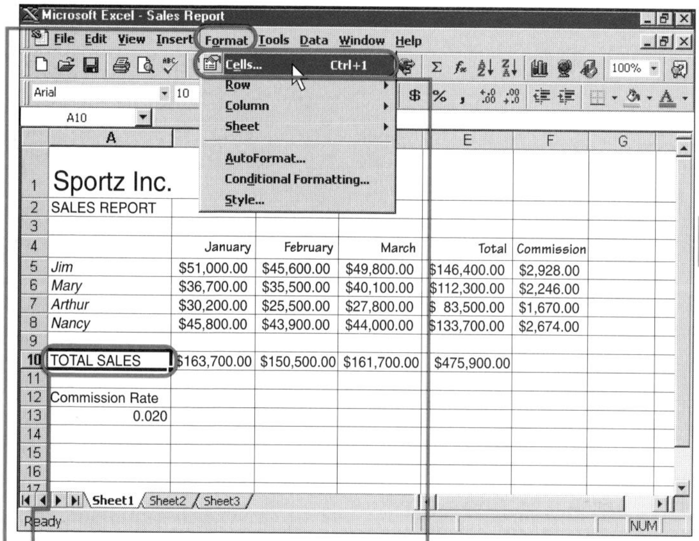

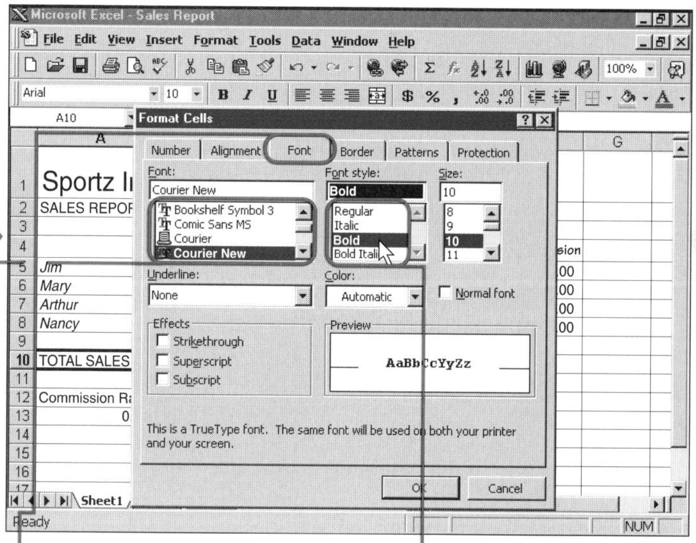

1 Select the cells containing the data you want to display differently. To select cells, refer to page 16.

2 Move the mouse over **Format** and then press the left mouse button.

3 Move the mouse over **Cells** and then press the left mouse button.

■ The **Format Cells** dialog box appears.

4 Move the mouse over the **Font** tab and then press the left mouse button.

5 To change the design of the data, move the mouse over the font you want to use and then press the left mouse button.

6 To change the style of the data, move the mouse over the style you want to use and then press the left mouse button.

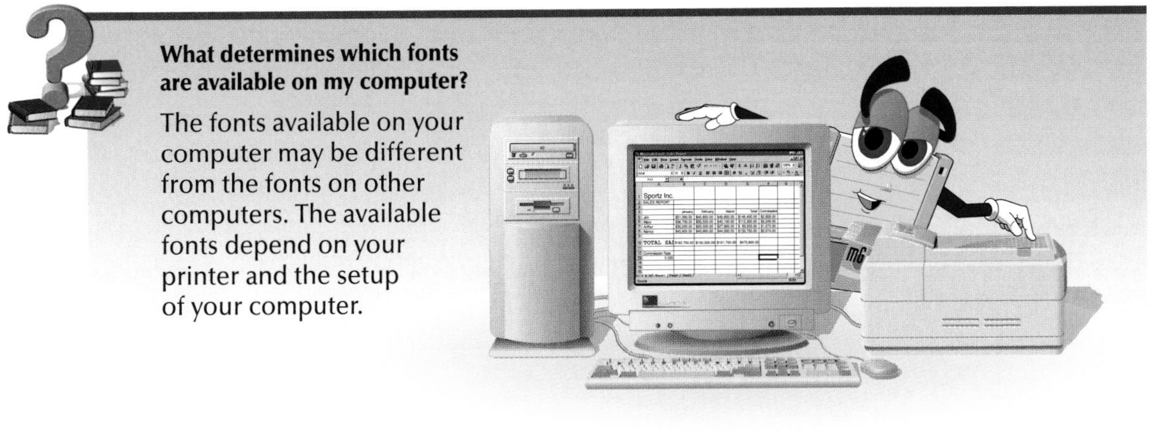

What determines which fonts are available on my computer?

The fonts available on your computer may be different from the fonts on other computers. The available fonts depend on your printer and the setup of your computer.

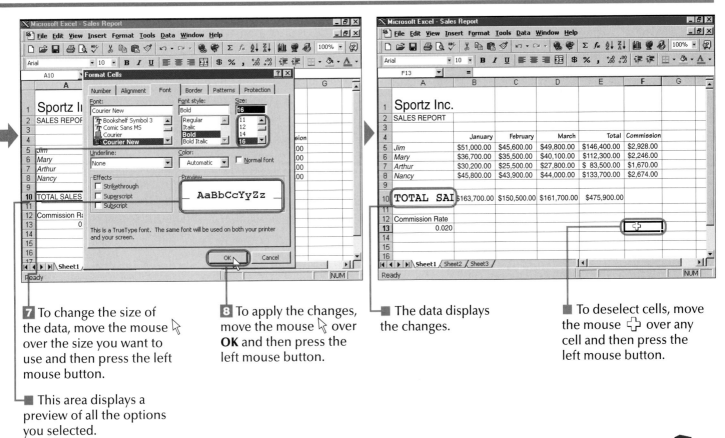

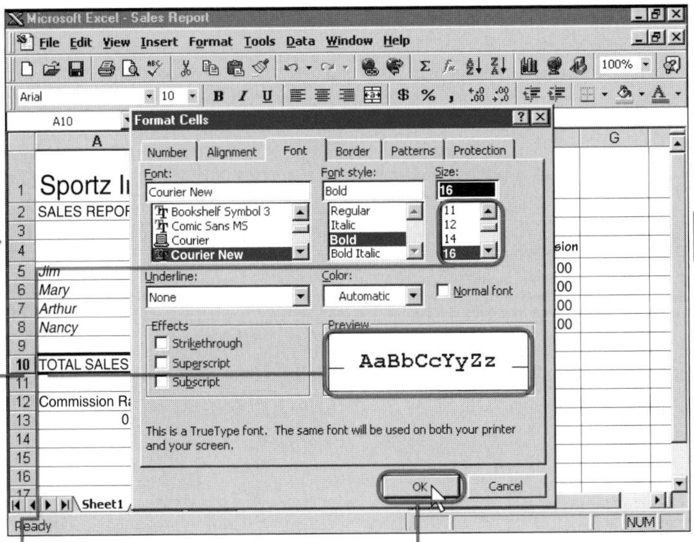

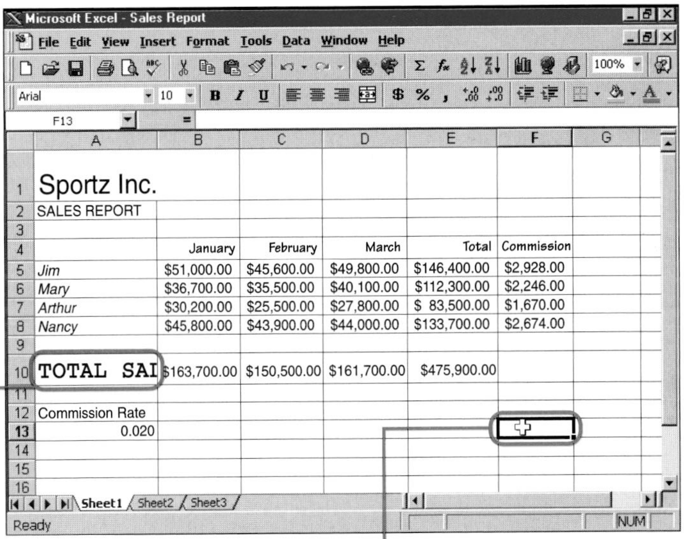

7 To change the size of the data, move the mouse over the size you want to use and then press the left mouse button.

■ This area displays a preview of all the options you selected.

8 To apply the changes, move the mouse over **OK** and then press the left mouse button.

■ The data displays the changes.

■ To deselect cells, move the mouse over any cell and then press the left mouse button.

INDENT DATA

You can use the Indent feature to move data away from the left edge of a cell.
FRUIT
Lemons
Limes
Oranges

INDENT DATA

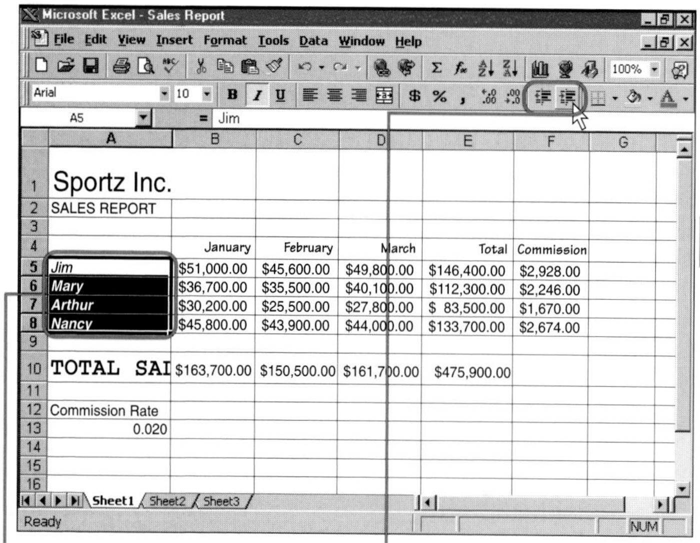

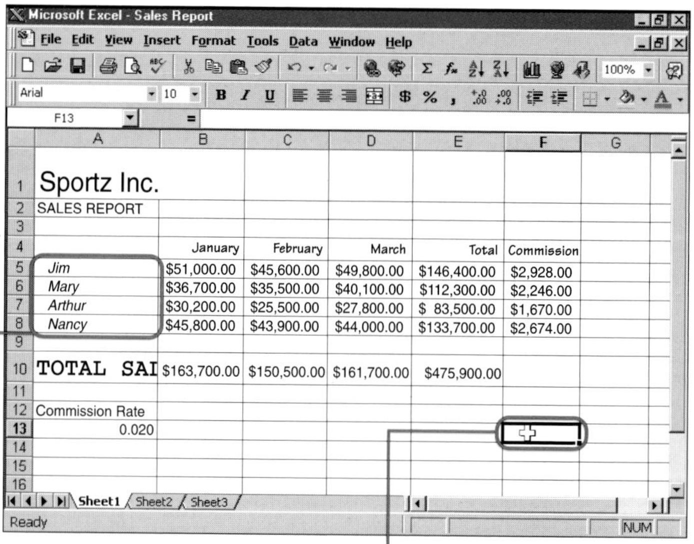

1 Select the cells containing the data you want to indent. To select cells, refer to page 16.

2 Move the mouse over one of the following options and then press the left mouse button.

- Move data to the left
- Move data to the right

■ Excel indents the data.

■ To deselect cells, move the mouse over any cell and then press the left mouse button.

CENTER DATA ACROSS COLUMNS

You can center data across several columns in your worksheet. This is useful for centering titles over your data.
Income Statement

CENTER DATA ACROSS COLUMNS

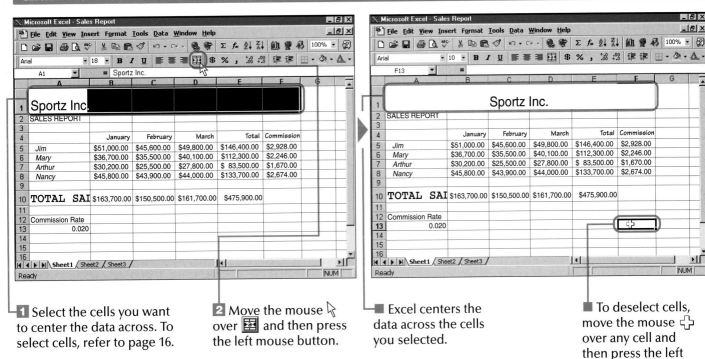

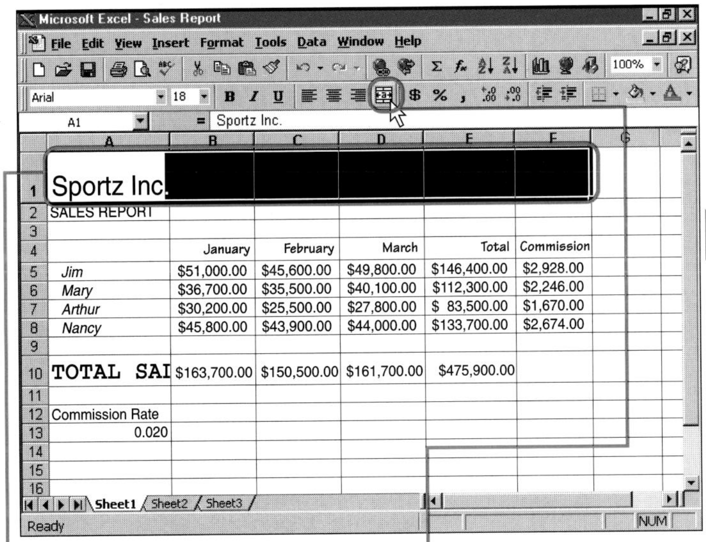

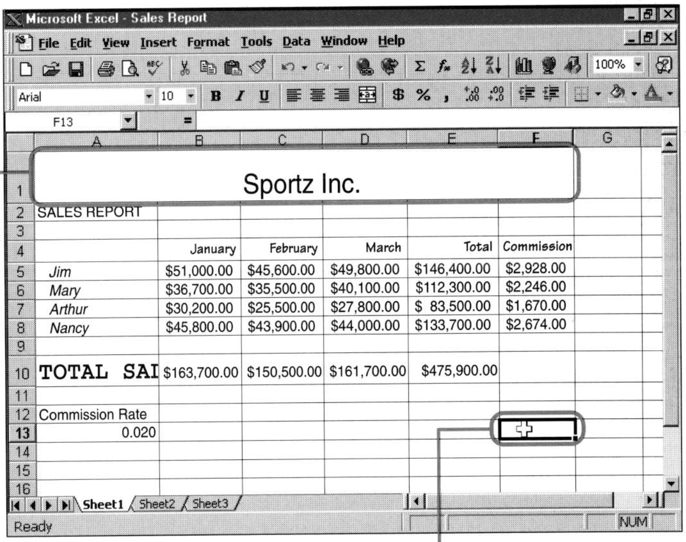

1 Select the cells you want to center the data across. To select cells, refer to page 16.

Note: The first cell you select should contain the data you want to center.

2 Move the mouse over and then press the left mouse button.

■ Excel centers the data across the cells you selected.

■ To deselect cells, move the mouse over any cell and then press the left mouse button.

WRAP TEXT IN CELLS

WRAP TEXT IN CELLS

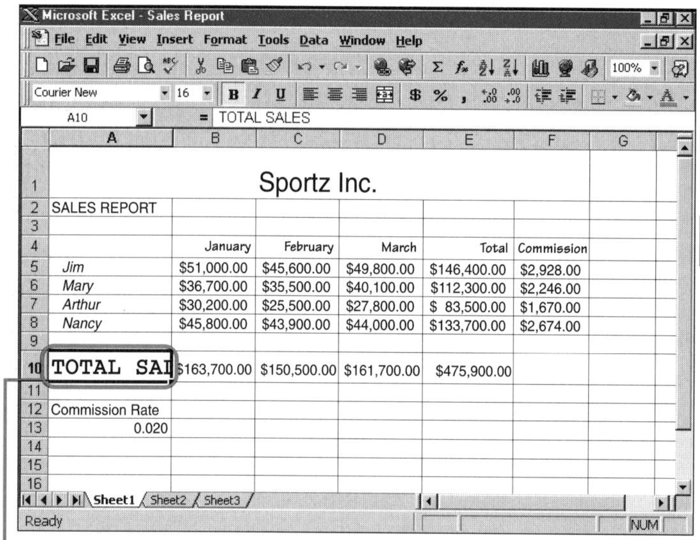

1 Select the cells containing the text you want to wrap. To select cells, refer to page 16.

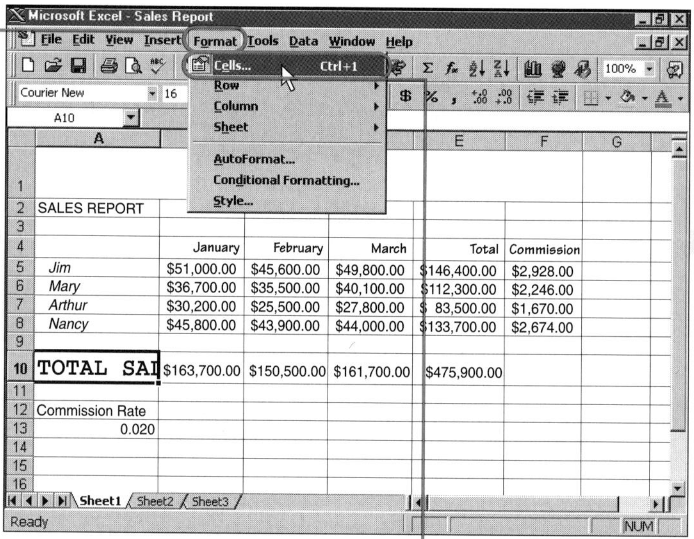

2 Move the mouse over **Format** and then press the left mouse button.

3 Move the mouse over **Cells** and then press the left mouse button.

■ The **Format Cells** dialog box appears.

Can I wrap text as I type?

When you want to start a new line of text as you type, press and hold down Alt and then press Enter on your keyboard. Then release both keys.

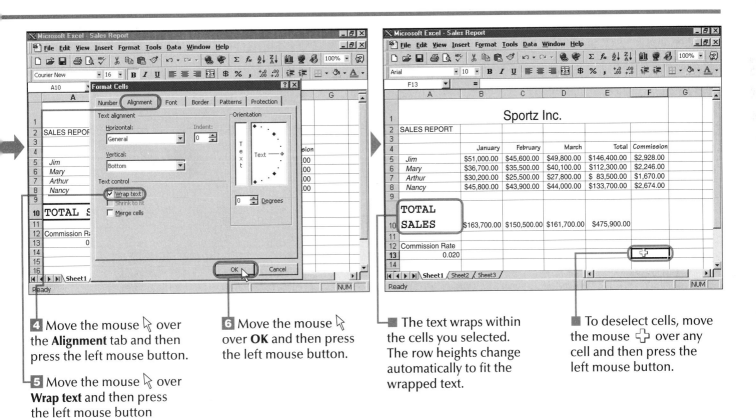

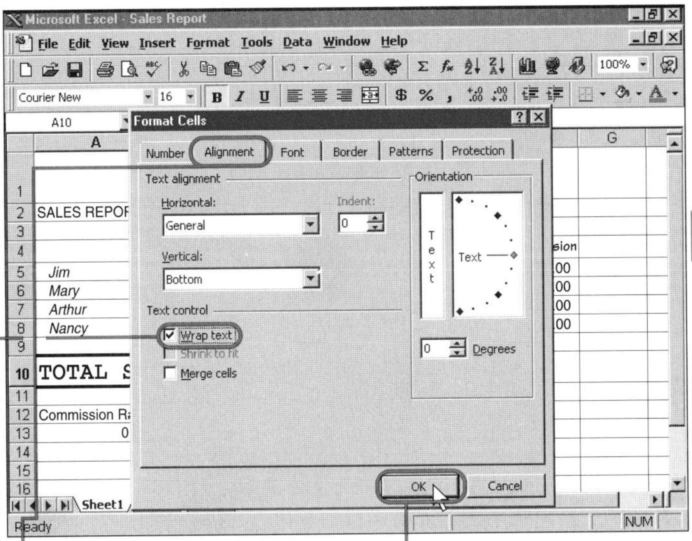

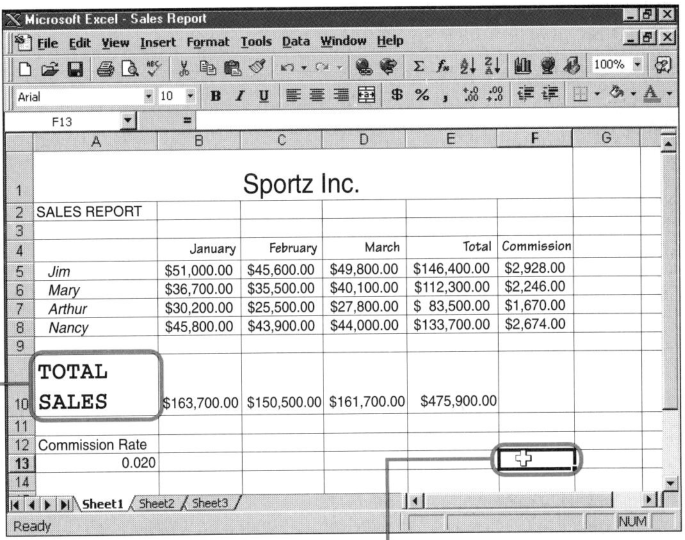

4 Move the mouse over the **Alignment** tab and then press the left mouse button.

5 Move the mouse over **Wrap text** and then press the left mouse button (☐ changes to ☑).

6 Move the mouse over **OK** and then press the left mouse button.

■ The text wraps within the cells you selected. The row heights change automatically to fit the wrapped text.

■ To deselect cells, move the mouse over any cell and then press the left mouse button.

ROTATE DATA IN CELLS

You can easily rotate data within cells in your worksheet. This helps you emphasize row and column headings.
Jan
Feb
Mar

ROTATE DATA IN CELLS

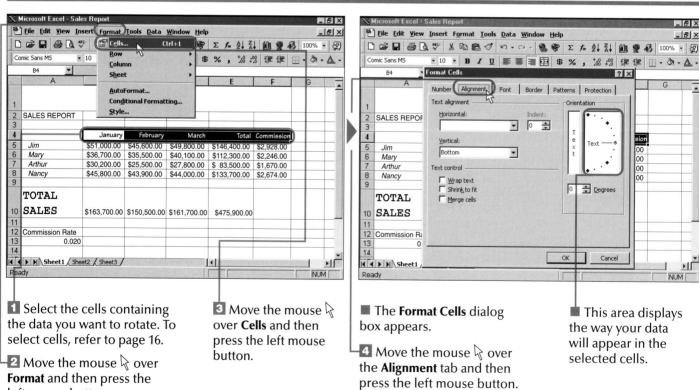

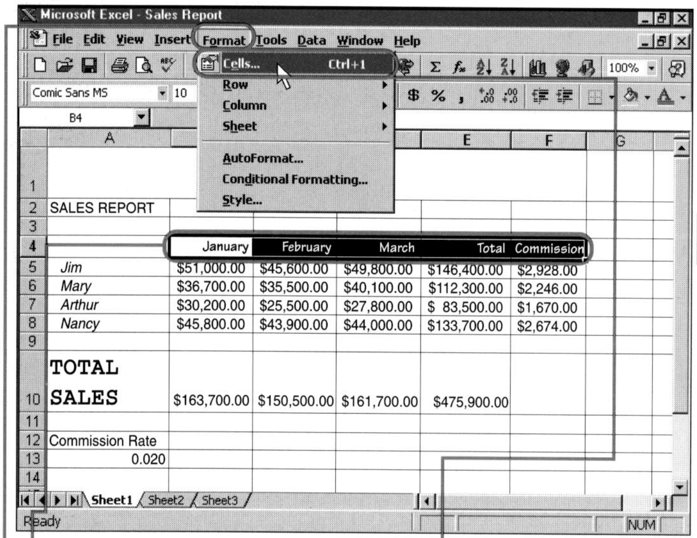

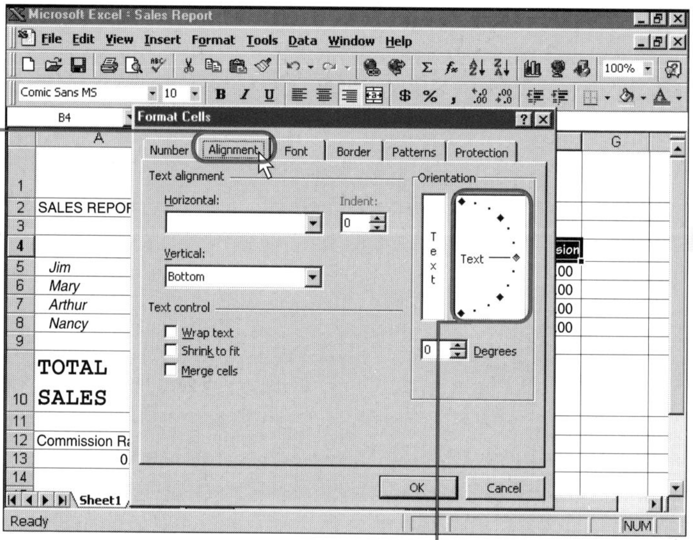

1 Select the cells containing the data you want to rotate. To select cells, refer to page 16.

2 Move the mouse over **Format** and then press the left mouse button.

3 Move the mouse over **Cells** and then press the left mouse button.

■ The **Format Cells** dialog box appears.

4 Move the mouse over the **Alignment** tab and then press the left mouse button.

■ This area displays the way your data will appear in the selected cells.

How can I display data vertically?

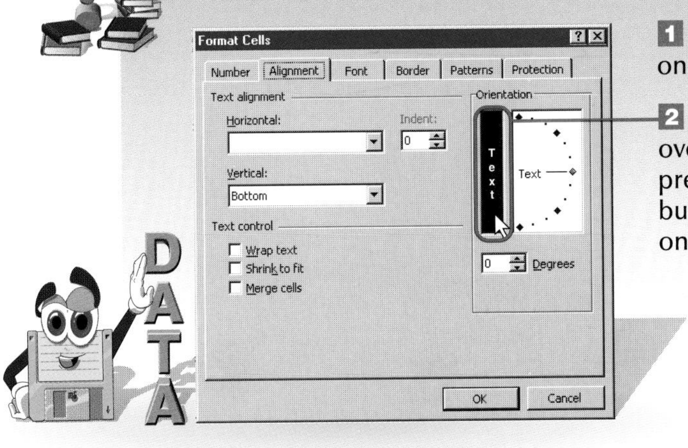

1 Perform steps 1 to 4 on page 106.

2 Move the mouse over this area and then press the left mouse button. Then press **Enter** on your keyboard.

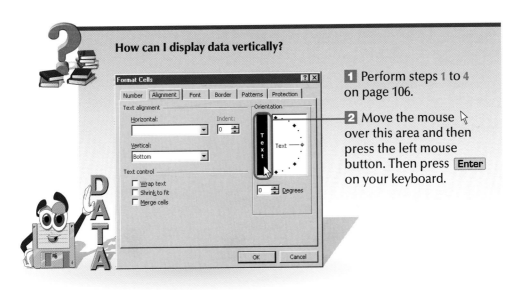

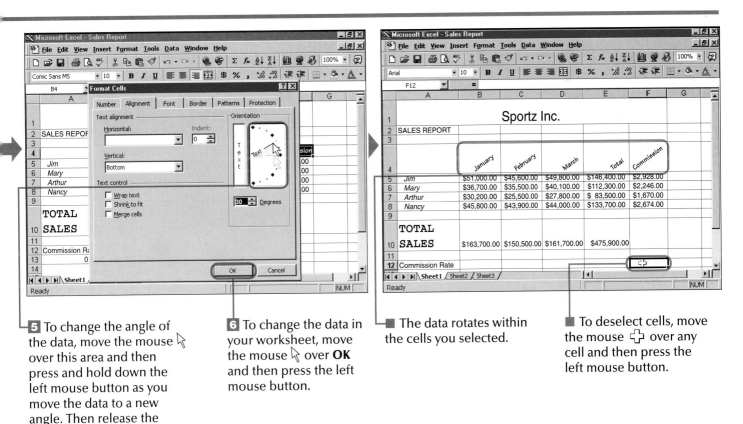

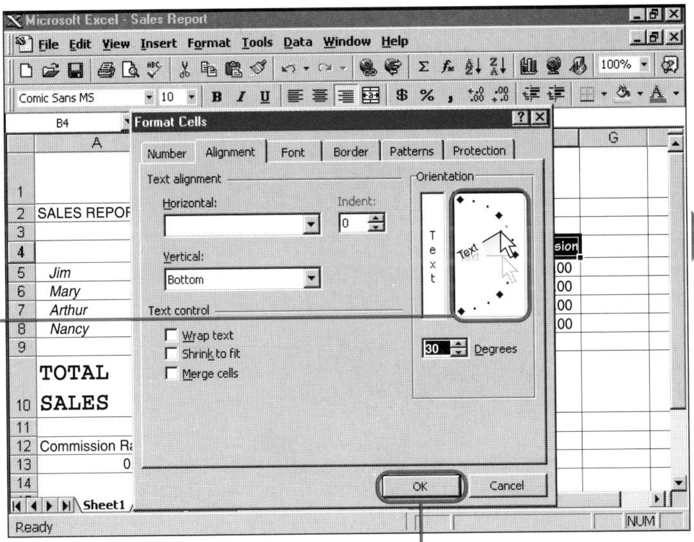

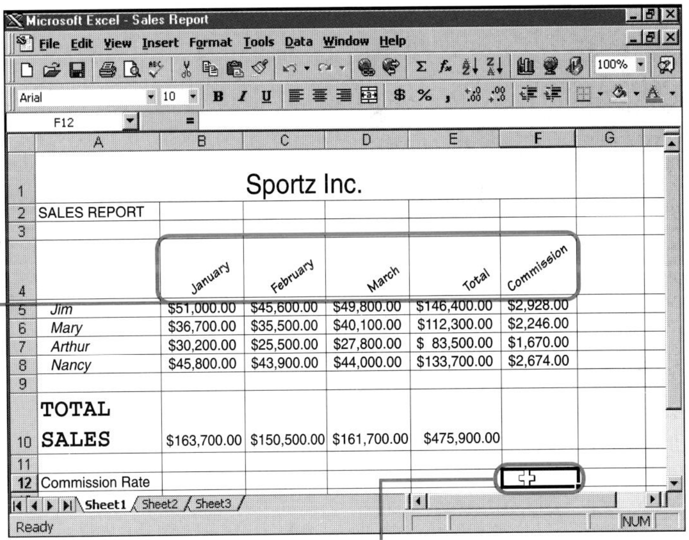

5 To change the angle of the data, move the mouse over this area and then press and hold down the left mouse button as you move the data to a new angle. Then release the mouse button.

6 To change the data in your worksheet, move the mouse over **OK** and then press the left mouse button.

■ The data rotates within the cells you selected.

■ To deselect cells, move the mouse over any cell and then press the left mouse button.

ADD BORDERS

ADD BORDERS

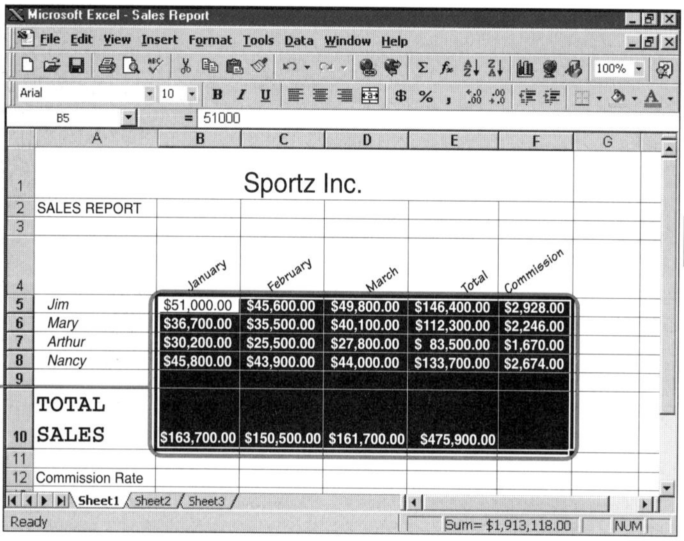

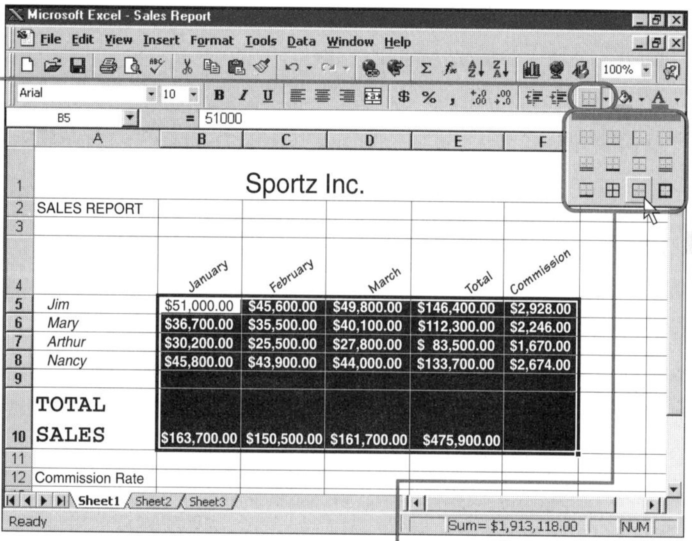

1 Select the cells you want to display borders. To select cells, refer to page 16.

2 Move the mouse over ▾ in this area and then press the left mouse button.

3 Move the mouse over the type of border you want to add and then press the left mouse button.

Can I print lines in my worksheet without adding borders?

Instead of adding borders to your worksheet, you can have Excel automatically print light lines, called gridlines, around each cell. To print gridlines, refer to page 128.

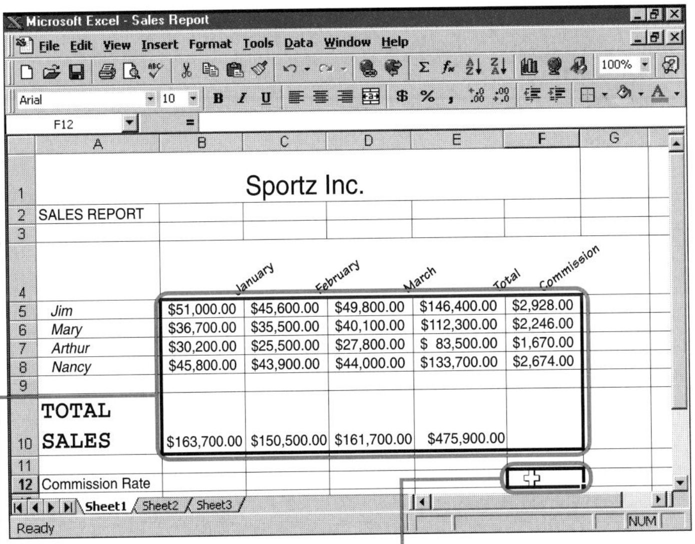

■ The cells display the border you selected.

■ To deselect cells, move the mouse ✥ over any cell and then press the left mouse button.

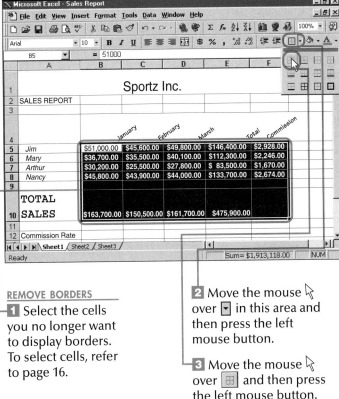

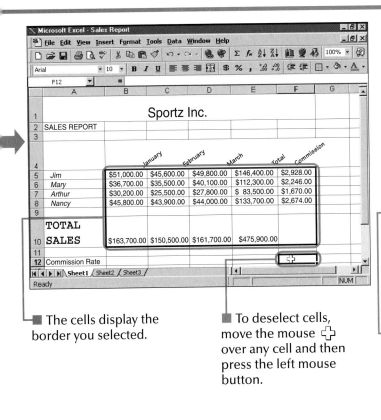

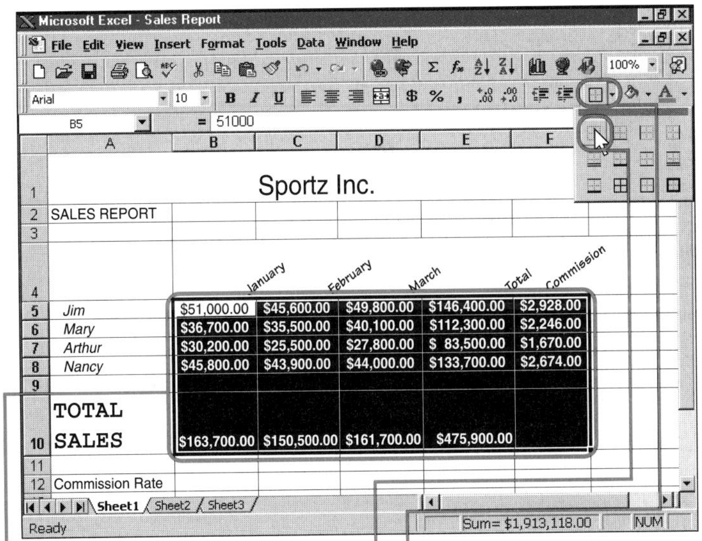

REMOVE BORDERS

1 Select the cells you no longer want to display borders. To select cells, refer to page 16.

2 Move the mouse over ▾ in this area and then press the left mouse button.

3 Move the mouse over ⊞ and then press the left mouse button.

CHANGE COLOR

CHANGE CELL COLOR

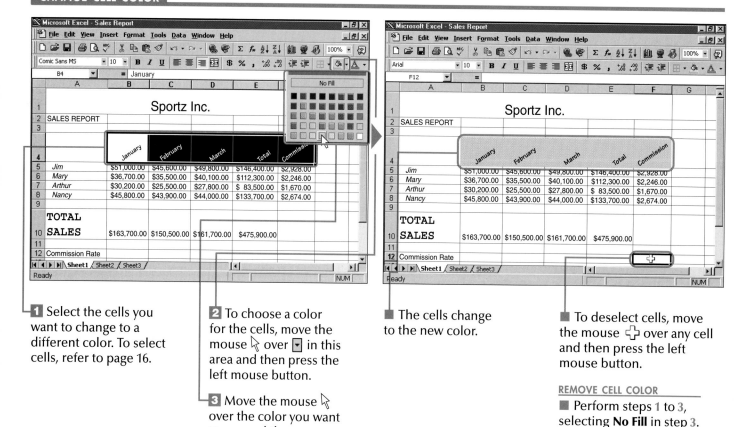

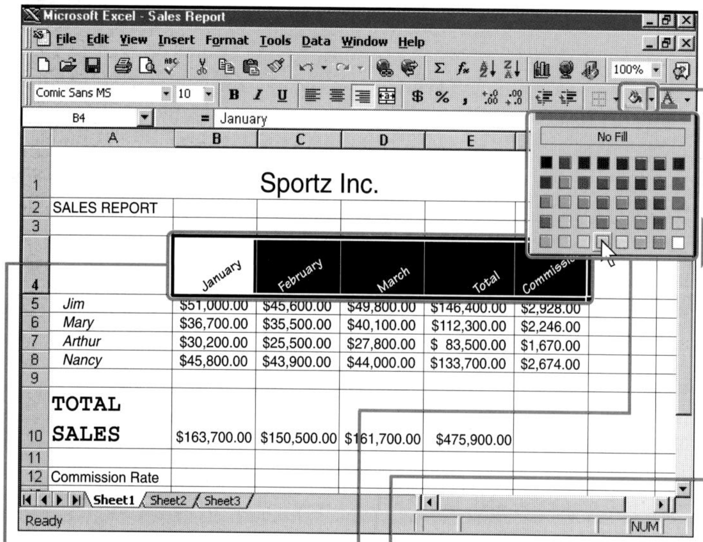

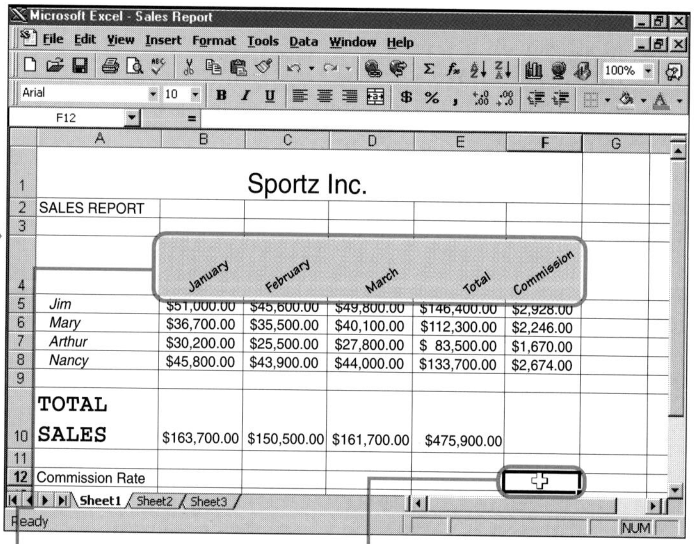

1 Select the cells you want to change to a different color. To select cells, refer to page 16.

2 To choose a color for the cells, move the mouse over ▾ in this area and then press the left mouse button.

3 Move the mouse over the color you want to use and then press the left mouse button.

■ The cells change to the new color.

■ To deselect cells, move the mouse over any cell and then press the left mouse button.

REMOVE CELL COLOR

■ Perform steps 1 to 3, selecting **No Fill** in step 3.

What colors should I choose?

When adding color to your worksheet, make sure you choose cell and data colors that work well together. For example, red text on a blue background is difficult to read. To choose from many ready-to-use designs offered by Excel, refer to page 116.

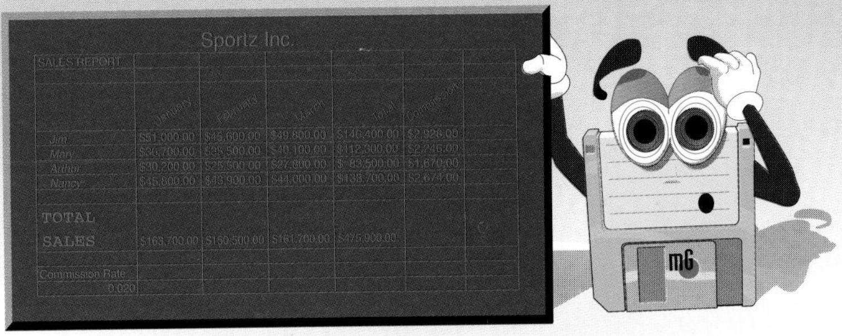

CHANGE DATA COLOR

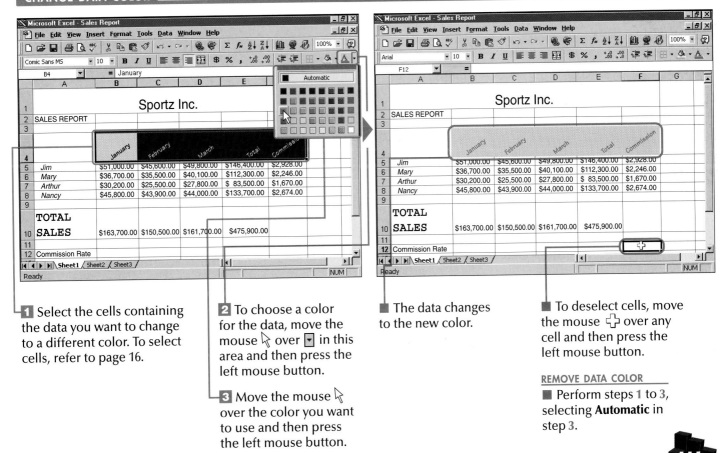

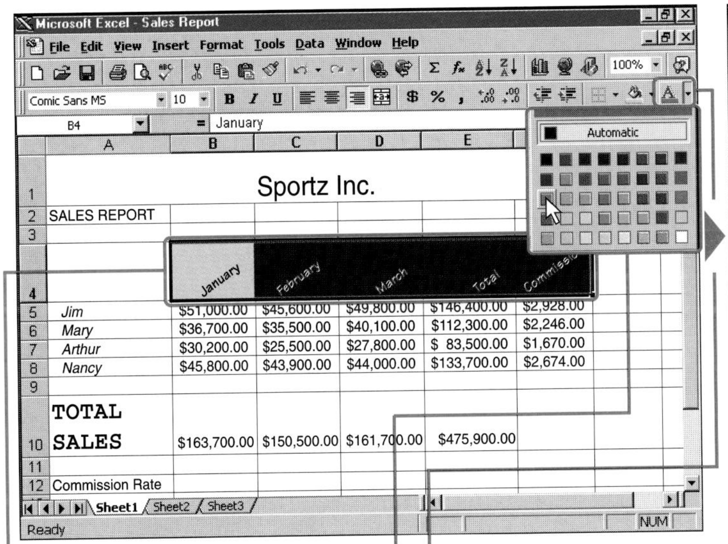

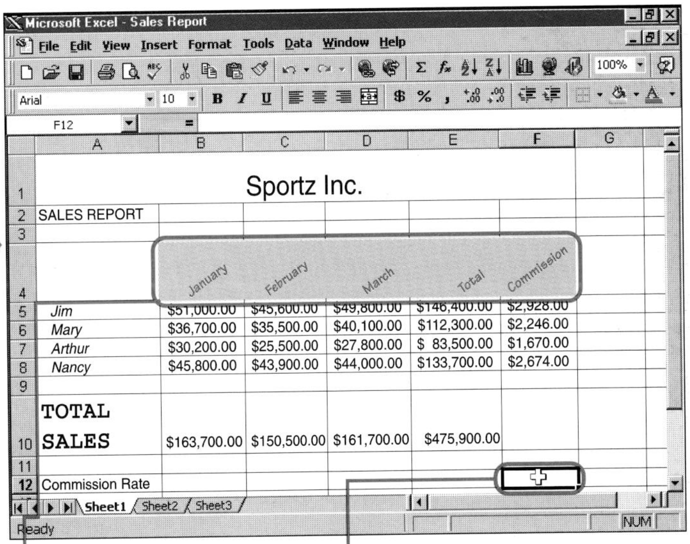

1 Select the cells containing the data you want to change to a different color. To select cells, refer to page 16.

2 To choose a color for the data, move the mouse over ▾ in this area and then press the left mouse button.

3 Move the mouse over the color you want to use and then press the left mouse button.

■ The data changes to the new color.

■ To deselect cells, move the mouse over any cell and then press the left mouse button.

REMOVE DATA COLOR

■ Perform steps 1 to 3, selecting **Automatic** in step 3.

COPY FORMATTING

If you like the appearance of a cell in your worksheet, you can make other cells look exactly the same.
Sales
1996
1997
Product A
3180
3210
Product B
3180
2740
Product C
3240
3140
Product D
2610
2750

COPY FORMATTING

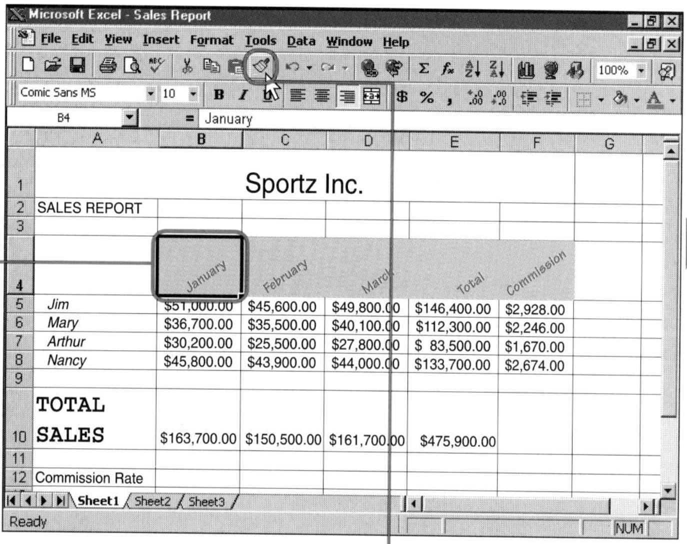

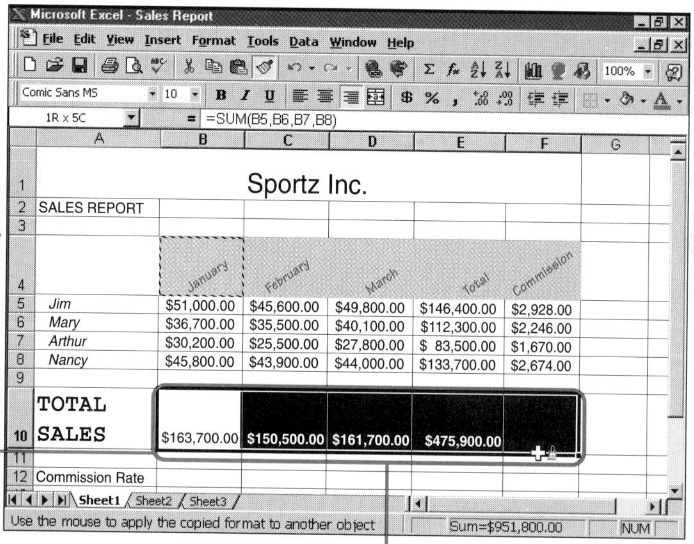

1 Move the mouse over a cell displaying the formatting you want to copy to other cells and then press the left mouse button.

2 Move the mouse over the Format Painter button and then press the left mouse button.

■ The mouse changes when over your worksheet.

3 Select the cells you want to display the same formatting. To select cells, refer to page 16.

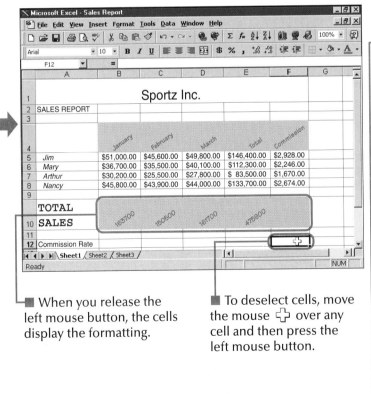

You can copy formatting to several locations in your worksheet at once.

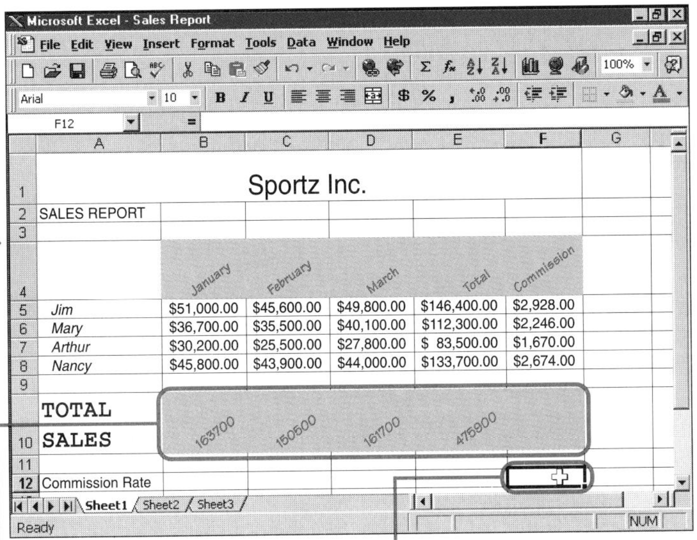

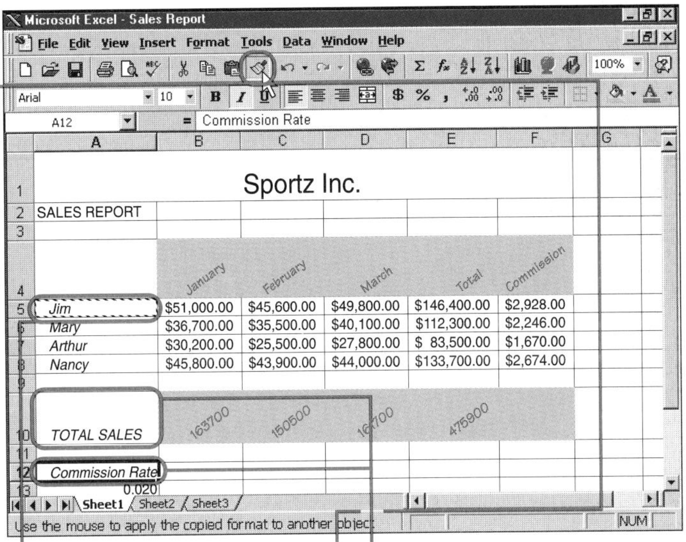

■ When you release the left mouse button, the cells display the formatting.

■ To deselect cells, move the mouse over any cell and then press the left mouse button.

1 Move the mouse over a cell displaying the formatting you want to copy to other cells and then press the left mouse button.

2 Move the mouse over and then quickly press the left mouse button twice.

3 Select the cells you want to display the same formatting. Repeat this step until you have selected all the cells you want to display the formatting.

4 Move the mouse over and then press the left mouse button.

CLEAR FORMATTING

CLEAR FORMATTING

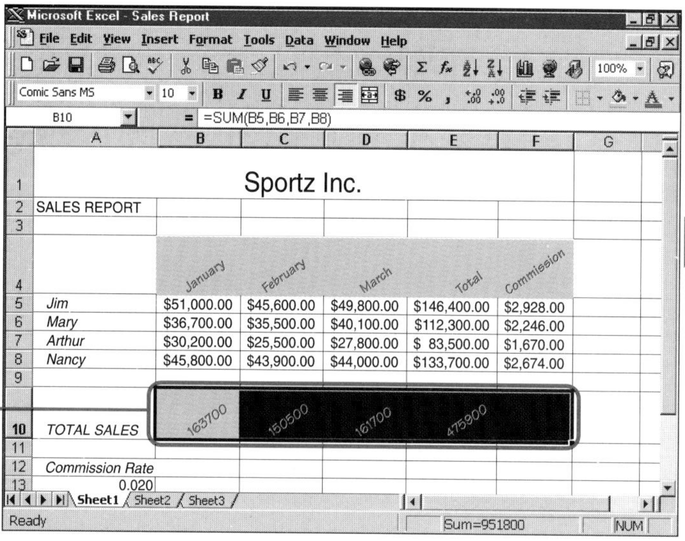

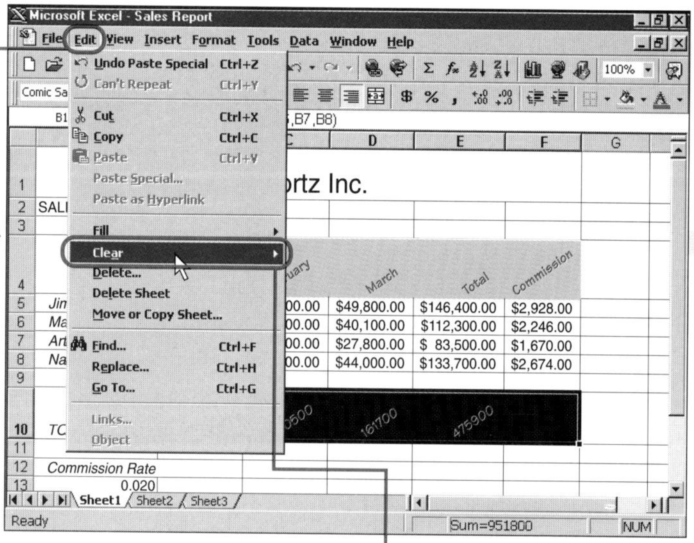

1 Select the cells containing the formatting you want to remove. To select cells, refer to page 16.

2 Move the mouse over **Edit** and then press the left mouse button.

3 Move the mouse over **Clear**.

How can I keep the formatting but remove the data from cells?

To keep the formatting but remove the data from cells, select the cells containing the data you want to remove. Then press Delete on your keyboard.

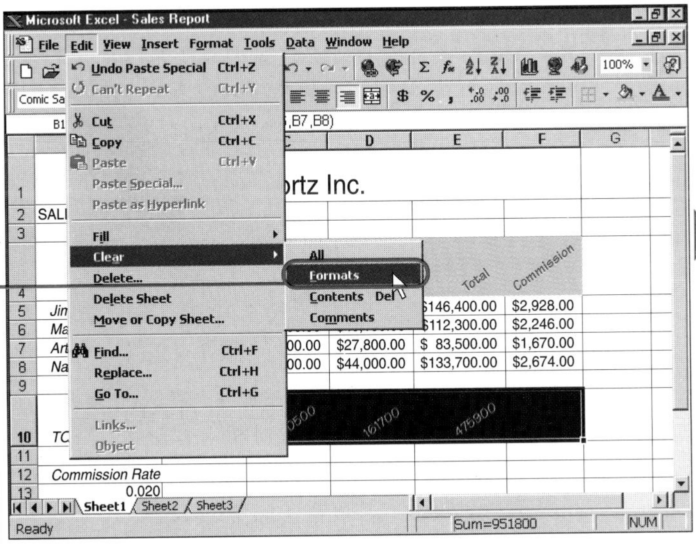

4 Move the mouse over **Formats** and then press the left mouse button.

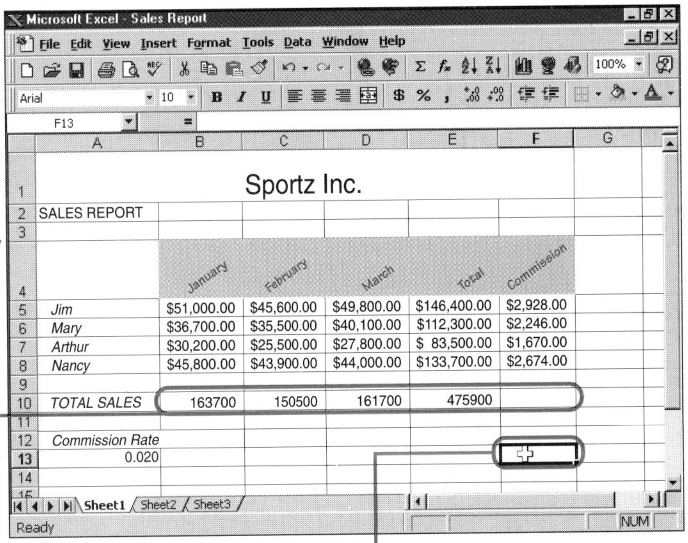

■ All the formatting disappears from the cells you selected.

■ To deselect cells, move the mouse over any cell and then press the left mouse button.

QUICKLY APPLY A DESIGN

Excel offers many ready-to-use designs you can choose from to give your worksheet a new appearance.

QUICKLY APPLY A DESIGN

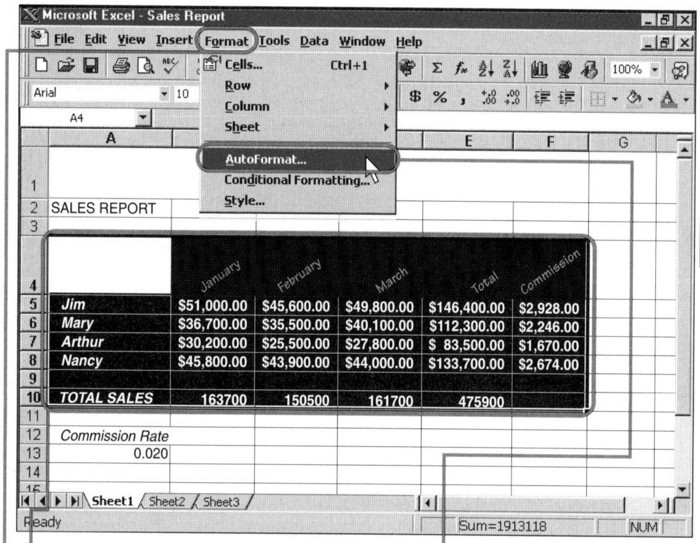

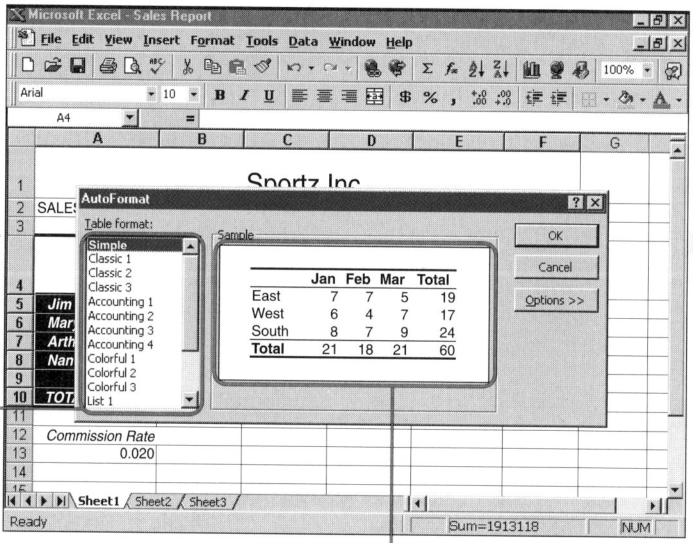

1 Select the cells you want to apply a design to. To select cells, refer to page 16.

2 Move the mouse over **Format** and then press the left mouse button.

3 Move the mouse over **AutoFormat** and then press the left mouse button.

■ The **AutoFormat** dialog box appears.

■ This area displays a list of the available designs.

■ This area displays a sample of the highlighted design.

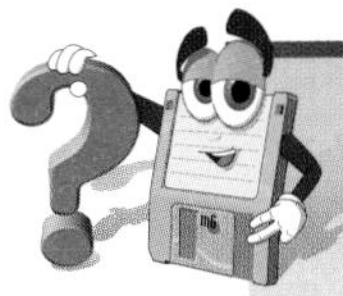

What are some designs offered by Excel?

	Jan	Feb	Mar	Total
East	7	7	5	19
West	6	4	7	17
South	8	7	9	24
Total	21	18	21	60

List 2

		Jan		Feb		Mar		Total
East	$	7	$	7	$	5	$	19
West		6		4		7		17
South		8		7		9		24
Total	$	21	$	18	$	21	$	60

Accounting 2

	Jan	*Feb*	*Mar*	*Total*
East	7	7	5	19
West	6	4	7	17
South	8	7	9	24
Total	21	18	21	60

Colorful 1

	Jan	Feb	Mar	Total
East	7	7	5	19
West	6	4	7	17
South	8	7	9	24
Total	21	18	21	60

3D Effects 1

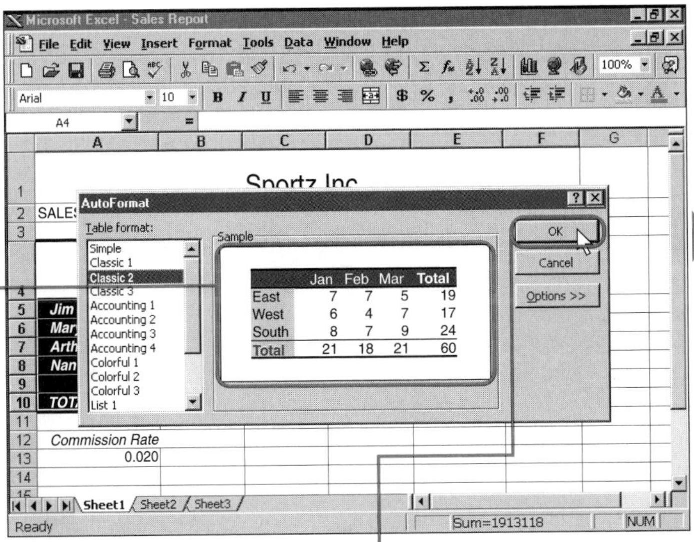

4 Press ↓ or ↑ on your keyboard until you see a design you like.

5 To apply the design to the cells you selected, move the mouse over **OK** and then press the left mouse button.

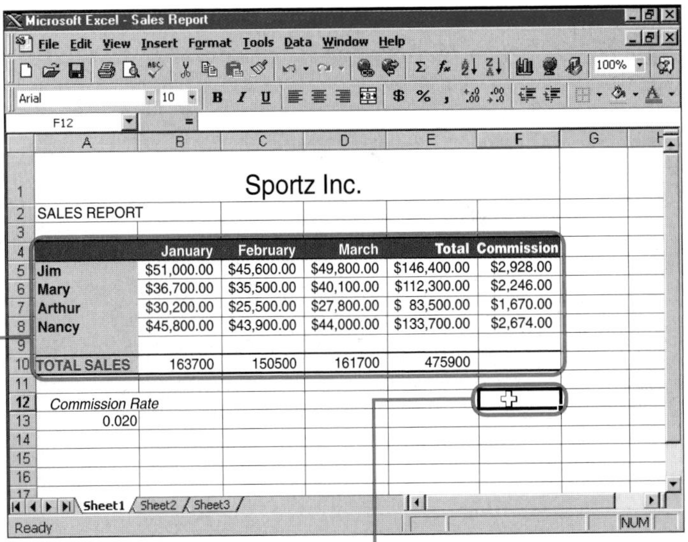

■ The cells display the design you selected.

■ To deselect cells, move the mouse over any cell and then press the left mouse button.

REMOVE AUTOFORMAT

■ Perform steps 1 to 5, selecting **None** in step 4.

PRODUCE SALES 1997
Oranges 25000
Apples 37000
Grapefruits 18000
Lemons 27000
Limes 15000
Lemons
Limes
Oranges
Grapefruits
Apples
mG

CHAPTER 7

PRINT YOUR WORKSHEETS

Are you ready to print your worksheet? In this chapter you will learn how to print your worksheet and change the way your worksheet appears on a printed page.

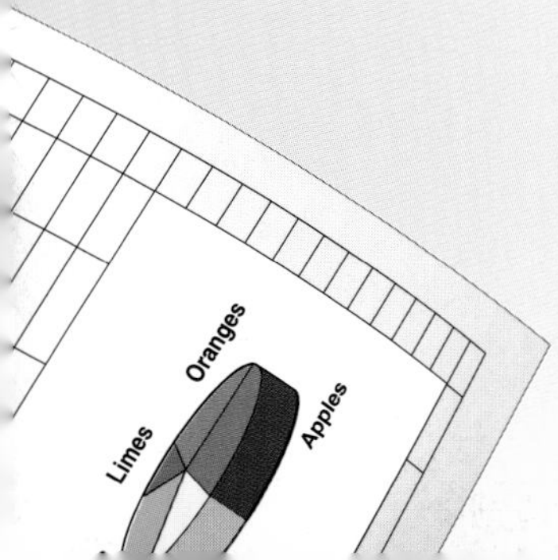

PREVIEW A WORKSHEET

You can see on your screen how your worksheet will look when printed.

PREVIEW A WORKSHEET

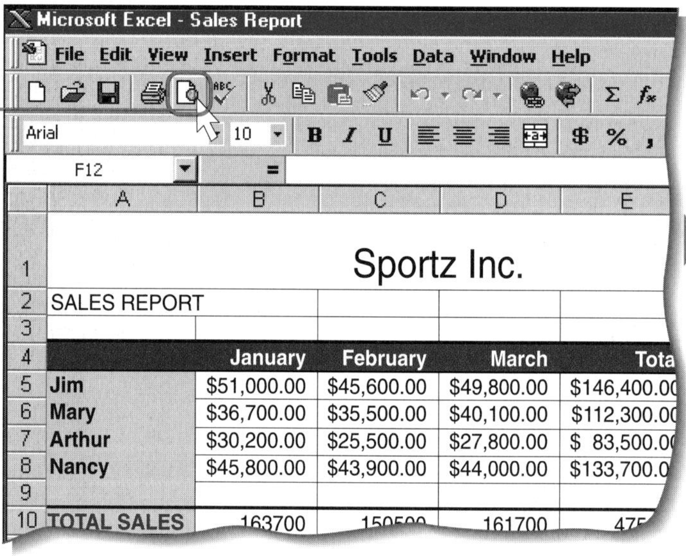

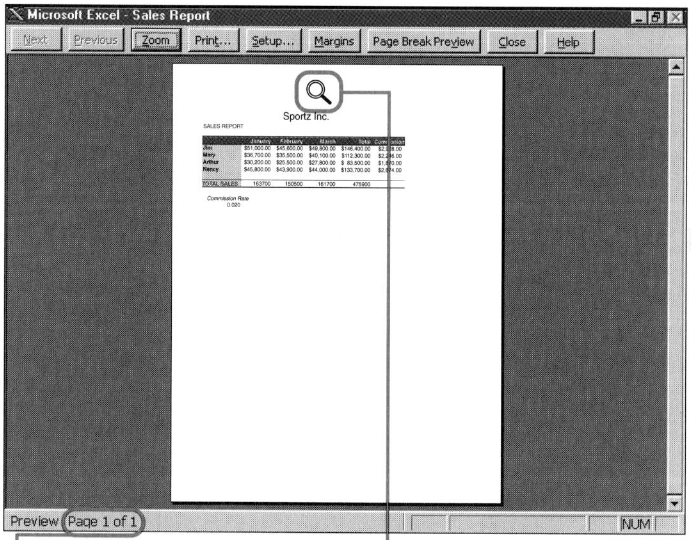

■1 Move the mouse over and then press the left mouse button.

■ The Print Preview window appears.

■ This area tells you which page is displayed and the total number of pages in your worksheet.

Note: If you have a black-and-white printer, Excel displays the page in black and white.

■2 To magnify an area of the page, move the mouse over the area (changes to) and then press the left mouse button.

What should I do before printing my worksheet?

Before printing your worksheet, preview the worksheet to ensure it will print the way you want. Also make sure your printer is turned on and contains paper.

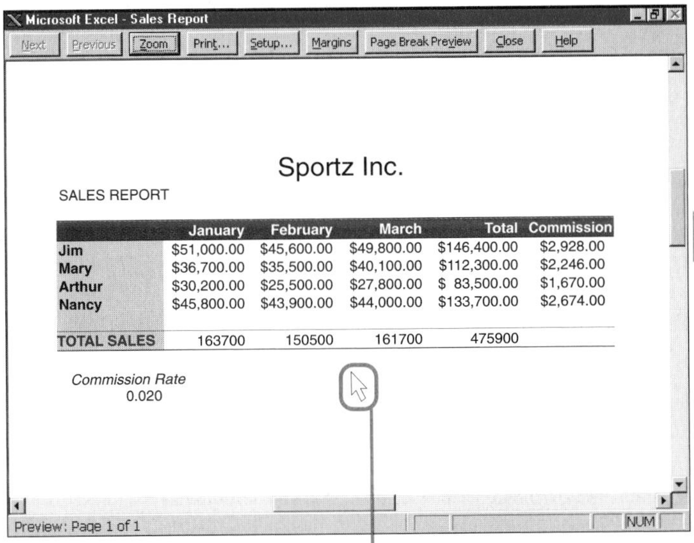

■ A magnified view of the area appears.

3 To display the entire page again, move the mouse anywhere over the page and then press the left mouse button.

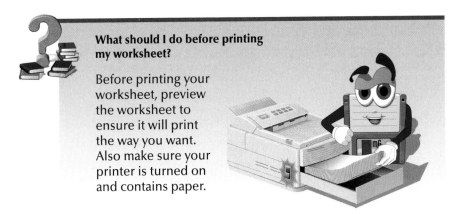

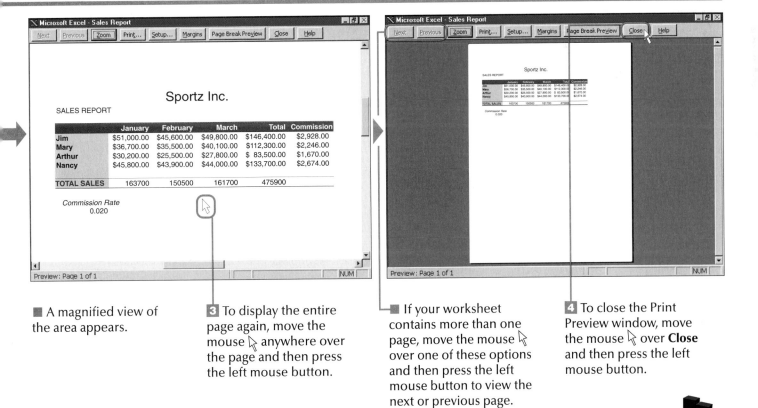

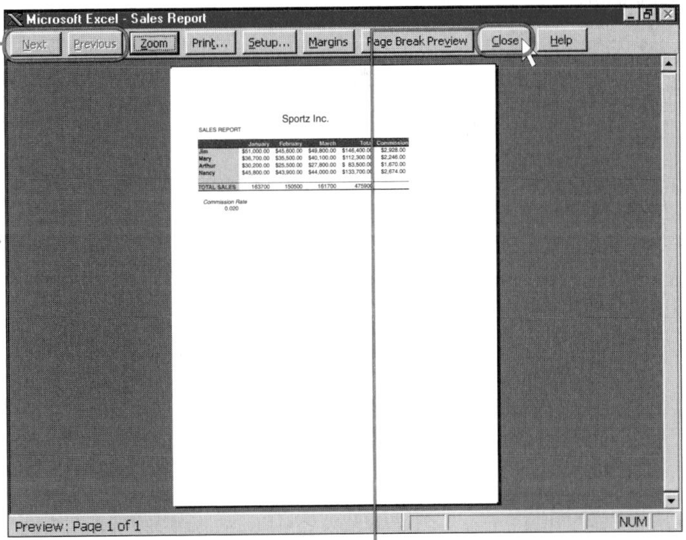

■ If your worksheet contains more than one page, move the mouse over one of these options and then press the left mouse button to view the next or previous page.

4 To close the Print Preview window, move the mouse over **Close** and then press the left mouse button.

PRINT A WORKSHEET

You can produce a paper copy of the worksheet displayed on your screen.

PRINT A WORKSHEET

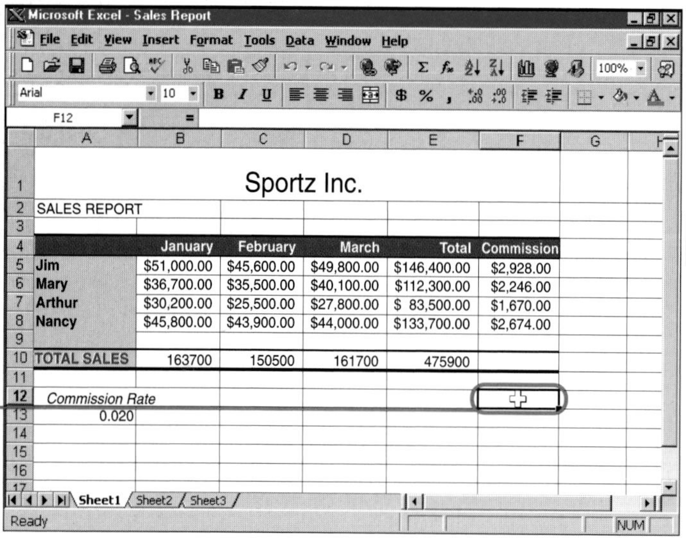

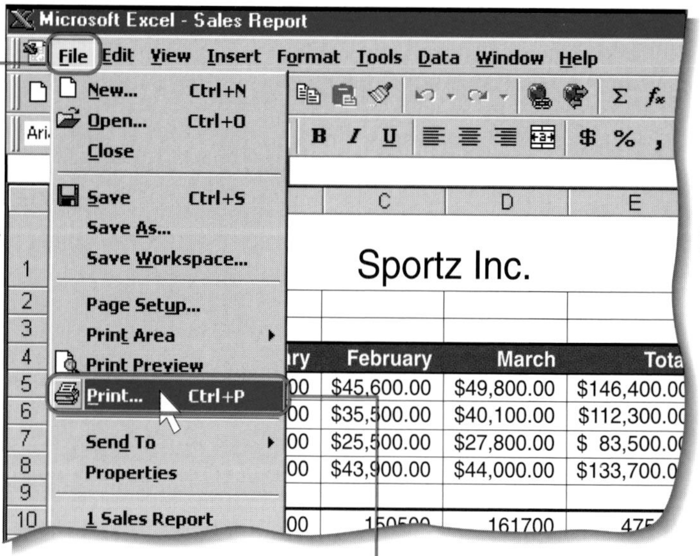

1 To print a worksheet, move the mouse over any cell in the worksheet and then press the left mouse button.

■ To print only part of the worksheet, select the cells you want to print. To select cells, refer to page 16.

2 Move the mouse over **File** and then press the left mouse button.

3 Move the mouse over **Print** and then press the left mouse button.

■ The **Print** dialog box appears.

What can I print?

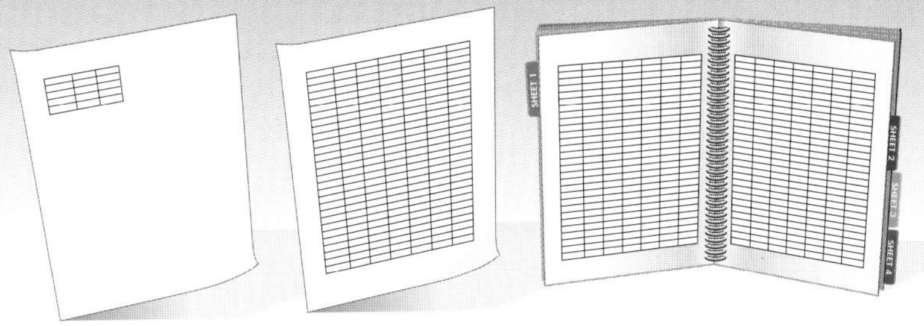

Selection
Print the cells you selected.

Active sheet(s)
Print the entire worksheet.

Entire workbook
Print every worksheet in the workbook.

For information on using multiple worksheets in a workbook, refer to pages 140 to 149.

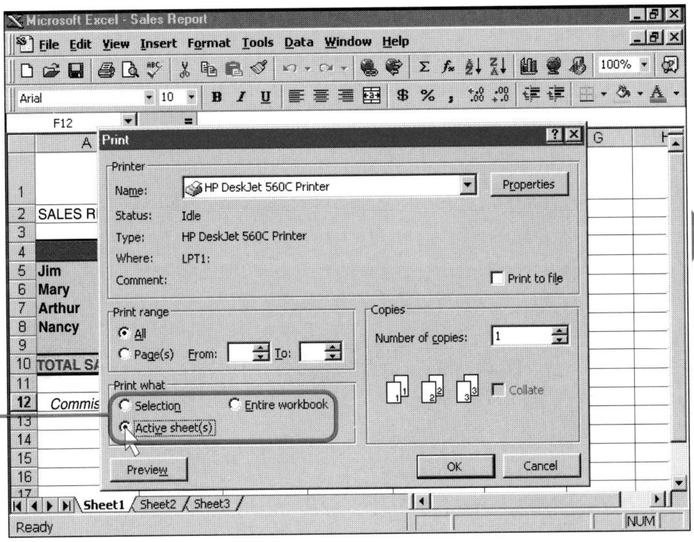

4 Move the mouse over what you want to print and then press the left mouse button (○ changes to ◉).

Note: For information on what you can print, refer to the top of this page.

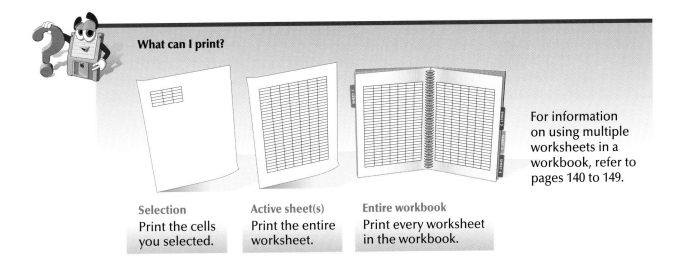

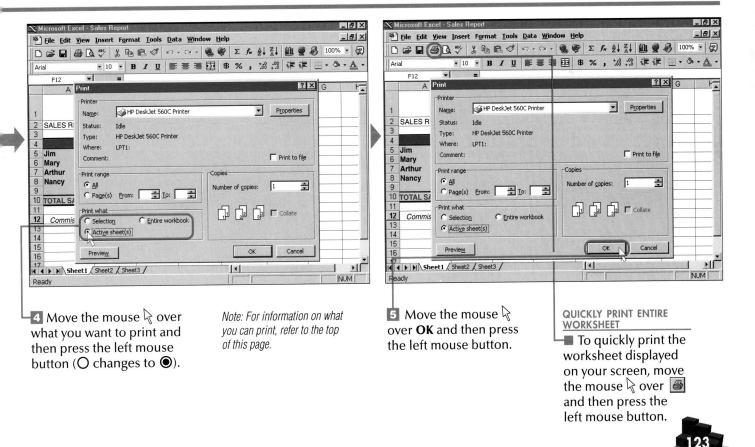

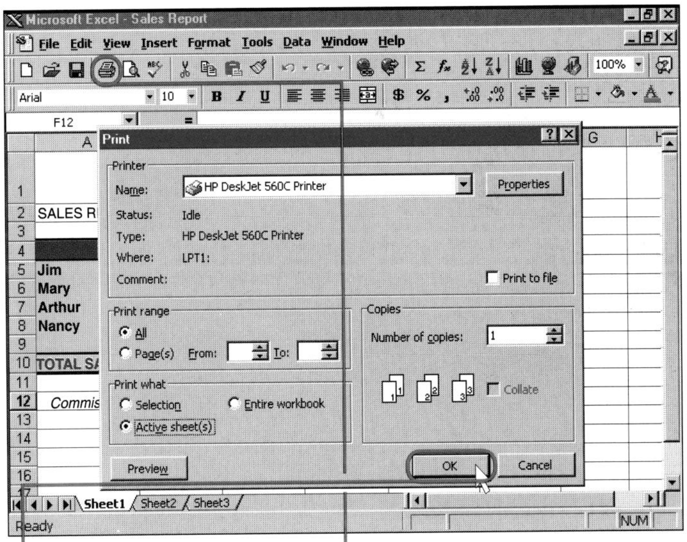

5 Move the mouse over **OK** and then press the left mouse button.

QUICKLY PRINT ENTIRE WORKSHEET

■ To quickly print the worksheet displayed on your screen, move the mouse over the print button and then press the left mouse button.

CHANGE MARGINS

CHANGE MARGINS

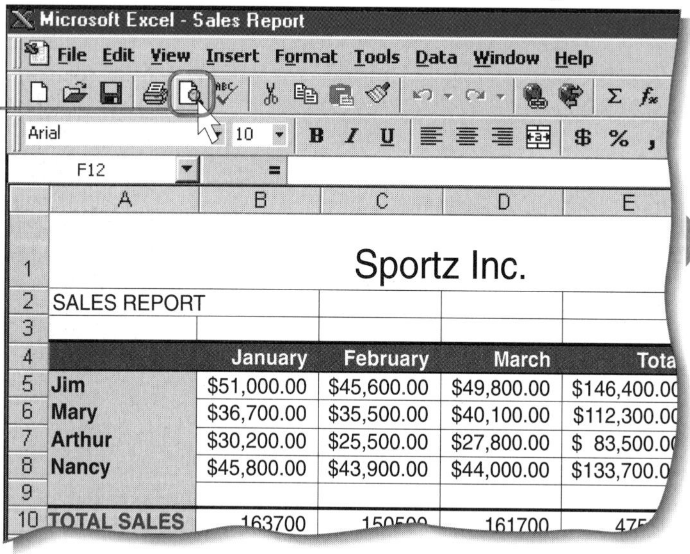

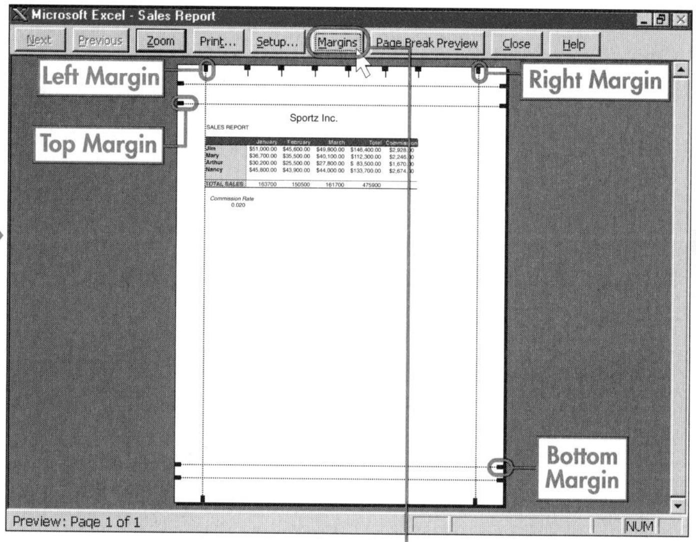

1 To display your worksheet in the Print Preview window, move the mouse over and then press the left mouse button.

■ Your worksheet appears in the Print Preview window. For information on previewing a worksheet, refer to page 120.

2 If the margins are not displayed, move the mouse over **Margins** and then press the left mouse button.

Why would I change the margins?

Changing margins lets you accommodate letterhead and other specialty paper.

You can also change the margins to fit more or less information on a page.

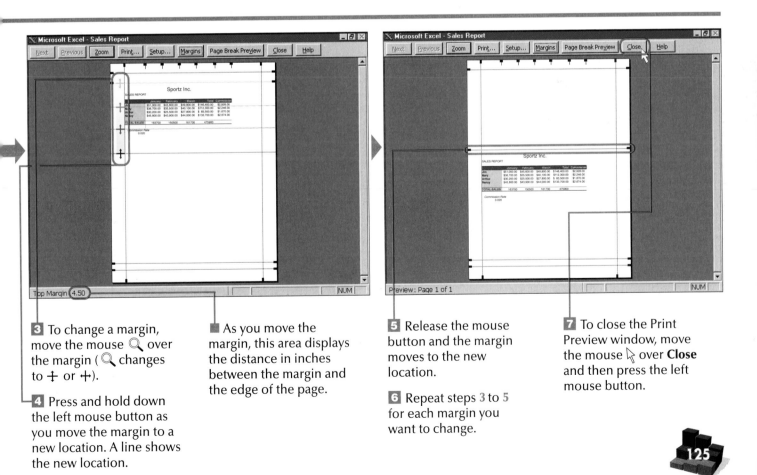

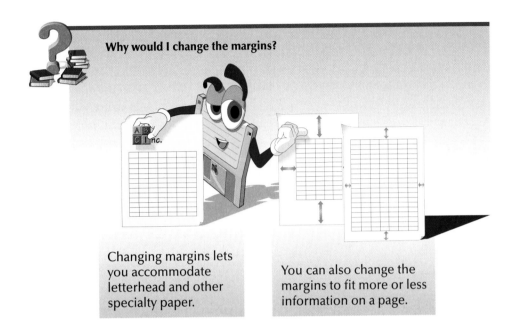

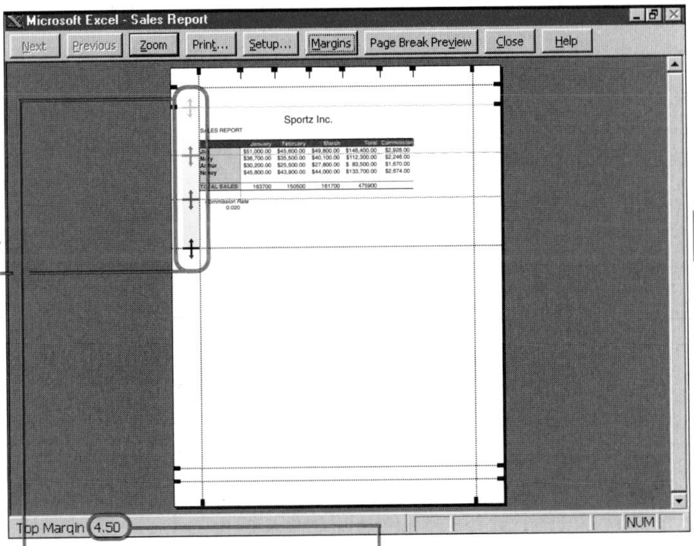

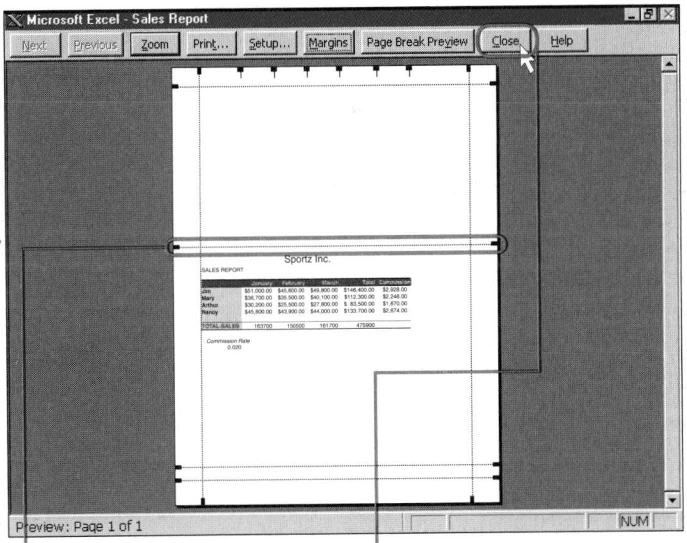

3 To change a margin, move the mouse 🔍 over the margin (🔍 changes to ╪ or ╫).

4 Press and hold down the left mouse button as you move the margin to a new location. A line shows the new location.

■ As you move the margin, this area displays the distance in inches between the margin and the edge of the page.

5 Release the mouse button and the margin moves to the new location.

6 Repeat steps 3 to 5 for each margin you want to change.

7 To close the Print Preview window, move the mouse ↖ over **Close** and then press the left mouse button.

CENTER DATA ON A PAGE

You can center data horizontally and vertically between the margins on a page.

CENTER DATA ON A PAGE

1 Move the mouse ᐅ over **File** and then press the left mouse button.

2 Move the mouse ᐅ over **Page Setup** and then press the left mouse button.

■ The **Page Setup** dialog box appears.

3 Move the mouse ᐅ over the **Margins** tab and then press the left mouse button.

4 Move the mouse ᐅ over the way you want to center the data and then press the left mouse button (☐ changes to ☑). You can select both center options if you wish.

5 Move the mouse ᐅ over **OK** and then press the left mouse button.

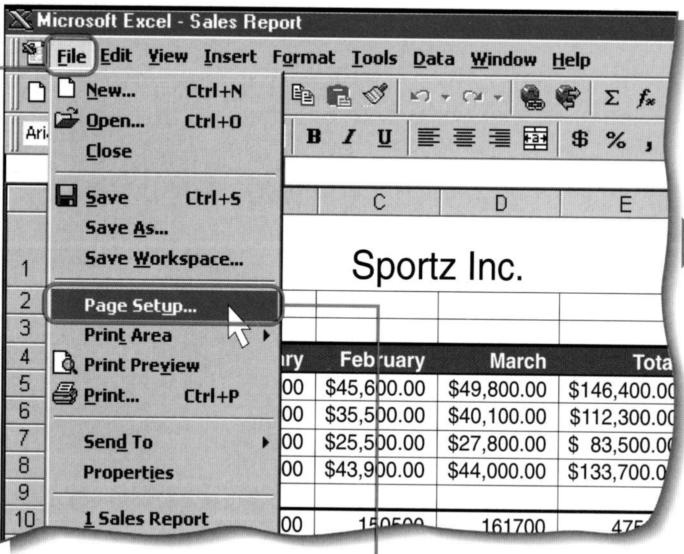

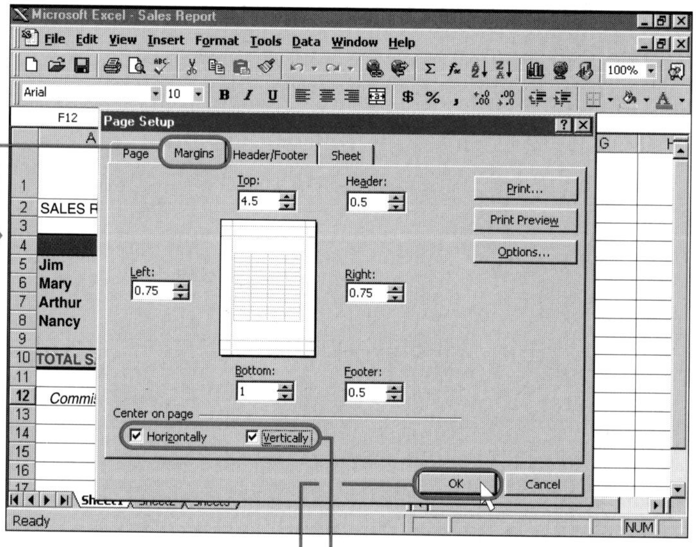

CHANGE PAGE ORIENTATION

The landscape orientation is ideal if you want a wide worksheet to fit on one page.

CHANGE PAGE ORIENTATION

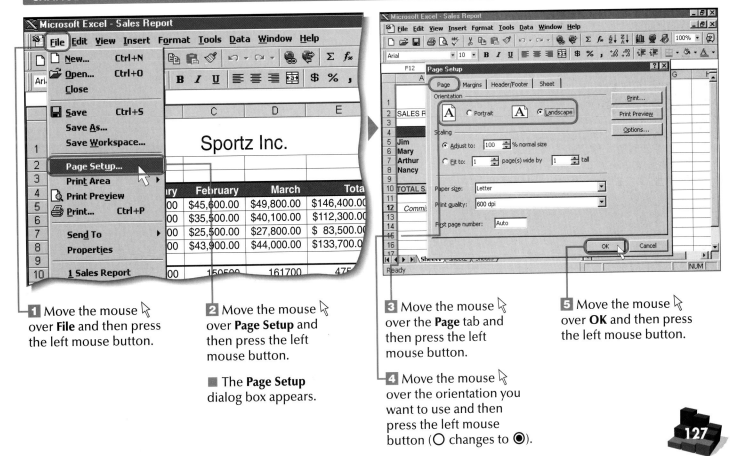

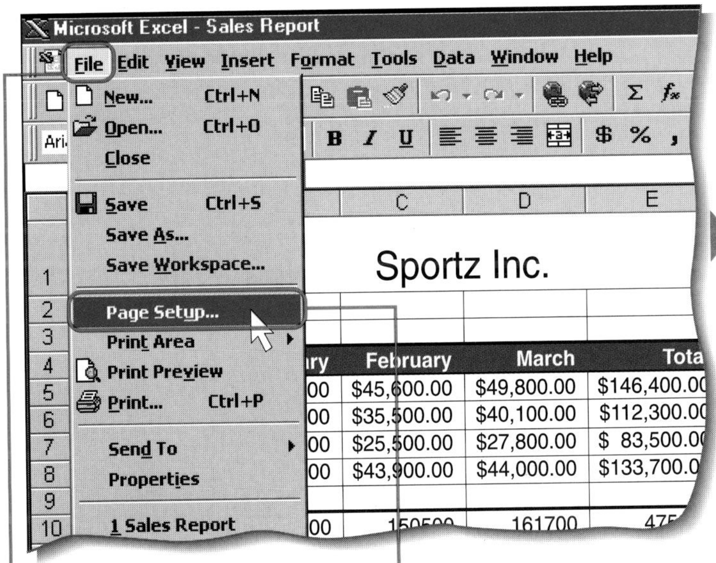

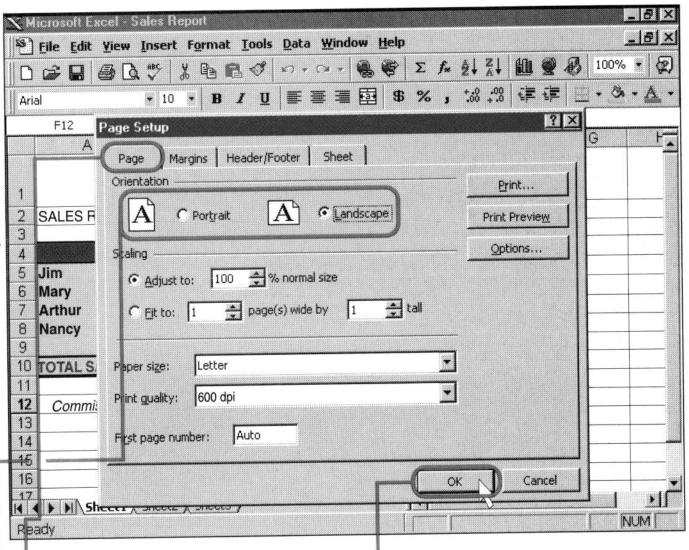

1 Move the mouse over **File** and then press the left mouse button.

2 Move the mouse over **Page Setup** and then press the left mouse button.

■ The **Page Setup** dialog box appears.

3 Move the mouse over the **Page** tab and then press the left mouse button.

4 Move the mouse over the orientation you want to use and then press the left mouse button (○ changes to ◉).

5 Move the mouse over **OK** and then press the left mouse button.

CHANGE PRINT OPTIONS

CHANGE PRINT OPTIONS

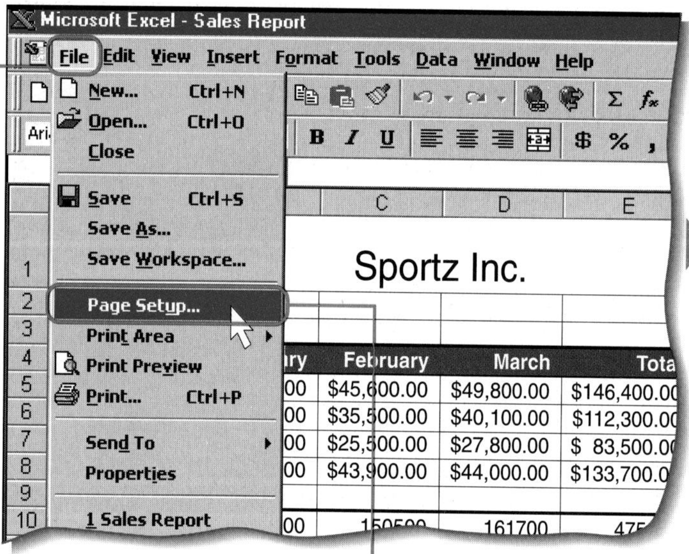

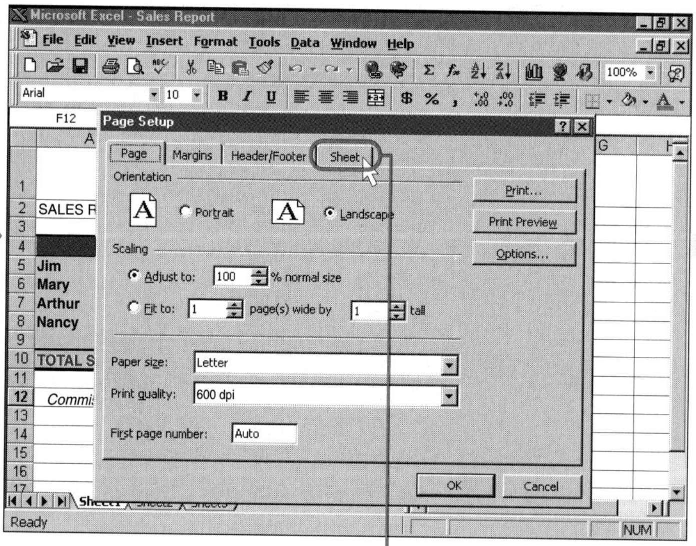

1 Move the mouse over **File** and then press the left mouse button.

2 Move the mouse over **Page Setup** and then press the left mouse button.

■ The **Page Setup** dialog box appears.

3 Move the mouse over the **Sheet** tab and then press the left mouse button.

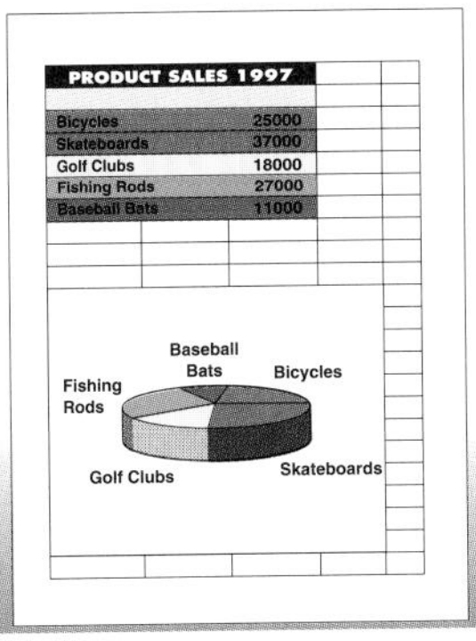

Gridlines

Prints lines around each cell in your worksheet.

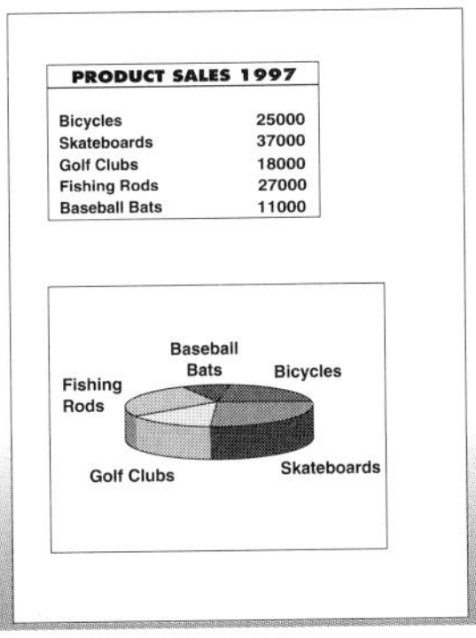

Black and white

Prints your worksheet in black and white. This can make a colored worksheet printed on a black-and-white printer easier to read.

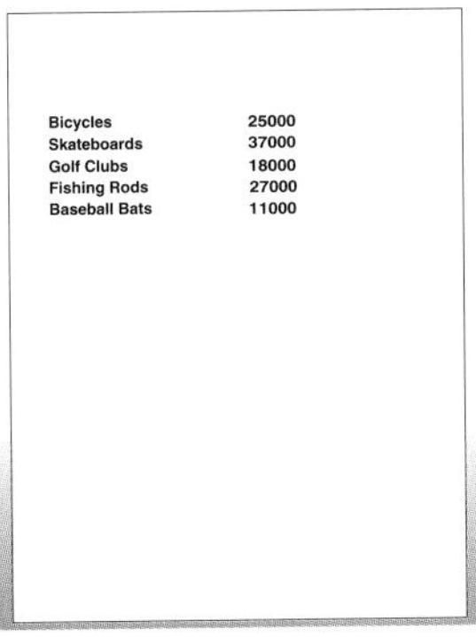

Draft quality

Does not print gridlines or most graphics to reduce printing time.

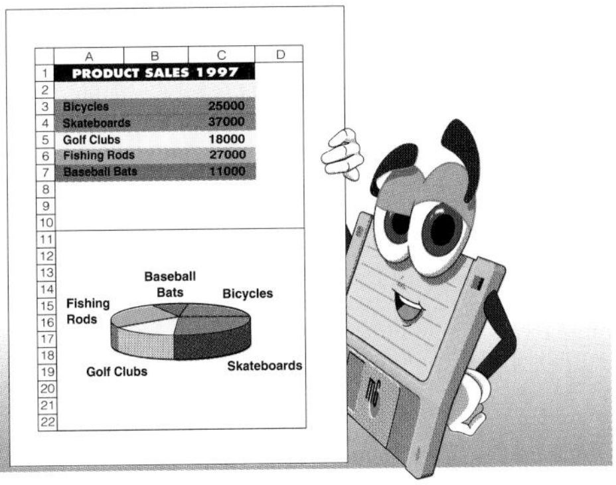

Row and column headings

Prints the row numbers and column letters.

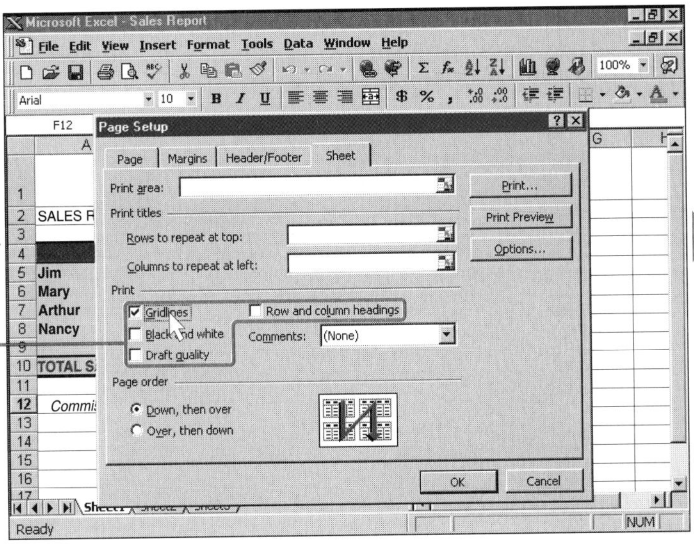

4 Move the mouse over the print option you want to select and then press the left mouse button (☐ changes to ☑).

Note: For information on the print options, refer to the top of this page.

5 Repeat step 4 for each print option you want to select.

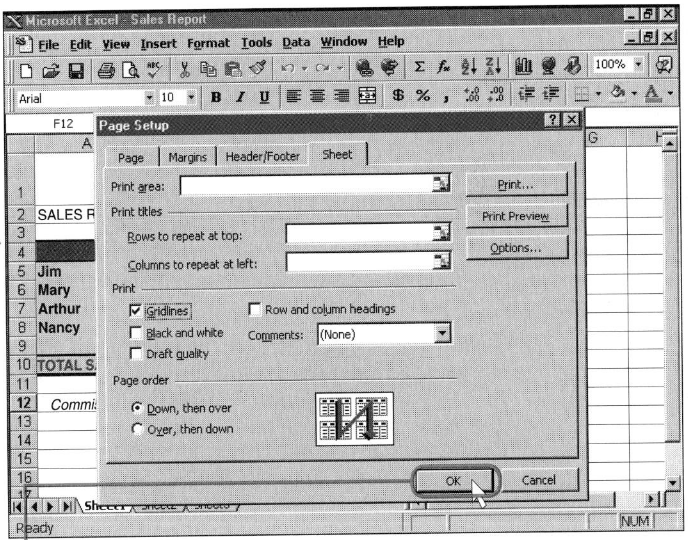

6 Move the mouse over **OK** and then press the left mouse button.

■ The print options you selected only change the way your worksheet appears on a printed page. The print options do not affect the way your worksheet appears on your screen.

INSERT A PAGE BREAK

If you want to start a new page at a specific place in your worksheet, you can add a page break. A page break defines where one page ends and another begins.

When you fill a page with data, Excel automatically starts a new page by inserting a page break for you.

INSERT A PAGE BREAK

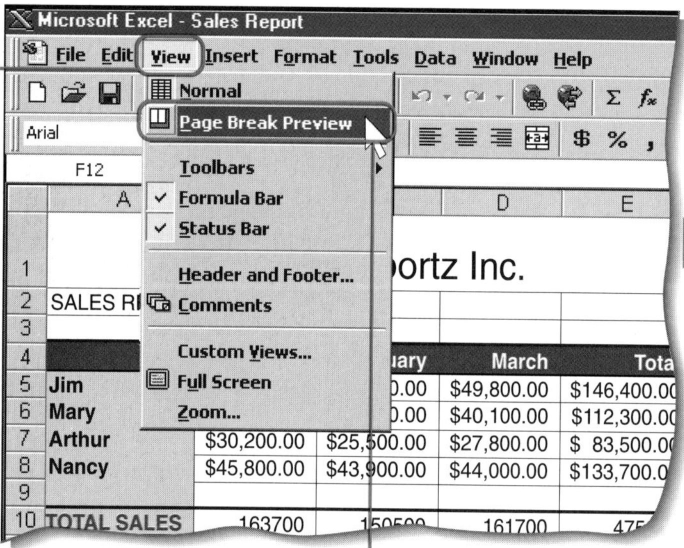

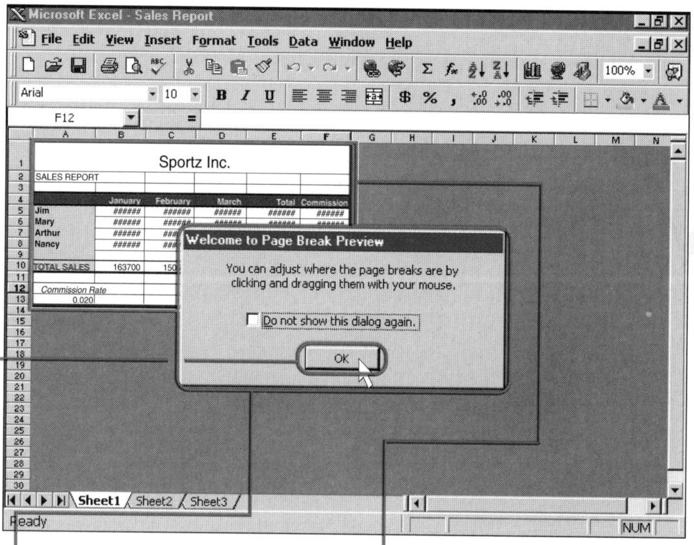

1 To display the page breaks in your worksheet, move the mouse over **View** and then press the left mouse button.

2 Move the mouse over **Page Break Preview** and then press the left mouse button.

■ A **Welcome** dialog box appears.

3 To close the dialog box, move the mouse over **OK** and then press the left mouse button.

■ Blue lines show where page breaks currently occur in your worksheet.

*Note: To return to the normal view at any time, repeat steps **1** and **2**, selecting **Normal** in step **2**.*

How can I move a page break?

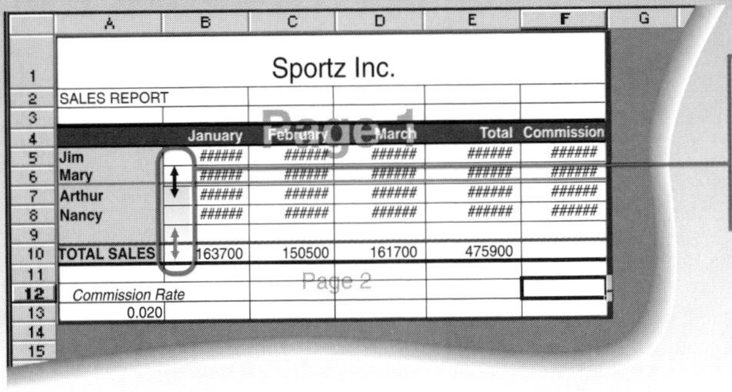

1 To move a page break, move the mouse ✥ over the page break line (✥ changes to ↕ or ↔).

2 Press and hold down the left mouse button as you move the page break line to a new location. Then release the mouse button.

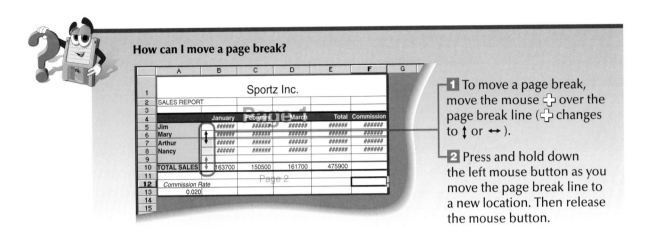

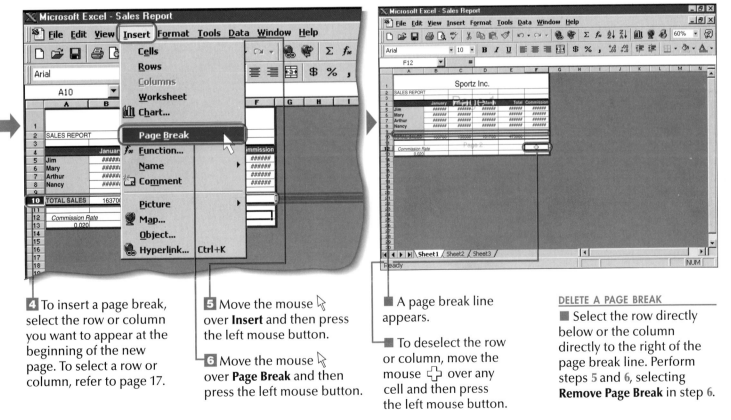

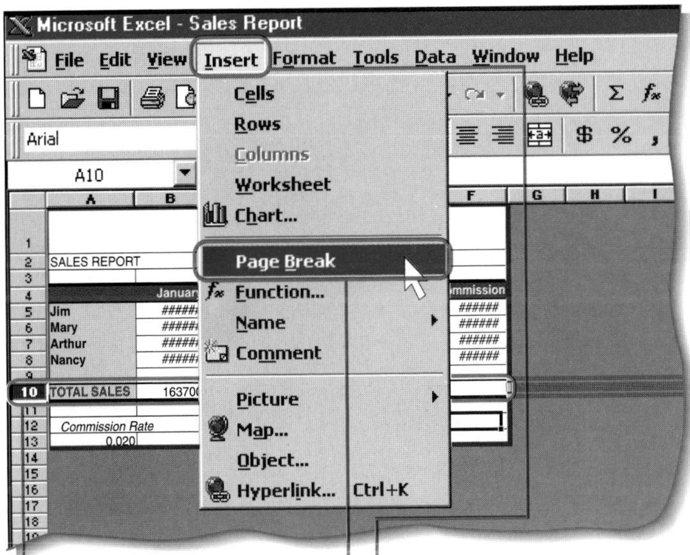

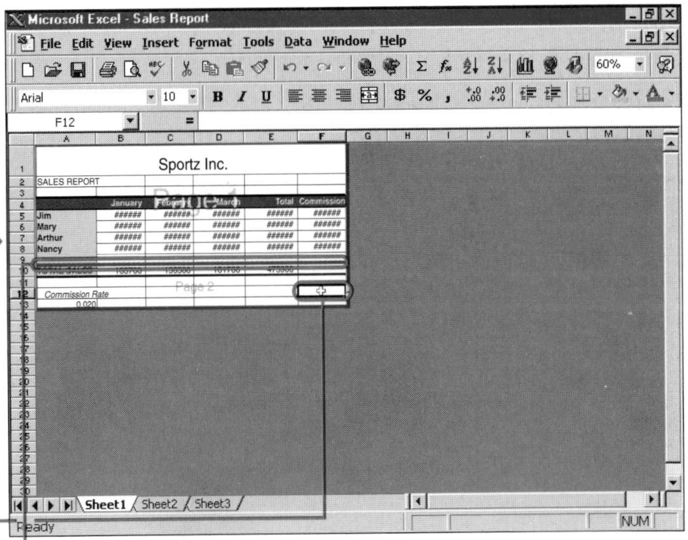

4 To insert a page break, select the row or column you want to appear at the beginning of the new page. To select a row or column, refer to page 17.

5 Move the mouse ↖ over **Insert** and then press the left mouse button.

6 Move the mouse ↖ over **Page Break** and then press the left mouse button.

■ A page break line appears.

■ To deselect the row or column, move the mouse ✥ over any cell and then press the left mouse button.

DELETE A PAGE BREAK

■ Select the row directly below or the column directly to the right of the page break line. Perform steps 5 and 6, selecting **Remove Page Break** in step 6.

ADD A HEADER OR FOOTER

ADD A HEADER OR FOOTER

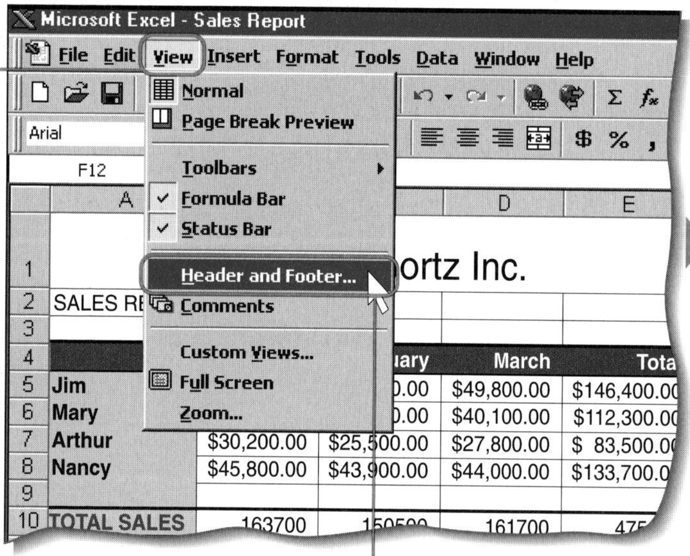

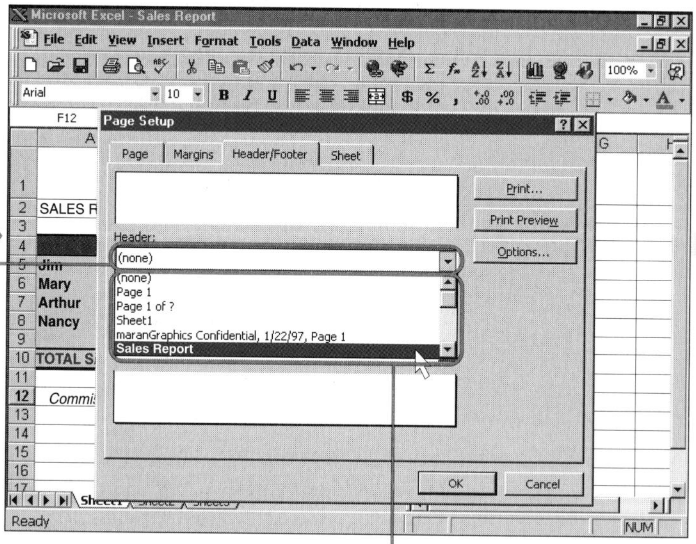

1 Move the mouse over **View** and then press the left mouse button.

2 Move the mouse over **Header and Footer** and then press the left mouse button.

■ The **Page Setup** dialog box appears.

3 To view a list of headers you can use, move the mouse over this area and then press the left mouse button.

4 Move the mouse over the header you want to use and then press the left mouse button.

How can I see what a header or footer will look like before I print my worksheet?

You can use the Print Preview feature to view a header or footer before you print your worksheet. To use the Print Preview feature, refer to page 120.

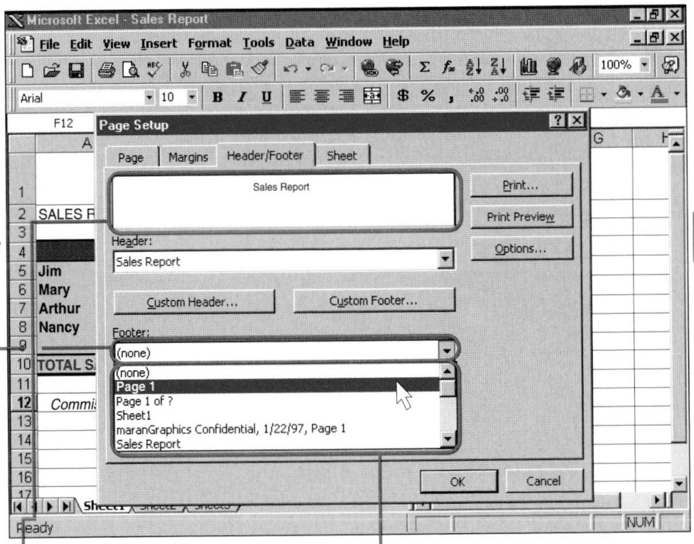

■ This area displays a sample of the header you selected.

5 To view a list of footers you can use, move the mouse over this area and then press the left mouse button.

6 Move the mouse over the footer you want to use and then press the left mouse button.

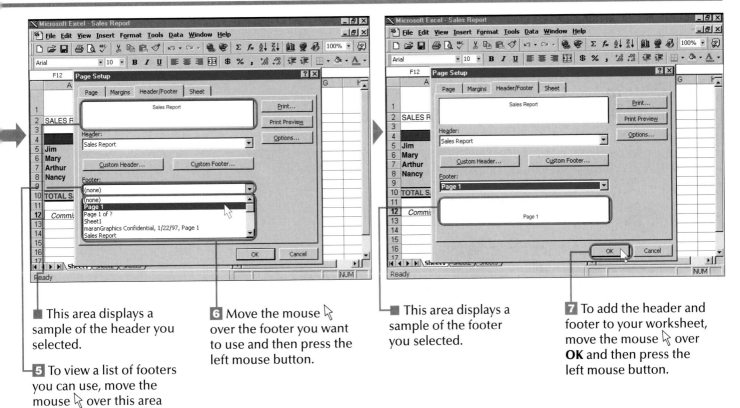

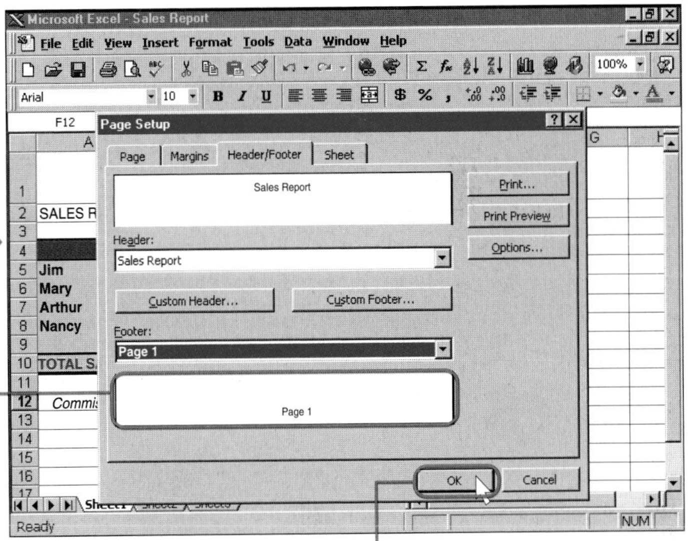

■ This area displays a sample of the footer you selected.

7 To add the header and footer to your worksheet, move the mouse over **OK** and then press the left mouse button.

CHANGE SIZE OF PRINTED DATA

You can reduce the size of printed data to print your worksheet on a specific number of pages.

This feature is useful when the last page of your worksheet contains a small amount of data that you want to fit on the second-last page.

CHANGE SIZE OF PRINTED DATA

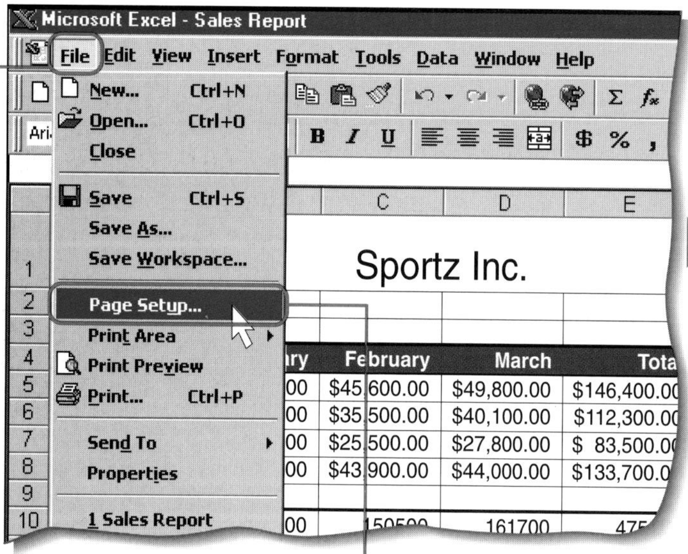

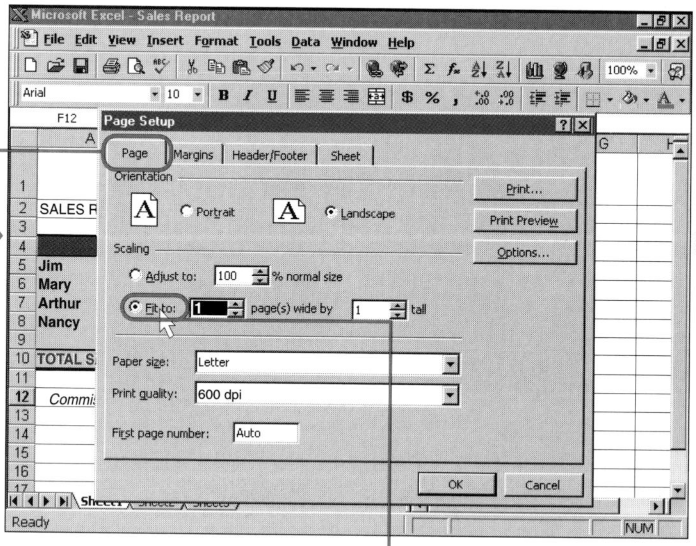

1 Move the mouse over **File** and then press the left mouse button.

2 Move the mouse over **Page Setup** and then press the left mouse button.

■ The **Page Setup** dialog box appears.

3 Move the mouse over the **Page** tab and then press the left mouse button.

4 Move the mouse over **Fit to** and then press the left mouse button (○ changes to ◉).

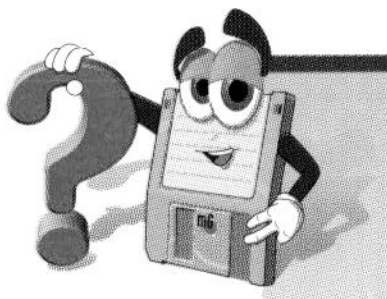

When I change the size of my printed data, what information does Excel require?

When you change the size of your printed data, you need to tell Excel how many pages you want the data to print across and down.

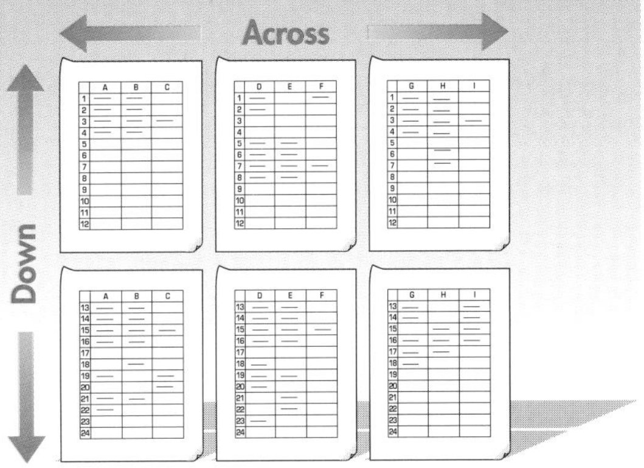

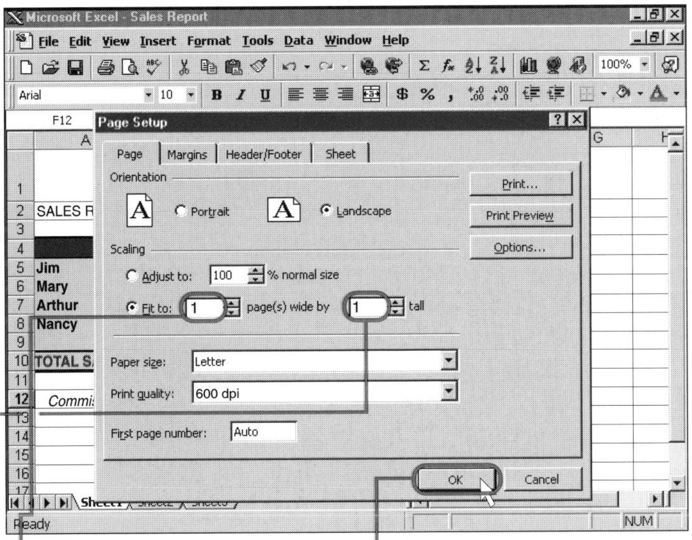

5 Type the number of pages you want your data to print across and then press **Tab** on your keyboard.

6 Type the number of pages you want your data to print down.

7 Move the mouse over **OK** and then press the left mouse button.

■ Excel will change the size of the printed data to fit on the number of pages you specified.

MANUALLY CHANGE SIZE OF PRINTED DATA

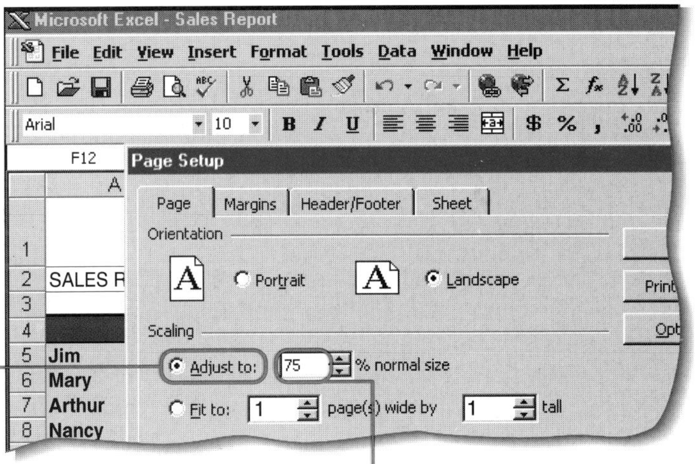

You can manually reduce or enlarge the size of printed data.

1 Perform steps 1 to 3 on page 134.

2 Move the mouse over **Adjust to** and then press the left mouse button (○ changes to ◉).

3 Type the percentage you want to use and then press **Enter** on your keyboard.

Note: A percentage over 100 will increase the size of the printed data. A percentage under 100 will decrease the size of the printed data.

REPEAT TITLES ON PRINTED PAGES

You can display the same rows or columns of titles on every printed page. This helps you review worksheets that print on more than one page.
Repeat a Row
Repeat a Column

REPEAT TITLES ON PRINTED PAGES

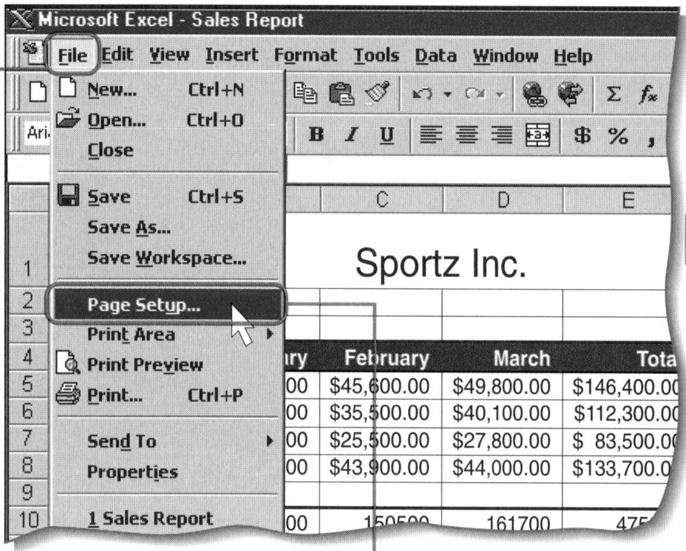

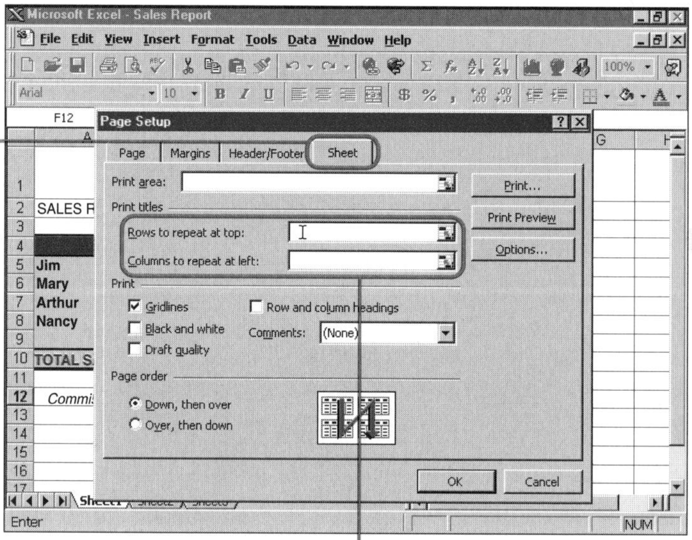

1 Move the mouse over **File** and then press the left mouse button.

2 Move the mouse over **Page Setup** and then press the left mouse button.

■ The **Page Setup** dialog box appears.

3 Move the mouse over the **Sheet** tab and then press the left mouse button.

4 Move the mouse I over the box beside one of the following options and then press the left mouse button.

Rows to repeat at top
Repeat titles across the top of each page.

Columns to repeat at left
Repeat titles down the left side of each page.

How can I see what the repeated titles will look like before I print my worksheet?

You can use the Print Preview feature to view the repeated titles before you print your worksheet. To use the Print Preview feature, refer to page 120.

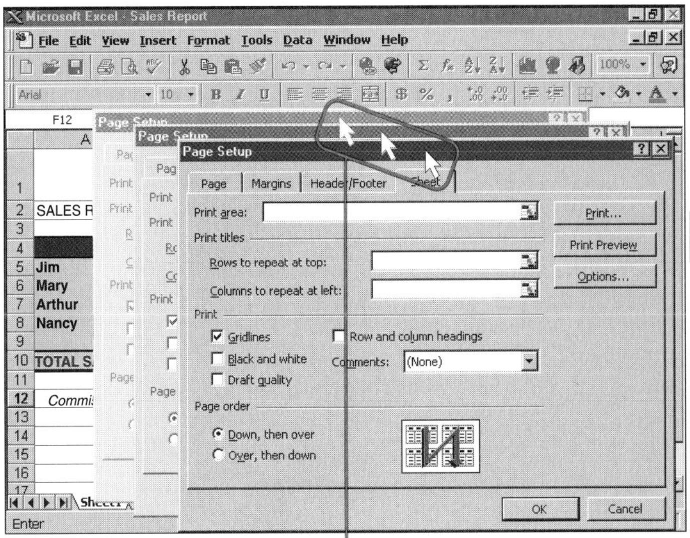

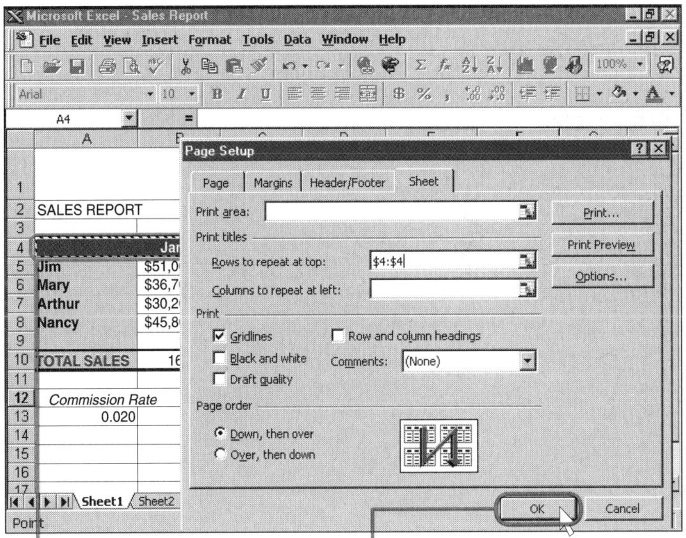

■ If the dialog box covers the rows or columns containing the titles you want to repeat, you can move the dialog box to a new location.

5 To move the dialog box, move the mouse over the title bar.

6 Press and hold down the left mouse button as you move the dialog box to a new location. Then release the mouse button.

7 Select one cell in each row or column containing the titles you want to repeat. To select cells, refer to page 16.

8 Move the mouse over **OK** and then press the left mouse button.

Sales
1996
1997
Product A
3180
3210
Product B
3180
2740
Product C
3240
3140
Product D
2610
2750
INCOME STATEMENT
January
February
March
REVENUE
8700
11500
13670
Payroll
Rent
Supplies
3850
1750
1920
4850
1750
1980
5250
1750
2030
TOTAL EXPENSES
INCOME
PRODUCE SALES 1997
Oranges
Apples
Grapefruits
Lemons
Limes
25000
37000
18000
27000
15000
Lemons
Limes
Oranges
Grapefruits
Apples
Week 1
Week 2
Week 3
Apples
Limes
Plums
550
830
535
540
465
670
540
600
580
540
465
670

CHAPTER 8

WORK WITH MULTIPLE WORKSHEETS

Would you like to work with more than one worksheet at a time? This chapter teaches you how.

SWITCH BETWEEN WORKSHEETS

SWITCH BETWEEN WORKSHEETS

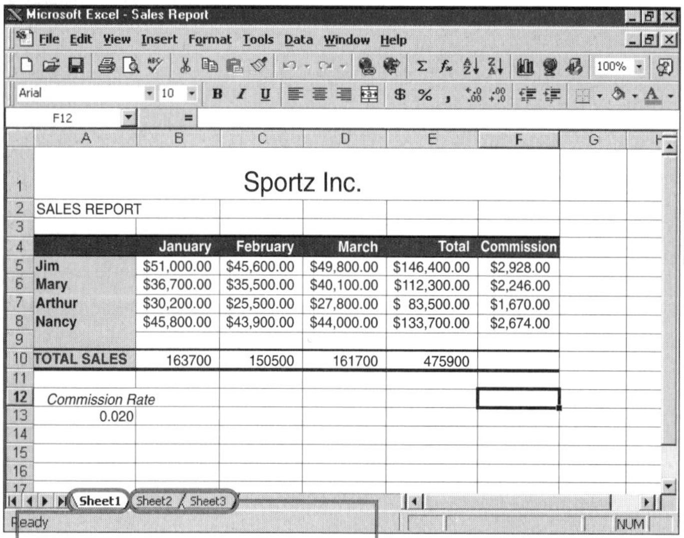

■ The worksheet displayed on your screen has a white tab.

■ The other worksheets in the workbook have gray tabs. The contents of these worksheets are hidden.

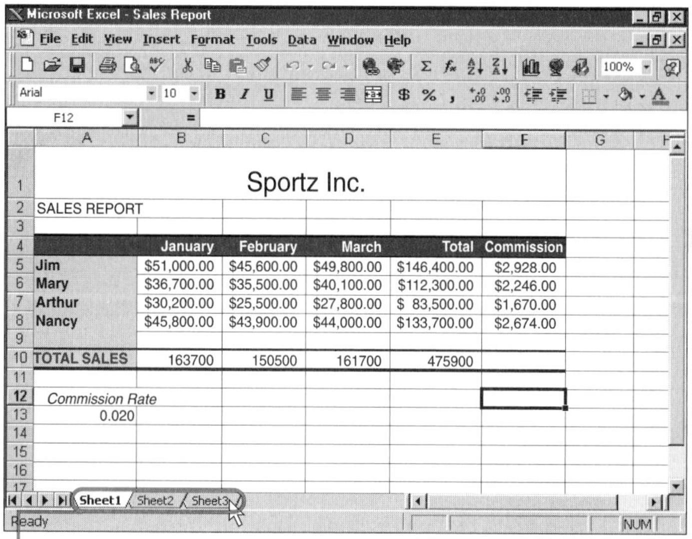

1 To display the contents of a worksheet, move the mouse over the tab of the worksheet and then press the left mouse button.

Why would I need more than one worksheet?

Worksheets allow you to keep related information in a single file, called a workbook. For example, information for each division of a company can be stored on a separate worksheet in one workbook.

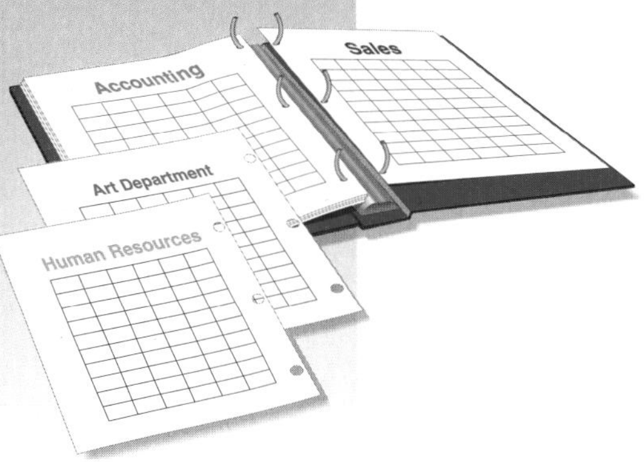

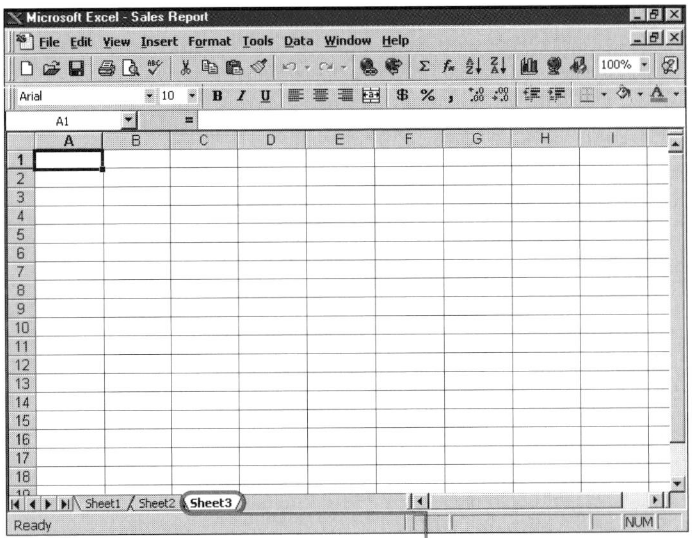

■ The contents of the worksheet appear. The contents of the other worksheets in the workbook are hidden.

■ The worksheet you selected now has a white tab.

BROWSE THROUGH TABS

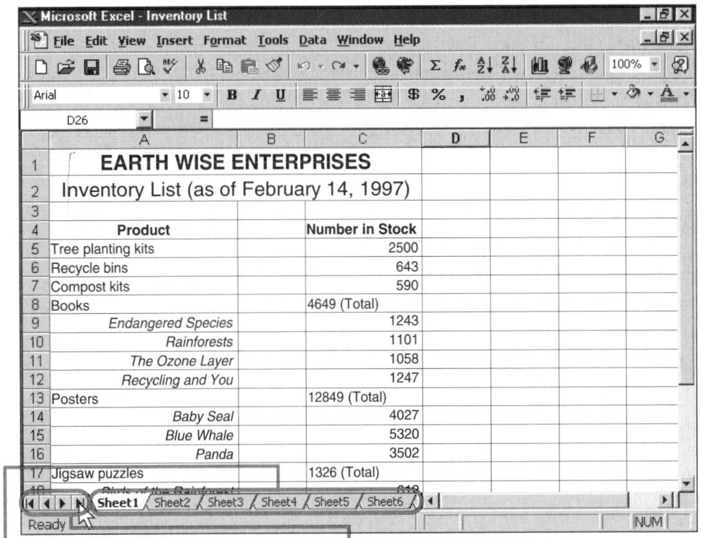

■ If you have many worksheets in your workbook, you may not be able to see all the tabs.

Note: To insert additional worksheets, refer to page 142.

1 To browse through the tabs, move the mouse over one of the following options and then press the left mouse button.

- ⏮ Display first tab
- ◀ Display tab to the left
- ▶ Display tab to the right
- ⏭ Display last tab

INSERT A WORKSHEET

You can easily insert a new worksheet to add related information to a workbook.

INSERT A WORKSHEET

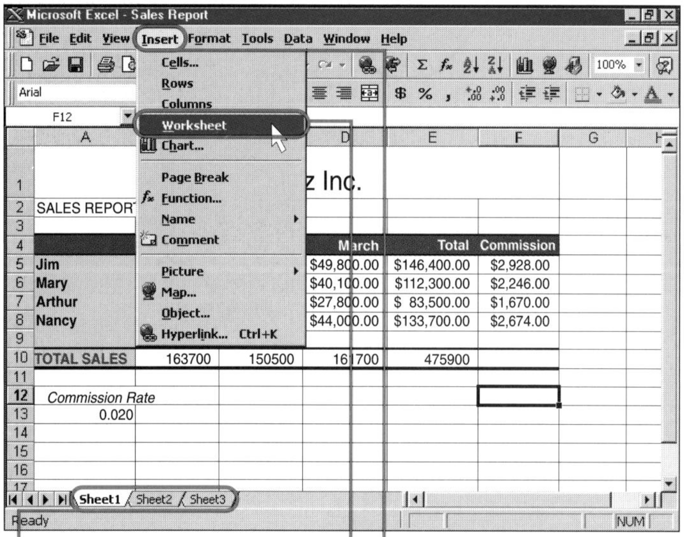

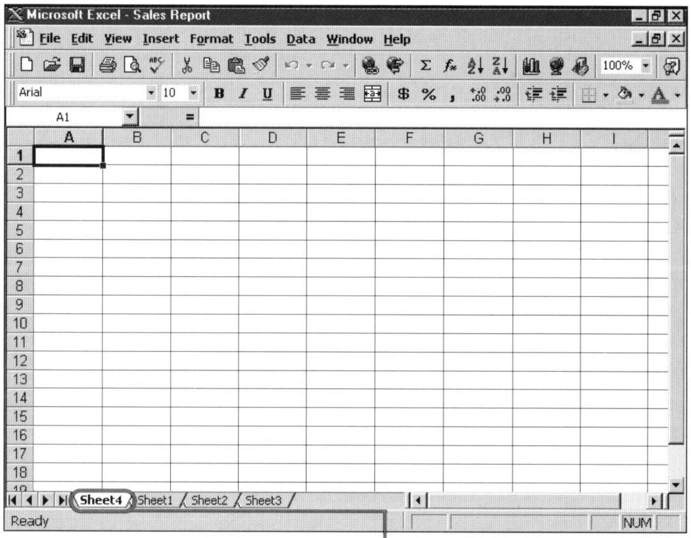

1 Move the mouse over the tab of the worksheet you want to appear after the new worksheet and then press the left mouse button.

2 Move the mouse over **Insert** and then press the left mouse button.

3 Move the mouse over **Worksheet** and then press the left mouse button.

■ The new worksheet appears.

■ Excel displays a tab for the new worksheet.

DELETE A WORKSHEET

You can permanently remove a worksheet you no longer need.

DELETE A WORKSHEET

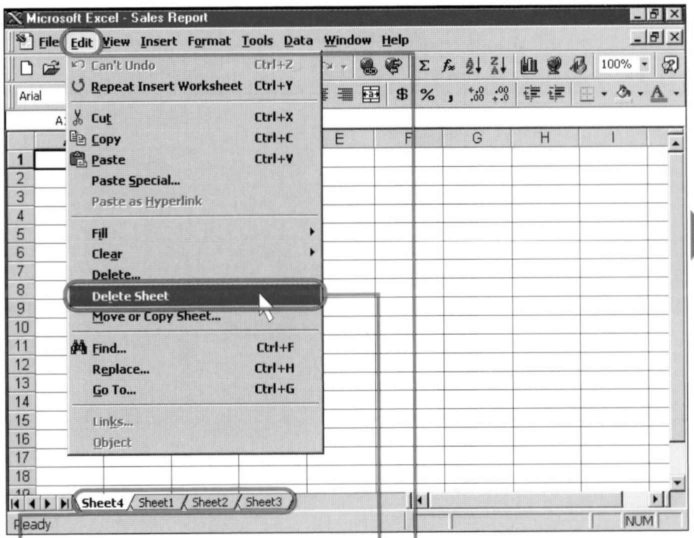

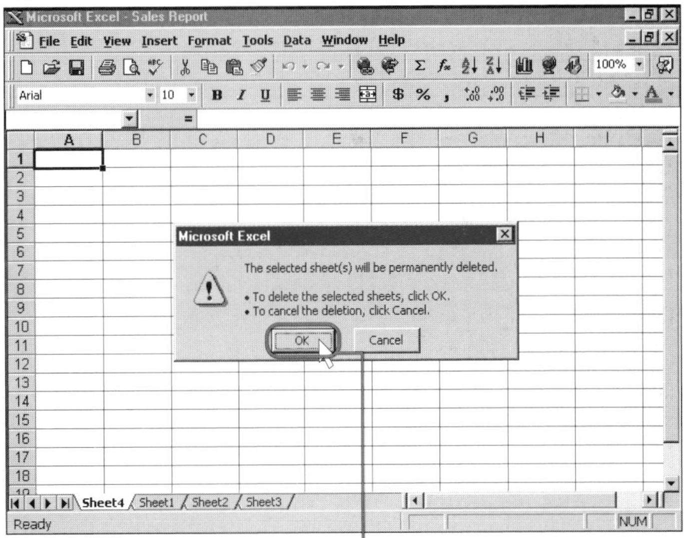

1 Move the mouse over the tab of the worksheet you want to delete and then press the left mouse button.

2 Move the mouse over **Edit** and then press the left mouse button.

3 Move the mouse over **Delete Sheet** and then press the left mouse button.

■ A warning dialog box appears.

4 To permanently delete the worksheet, move the mouse over **OK** and then press the left mouse button.

RENAME A WORKSHEET

RENAME A WORKSHEET

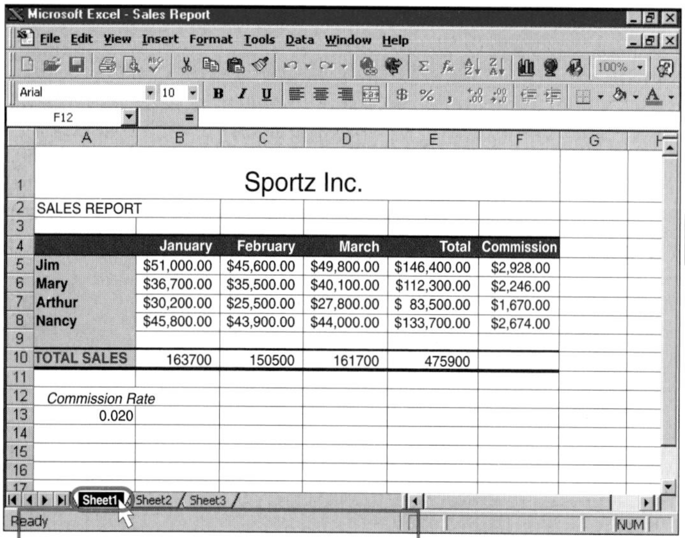

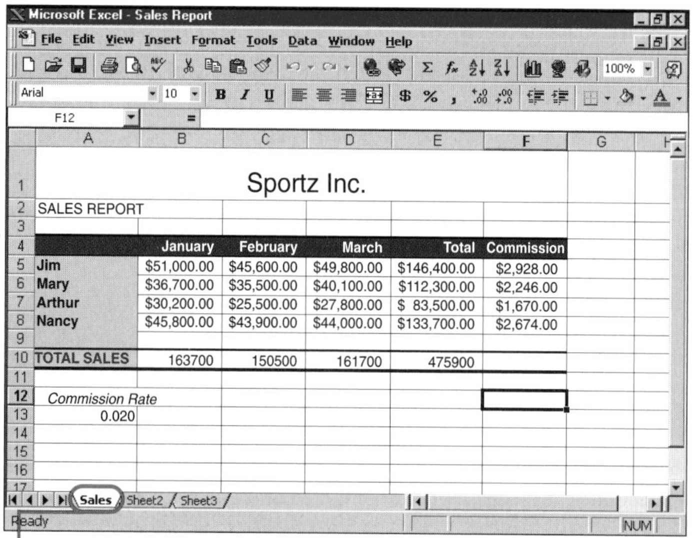

1 Move the mouse over the tab of the worksheet you want to rename and then quickly press the left mouse button twice.

■ The current name is highlighted.

2 Type a new name and then press **Enter** on your keyboard. A worksheet name can contain up to 31 characters, including spaces.

MOVE A WORKSHEET

MOVE A WORKSHEET

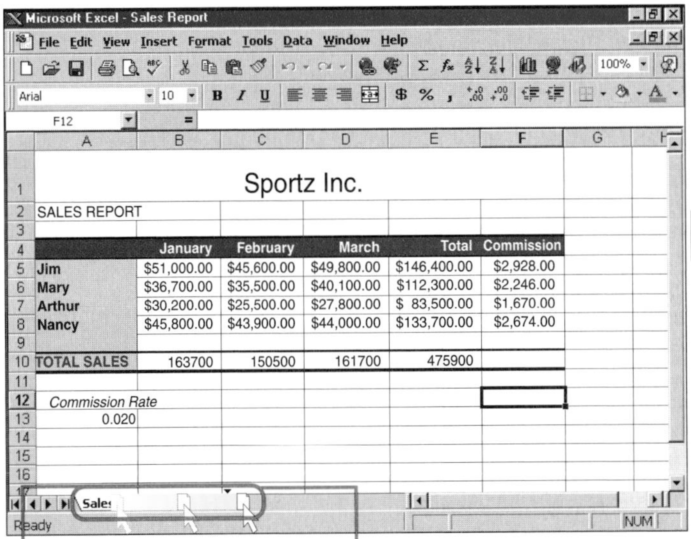

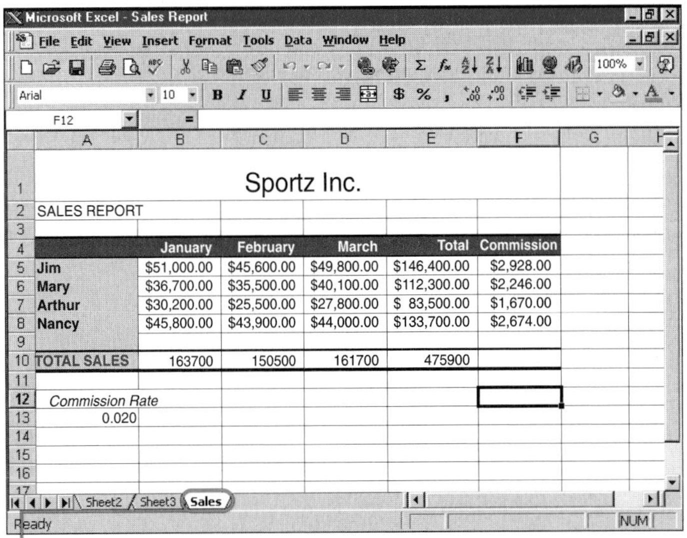

1 Move the mouse over the tab of the worksheet you want to move.

2 Press and hold down the left mouse button as you move the worksheet to a new location.

■ An arrow (▾) shows where the worksheet will appear.

3 Release the mouse button and the worksheet appears in the new location.

COPY OR MOVE DATA BETWEEN WORKSHEETS

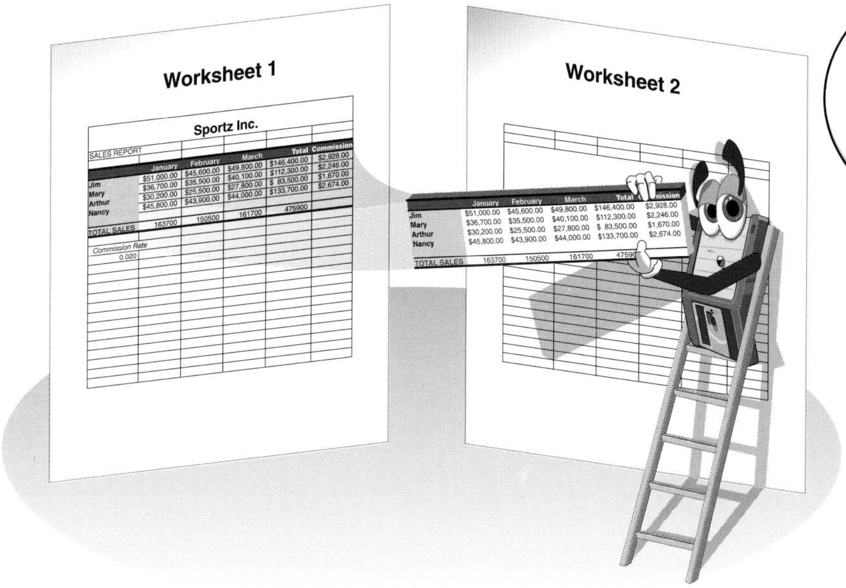

You can copy or move data from one worksheet to another. This will save you time when you want to use data from another worksheet.

COPY OR MOVE DATA BETWEEN WORKSHEETS

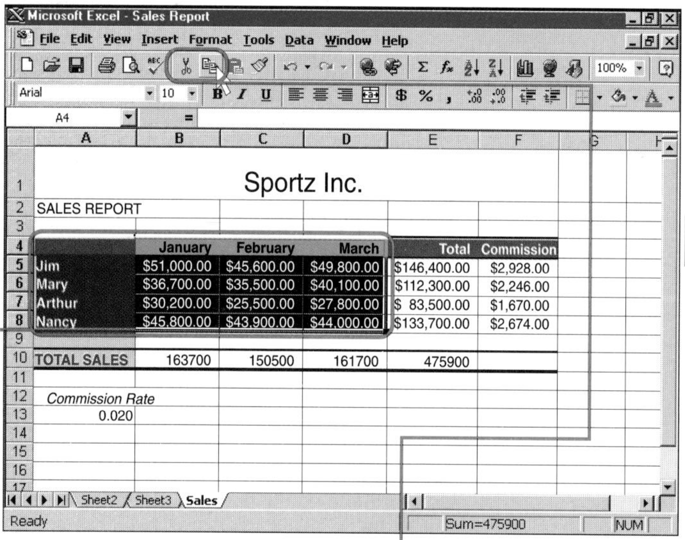

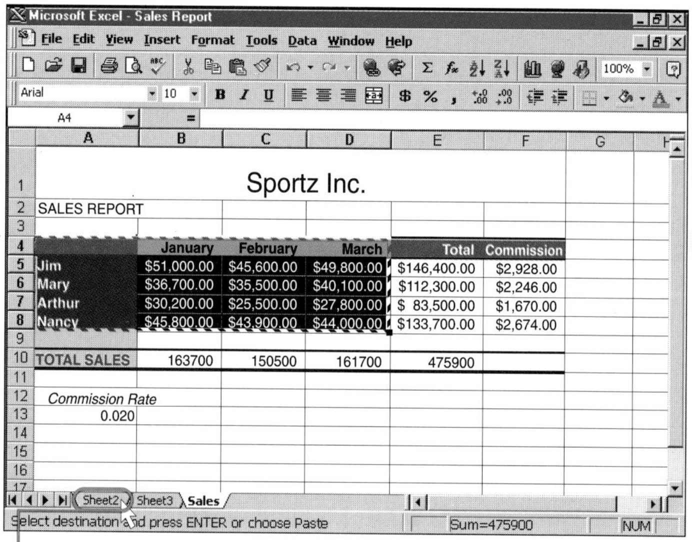

1 Select the cells containing the data you want to place in another worksheet. To select cells, refer to page 16.

2 Move the mouse over one of the following options and then press the left mouse button.

- Move the data
- Copy the data

3 Move the mouse over the tab of the worksheet where you want to place the data and then press the left mouse button.

Note: To place the data in another workbook, open the workbook and then perform step 3. To open a workbook, refer to page 32.

What is the difference between copying and moving data?

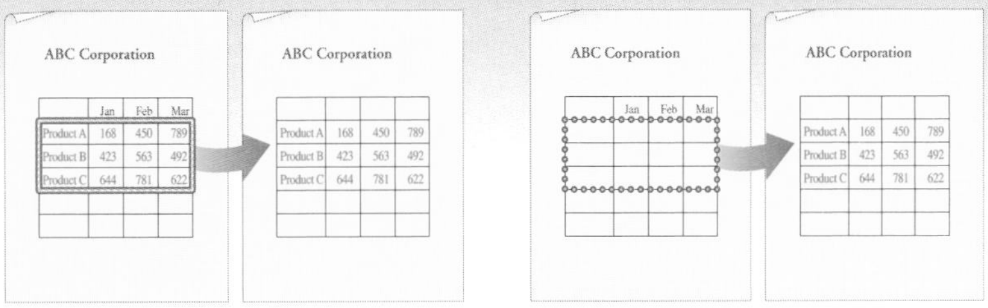

Copy Data

When you copy data, the original data remains in its place.

Move Data

When you move data, the original data disappears.

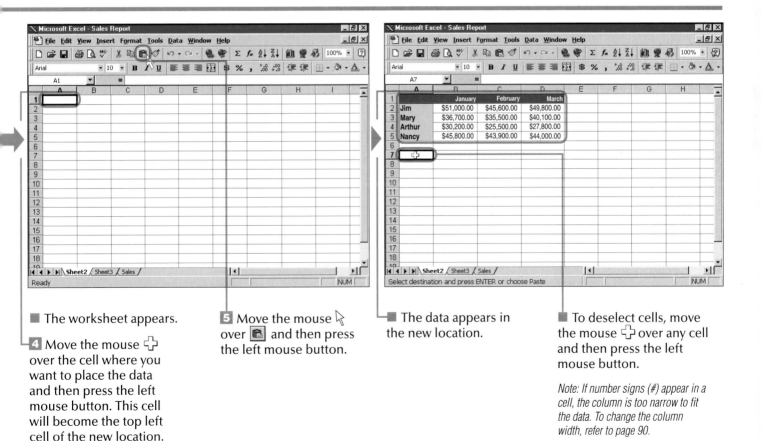

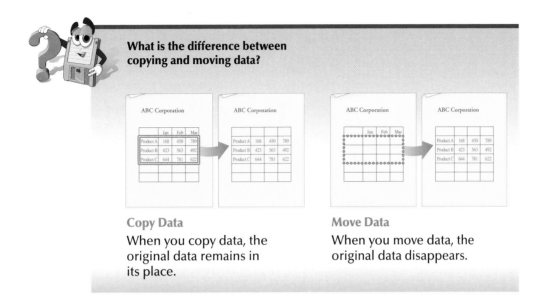

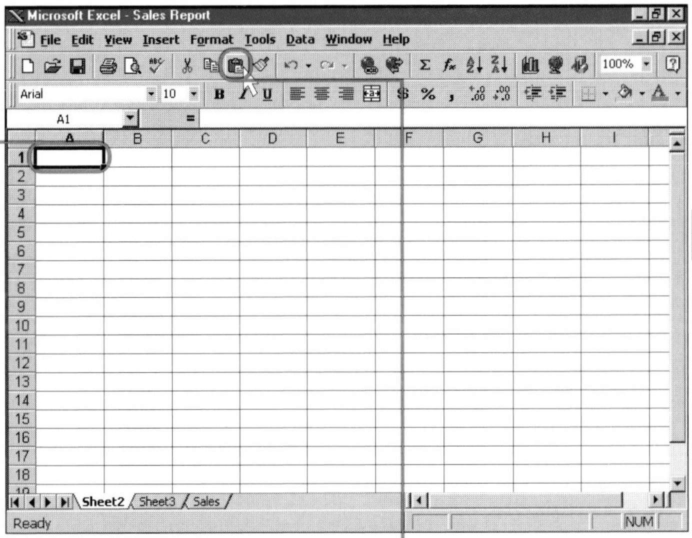

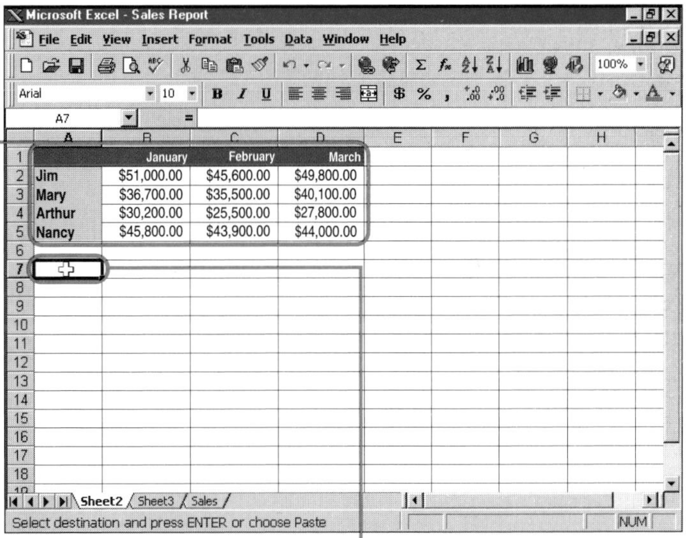

■ The worksheet appears.

4 Move the mouse ✣ over the cell where you want to place the data and then press the left mouse button. This cell will become the top left cell of the new location.

5 Move the mouse ↖ over 📋 and then press the left mouse button.

■ The data appears in the new location.

■ To deselect cells, move the mouse ✣ over any cell and then press the left mouse button.

Note: If number signs (#) appear in a cell, the column is too narrow to fit the data. To change the column width, refer to page 90.

ENTER A FORMULA ACROSS WORKSHEETS

ENTER A FORMULA ACROSS WORKSHEETS

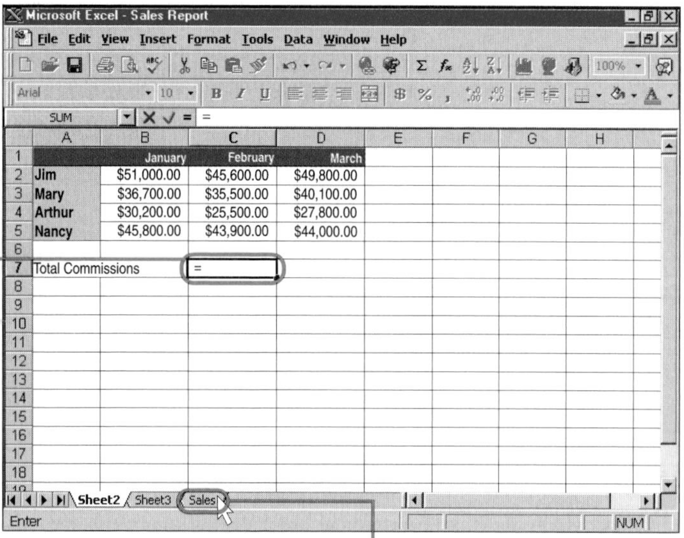

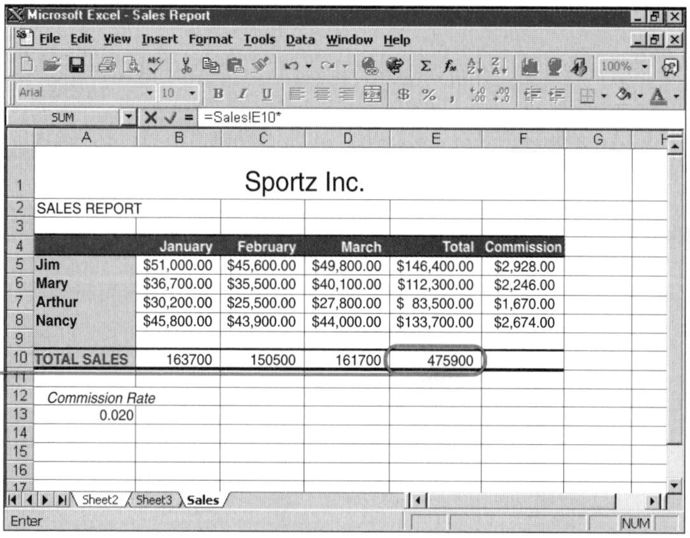

1 Move the mouse ✚ over the cell where you want to enter a formula and then press the left mouse button.

2 Type an equal sign (=) to begin the formula.

3 Move the mouse ↖ over the tab of a worksheet containing data you want to use in the formula and then press the left mouse button.

■ The worksheet appears.

4 Move the mouse ✚ over a cell containing data you want to use in the formula and then press the left mouse button.

5 Type an operator (example: *).

What happens if I change a number used in a formula?

If you change a number used in a formula, Excel will automatically calculate a new result. This ensures that your calculations are always up-to-date.

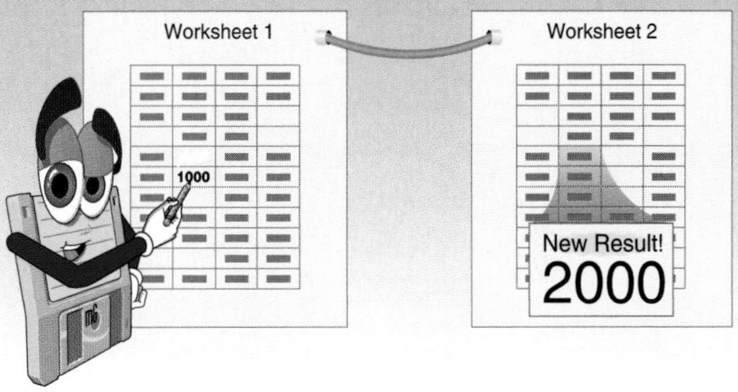

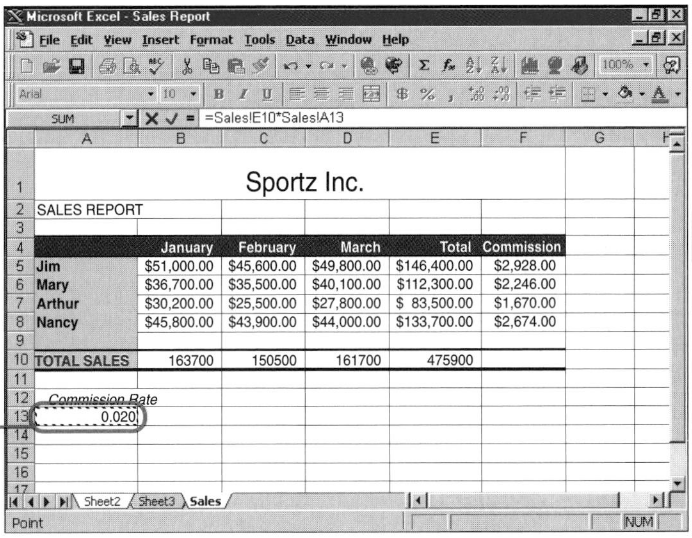

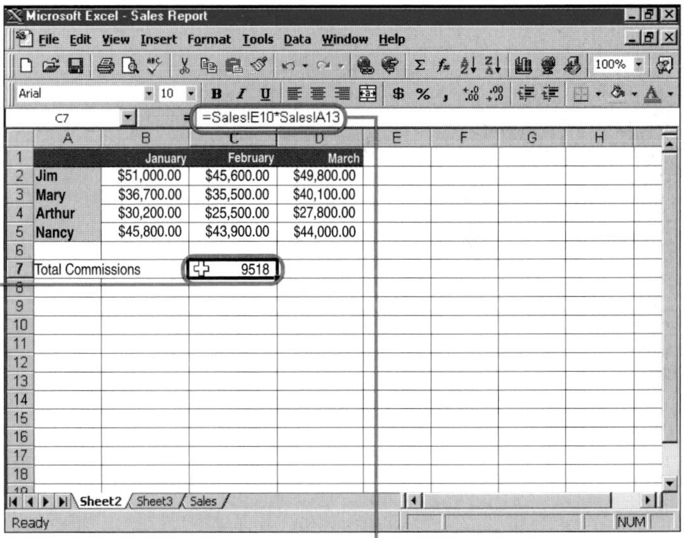

6 Repeat steps 3 to 5 until you have selected all the cells containing data you want to use in the formula.

*Note: In this example, cells **E10** and **A13** are multiplied together.*

7 Press Enter on your keyboard to complete the formula.

■ The result of the calculation appears in the cell you selected in step 1.

8 To view the formula you entered, move the mouse ✥ over the cell containing the formula and then press the left mouse button.

■ The formula bar displays the worksheet name and the cell reference for each cell used in the formula.

EMPLOYEE of the MONTH
Jan
Feb
Mar
Apr
May
Jun
Jul
Aug
Sep
Oct
Nov
Dec
Records & Information
PAYROLL 1997
PAYROLL 1996
PAYROLL 1995

CHAPTER 9

WORK WITH CHARTS

Do you want to visually display your worksheet data in a chart? In this chapter you will learn how to create, change and print charts.

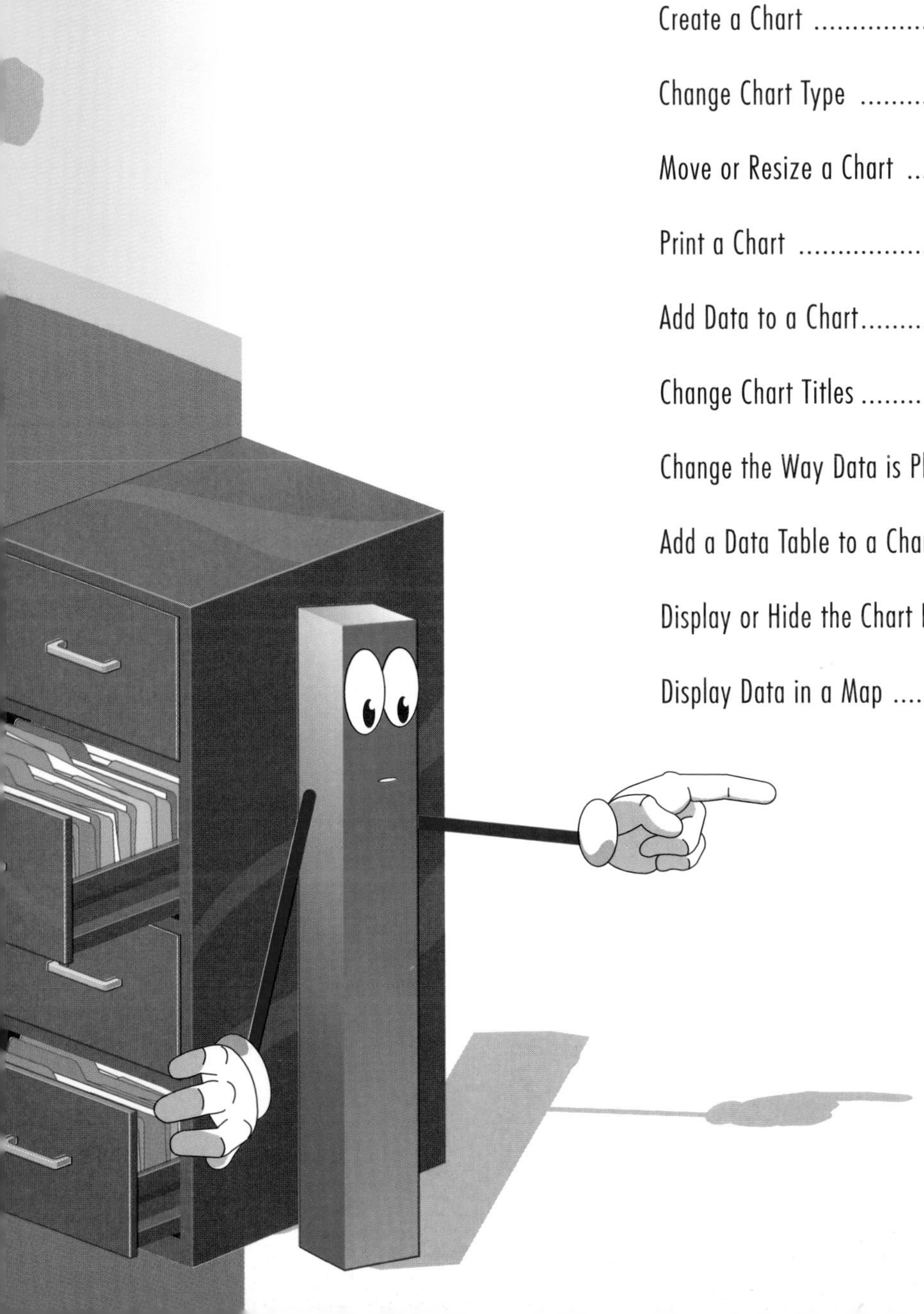

INTRODUCTION TO CHARTS

A chart allows you to visually display your worksheet data. Excel offers many different chart types.

PARTS OF A CHART

Data Series

A group of related data representing one row or column from your worksheet. Each data series is a specific color, pattern or symbol.

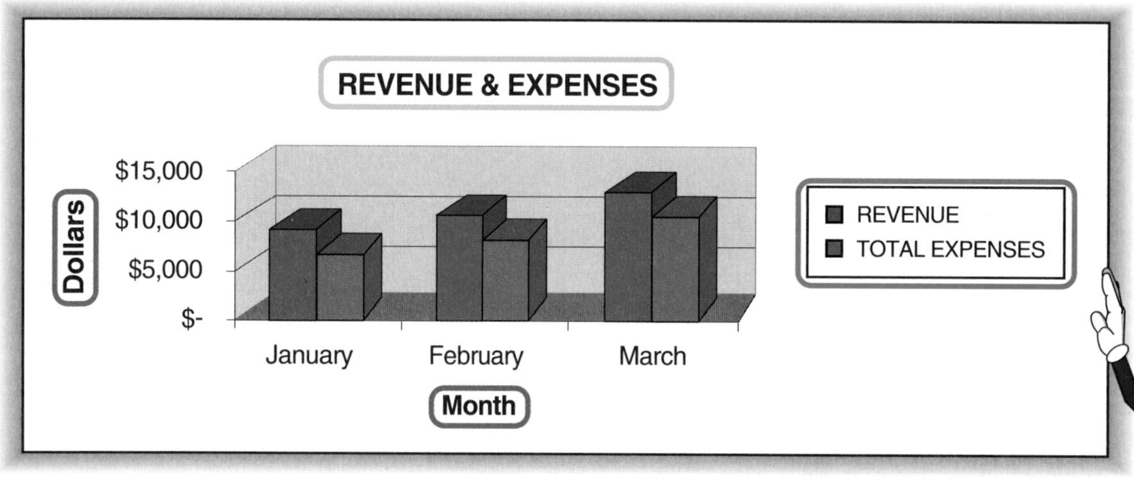

Chart Title

Identifies the subject of your chart.

Y-Axis Title

Indicates the unit of measure used in your chart.

X-Axis Title

Indicates the categories used in your chart.

Legend

Identifies the color, pattern or symbol used for each data series in your chart.

COMMON CHART TYPES

Area

An area chart is useful for showing the amount of change in data over time. Each line represents a data series.

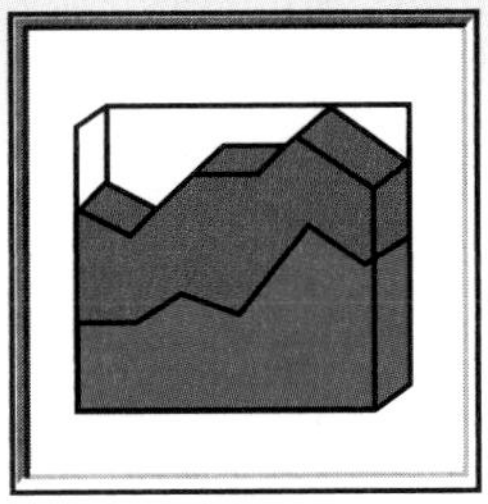

Line

A line chart is useful for showing changes to data at regular intervals. Each line represents a data series.

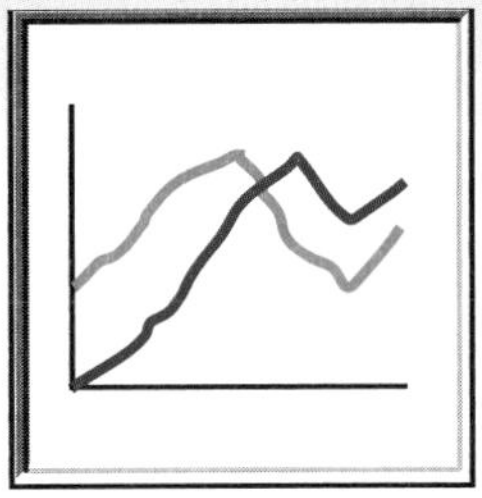

Bar

A bar chart is useful for comparing individual items. Each bar represents an item in a data series.

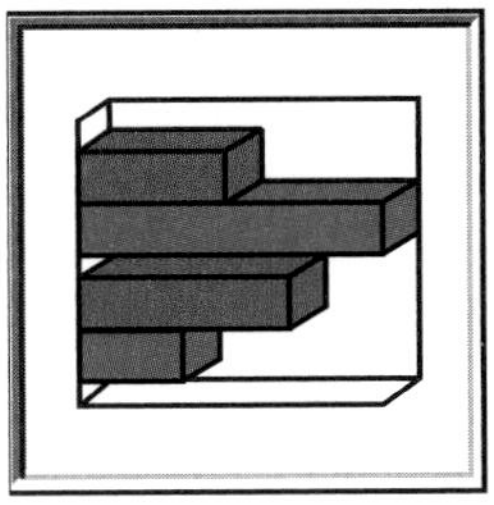

Pie

A pie chart is useful for showing the relationship of parts to a whole. Each piece of a pie represents an item in a data series. A pie chart can show only one data series at a time.

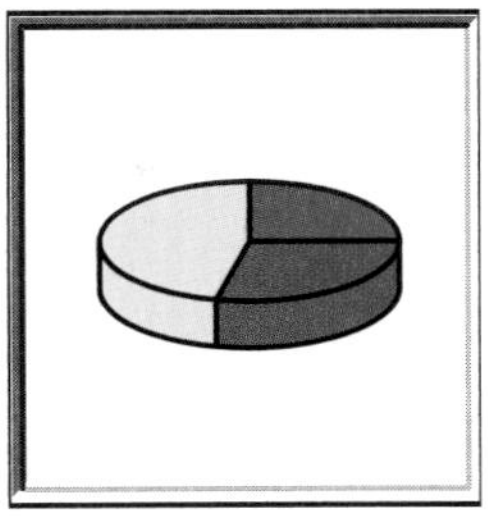

Column

A column chart is useful for showing changes to data over time or comparing individual items. Each bar represents an item in a data series.

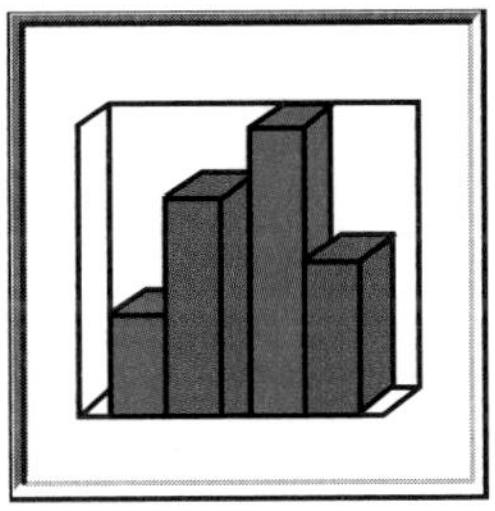

Radar

A radar chart is useful for comparing the items in several data series. Each data series is shown as a line around a central point.

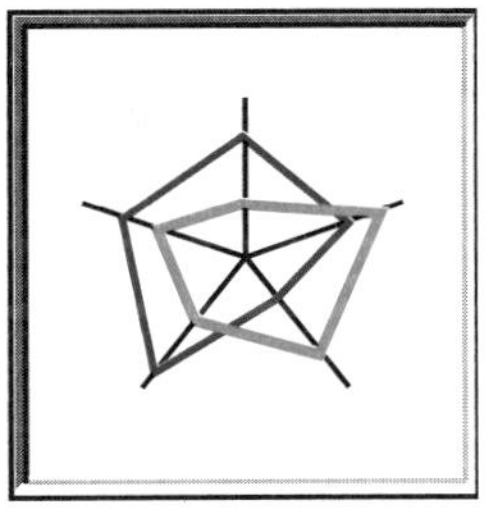

Doughnut

A doughnut chart is useful for showing the relationship of parts to a whole. Unlike a pie chart, a doughnut chart can display more than one data series. Each ring represents a data series.

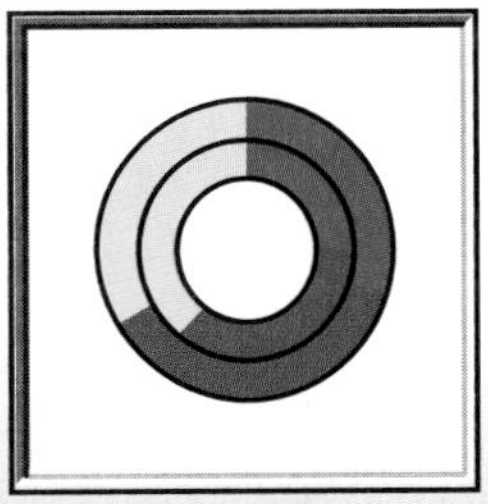

XY (Scatter)

An xy (scatter) chart is useful for showing the relationship between two or more data series measured at uneven intervals.

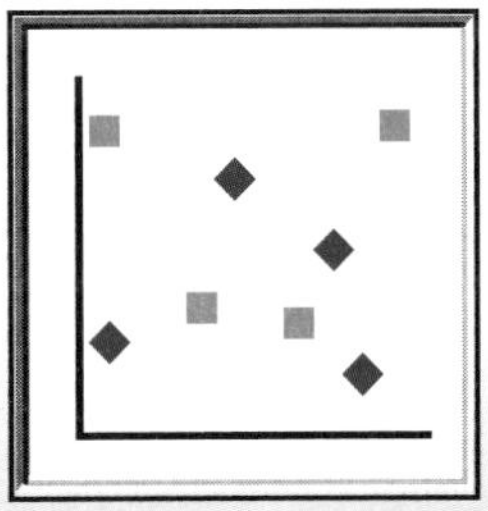

CREATE A CHART

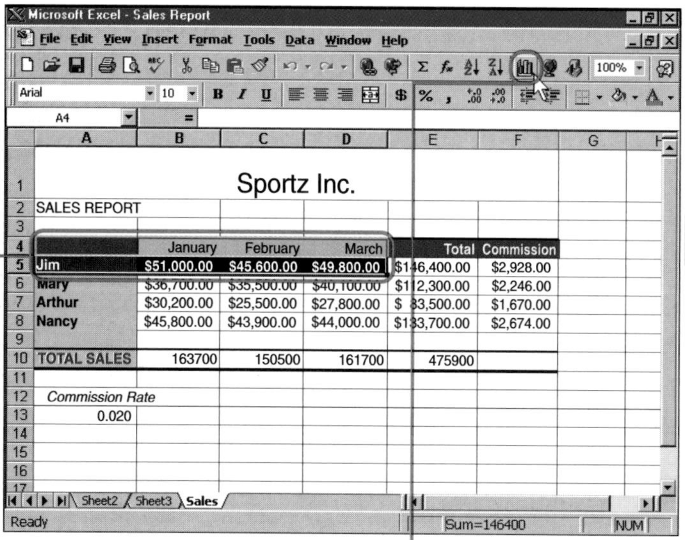

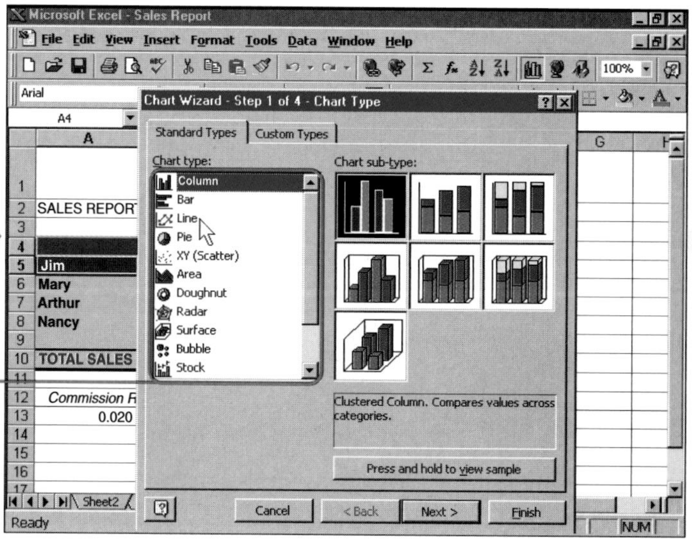

1 Select the cells containing the data you want to display in a chart, including the row and column labels. To select cells, refer to page 16.

2 Move the mouse over the chart button and then press the left mouse button.

■ The **Chart Wizard** dialog box appears.

3 Move the mouse over the type of chart you want to create and then press the left mouse button.

Note: After you create a chart, you can easily change the type of chart. For information, refer to page 158.

Can I change my selections?

While creating a chart, you can return to a previous step at any time to change the choices you made.

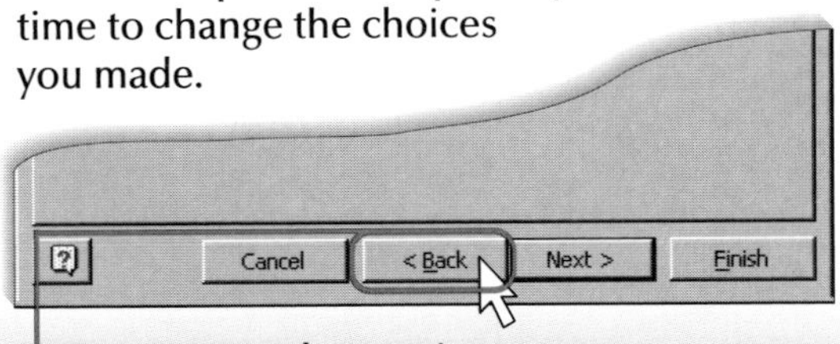

■ To return to the previous step, move the mouse ↖ over **Back** and then press the left mouse button.

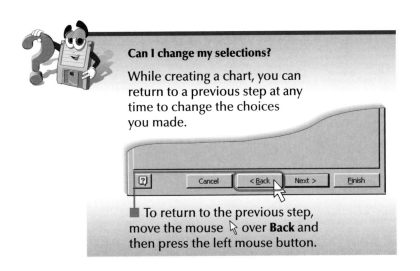

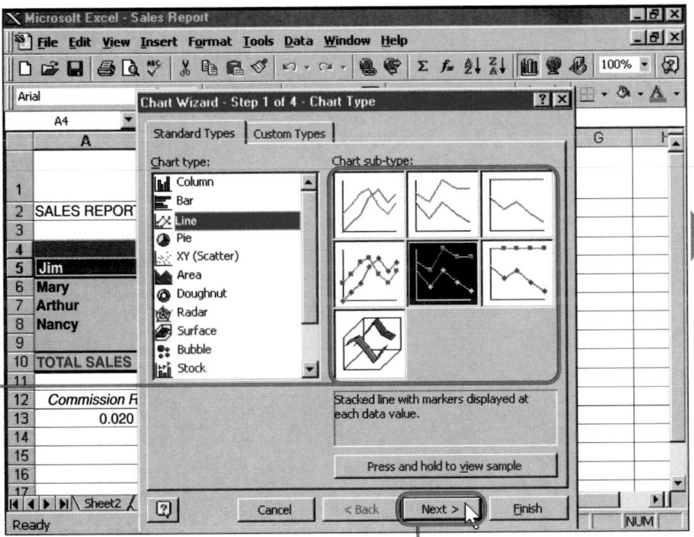

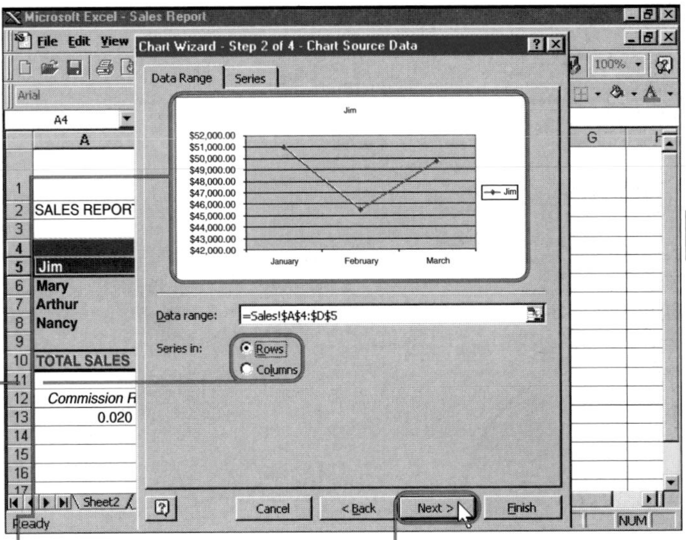

4 Move the mouse ↖ over the chart design you want to use and then press the left mouse button.

Note: The available designs depend on the type of chart you selected in step 3.

5 To continue, move the mouse ↖ over **Next** and then press the left mouse button.

■ This area displays a sample of the chart.

6 To select the way you want Excel to plot the data from your worksheet, move the mouse ↖ over one of these options and then press the left mouse button (○ changes to ◉).

7 To continue, move the mouse ↖ over **Next** and then press the left mouse button.

CONTINUED

CREATE A CHART

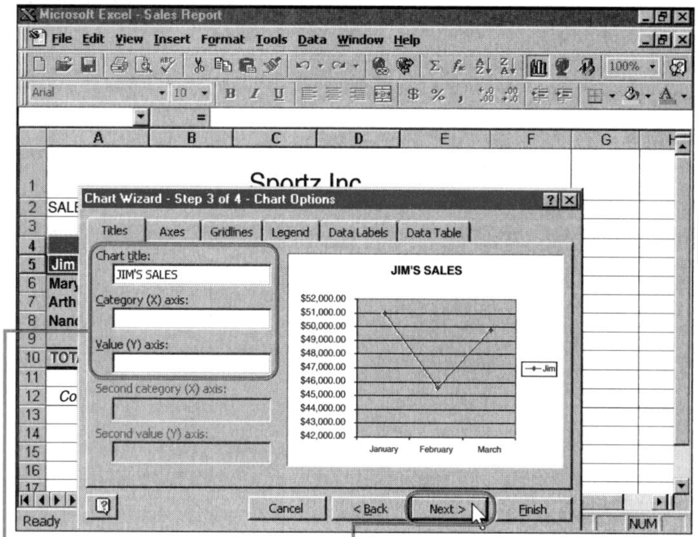

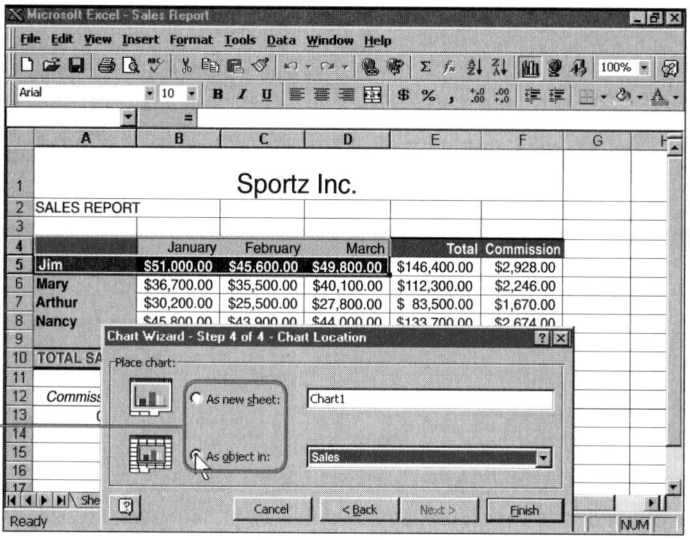

8 To add a title to the chart, move the mouse I over the box for the title you want to add and then press the left mouse button. Then type the title.

9 Repeat step 8 for each title you want to add.

10 To continue, move the mouse over **Next** and then press the left mouse button.

11 To choose where you want to display the chart, move the mouse over one of these options and then press the left mouse button (○ changes to ◉).

As new sheet

Display chart on its own sheet, called a chart sheet.

As object in

Display chart on the same worksheet as the data.

What happens if I change data used in a chart?

If you change data used in a chart, Excel will automatically update the chart.

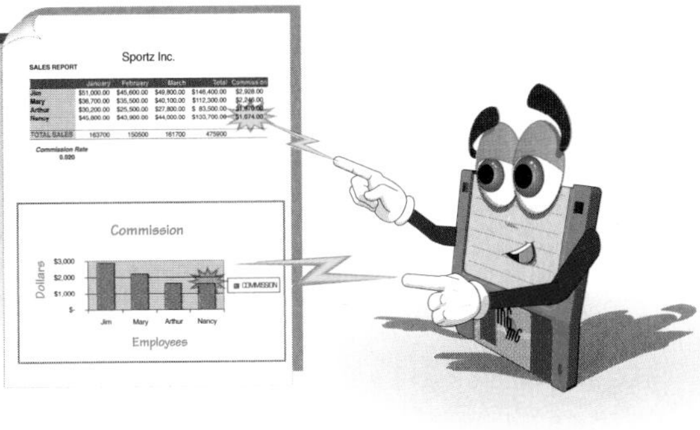

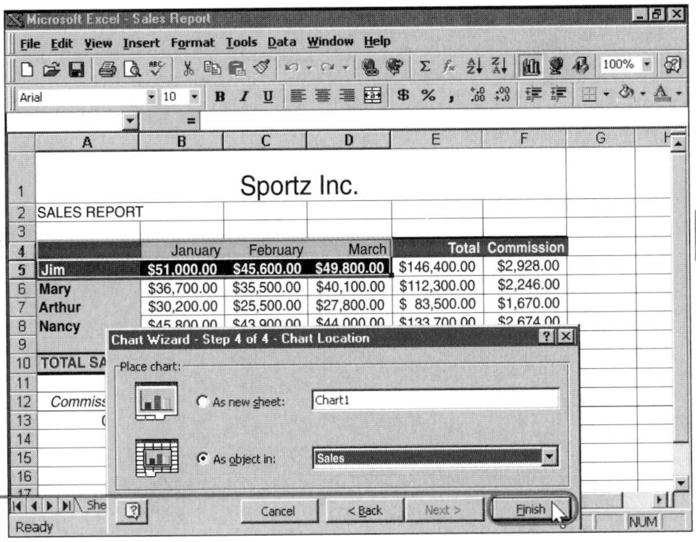

12 To complete the chart, move the mouse over **Finish** and then press the left mouse button.

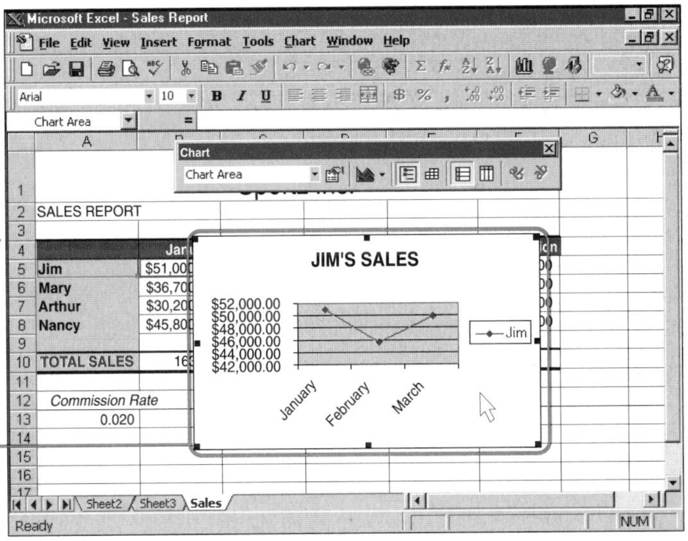

■ The chart appears.

DELETE A CHART

1 Move the mouse over a blank area in the chart and then press the left mouse button. Handles (■) appear around the chart.

2 Press Delete on your keyboard.

Note: To delete a chart displayed on a chart sheet, follow the steps to delete a worksheet. To delete a worksheet, refer to page 143.

CHANGE CHART TYPE

You can easily change the chart type to improve the way data is displayed in your chart.

CHANGE CHART TYPE

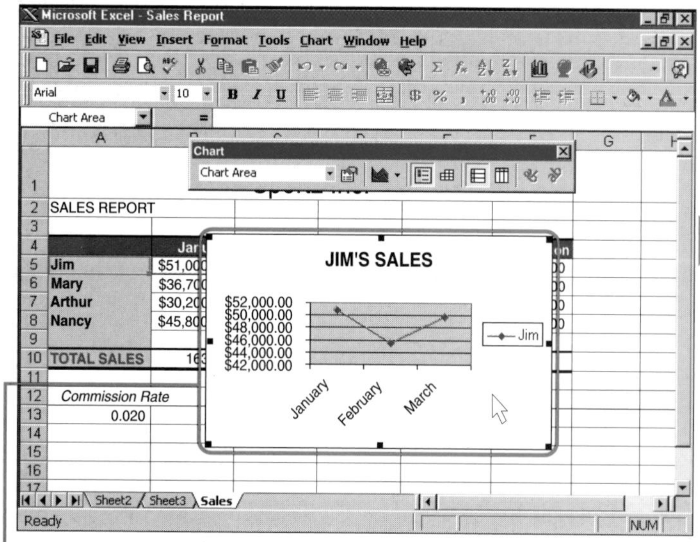

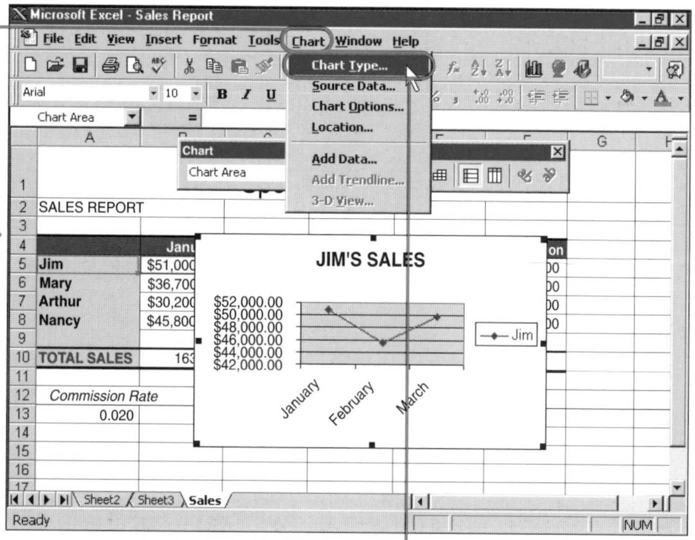

1 To change a chart on a worksheet, move the mouse ⇖ over a blank area in the chart and then press the left mouse button. Handles (■) appear around the chart.

■ To change a chart on a chart sheet, move the mouse ⇖ over the tab for the chart sheet and then press the left mouse button.

2 Move the mouse ⇖ over **Chart** and then press the left mouse button.

3 Move the mouse ⇖ over **Chart Type** and then press the left mouse button.

■ The **Chart Type** dialog box appears.

What type of chart should I choose?

The type of chart you should choose depends on your data. For example, area, column and line charts are ideal for showing changes to values over time, whereas pie charts are ideal for showing percentages.

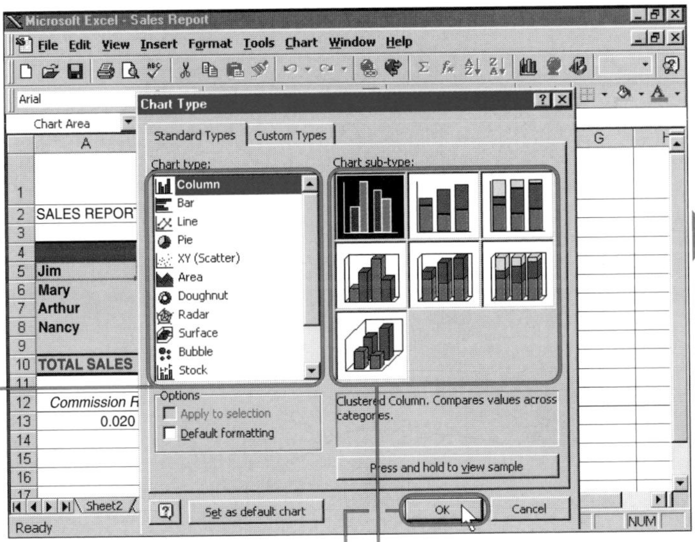

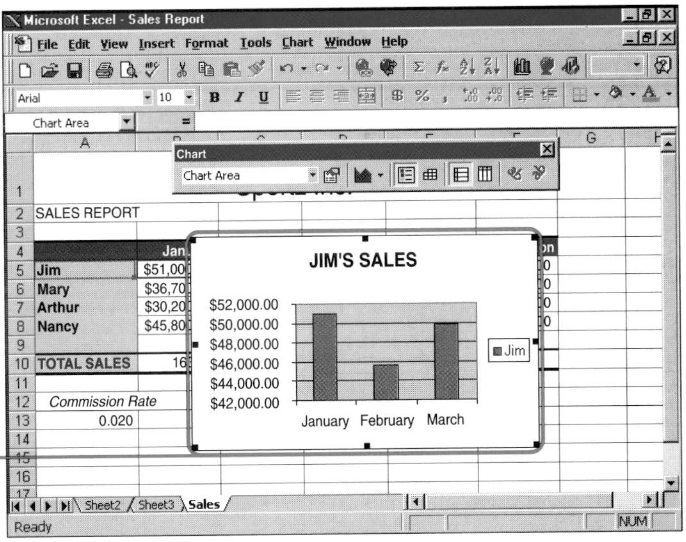

4 Move the mouse over the chart type you want to use and then press the left mouse button.

5 Move the mouse over the chart design you want to use and then press the left mouse button.

6 Move the mouse over **OK** and then press the left mouse button.

■ The chart displays the chart type you selected.

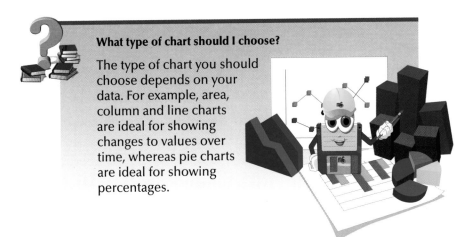

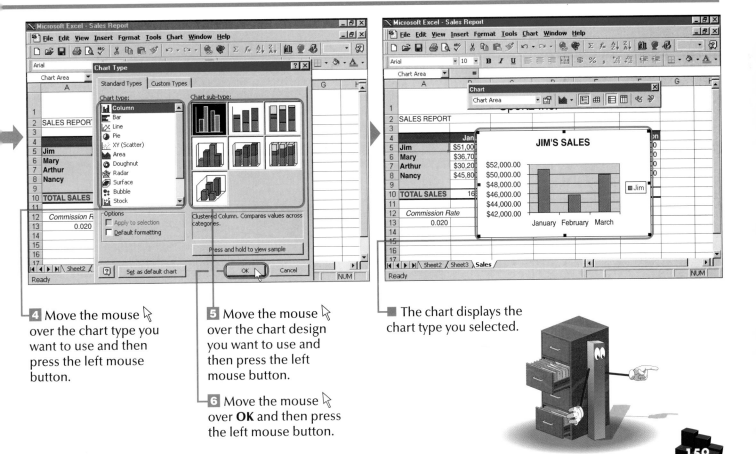

MOVE OR RESIZE A CHART

MOVE A CHART

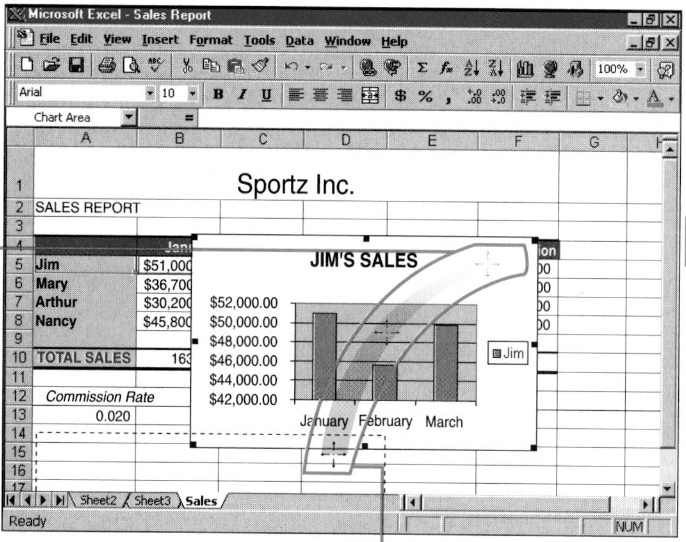

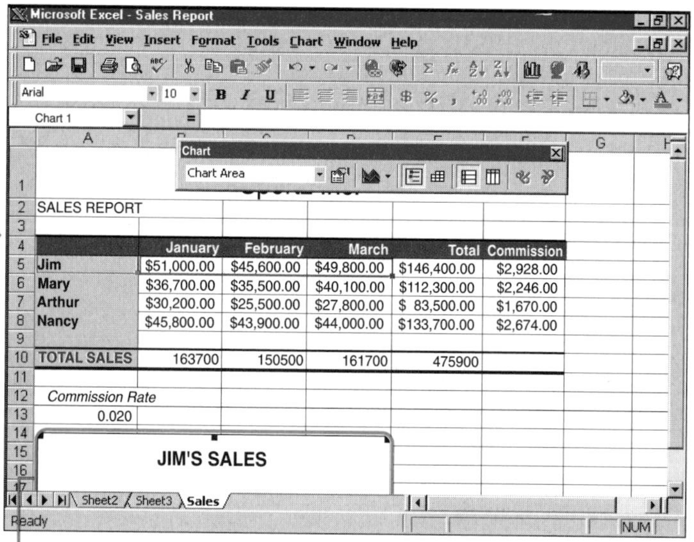

1 Move the mouse over a blank area in your chart.

2 Press and hold down the left mouse button as you move your chart to a new location.

■ A dotted line shows the new location.

3 Release the mouse button and your chart appears in the new location.

What are the handles (■) that appear around a chart?

The handles around a chart let you change the size of the chart.

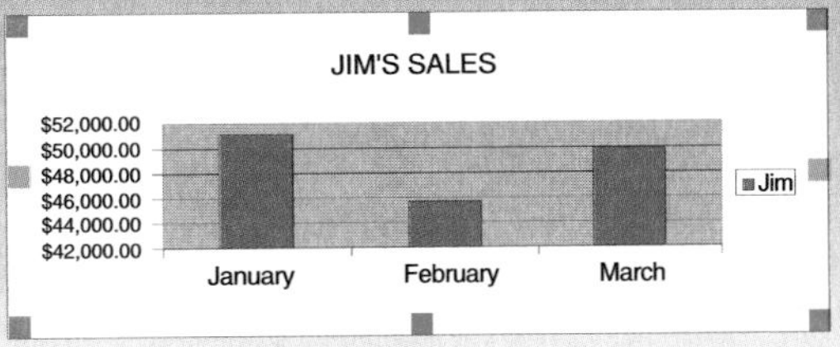

■ Change the height of a chart.

■ Change the width of a chart.

■ Change the height and width of a chart at the same time.

RESIZE A CHART

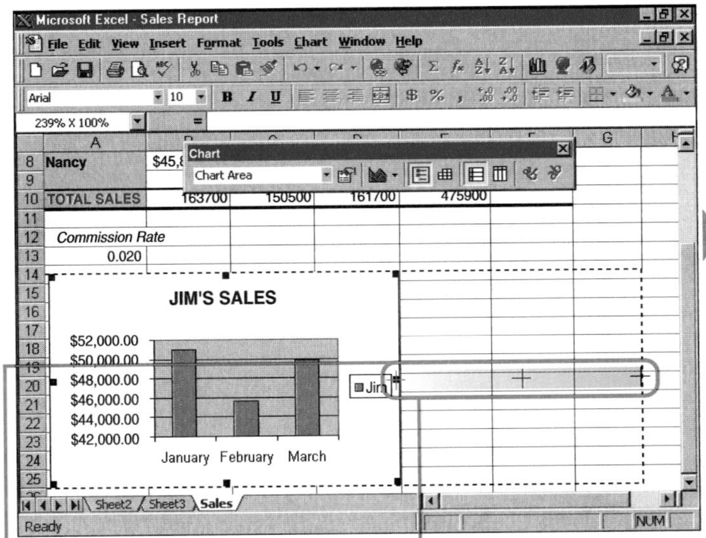

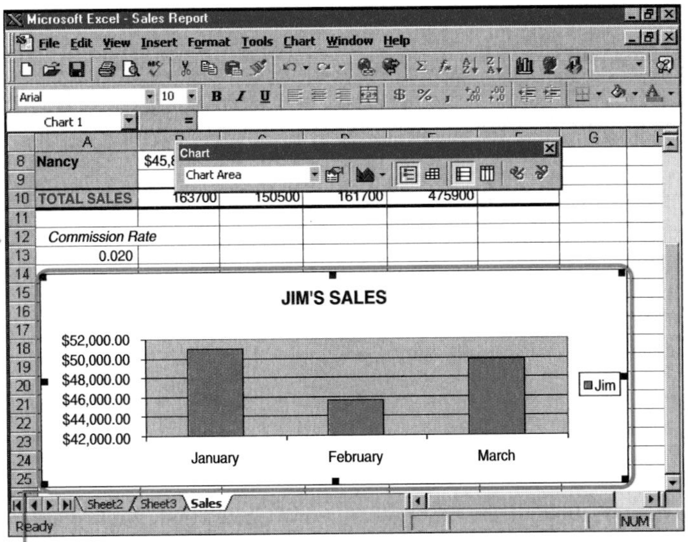

1 Move the mouse over a blank area in your chart and then press the left mouse button. Handles (■) appear around the chart.

2 Move the mouse over one of the handles (■) (changes to ↕ or ↔).

3 Press and hold down the left mouse button as you move the edge of your chart until the chart is the size you want.

■ A dotted line shows the new size.

4 Release the mouse button and your chart appears in the new size.

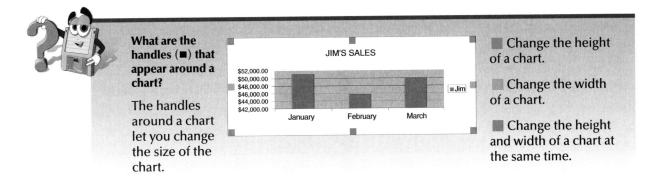

PRINT A CHART

PRINT A CHART WITH WORKSHEET DATA

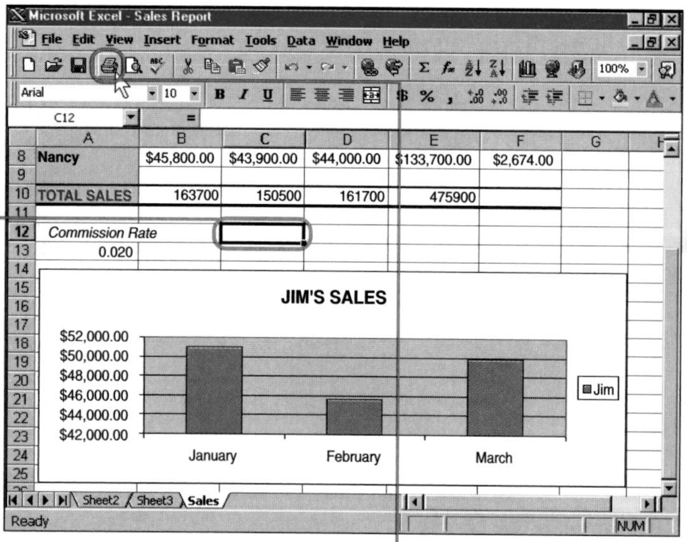

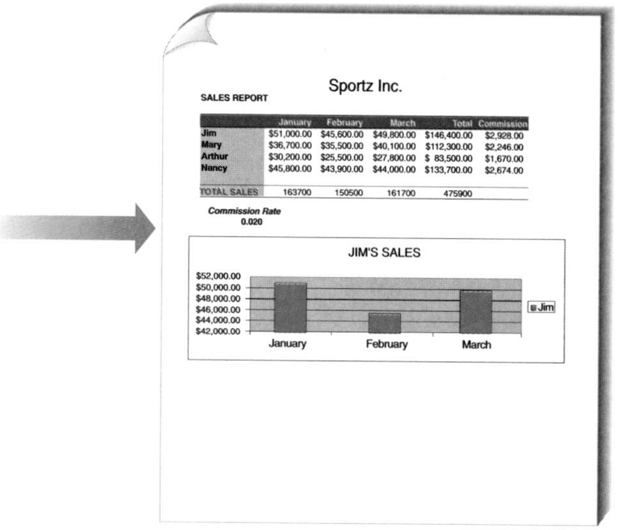

1 Move the mouse ✥ over any cell outside your chart and then press the left mouse button.

2 Move the mouse ↖ over 🖨 and then press the left mouse button.

Note: For more information on printing, refer to pages 120 to 137.

Can I see what my chart will look like when printed?

You can preview your chart to see what the chart will look like when printed. To preview a chart, refer to page 120.

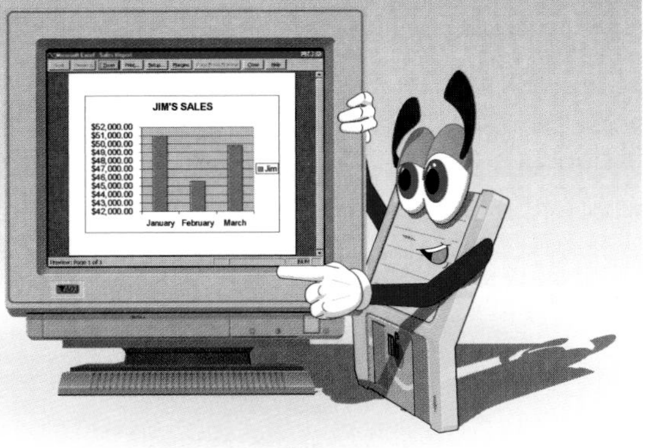

PRINT A CHART ON ITS OWN PAGE

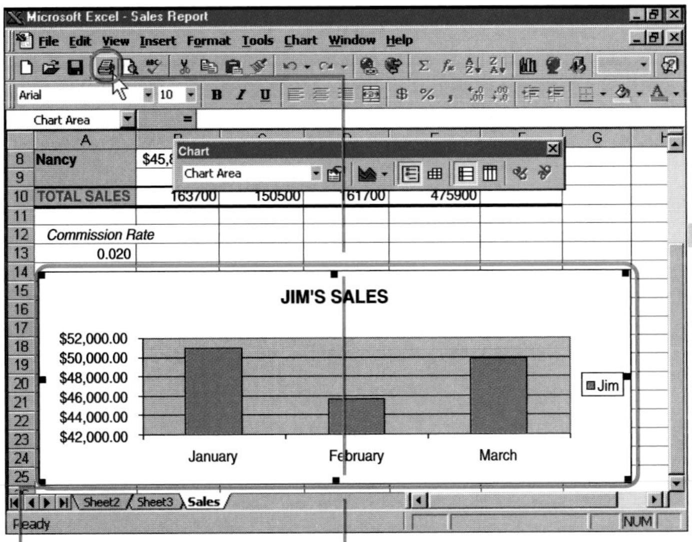

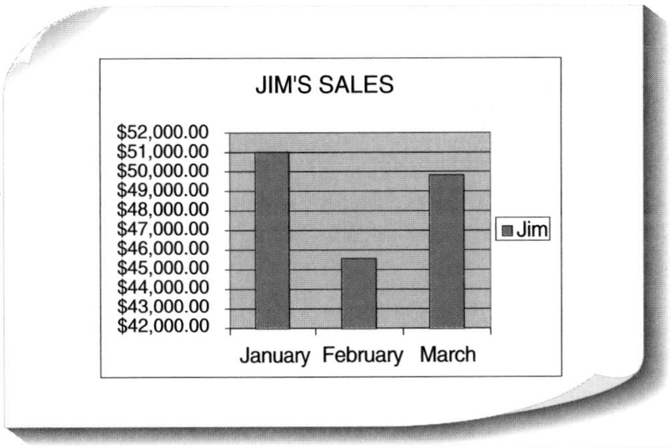

1 To print a chart displayed on a worksheet, move the mouse over a blank area in the chart and then press the left mouse button.

■ To print a chart displayed on a chart sheet, move the mouse over the tab for the chart sheet and then press the left mouse button.

2 Move the mouse over and then press the left mouse button.

Note: When you print a chart on its own page, the chart will expand to fill the page. The printed chart may look different from the chart on the worksheet.

ADD DATA TO A CHART

ADD DATA TO A CHART

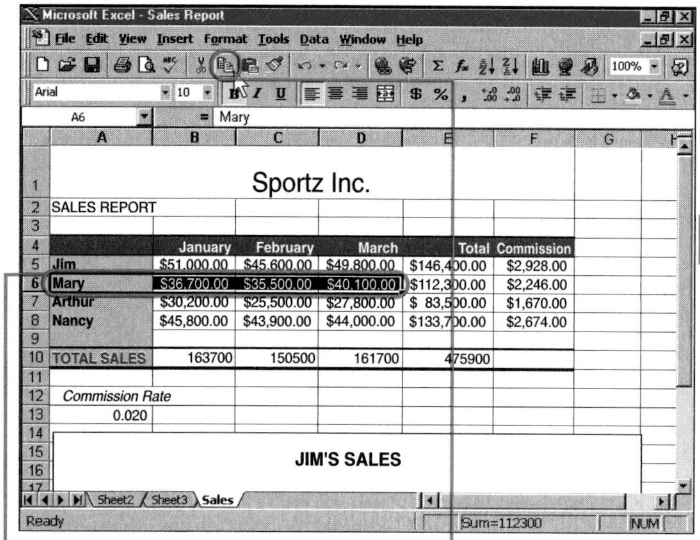

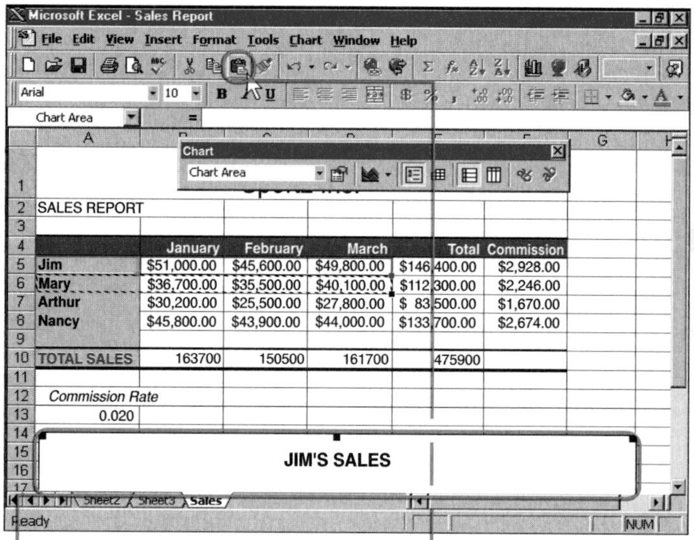

1 Select the cells containing the data you want to add to your chart, including the row or column headings. To select cells, refer to page 16.

2 To copy the data, move the mouse over and then press the left mouse button.

3 To select the chart you want to add the data to, move the mouse over the chart and then press the left mouse button.

4 To add the data to the chart, move the mouse over and then press the left mouse button.

Can I add a data series to a pie chart?

A pie chart can display only one data series. You cannot add another data series to a pie chart.

DELETE DATA FROM A CHART

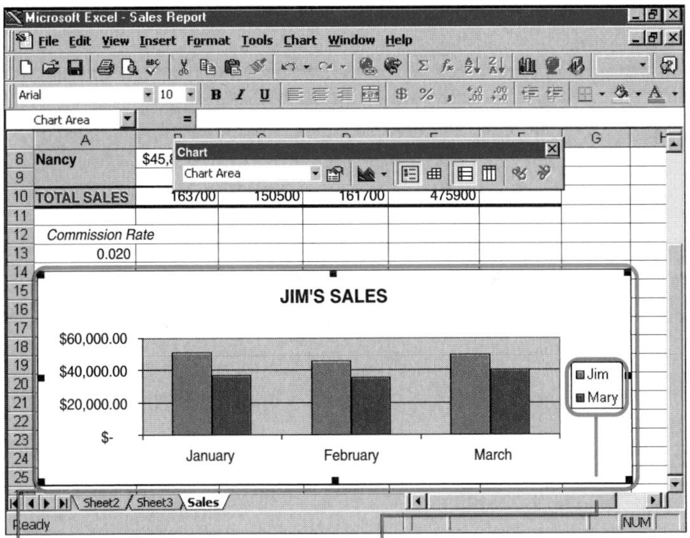

■ The data appears in the chart.

■ When you add data to a chart, Excel automatically updates the chart legend.

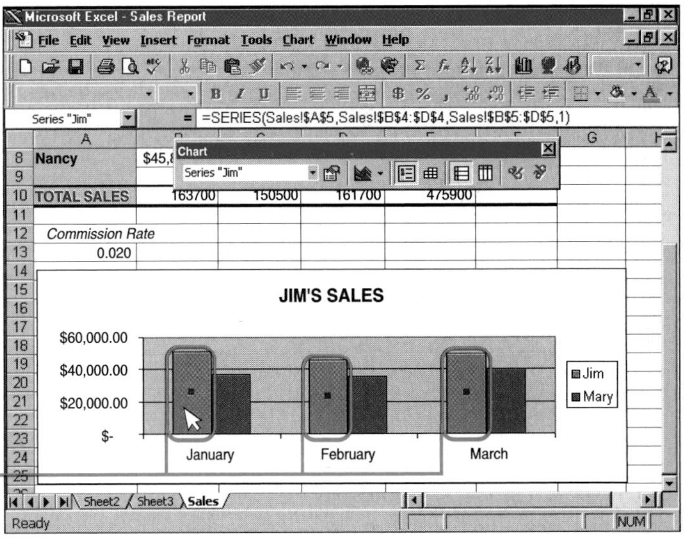

1 Move the mouse over the data series you want to delete from your chart and then press the left mouse button.

■ Small squares (■) appear in the data series you selected.

2 To delete the data series from your chart, press Delete on your keyboard.

CHANGE CHART TITLES

CHANGE CHART TITLES

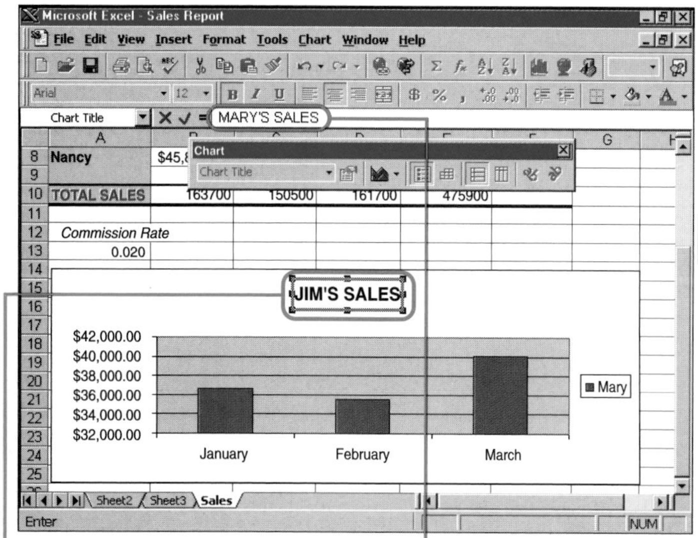

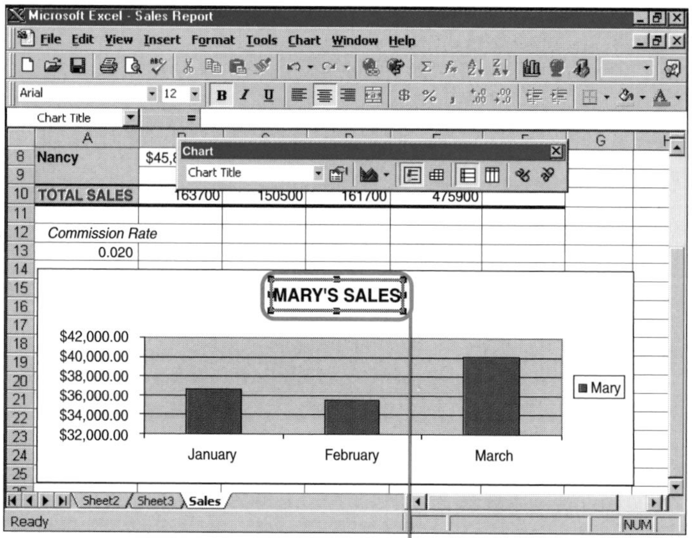

1 Move the mouse over the title you want to change and then press the left mouse button. A border appears around the title.

2 Type the new title.

■ This area displays the text as you type.

3 Press **Enter** on your keyboard.

■ Your chart displays the new title.

CHANGE THE WAY DATA IS PLOTTED

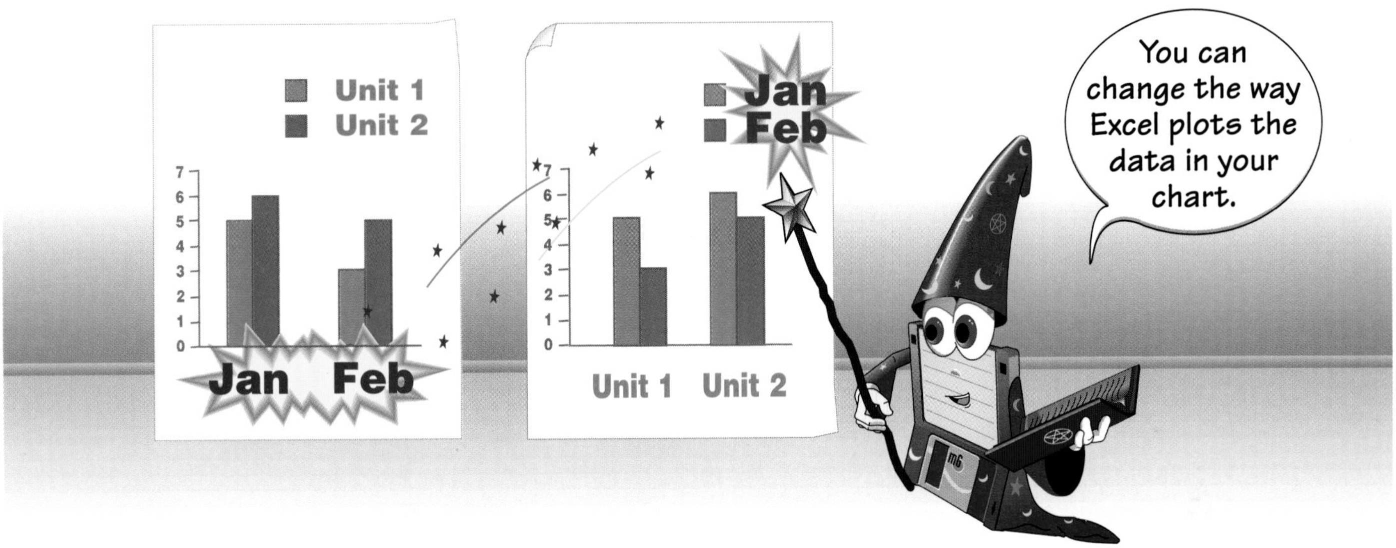

CHANGE THE WAY DATA IS PLOTTED

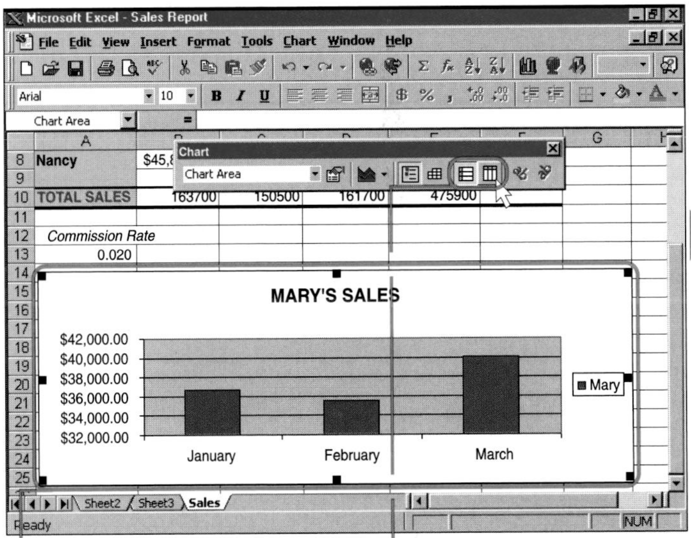

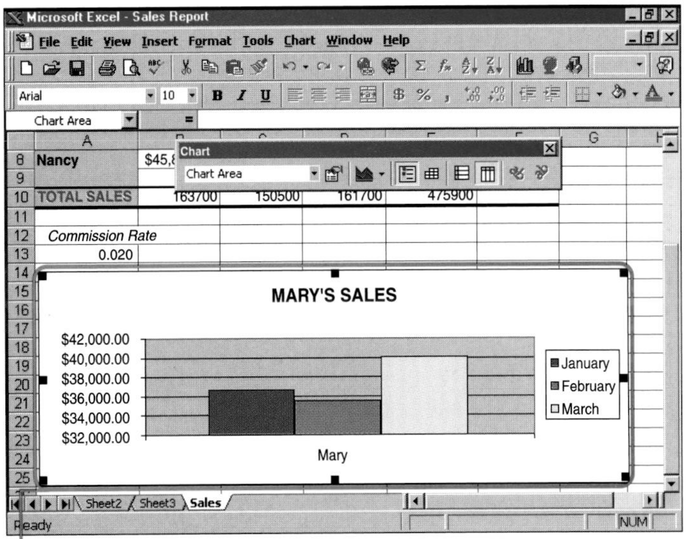

1 Move the mouse over your chart and then press the left mouse button.

2 Move the mouse over one of the following options and then press the left mouse button.

- Plot data by row
- Plot data by column

*Note: If and are not displayed, refer to page 82 to display the **Chart** toolbar.*

■ Your chart displays the changes.

■ To once again change the way data is plotted, repeat steps 1 and 2.

ADD A DATA TABLE TO A CHART

ADD A DATA TABLE TO A CHART

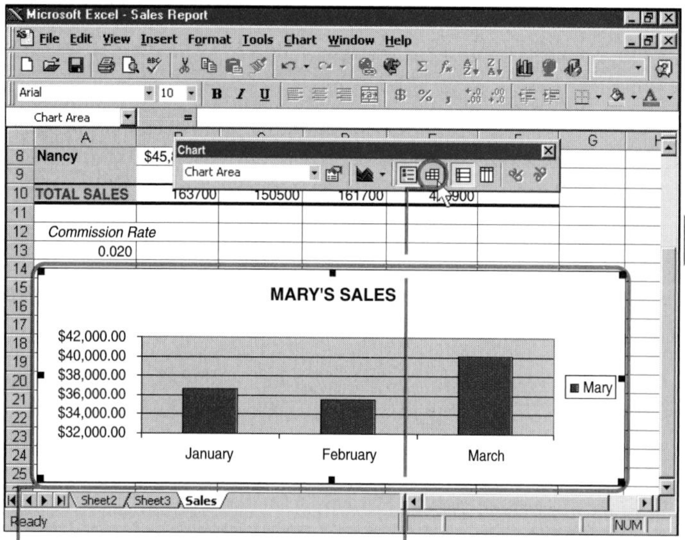

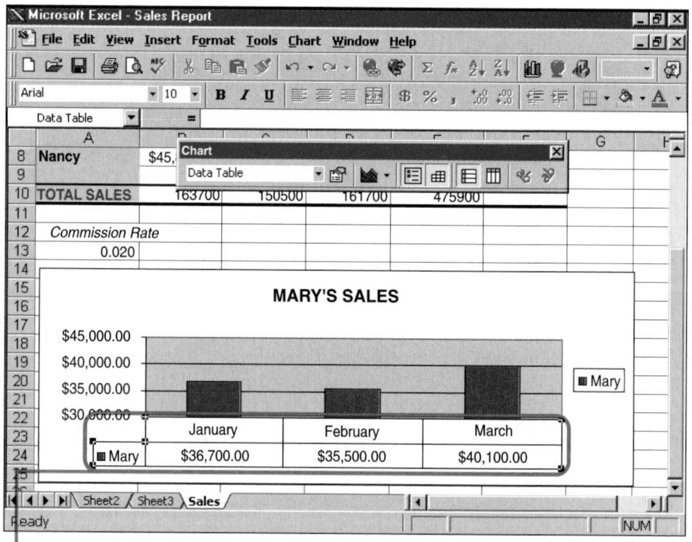

1 Move the mouse over the chart you want to display a data table and then press the left mouse button.

Note: You cannot add a data table to some chart types.

2 Move the mouse over ▦ and then press the left mouse button.

*Note: If ▦ is not displayed, refer to page 82 to display the **Chart** toolbar.*

■ The data table appears in the chart.

■ To hide the data table, repeat steps **1** and **2**.

DISPLAY OR HIDE THE CHART LEGEND

DISPLAY OR HIDE THE CHART LEGEND

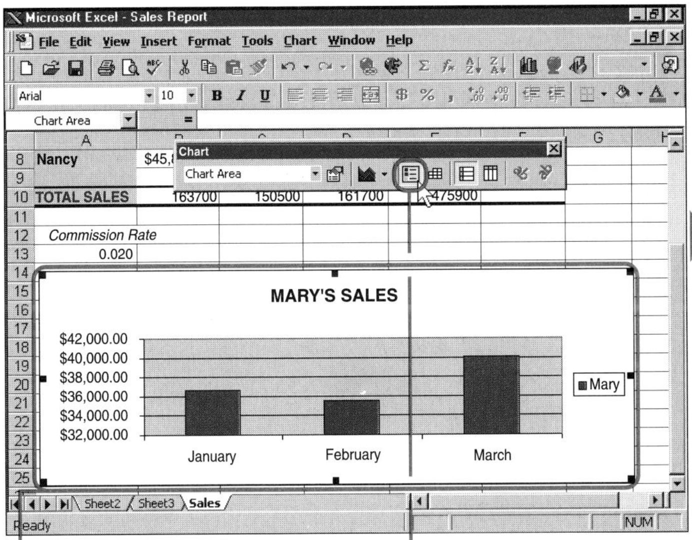

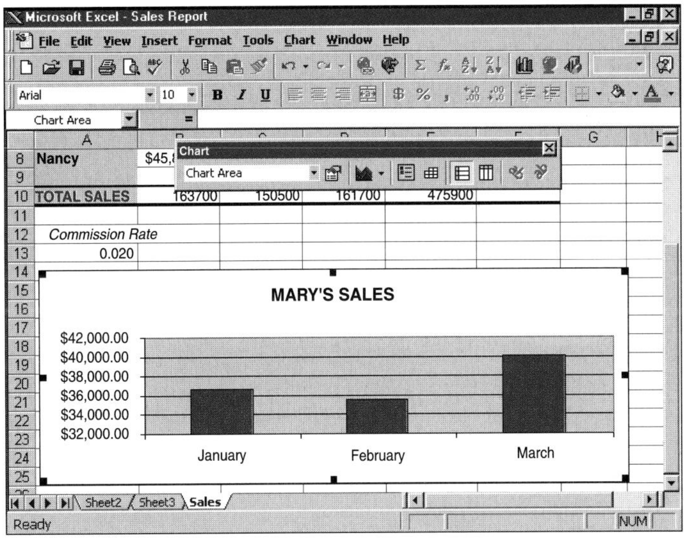

1 To display or hide the legend in a chart, move the mouse over the chart and then press the left mouse button.

2 Move the mouse over and then press the left mouse button.

*Note: If is not displayed, refer to page 82 to display the **Chart** toolbar.*

■ Excel displays or hides the chart legend.

DISPLAY DATA IN A MAP

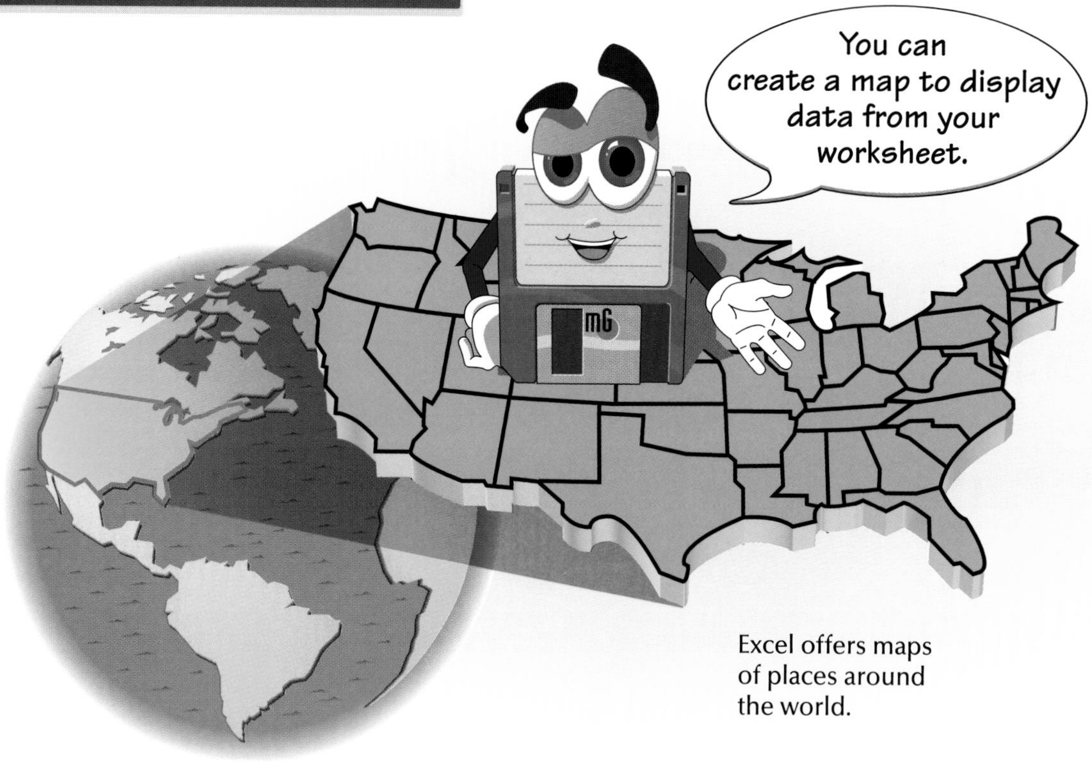

You can create a map to display data from your worksheet.

Excel offers maps of places around the world.

CREATE A MAP

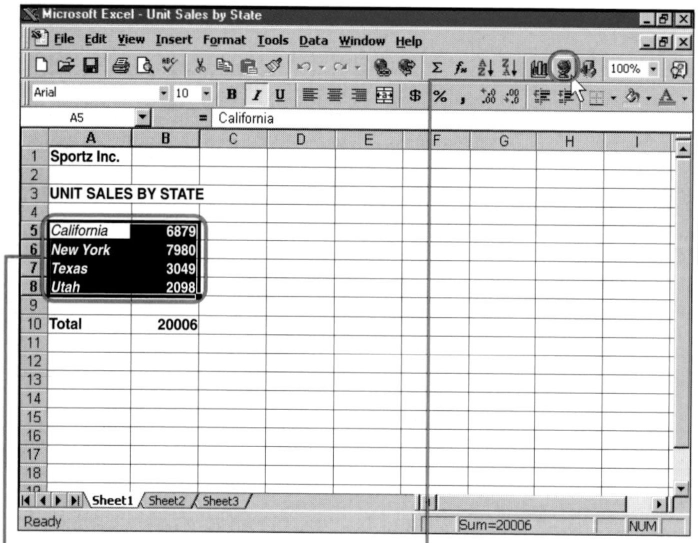

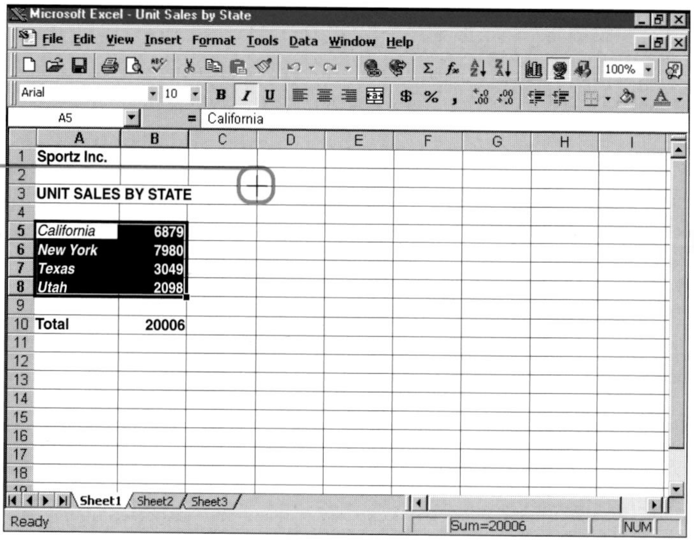

1 Select the cells containing the data you want to display in a map. To select cells, refer to page 16.

Note: One column must contain geographic data, such as country or state names.

2 Move the mouse over the map button and then press the left mouse button.

■ The mouse changes to + when over your worksheet.

3 Move the mouse + over the location where you want the top left corner of the map to appear and then press the left mouse button.

Note: If an error message appears, you need to add the Microsoft Map feature from the Microsoft Excel or Microsoft Office CD-ROM disc.

Can I move or resize a map?

You can move or resize a map as you would move or resize a chart. To move or resize a chart, refer to page 160.

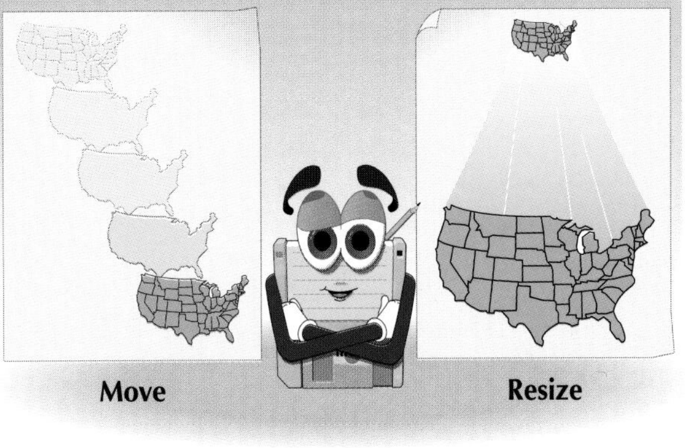

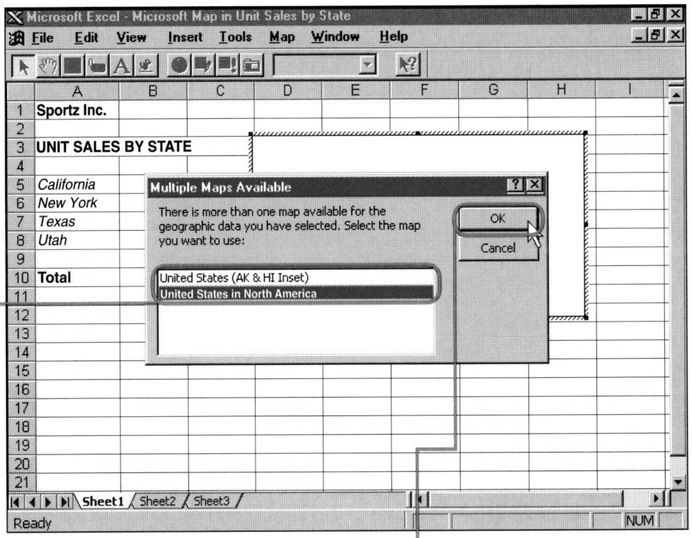

■ A dialog box appears if more than one map is available for your data.

4 Move the mouse over the map you want to create and then press the left mouse button.

5 Move the mouse over **OK** and then press the left mouse button.

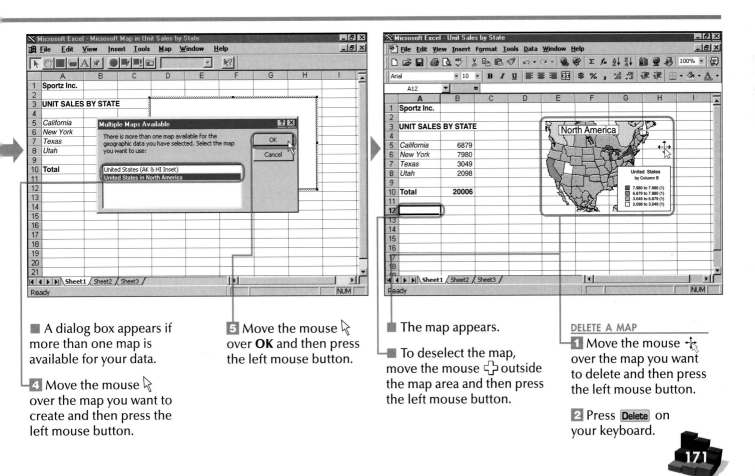

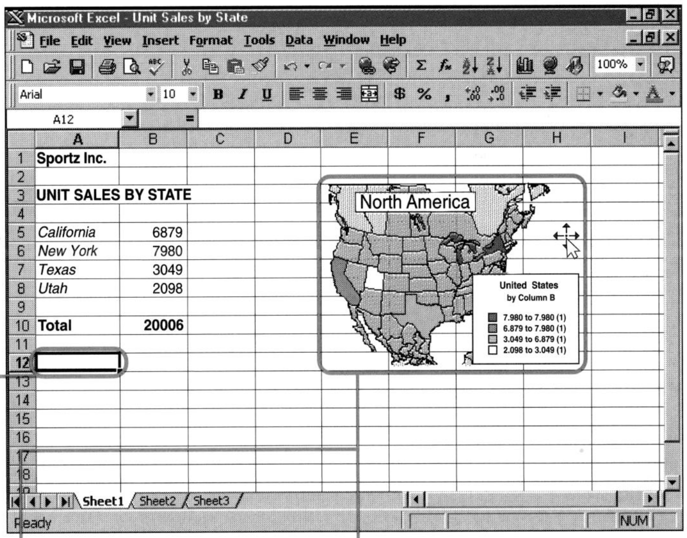

■ The map appears.

■ To deselect the map, move the mouse outside the map area and then press the left mouse button.

DELETE A MAP

1 Move the mouse over the map you want to delete and then press the left mouse button.

2 Press Delete on your keyboard.

DISPLAY DATA IN A MAP

UPDATE A MAP

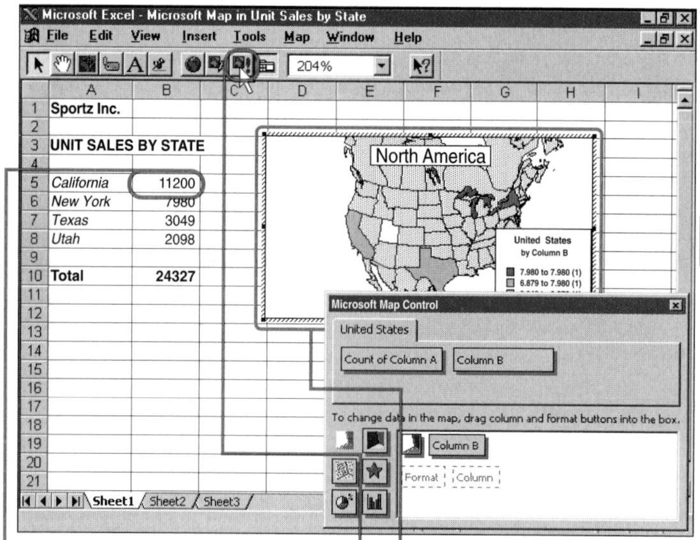

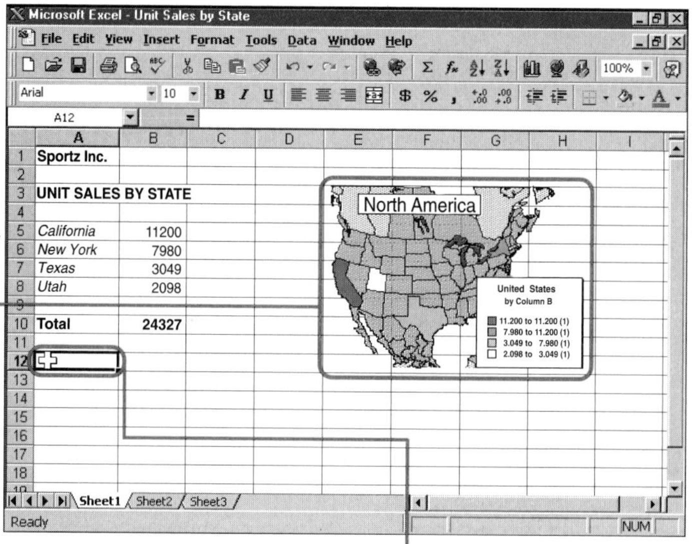

■ In this example, **6879** was changed to **11200**.

1 Move the mouse over the map you want to update and then quickly press the left mouse button twice.

2 To update the map, move the mouse over and then press the left mouse button.

■ The map updates to reflect the changes.

■ To deselect the map, move the mouse outside the map area and then press the left mouse button.

ADD TEXT TO A MAP

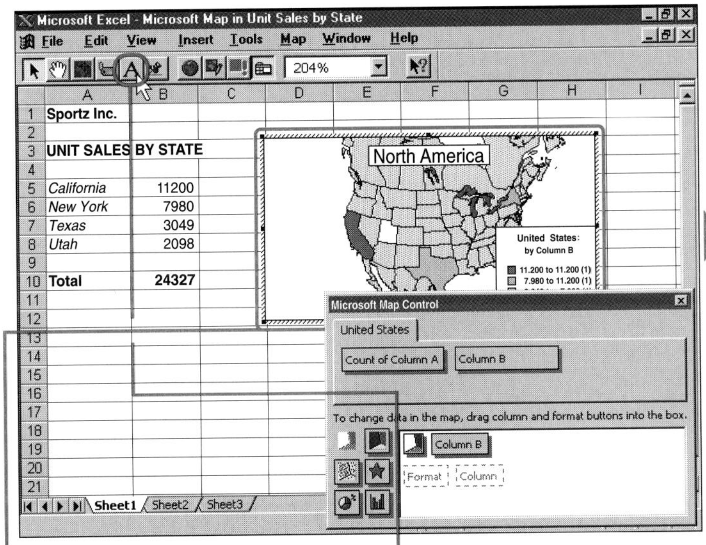

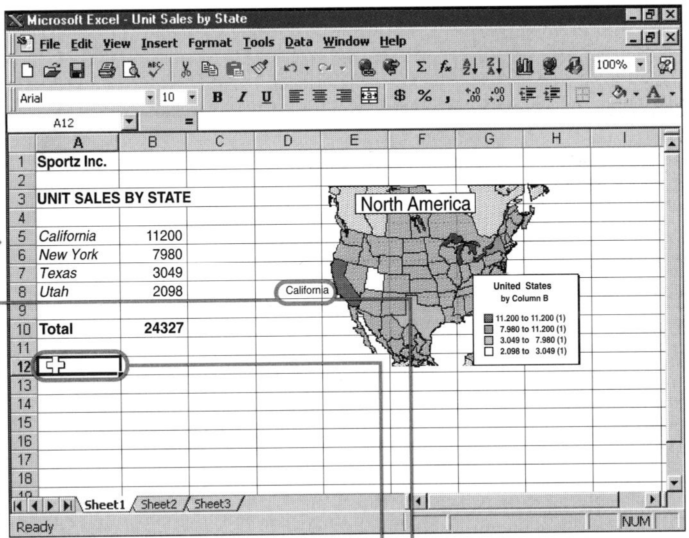

1 Move the mouse over the map you want to add text to and then quickly press the left mouse button twice.

2 To add text to the map, move the mouse over **A** and then press the left mouse button.

3 Move the mouse over the location where you want the text to appear and then press the left mouse button.

4 Type the text and then press **Enter** on your keyboard.

■ To deselect the map, move the mouse outside the map area and then press the left mouse button.

Hello
Hello
mG

CHAPTER 10

WORK WITH GRAPHICS

Are you wondering how to use graphics to enhance the appearance of your worksheet? This chapter shows you how.

ADD A SIMPLE SHAPE

Excel provides many ready-made shapes, called AutoShapes, that you can easily add to your worksheet or chart.

ADD A SIMPLE SHAPE

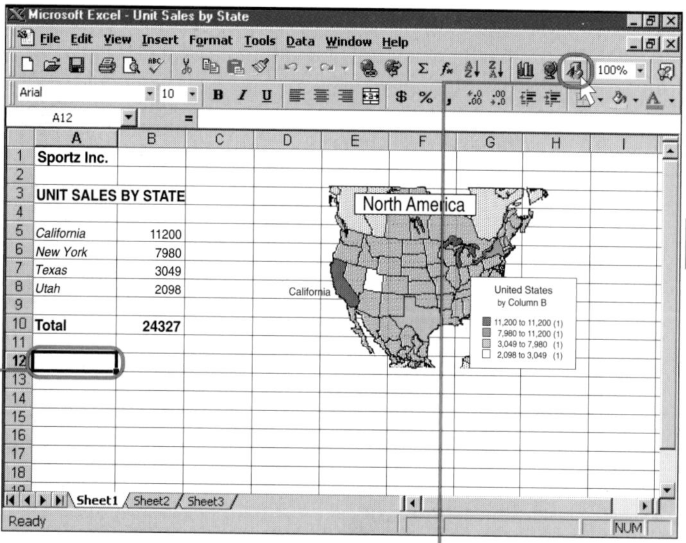

1 To add a simple shape to your worksheet, move the mouse over any cell and then press the left mouse button.

■ To add a simple shape to your chart, move the mouse over the chart and then press the left mouse button.

2 To display the **Drawing** toolbar, move the mouse over and then press the left mouse button.

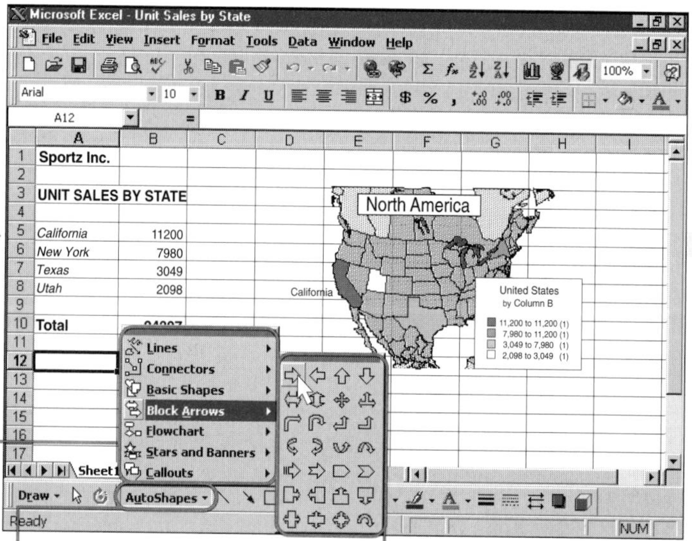

3 To add a simple shape, move the mouse over **AutoShapes** and then press the left mouse button.

4 Move the mouse over the type of shape you want to add.

5 Move the mouse over the shape you want to add and then press the left mouse button.

Can I add text to a simple shape?

1 To add text to a simple shape, move the mouse over the shape and then press the left mouse button.

2 Type the text.

Note: You cannot add text to some simple shapes.

3 To deselect the shape, move the mouse outside the shape area and then press the left mouse button.

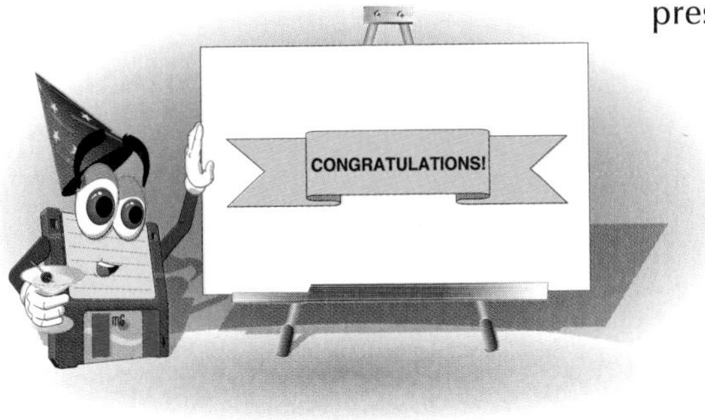

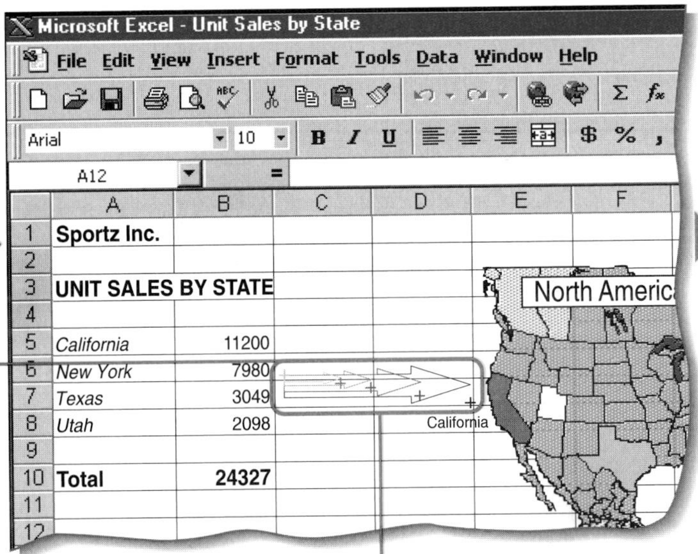

6 Move the mouse to where you want the top left corner of the shape to appear (changes to +).

7 Press and hold down the left mouse button as you move the mouse + until the shape is the size you want. Then release the mouse button.

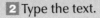

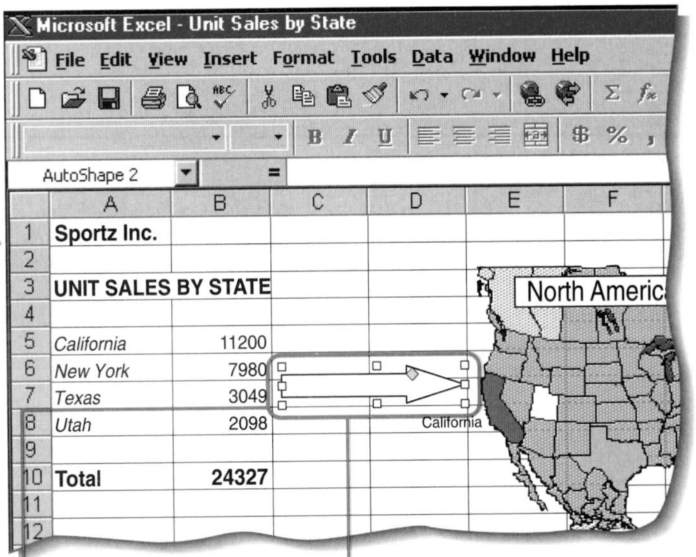

■ The shape appears. The handles (□) around the shape let you change the size of the shape. To resize a graphic, refer to page 183.

■ To hide the **Drawing** toolbar, repeat step **2**.

DELETE A SHAPE

■ Move the mouse over an edge of the shape (changes to) and then press the left mouse button. Then press Delete on your keyboard.

ADD A TEXT BOX

ADD A TEXT BOX

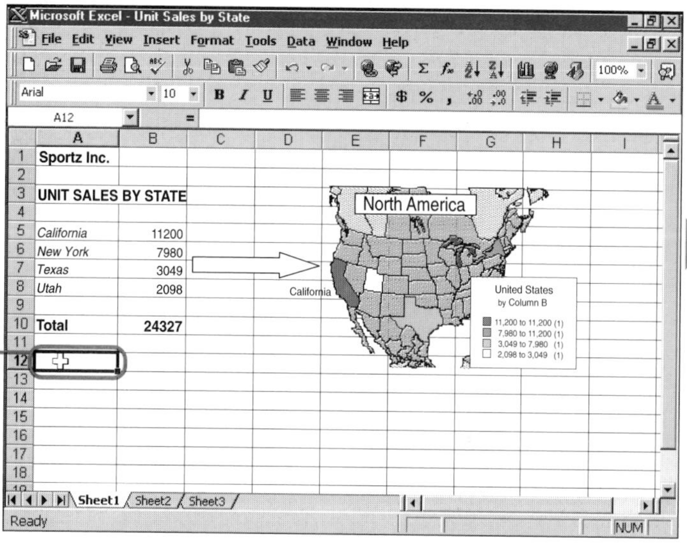

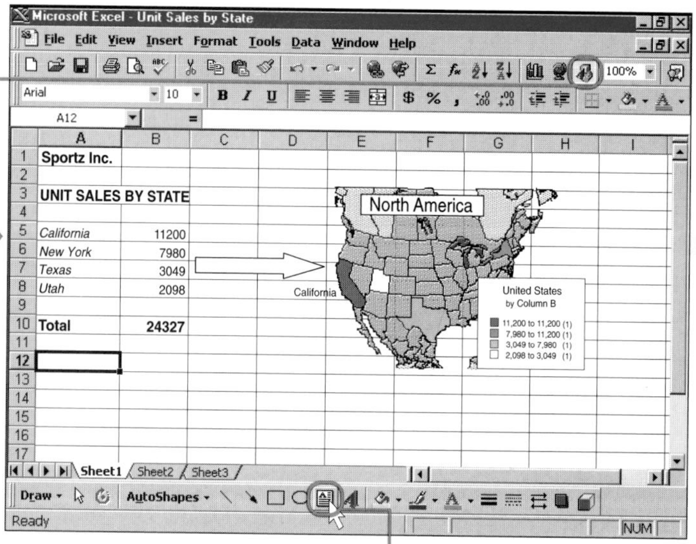

1 To add a text box to your worksheet, move the mouse ✥ over any cell and then press the left mouse button.

■ To add a text box to your chart, move the mouse ↖ over the chart and then press the left mouse button.

2 To display the **Drawing** toolbar, move the mouse ↖ over the Drawing button and then press the left mouse button.

3 To add a text box, move the mouse ↖ over the Text Box button and then press the left mouse button.

How do I delete a text box?

1 To delete a text box, move the mouse over an edge of the text box and then press the left mouse button.

2 Press Delete on your keyboard.

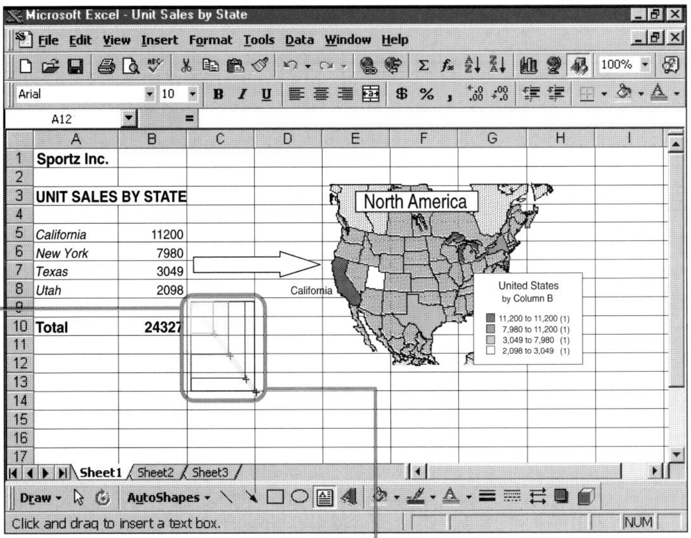

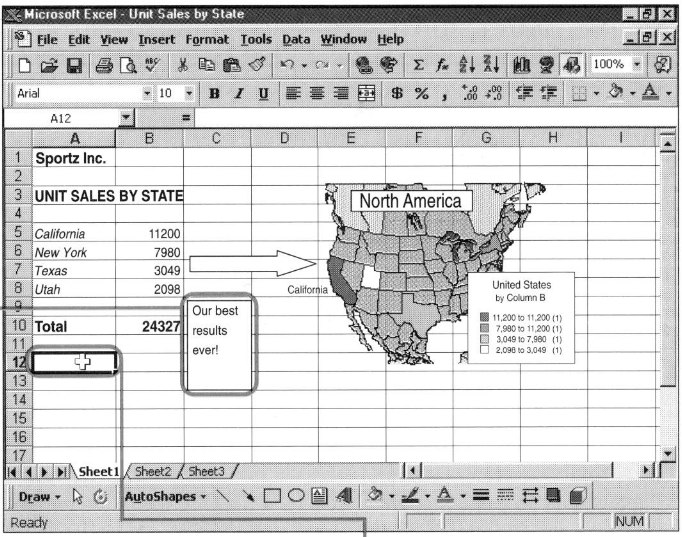

4 Move the mouse to where you want the top left corner of the text box to appear (changes to).

5 Press and hold down the left mouse button as you move the mouse + until the text box is the size you want. Then release the mouse button.

■ The text box appears.

6 Type the text you want to appear in the text box.

7 To deselect the text box, move the mouse outside the text box area and then press the left mouse button.

■ To hide the **Drawing** toolbar, repeat step **2**.

ADD A TEXT EFFECT

You can use the WordArt feature to add special text effects to your worksheet or chart.

ADD A TEXT EFFECT

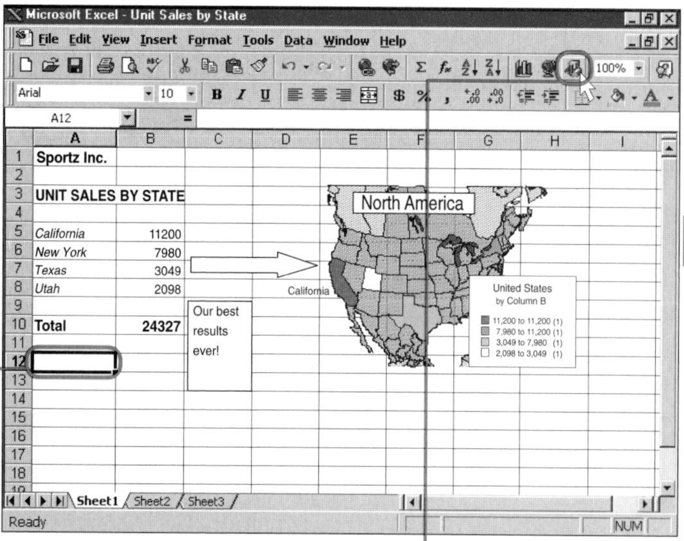

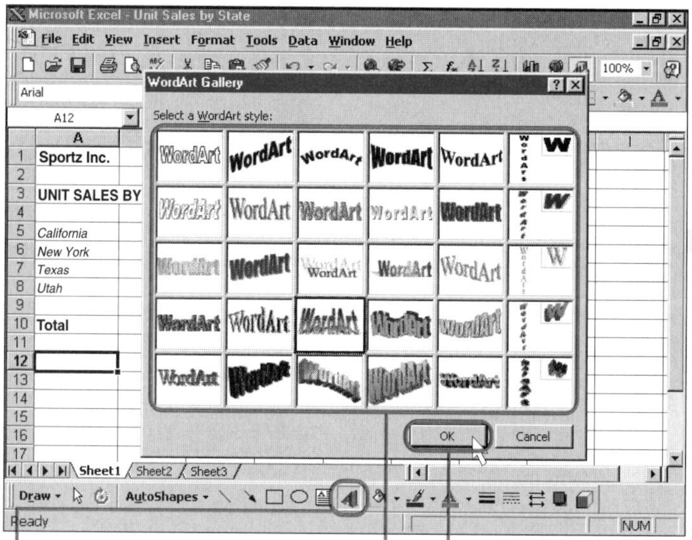

1 To add a text effect to your worksheet, move the mouse over any cell and then press the left mouse button.

■ To add a text effect to your chart, move the mouse over the chart and then press the left mouse button.

2 To display the **Drawing** toolbar, move the mouse over and then press the left mouse button.

3 To add a text effect, move the mouse over and then press the left mouse button.

■ The **WordArt Gallery** dialog box appears.

4 Move the mouse over the type of text effect you want to add and then press the left mouse button.

5 Move the mouse over **OK** and then press the left mouse button.

How do I delete a text effect?

1 To delete a text effect, move the mouse ✥ over the text effect and then press the left mouse button.

2 Press **Delete** on your keyboard.

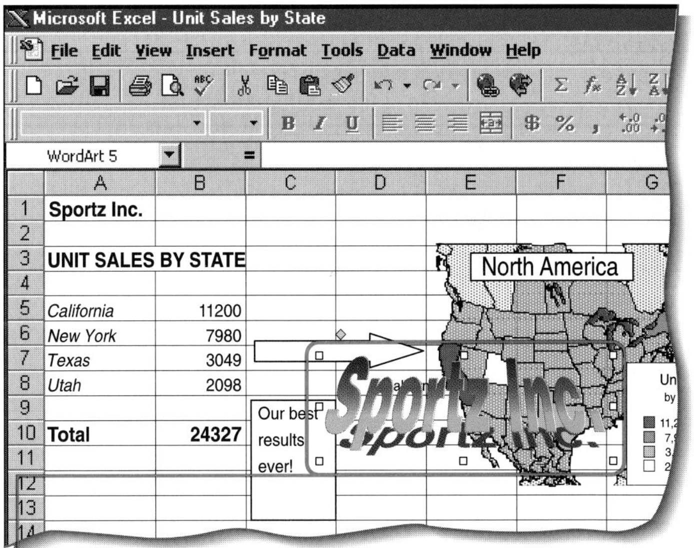

■ The **Edit WordArt Text** dialog box appears.

6 Type the text you want to display the effect you selected.

7 Move the mouse ↖ over **OK** and then press the left mouse button.

■ The text effect appears. The handles (□) around the text effect let you change the size of the effect. To resize a graphic, refer to page 183.

■ To deselect the text effect, move the mouse ✚ outside the text effect area and then press the left mouse button.

■ To hide the **Drawing** toolbar, repeat step **2**.

MOVE OR RESIZE A GRAPHIC

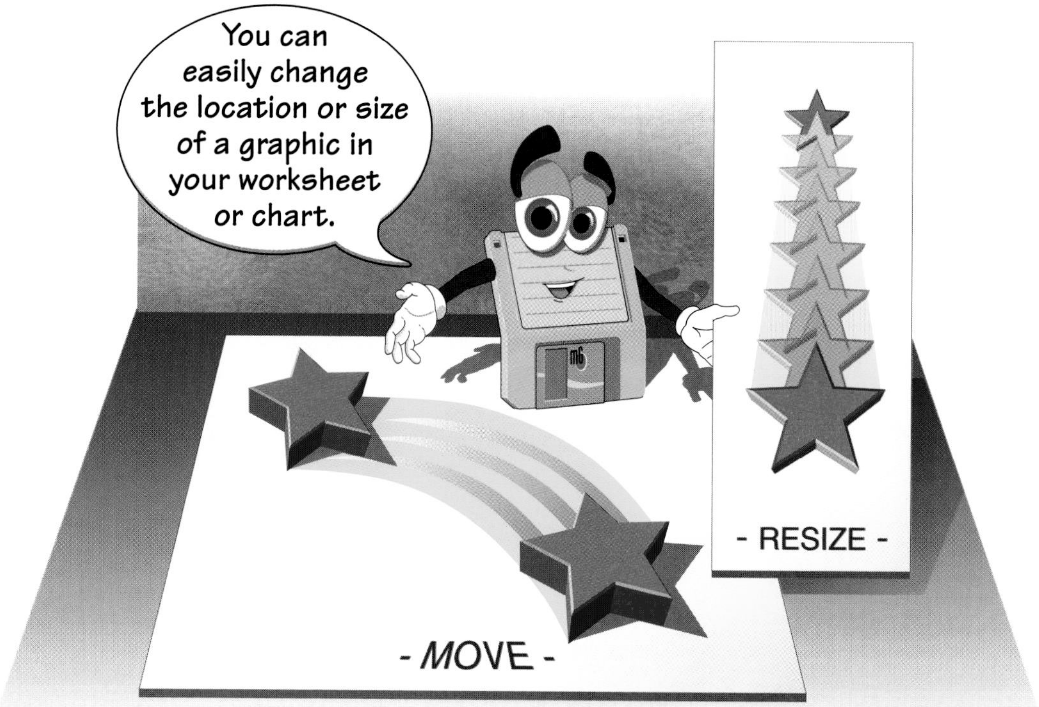

You can easily change the location or size of a graphic in your worksheet or chart.
- RESIZE -
- MOVE -

MOVE A GRAPHIC

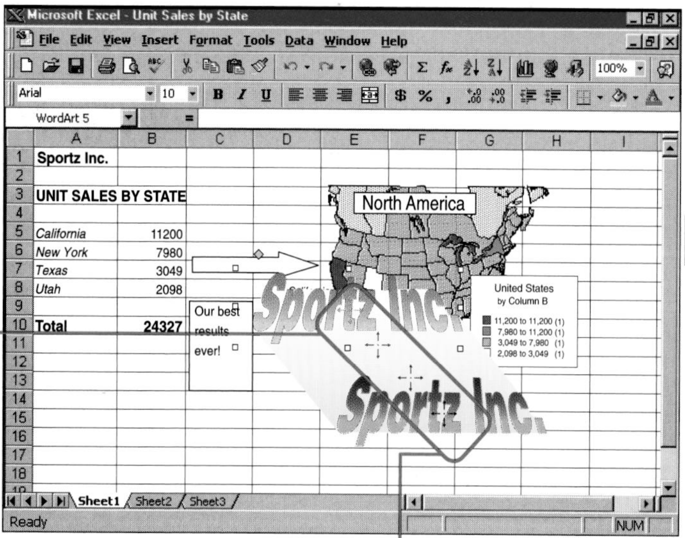

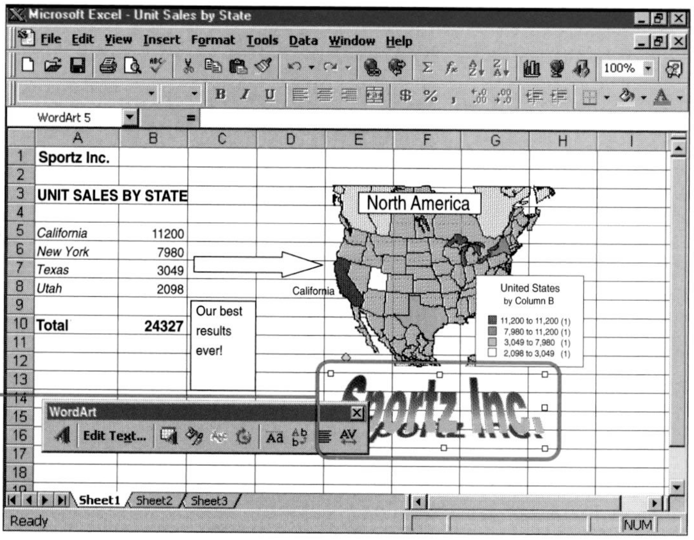

1 Move the mouse ✥ over the graphic you want to move (✥ changes to ✥).

2 Press and hold down the left mouse button as you move the graphic to a new location. Then release the mouse button.

■ The graphic appears in the new location.

Note: You cannot move a graphic you added to a chart outside of the chart area.

What are the handles (□) that appear around a selected graphic?

The handles around a graphic let you change the size of the graphic.

■ Change the height of a graphic.

■ Change the width of a graphic.

□ Change the height and width of a graphic at the same time.

RESIZE A GRAPHIC

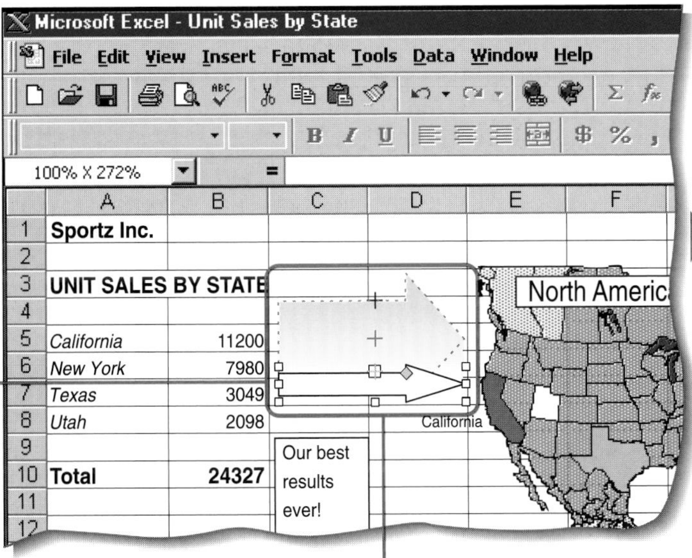

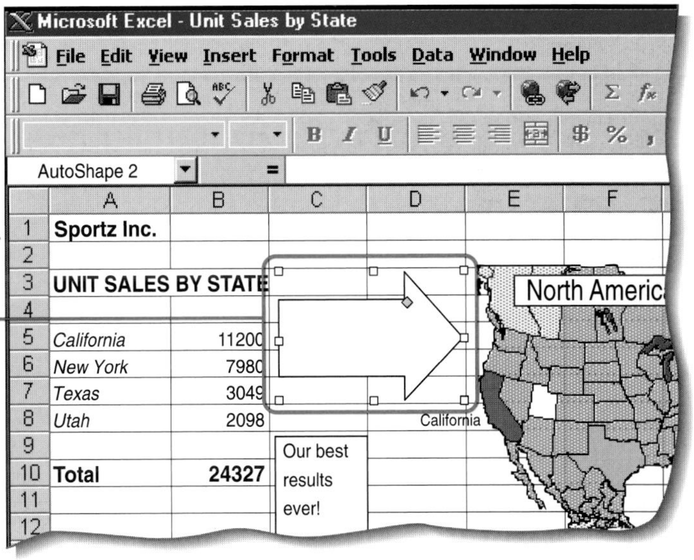

1 Move the mouse ✥ over the graphic you want to resize (✥ changes to ✥) and then press the left mouse button. Handles (□) appear around the graphic.

2 Move the mouse ✥ over one of the handles (✥ changes to ↔ or ↕).

3 Press and hold down the left mouse button as you move the mouse + until the graphic is the size you want. Then release the mouse button.

■ The graphic appears in the new size.

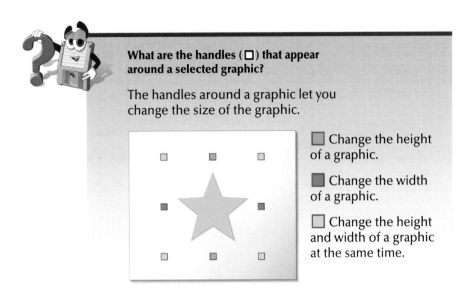

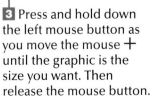

CHANGE COLOR OF GRAPHIC

CHANGE COLOR OF GRAPHIC

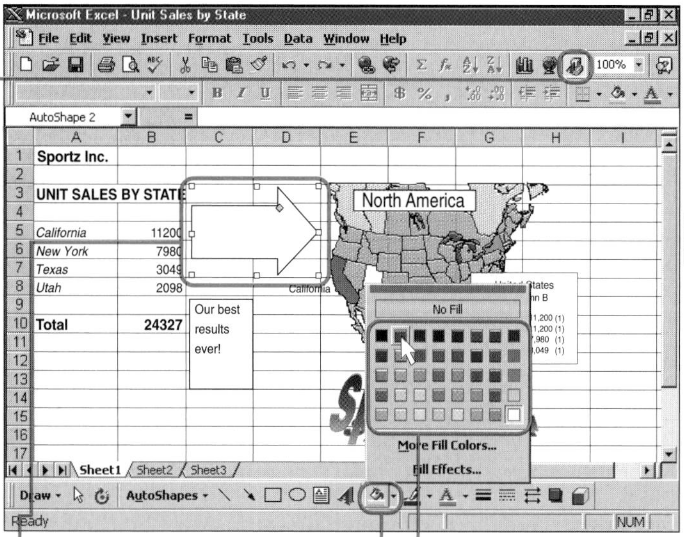

1 Move the mouse over the graphic you want to display a different color (changes to) and then press the left mouse button.

2 To display the **Drawing** toolbar, move the mouse over and then press the left mouse button.

3 Move the mouse over in this area and then press the left mouse button.

4 Move the mouse over the color you want to use and then press the left mouse button.

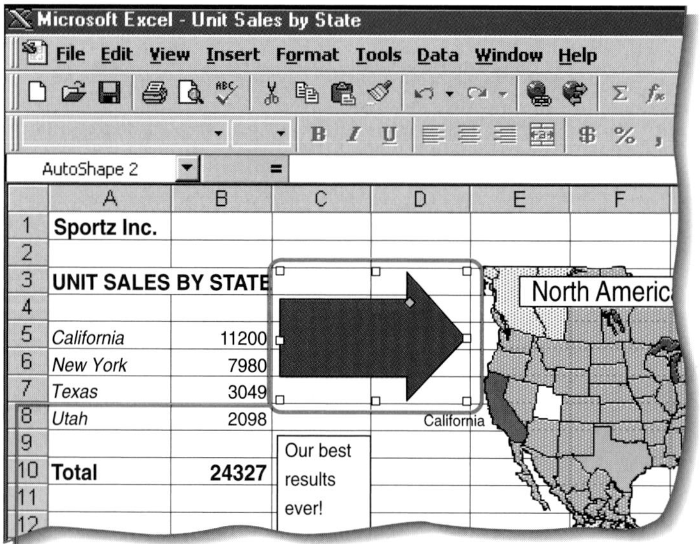

■ The graphic displays the color you selected.

■ To hide the **Drawing** toolbar, repeat step 2.

MAKE A GRAPHIC 3-D

MAKE A GRAPHIC 3-D

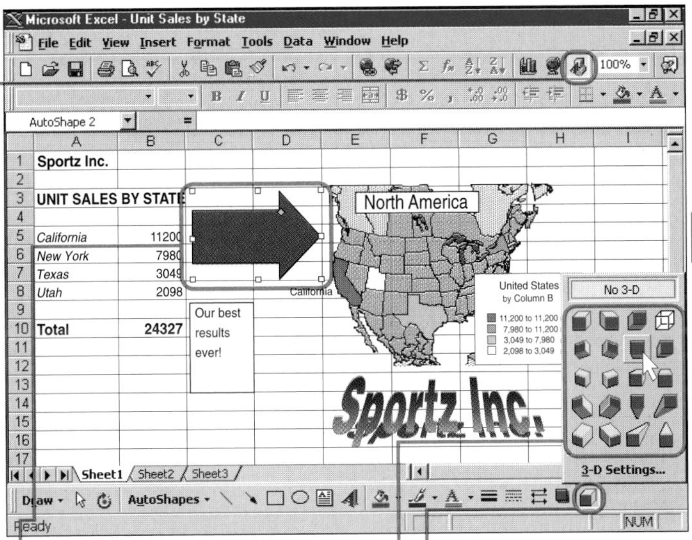

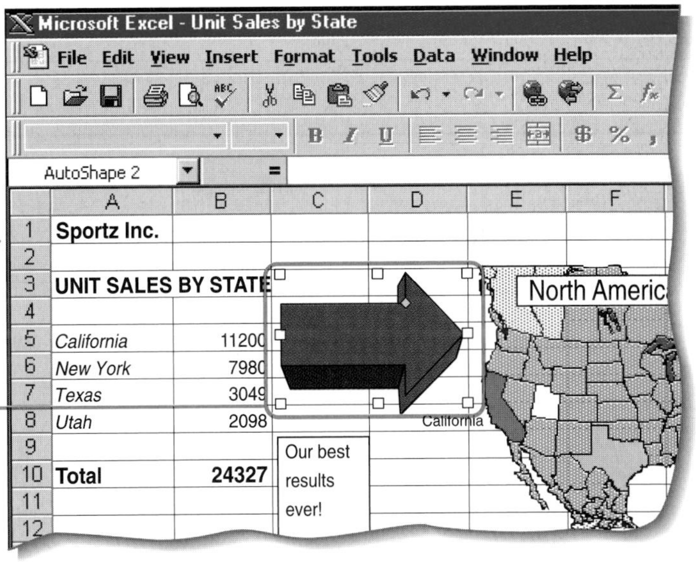

1 Move the mouse (✥) over the graphic you want to make 3-D (✥ changes to ✥) and then press the left mouse button.

2 To display the **Drawing** toolbar, move the mouse (↖) over (Drawing button) and then press the left mouse button.

3 Move the mouse (↖) over (3-D button) and then press the left mouse button.

4 Move the mouse (↖) over the 3-D effect you want to use and then press the left mouse button.

■ The graphic appears in 3-D.

■ To hide the **Drawing** toolbar, repeat step 2.

Maxine Maran
Richard Maran
Rob Maran
Ruth Maran
Judy Maran
Kelleigh Wing
Christie Van Duin
Tamara Poliquin
Chris K.C. Leung
Brad Hilderley
Russ Marini
Frank Ferreira
Alison MacAlpine
Paul Whitehead
Jamie Bell
Ben Lee
Wanda Lawrie
Jill Maran
Sherry Maran
Jeff Jones

CHAPTER 11

MANAGE DATA IN A LIST

Would you like Excel to help you organize and analyze a large collection of data? In this chapter you will learn how to sort data in a list, add subtotals to a list and more.

INTRODUCTION TO LISTS

Excel provides powerful tools for organizing and analyzing a large collection of data.

COMMON LISTS

Common lists include mailing lists, phone directories, product lists, library book catalogs, music collections and wine lists.

PARTS OF A LIST

Column Labels

The first row in a list contains column labels. Column labels describe the data in each column.

Records

Each row in a list contains one record. A record is a group of related data.

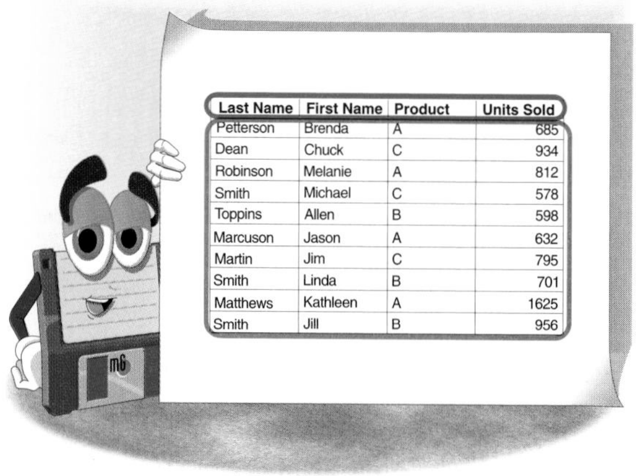

Last Name	First Name	Product	Units Sold
Petterson	Brenda	A	685
Dean	Chuck	C	934
Robinson	Melanie	A	812
Smith	Michael	C	578
Toppins	Allen	B	598
Marcuson	Jason	A	632
Martin	Jim	C	795
Smith	Linda	B	701
Matthews	Kathleen	A	1625
Smith	Jill	B	956

CREATE A LIST

CREATE A LIST

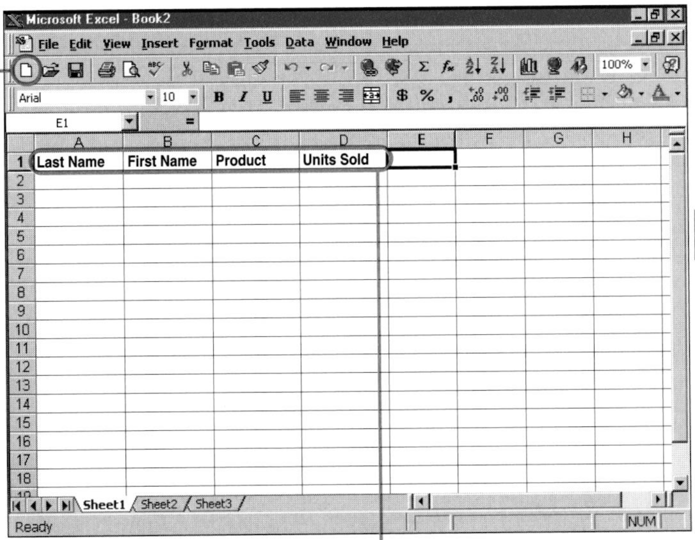

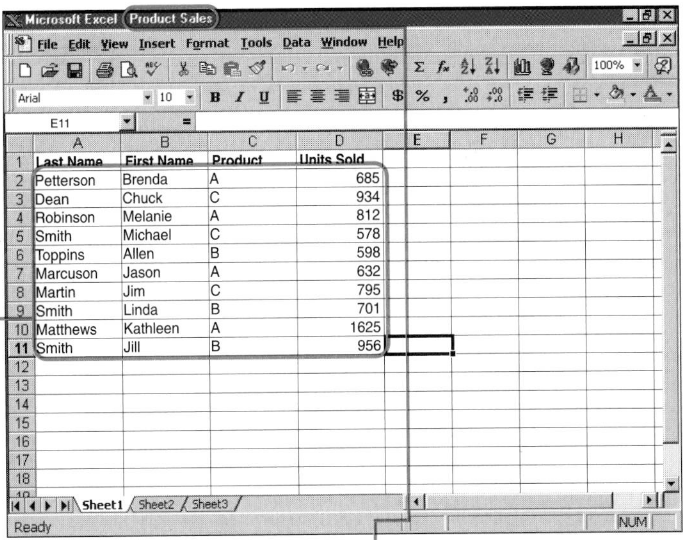

1 To create a new workbook for your list, move the mouse over ▢ and then press the left mouse button.

2 Type the column labels that describe the data you will enter into each column.

Note: To bold the column labels, refer to page 92. To change the width of the columns, refer to page 90.

3 Type the information for each record. Do not leave any blank rows in your list.

4 Save your workbook. To save a workbook, refer to page 24.

SORT DATA IN A LIST

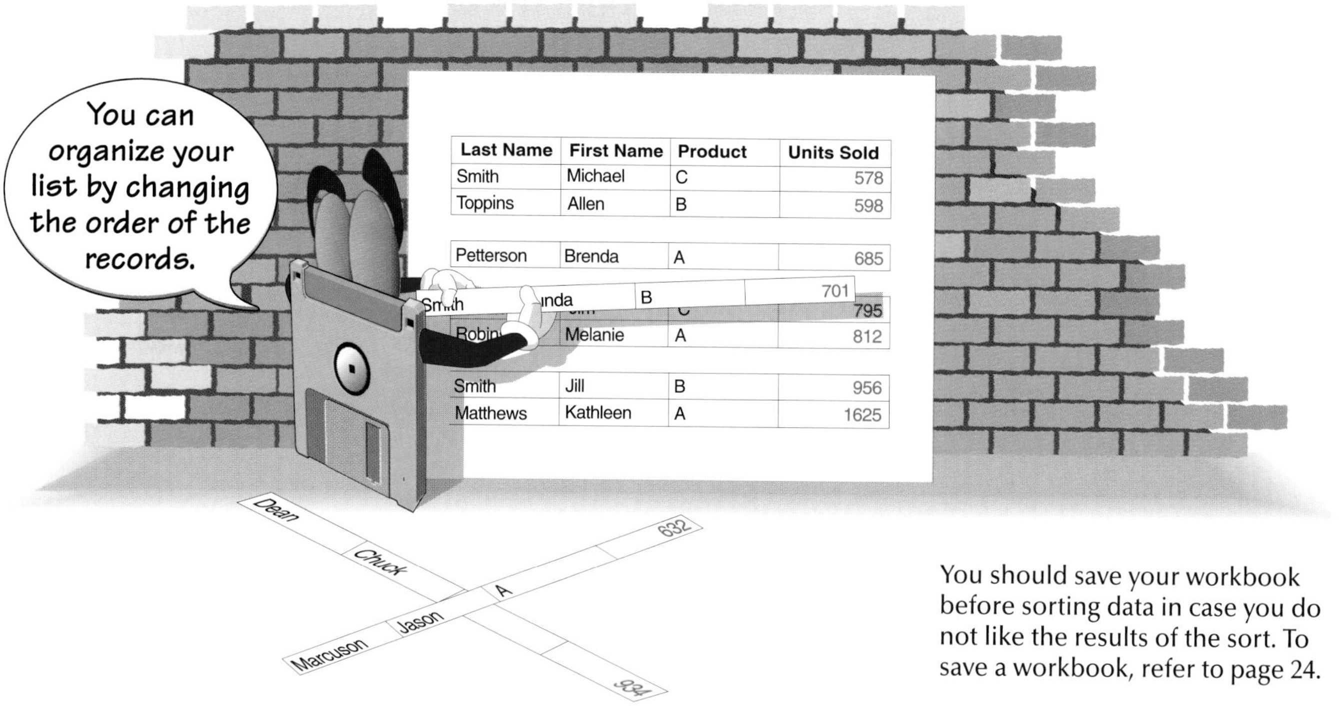

You can organize your list by changing the order of the records.
Last Name | First Name | Product | Units Sold
Smith | Michael | C | 578
Toppins | Allen | B | 598
Petterson | Brenda | A | 685
Melanie | A | 812
Smith | Jill | B | 956
Matthews | Kathleen | A | 1625
Dean
Chuck
Marcuson
Jason
A
632
934

You should save your workbook before sorting data in case you do not like the results of the sort. To save a workbook, refer to page 24.

SORT DATA BY ONE COLUMN

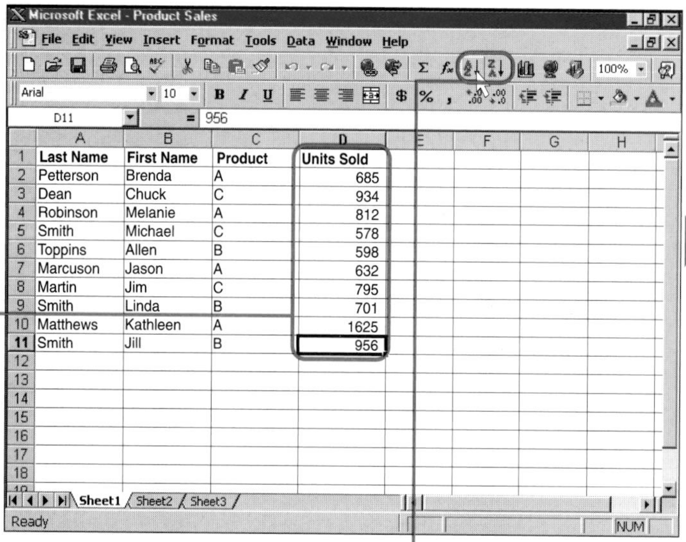

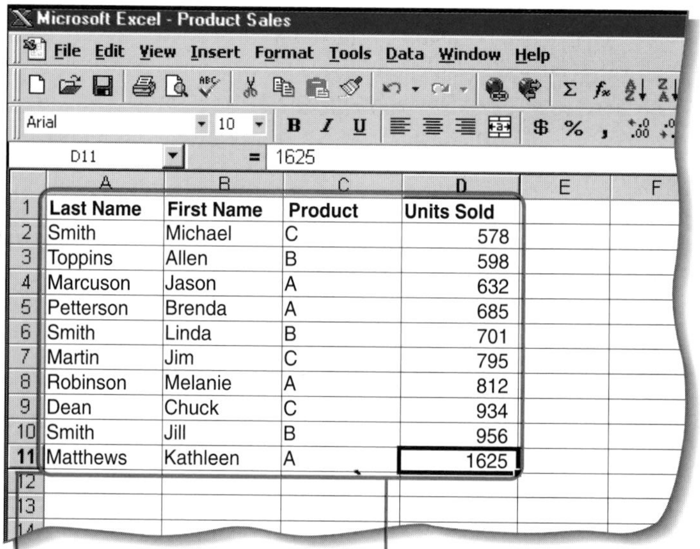

1 Move the mouse over any cell in the column you want to sort by and then press the left mouse button.

2 Move the mouse over the way you want to sort the data and then press the left mouse button.

Sort 0 to 9, A to Z

Sort 9 to 0, Z to A

■ The list appears in the new order.

■ In this example, the data is sorted by units sold.

	A	B
1	Last Name	First Name
2	Carter	Michael
3	Jones	Beatrice
4	Jones	Allan
5	Jones	Cathy
6	Thompson	Mary

■ In this example, the records are sorted alphabetically by last name.

	A	B
1	Last Name	First Name
2	Carter	Michael
3	Jones	Allan
4	Jones	Beatrice
5	Jones	Cathy
6	Thompson	Mary

■ If a last name appears more than once in your list, you can sort by a second column, such as first name.

SORT DATA BY TWO COLUMNS

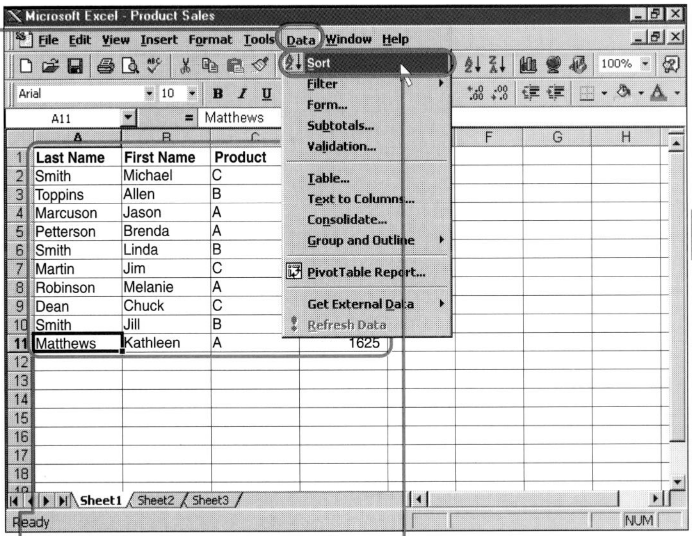

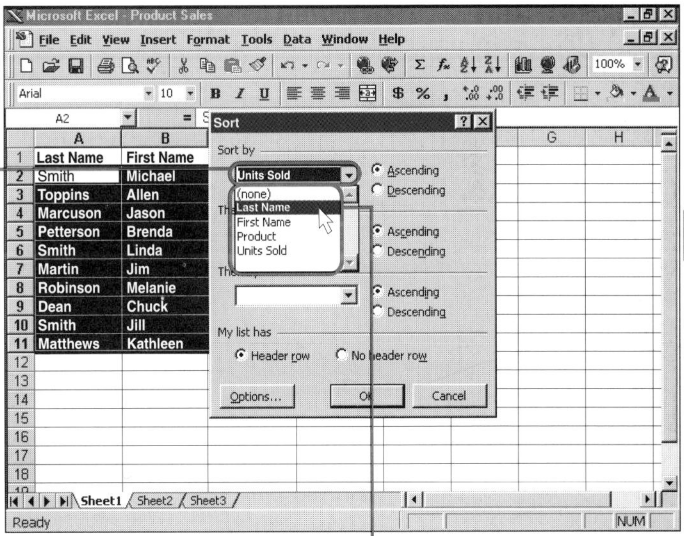

1 Move the mouse over any cell in your list and then press the left mouse button.

2 Move the mouse over **Data** and then press the left mouse button.

3 Move the mouse over **Sort** and then press the left mouse button.

■ The **Sort** dialog box appears.

4 To identify the first column you want to sort by, move the mouse over ▾ in this area and then press the left mouse button.

5 Move the mouse over the label for the first column you want to sort by and then press the left mouse button.

CONTINUED

SORT DATA IN A LIST

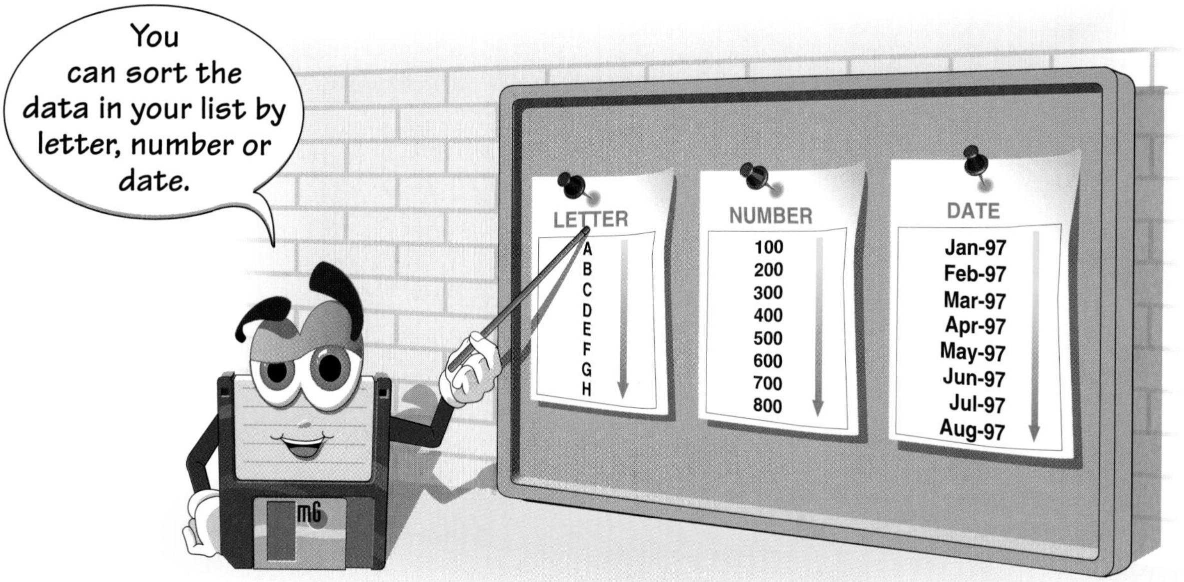

SORT DATA BY TWO COLUMNS (CONTINUED)

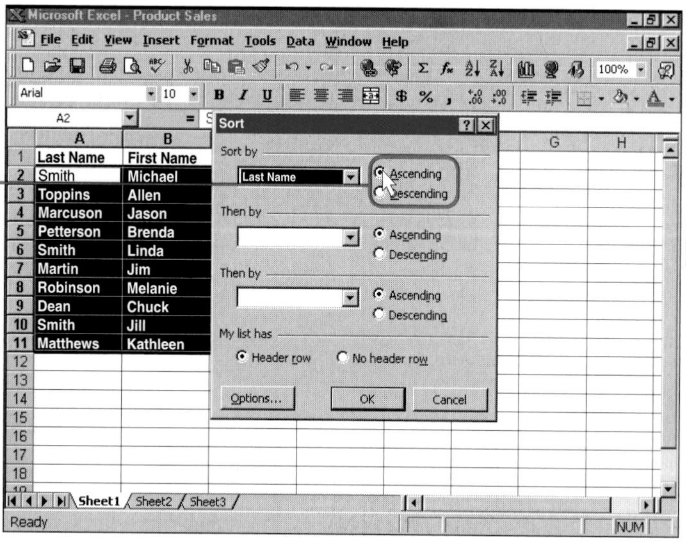

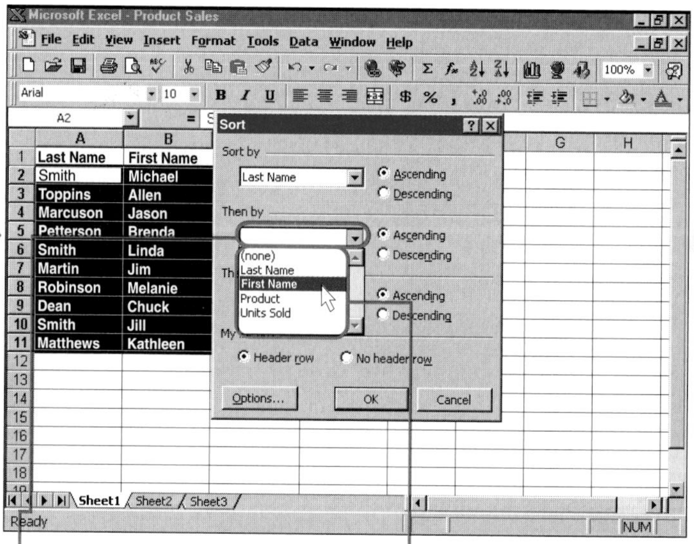

6 Move the mouse over the way you want to sort the first column and then press the left mouse button (○ changes to ◉).

Ascending
Sort 0 to 9, A to Z

Descending
Sort 9 to 0, Z to A

7 To identify the second column you want to sort by, move the mouse over ▼ in this area and then press the left mouse button.

8 Move the mouse over the label for the second column you want to sort by and then press the left mouse button.

How often can I sort my list?

You can sort your list as often as you like. This is ideal if you are constantly adding new records to the list.

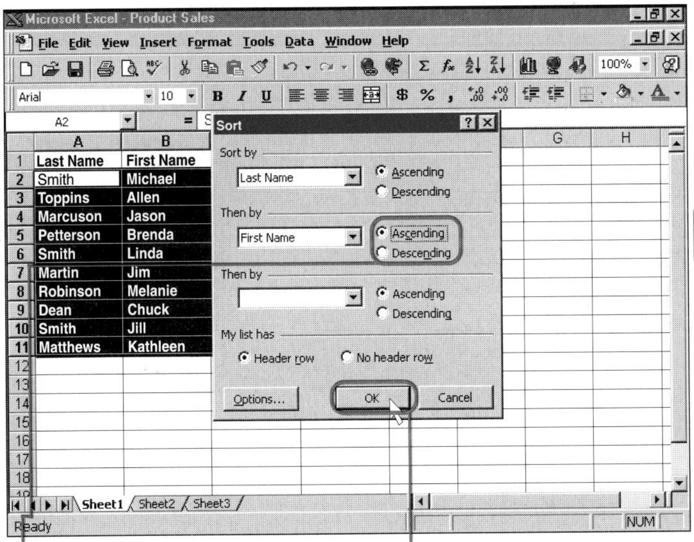

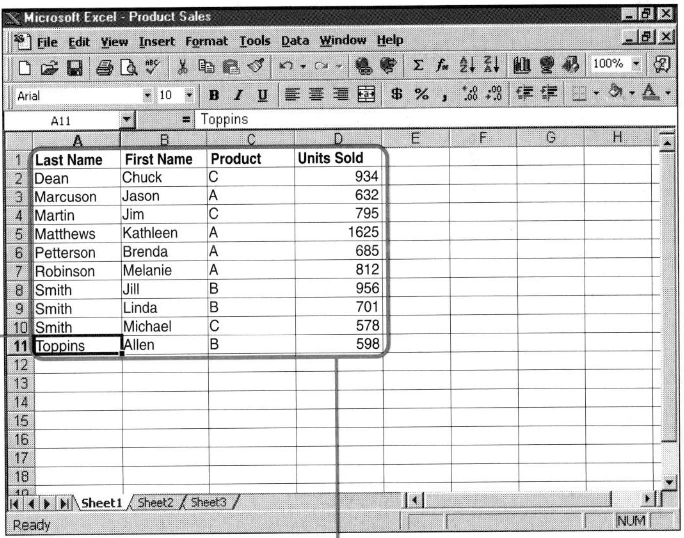

9 Move the mouse over the way you want to sort the second column and then press the left mouse button (○ changes to ◉).

10 To sort the data, move the mouse over **OK** and then press the left mouse button.

■ The list appears in the new order.

■ In this example, the data is sorted by last name. All records with the same last name are then sorted by first name.

FILTER DATA IN A LIST

FILTER DATA IN A LIST

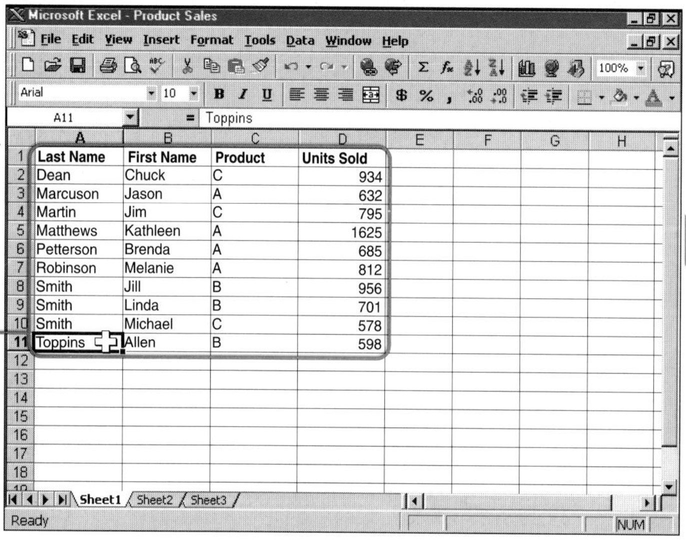

1 Move the mouse over any cell in your list and then press the left mouse button.

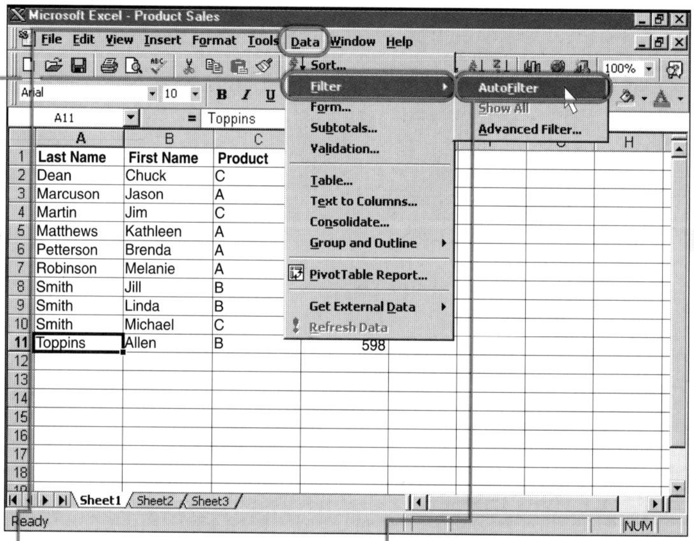

2 Move the mouse over **Data** and then press the left mouse button.

3 Move the mouse over **Filter**.

4 Move the mouse over **AutoFilter** and then press the left mouse button.

How does the AutoFilter feature help me analyze data?

The AutoFilter feature lets you easily analyze your data by placing related records together and hiding the records you do not want to review.

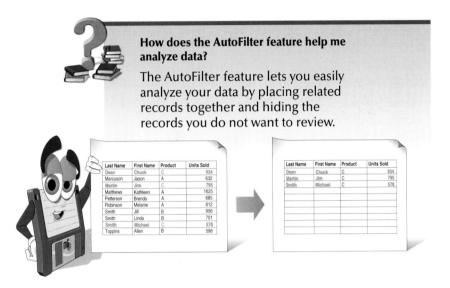

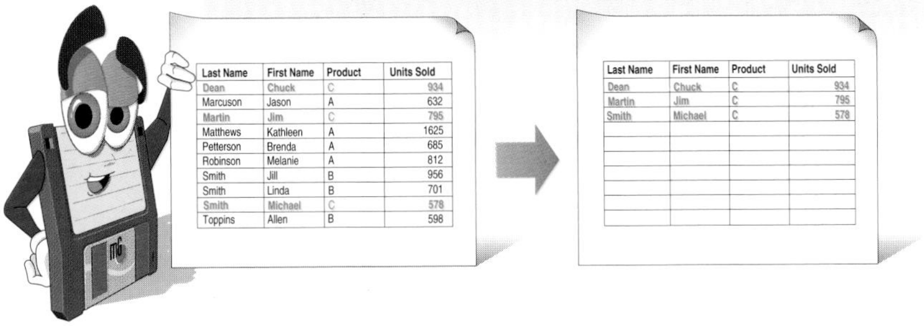

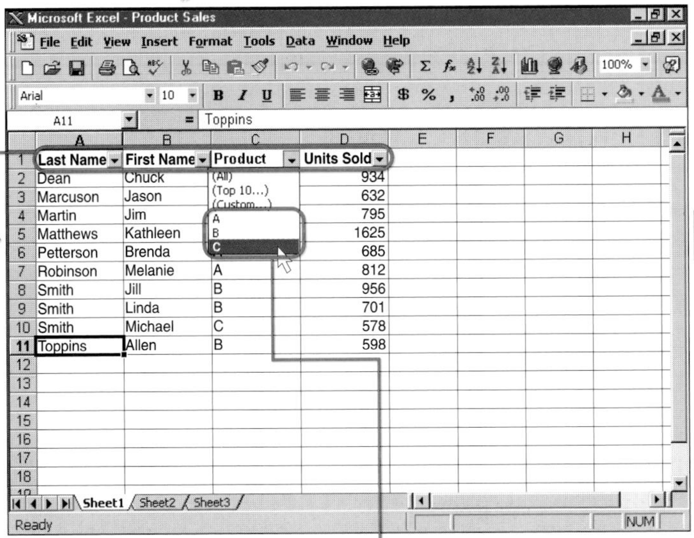

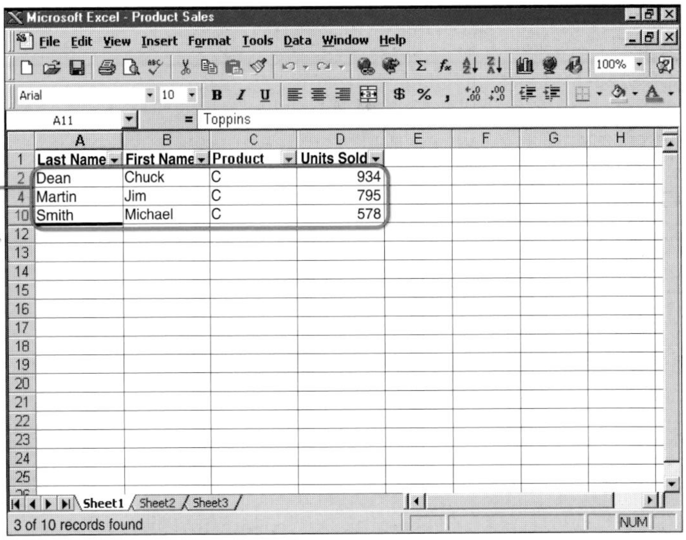

■ An arrow (▼) appears beside each column label.

5 Move the mouse over ▼ in the column containing the data you want to use to filter the list and then press the left mouse button.

6 Move the mouse over the data you want to use to filter the list and then press the left mouse button.

■ The list displays only the records containing the data you specified. The other records are temporarily hidden.

■ In this example, the list displays only the records containing product C.

■ To turn off the AutoFilter feature and redisplay the entire list, repeat steps **2** to **4**.

FILTER DATA IN A LIST

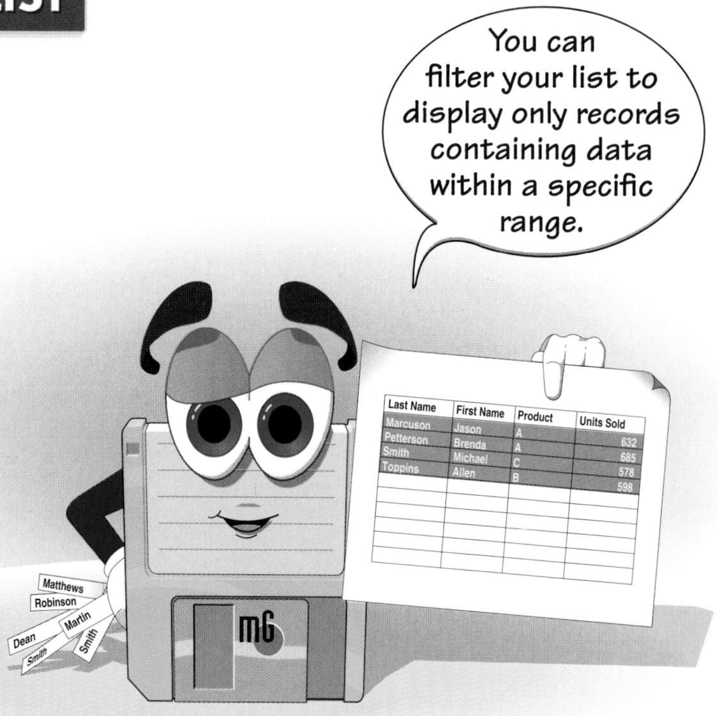

You can filter your list to display only records containing data within a specific range.

FILTER DATA—BY COMPARING VALUES

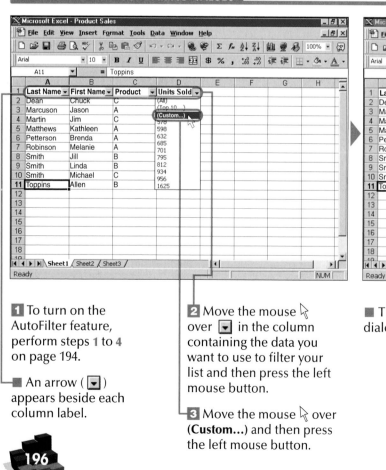

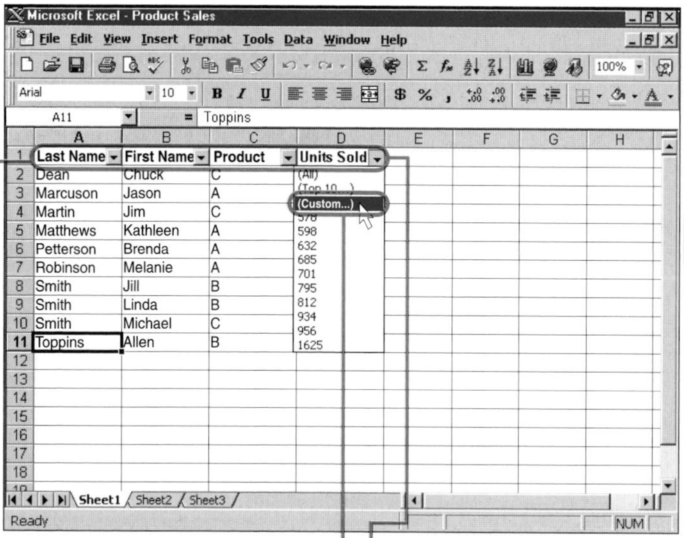

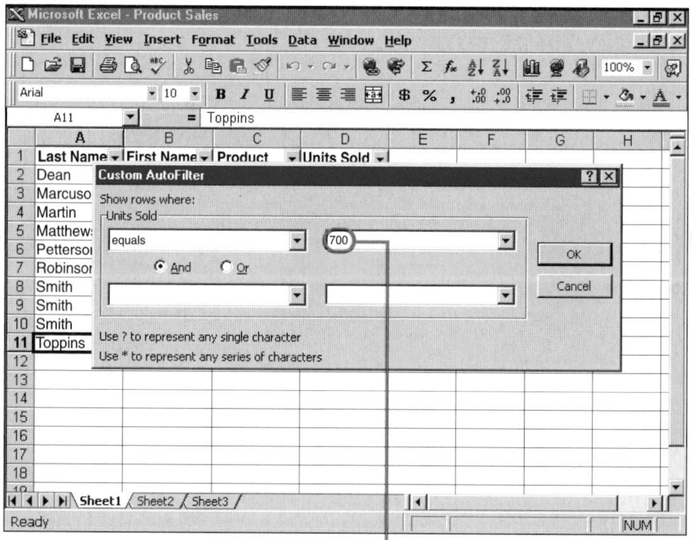

■1 To turn on the AutoFilter feature, perform steps 1 to 4 on page 194.

■ An arrow (▾) appears beside each column label.

■2 Move the mouse over ▾ in the column containing the data you want to use to filter your list and then press the left mouse button.

■3 Move the mouse over **(Custom...)** and then press the left mouse button.

■ The **Custom AutoFilter** dialog box appears.

■4 Type the data you want Excel to compare to each record in the list.

How can I compare data in my list?

Excel offers many ways you can compare data to help you analyze the information in your list.

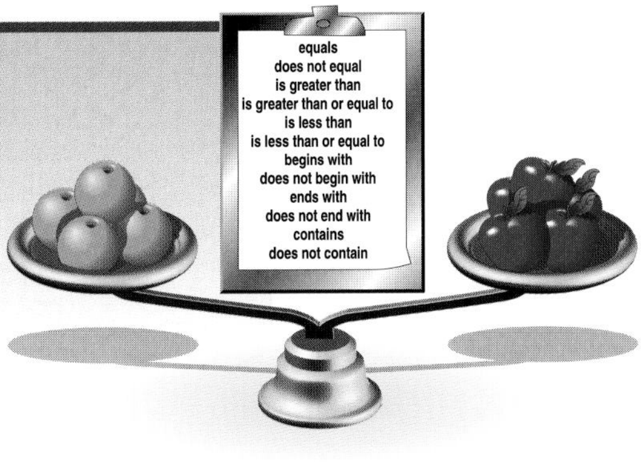

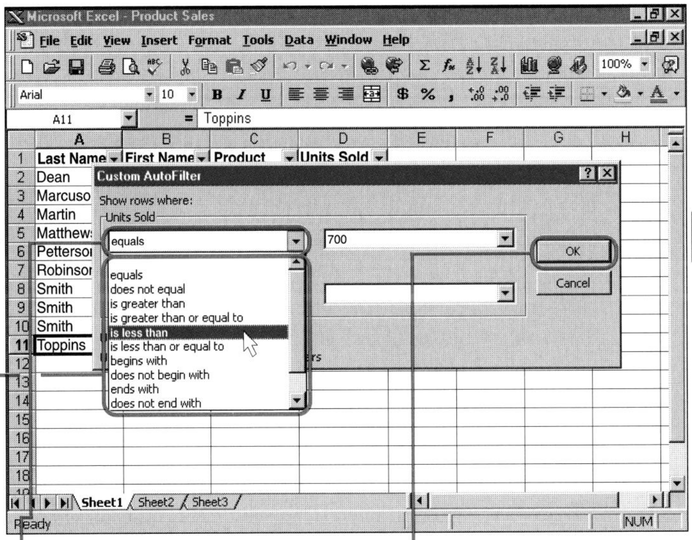

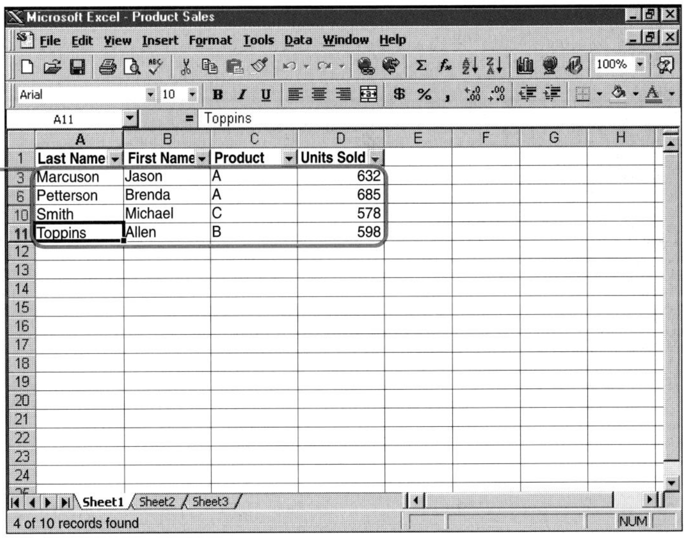

5 To select how you want Excel to compare the data, move the mouse over this area and then press the left mouse button.

6 Move the mouse over the way you want Excel to compare the data and then press the left mouse button.

7 To filter the data, move the mouse over **OK** and then press the left mouse button.

■ The list displays only the records containing the data you specified. The other records are temporarily hidden.

■ In this example, the list displays only the records containing less than 700 units sold.

■ To turn off the AutoFilter feature and redisplay the entire list, perform steps 2 to 4 on page 194.

ADD SUBTOTALS TO A LIST

You can quickly summarize data by adding subtotals to your list.

ADD SUBTOTALS TO A LIST

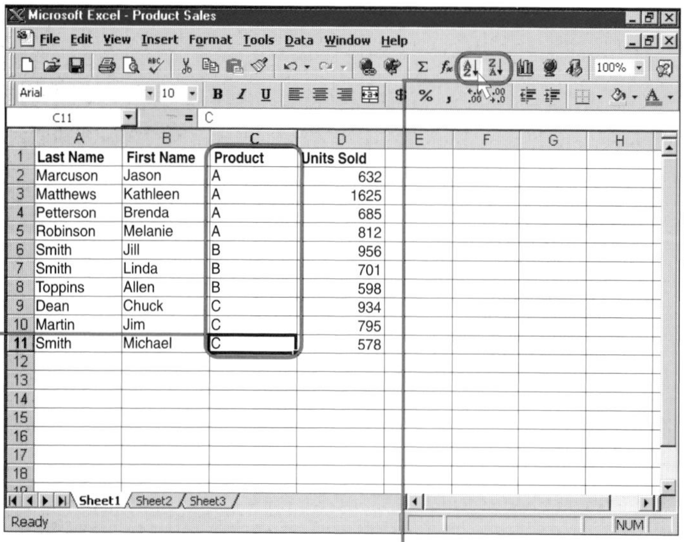

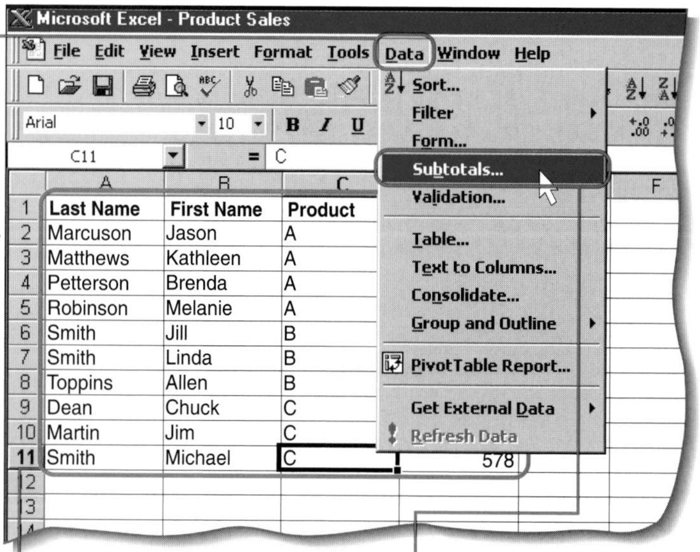

1 To sort the column you want to display subtotals for, move the mouse over any cell in the column and then press the left mouse button.

2 Move the mouse over the way you want to sort the data and then press the left mouse button.

- Sort 0 to 9, A to Z
- Sort 9 to 0, Z to A

3 Move the mouse over any cell in your list and then press the left mouse button.

4 Move the mouse over **Data** and then press the left mouse button.

5 Move the mouse over **Subtotals** and then press the left mouse button.

How can subtotals help me?

You can use subtotals to help you analyze the data in your list and quickly create reports and charts to summarize the data.

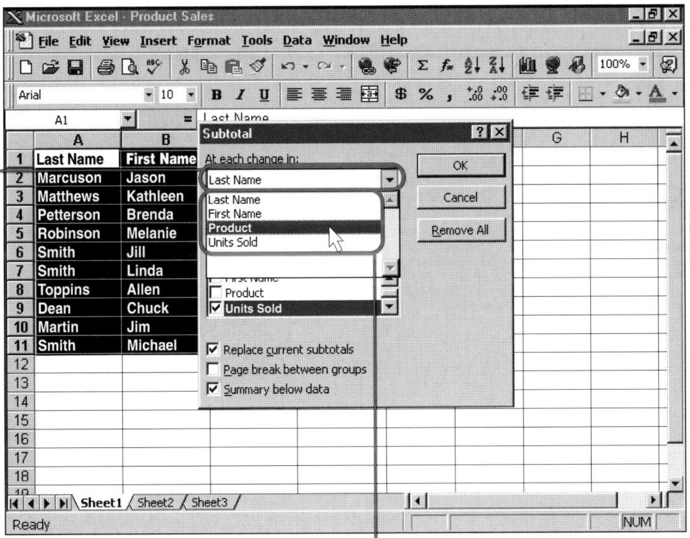

■ The **Subtotal** dialog box appears.

6 To identify the column you want to display subtotals for, move the mouse over this area and then press the left mouse button.

7 Move the mouse over the label of the column and then press the left mouse button.

*Note: The column you identify should be the same column you sorted in step **1**.*

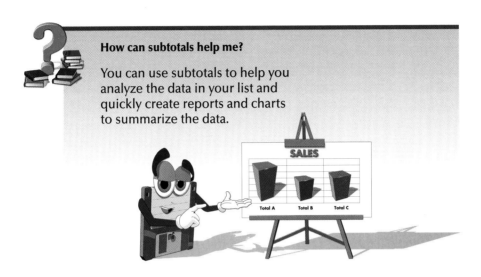

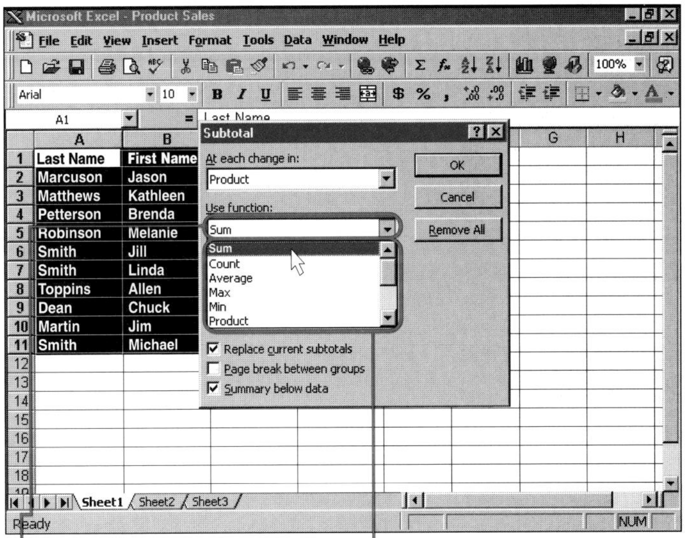

8 To select the calculation you want to perform, move the mouse over this area and then press the left mouse button.

9 Move the mouse over the calculation and then press the left mouse button.

CONTINUED

ADD SUBTOTALS TO A LIST

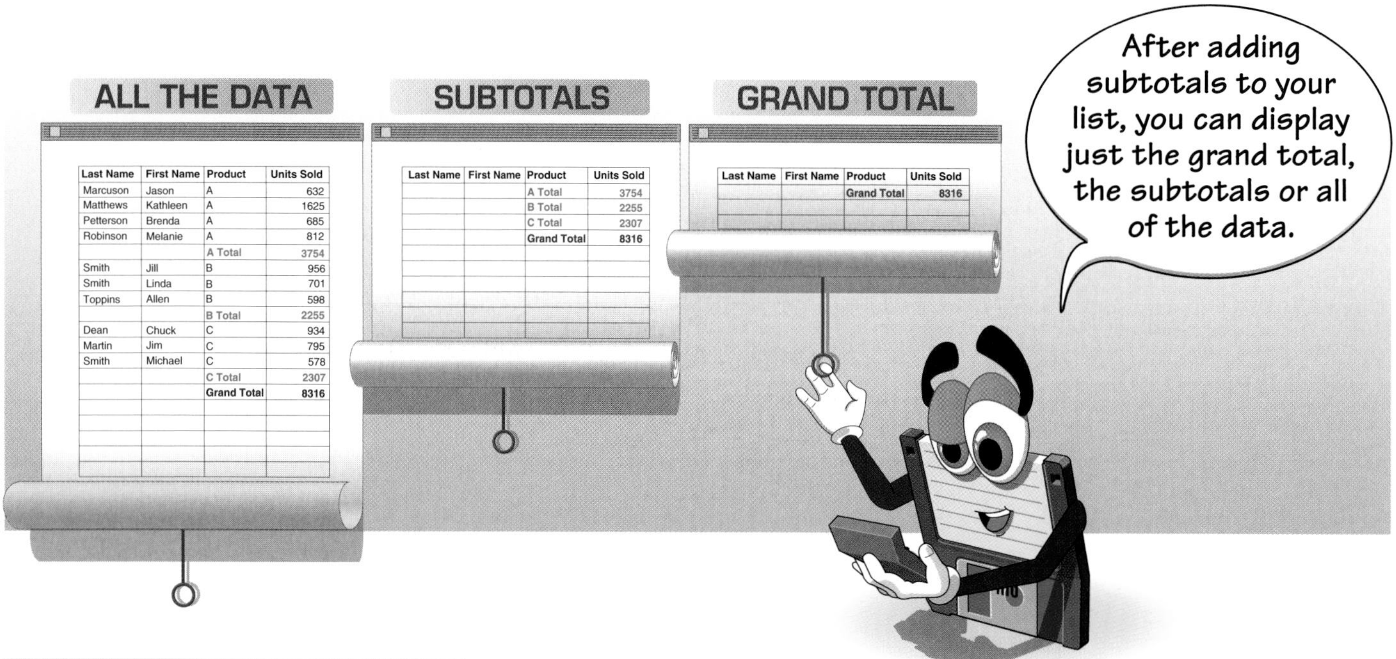

ALL THE DATA
SUBTOTALS
GRAND TOTAL
Last Name First Name Product Units Sold
Marcuson Jason A 632
Matthews Kathleen A 1625
Petterson Brenda A 685
Robinson Melanie A 812
A Total 3754
Smith Jill B 956
Smith Linda B 701
Toppins Allen B 598
B Total 2255
Dean Chuck C 934
Martin Jim C 795
Smith Michael C 578
C Total 2307
Grand Total 8316
After adding subtotals to your list, you can display just the grand total, the subtotals or all of the data.

ADD SUBTOTALS TO A LIST (CONTINUED)

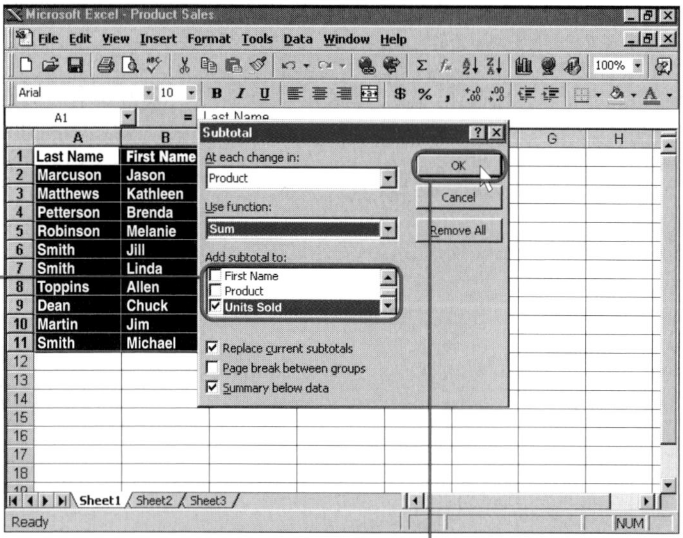

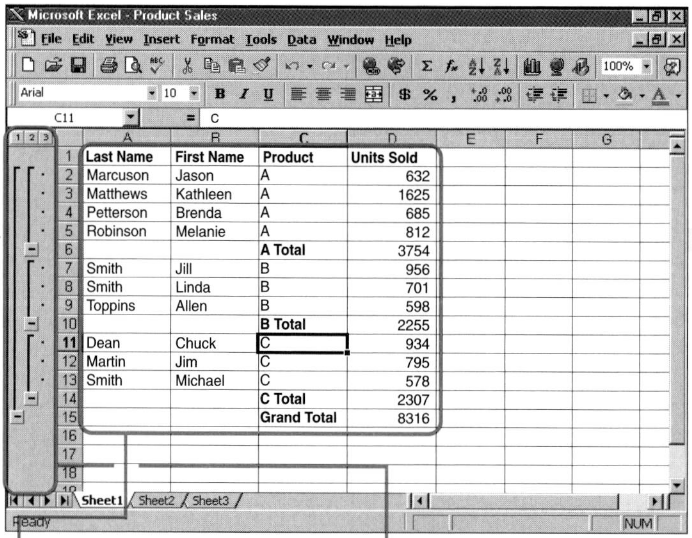

Microsoft Excel - Product Sales
Last Name First Name Product Units Sold
Marcuson Jason A 632
Matthews Kathleen A 1625
Petterson Brenda A 685
Robinson Melanie A 812
A Total 3754
Smith Jill B 956
Smith Linda B 701
Toppins Allen B 598
B Total 2255
Dean Chuck C 934
Martin Jim C 795
Smith Michael C 578
C Total 2307
Grand Total 8316

■ This area displays a check mark (✓) beside the column that Excel will subtotal.

10 To add or remove a check mark, move the mouse over the box beside the column and then press the left mouse button.

11 To add the subtotals to your list, move the mouse over **OK** and then press the left mouse button.

■ The list displays the subtotals and a grand total.

■ These symbols help you work with the data.

How do I remove subtotals from my list?

1 To remove subtotals from your list, perform steps 3 to 5 on page 198.

2 Move the mouse over **Remove All** and then press the left mouse button.

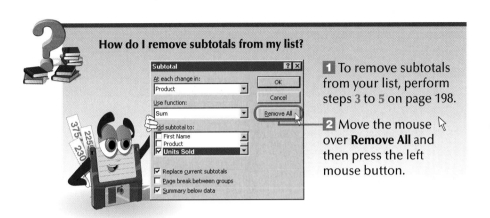

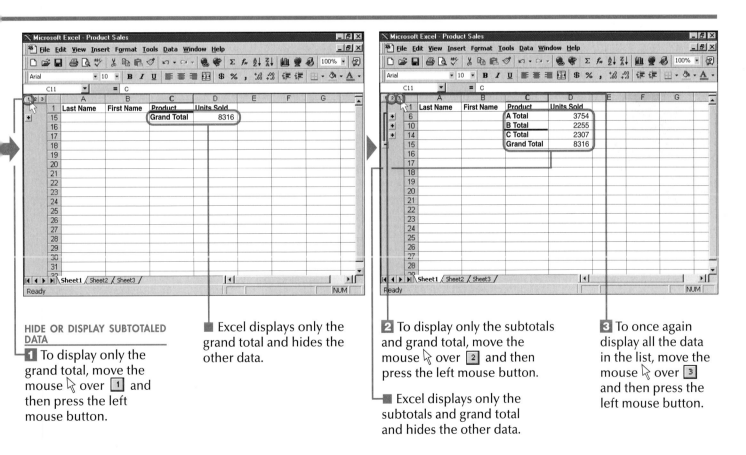

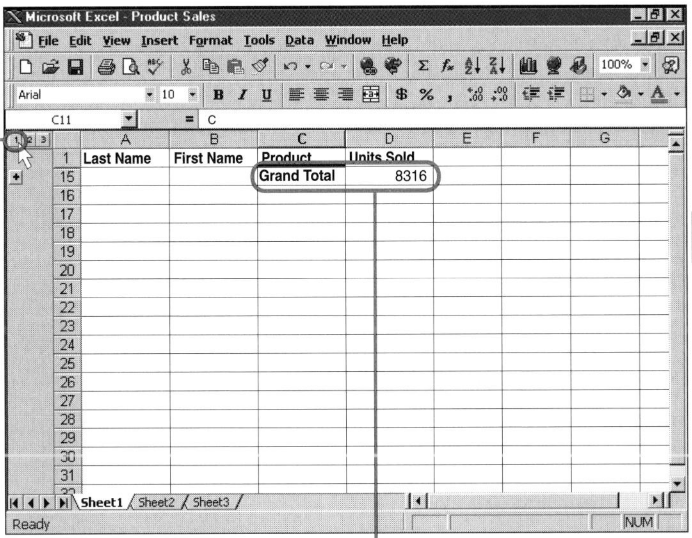

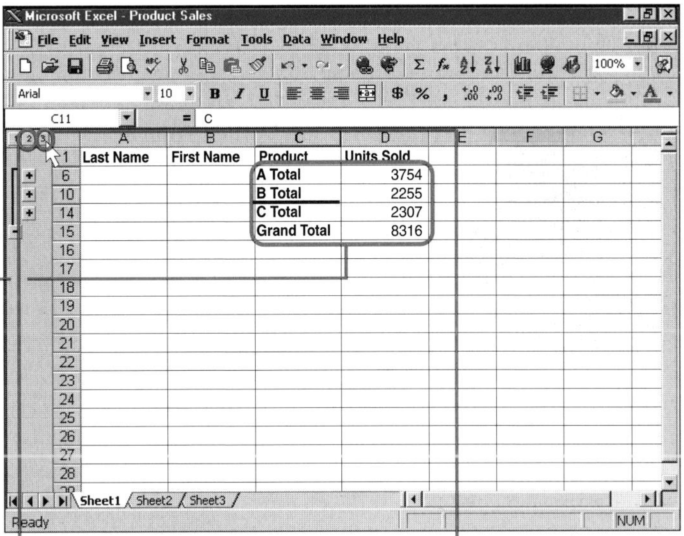

HIDE OR DISPLAY SUBTOTALED DATA

1 To display only the grand total, move the mouse over 1 and then press the left mouse button.

■ Excel displays only the grand total and hides the other data.

2 To display only the subtotals and grand total, move the mouse over 2 and then press the left mouse button.

■ Excel displays only the subtotals and grand total and hides the other data.

3 To once again display all the data in the list, move the mouse over 3 and then press the left mouse button.

maranGraphics - Microsoft Internet Explorer
File Edit View Go Favorites Help
Back
Forward
Stop
Refresh
Home
Search
Favori...
Print
Font
Mail
Edit
Links
Address http://www.maran.com/
maranGraphics™
COMPUTER BOOKS
SERVICES
Windows 95 Simplified
OUR COMPANY

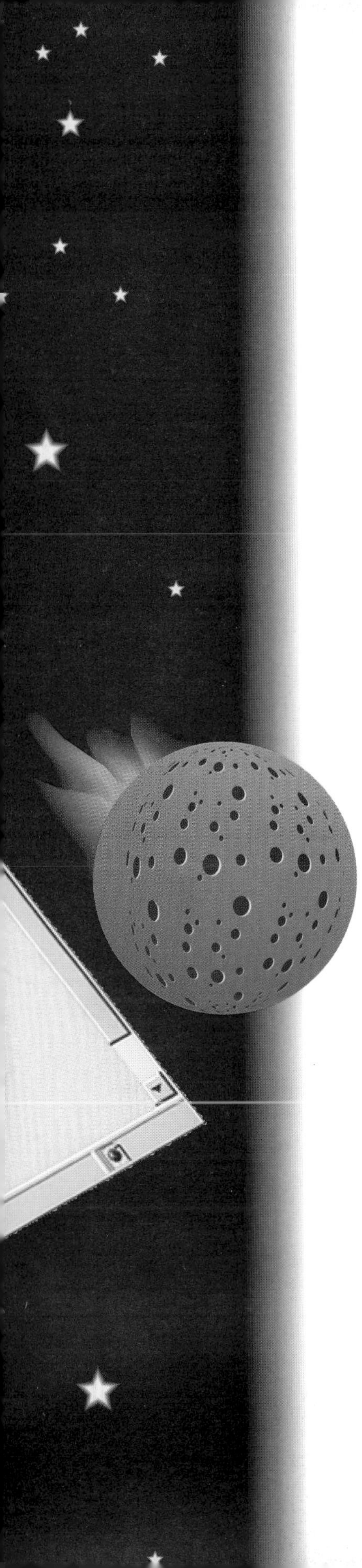

CHAPTER 12

EXCEL AND THE INTERNET

Do you want to make your worksheet available on your company's intranet or the Web? Find out how in this chapter.

CREATE A HYPERLINK

CREATE A HYPERLINK

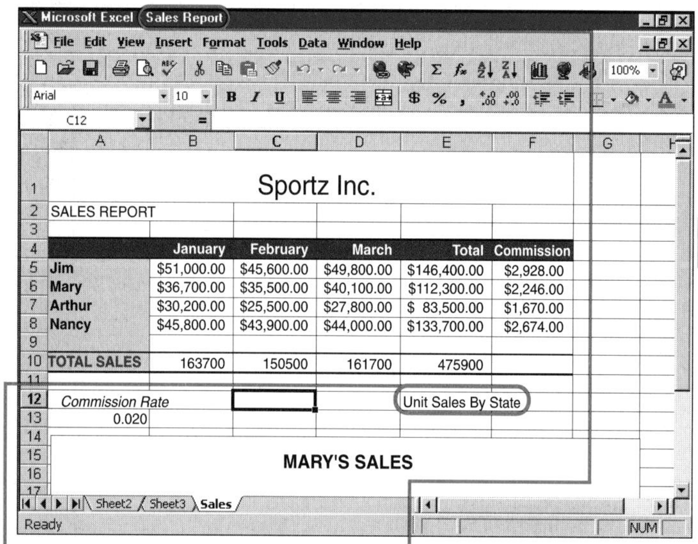

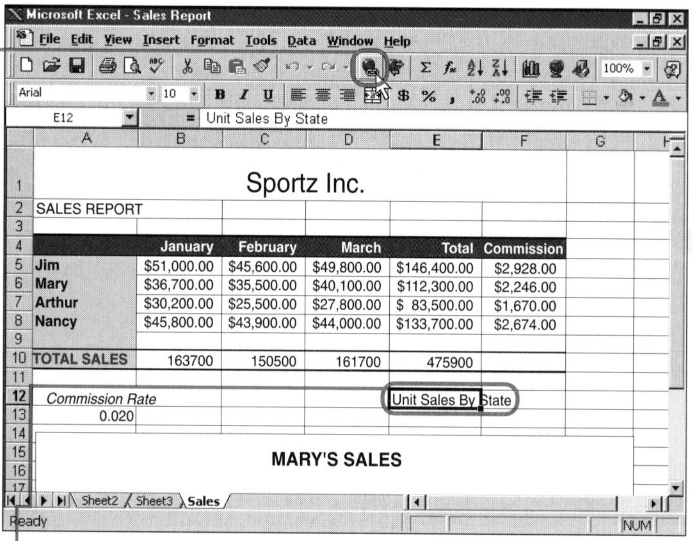

1 Enter the information you want to link to another document.

2 Save your workbook. To save a workbook, refer to page 24.

3 Select the cell(s) containing the information you entered in step **1**. To select cells, refer to page 16.

4 Move the mouse over the hyperlink button and then press the left mouse button.

■ The **Insert Hyperlink** dialog box appears.

Where can a hyperlink take me?

You can create a hyperlink that takes you to another document on your computer, network, corporate intranet or the Internet.

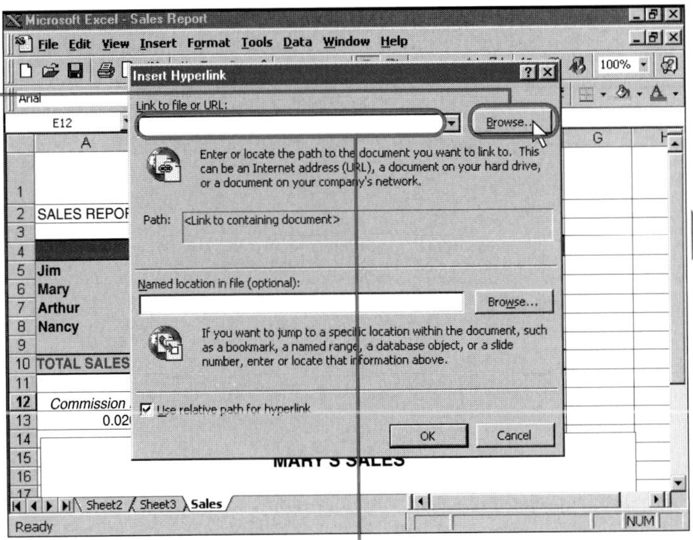

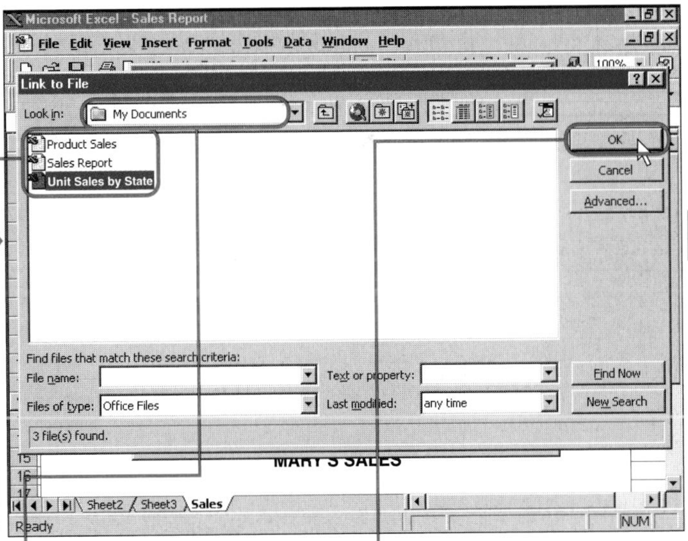

5 To link the information to a document on your computer or network, move the mouse over **Browse** and then press the left mouse button.

■ To link the information to a Web page, type the address of the Web page (example: http://www.maran.com). Then skip to step **8** on page 206.

■ The **Link to File** dialog box appears.

■ This area indicates where the documents listed in the dialog box are located.

6 Move the mouse over the document you want the information to link to and then press the left mouse button.

7 Move the mouse over **OK** and then press the left mouse button.

CONTINUED

CREATE A HYPERLINK

CREATE A HYPERLINK (CONTINUED)

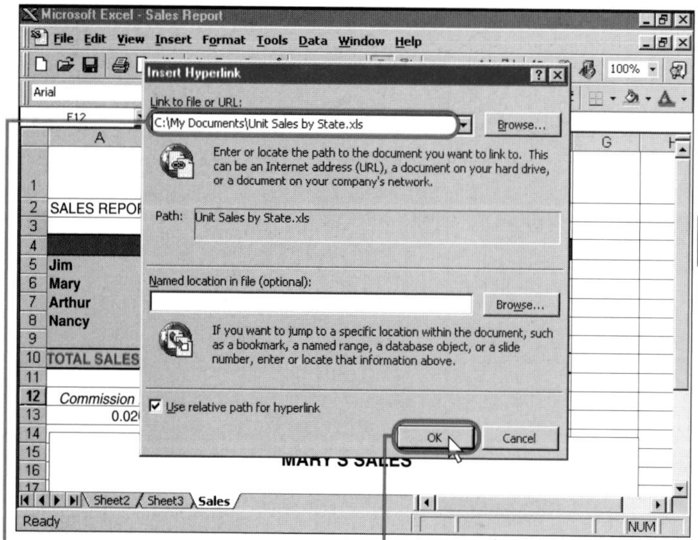

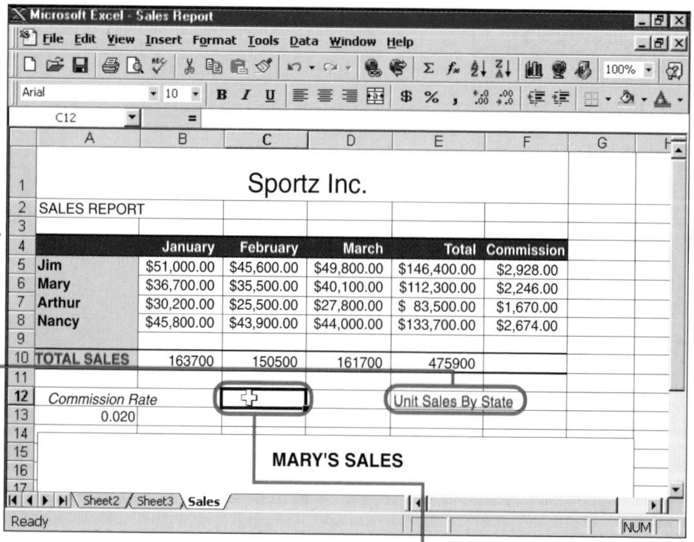

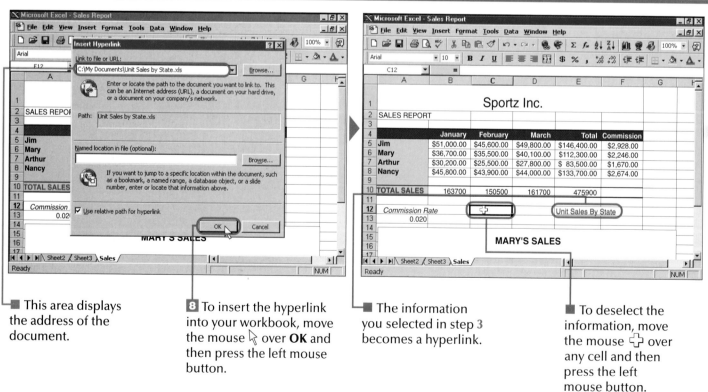

■ This area displays the address of the document.

8 To insert the hyperlink into your workbook, move the mouse ↖ over **OK** and then press the left mouse button.

■ The information you selected in step 3 becomes a hyperlink.

■ To deselect the information, move the mouse ✚ over any cell and then press the left mouse button.

What information can I use as a hyperlink?

You can use any information in a workbook as a hyperlink, including worksheet data, charts and maps. Make sure the information you choose clearly indicates where the hyperlink will take you. Avoid the phrase "click here" since this is not very informative.

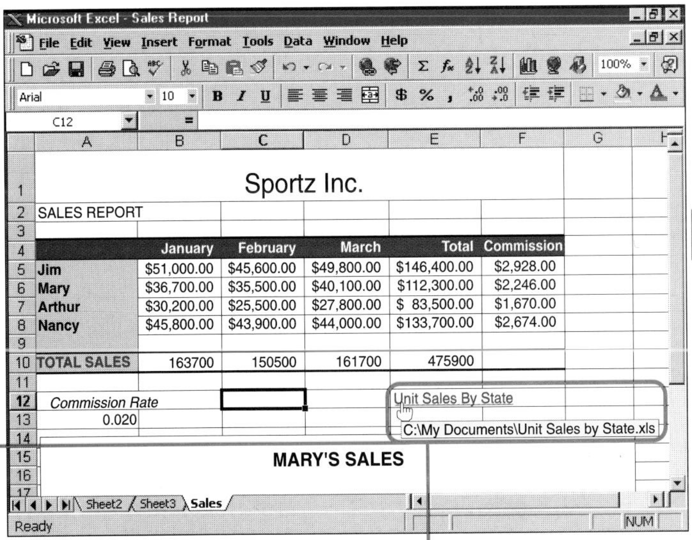

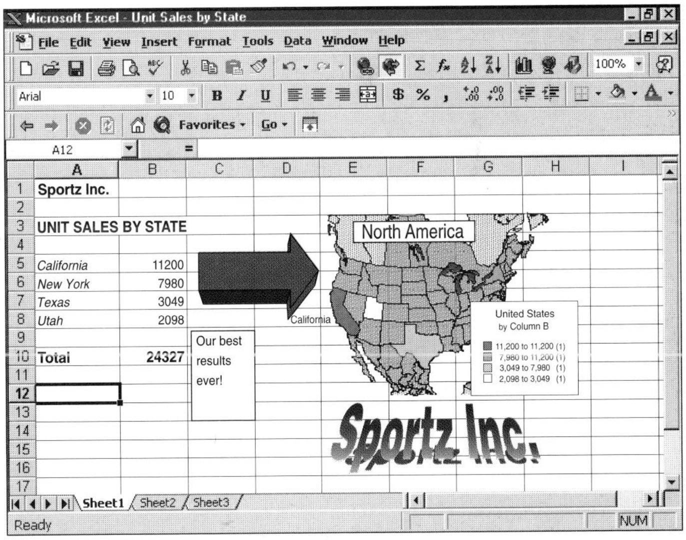

SELECT A HYPERLINK

1 To display the destination address of a hyperlink, move the mouse ✥ over the hyperlink (✥ changes to ☝). After a few seconds, the address appears.

2 To select a hyperlink, move the mouse ✥ over the hyperlink (✥ changes to ☝) and then press the left mouse button.

■ The document connected to the hyperlink appears.

■ If the hyperlink is connected to a Web page, your Web browser opens and displays the Web page.

DISPLAY THE WEB TOOLBAR

DISPLAY THE WEB TOOLBAR

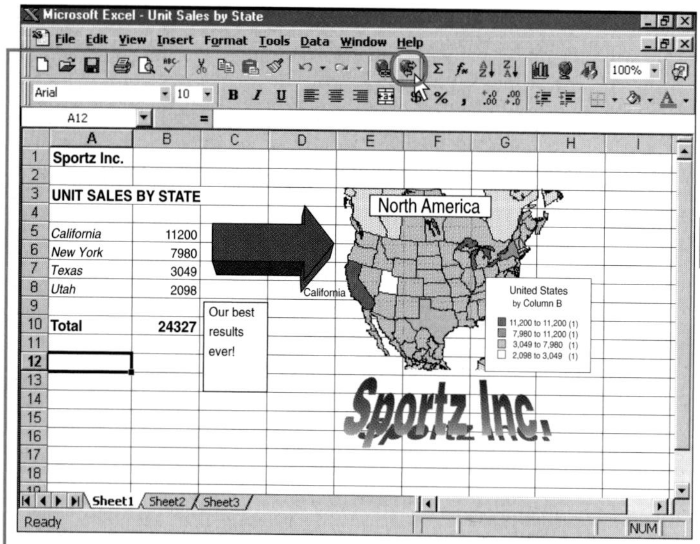

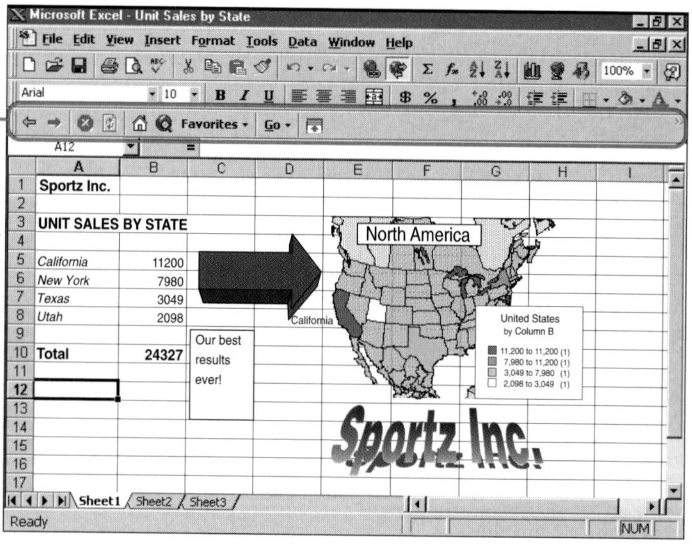

1 To display the **Web** toolbar, move the mouse over and then press the left mouse button.

■ The **Web** toolbar appears.

■ To hide the **Web** toolbar, repeat step **1**.

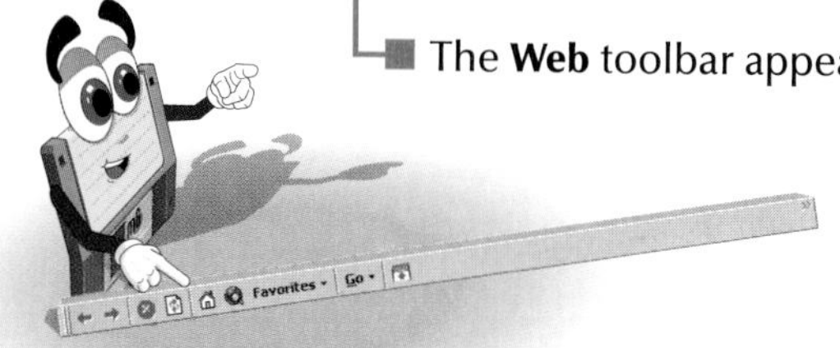

MOVE BETWEEN DOCUMENTS

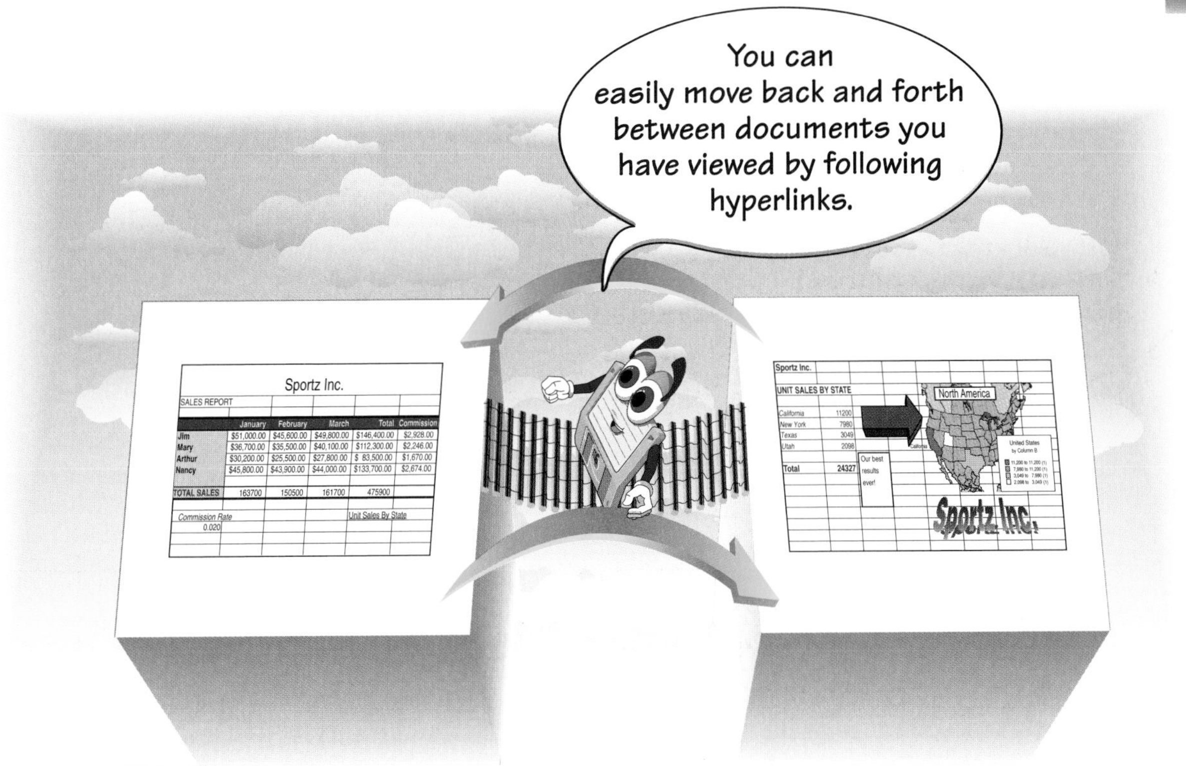

You can easily move back and forth between documents you have viewed by following hyperlinks.

MOVE BETWEEN DOCUMENTS

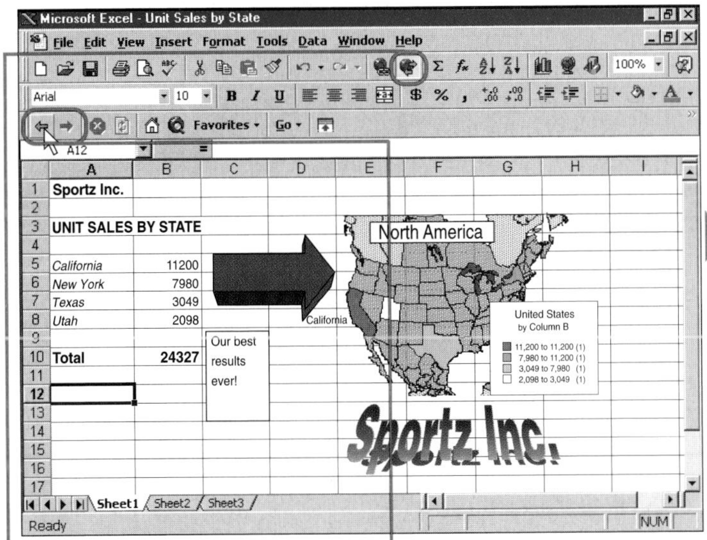

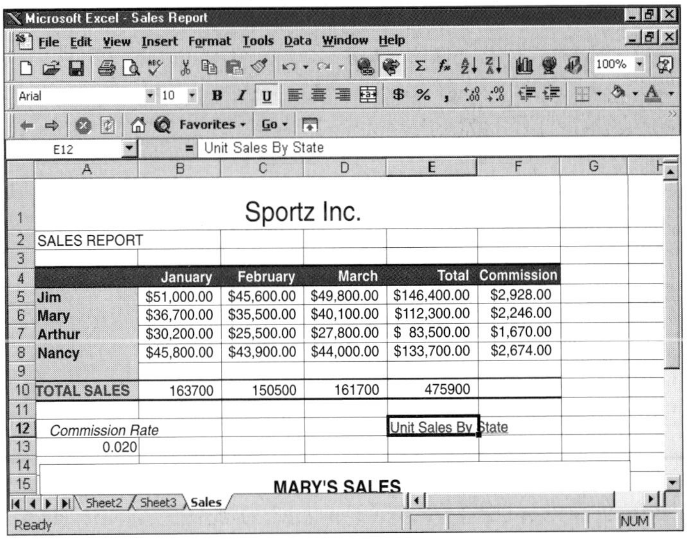

1 To display the **Web** toolbar, move the mouse over and then press the left mouse button.

2 Move the mouse over one of the following options and then press the left mouse button.

Move back

Move forward

■ The document you selected appears.

■ To hide the **Web** toolbar, repeat step **1**.

OPEN A DOCUMENT

You can quickly open a document that is on your computer, network, corporate intranet or the Internet.

OPEN A DOCUMENT

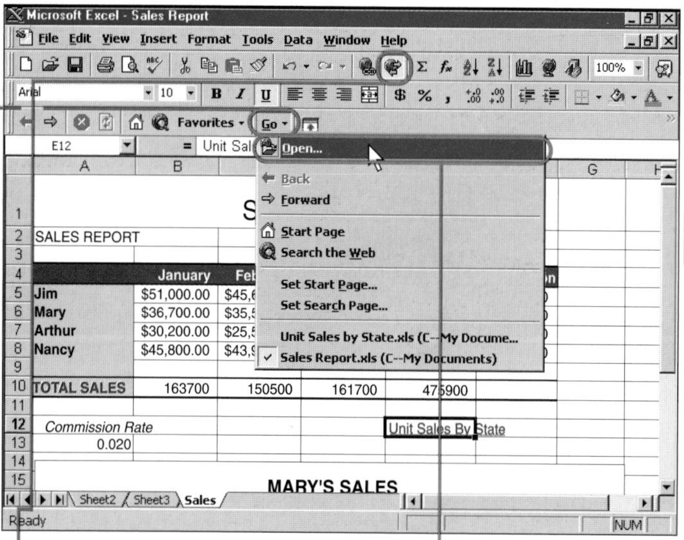

1 To display the **Web** toolbar, move the mouse over [Web toolbar button] and then press the left mouse button.

2 To open a document, move the mouse over **Go** and then press the left mouse button.

3 Move the mouse over **Open** and then press the left mouse button.

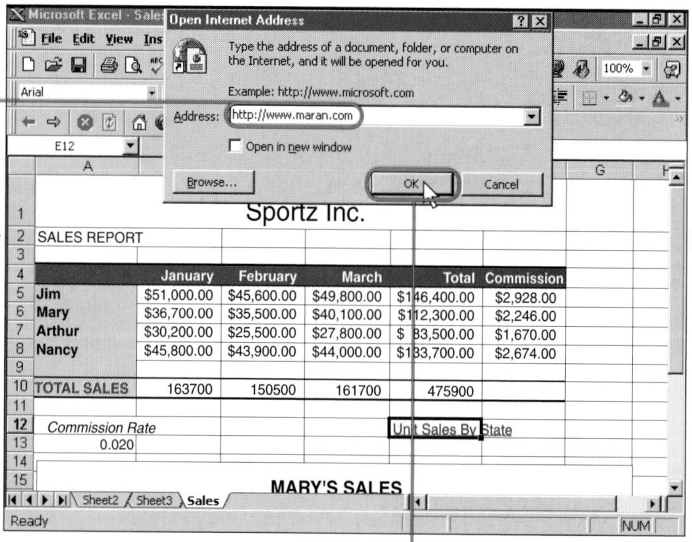

■ The **Open Internet Address** dialog box appears.

4 Type the address of the document you want to open.

5 Move the mouse over **OK** and then press the left mouse button.

STOP THE CONNECTION

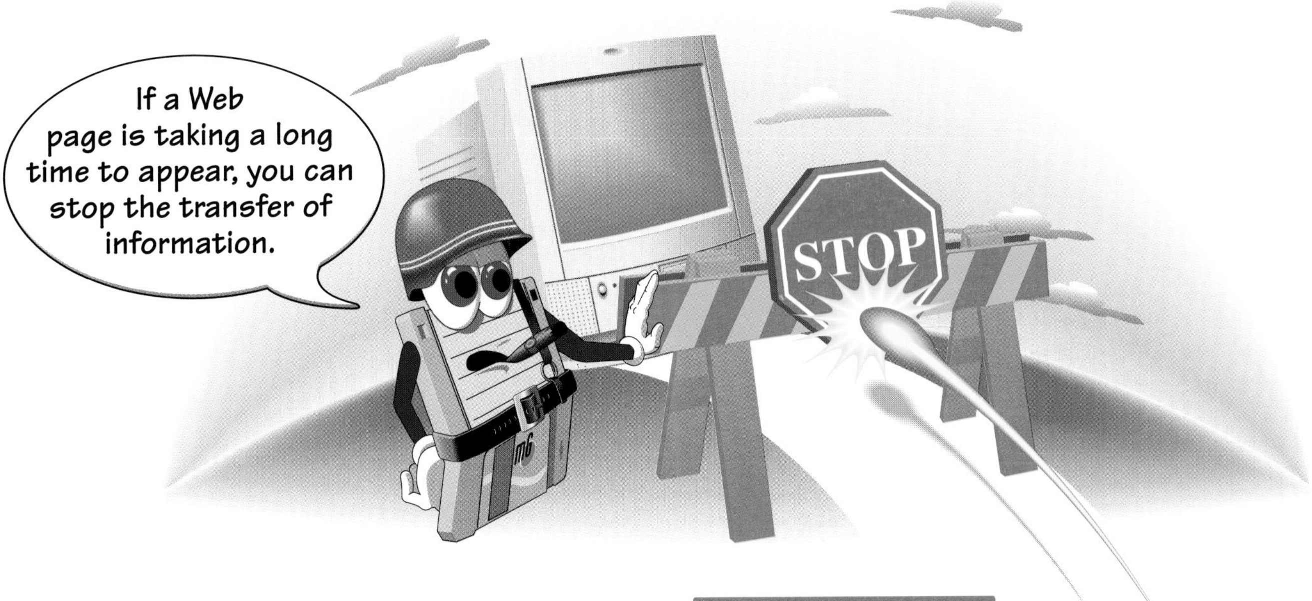

If a Web page is taking a long time to appear, you can stop the transfer of information.
STOP

STOP THE CONNECTION

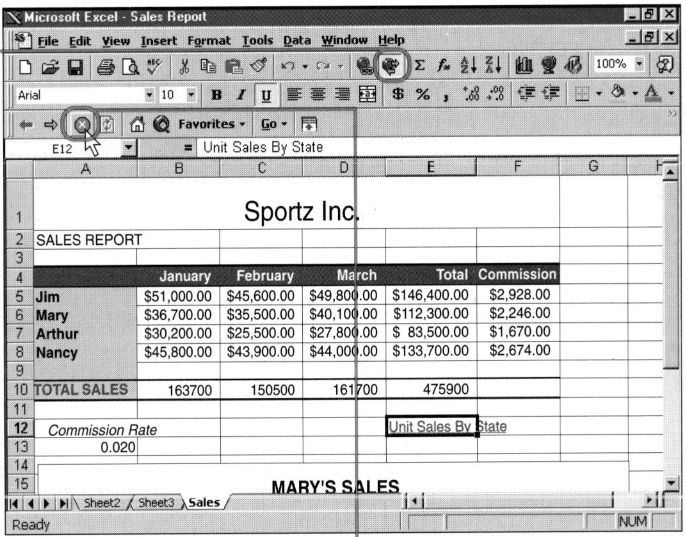

■ The document appears.

■ If you typed a Web page address in step 4, your Web browser opens and displays the Web page.

1 To display the **Web** toolbar, move the mouse over the Web toolbar button and then press the left mouse button.

■ The **Stop** button is red when information is transferring to your computer.

2 To stop the transfer of information, move the mouse over the Stop button and then press the left mouse button (the button changes to gray).

DISPLAY THE START PAGE

The start page includes instructions and hyperlinks that let you quickly connect to interesting documents.

DISPLAY THE START PAGE

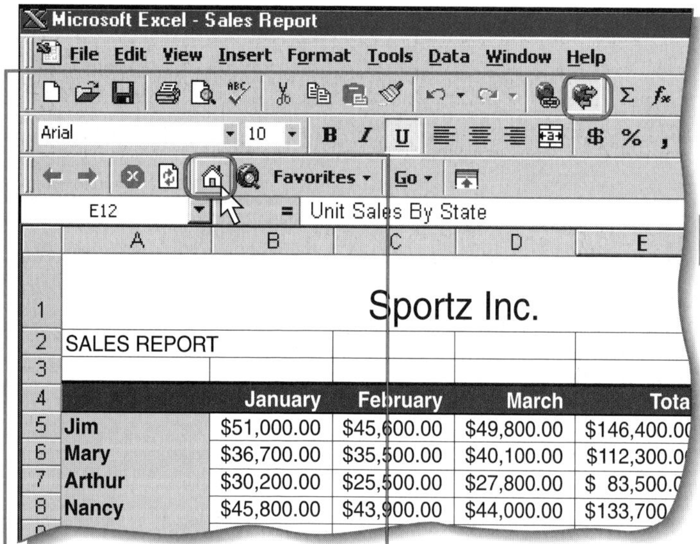

1 To display the **Web** toolbar, move the mouse over the Web toolbar button and then press the left mouse button.

2 To display the start page, move the mouse over the Start Page button and then press the left mouse button.

■ Your Web browser opens and displays the start page.

■ This page is automatically set as your start page.

DISPLAY THE SEARCH PAGE

DISPLAY THE SEARCH PAGE

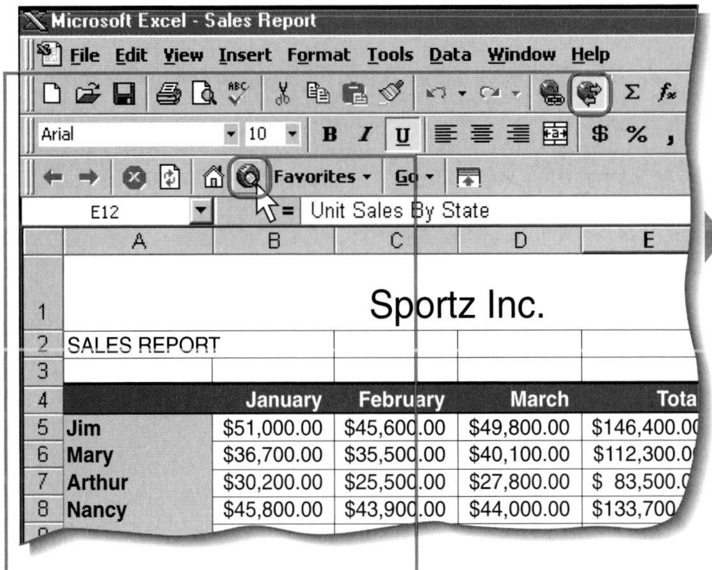

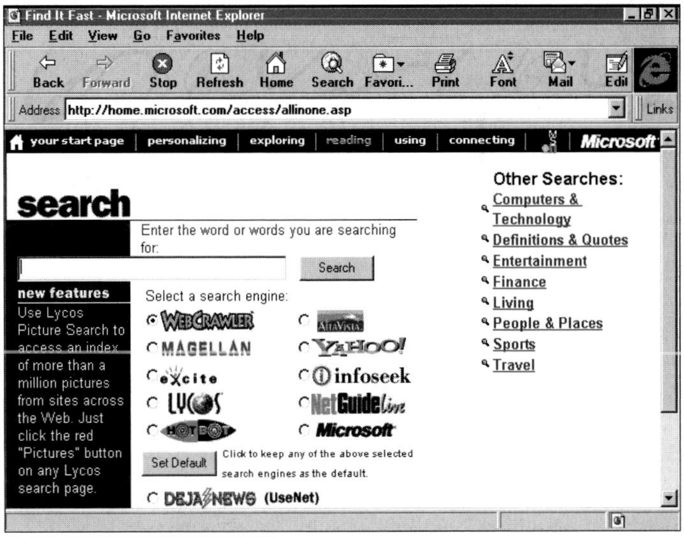

1 To display the **Web** toolbar, move the mouse over the toolbar button and then press the left mouse button.

2 To display the search page, move the mouse over the search button and then press the left mouse button.

■ Your Web browser opens and displays the search page.

■ This page is automatically set as your search page.

ADD WORKBOOK TO FAVORITES

ADD WORKBOOK TO FAVORITES

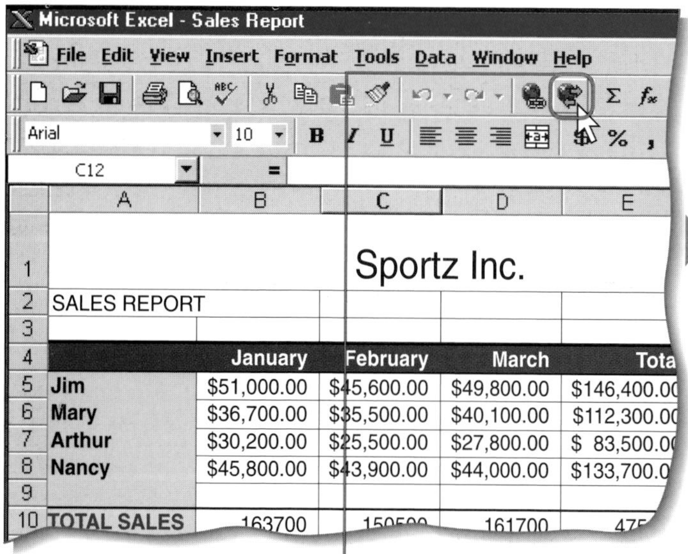

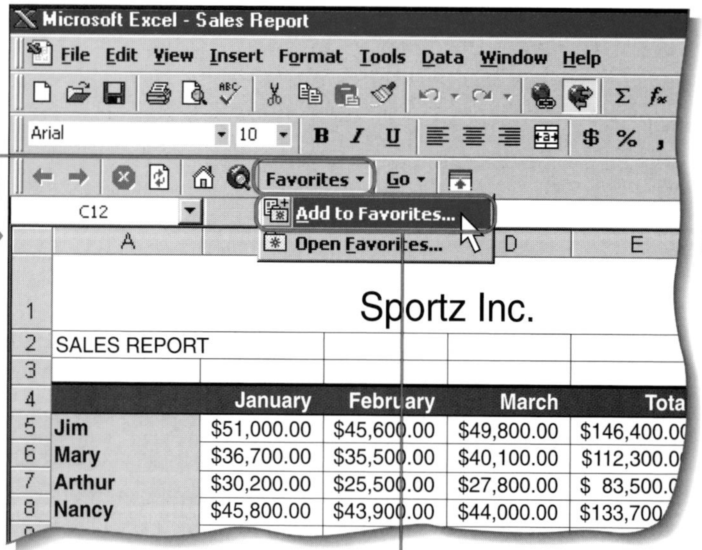

1 Open the workbook you want to add to the Favorites folder. To open a workbook, refer to page 32.

2 To display the **Web** toolbar, move the mouse over and then press the left mouse button.

3 Move the mouse over **Favorites** and then press the left mouse button.

4 Move the mouse over **Add to Favorites** and then press the left mouse button.

When I add a workbook to the Favorites folder, does the workbook change locations on my computer?

When you add a workbook to the Favorites folder, you create a shortcut to the original workbook. The original workbook does not change locations on your computer.

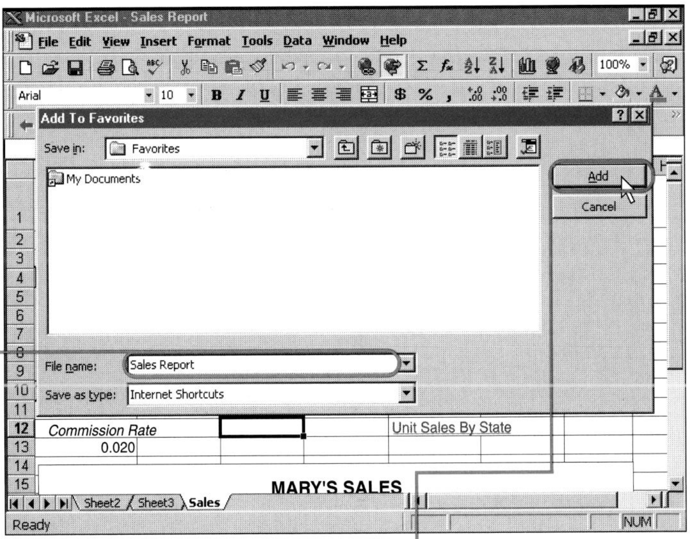

■ The **Add To Favorites** dialog box appears.

5 This area displays a name for the workbook. To change the name, type a new name.

6 Move the mouse over **Add** and then press the left mouse button.

OPEN WORKBOOK IN FAVORITES

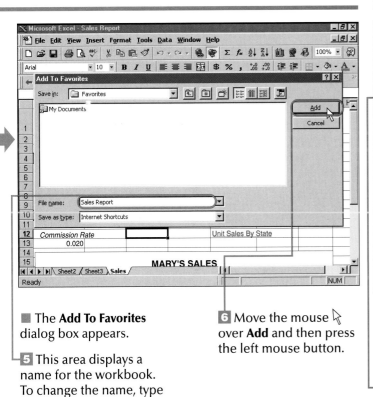

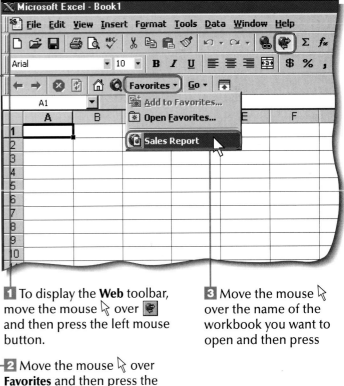

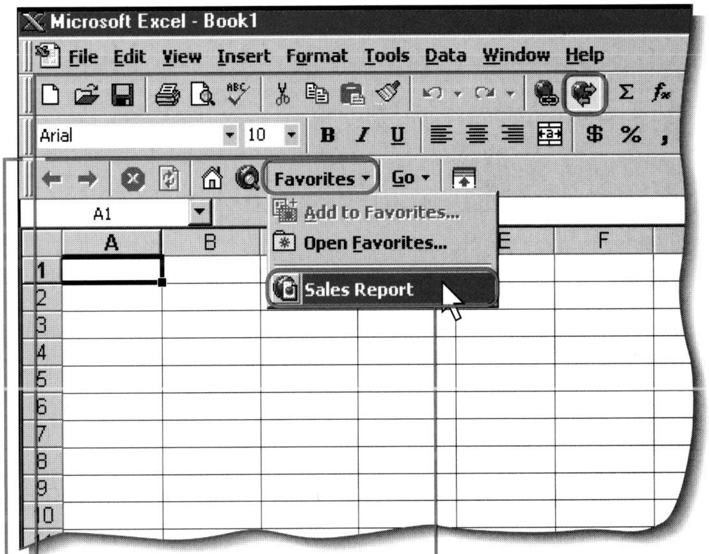

1 To display the **Web** toolbar, move the mouse over the Web toolbar button and then press the left mouse button.

2 Move the mouse over **Favorites** and then press the left mouse button.

3 Move the mouse over the name of the workbook you want to open and then press

SAVE INFORMATION AS A WEB PAGE

You can create a Web page from your worksheet data or chart. This lets you place the information on your company's intranet or the Web.
Web Page
Sportz Inc.

SAVE INFORMATION AS A WEB PAGE

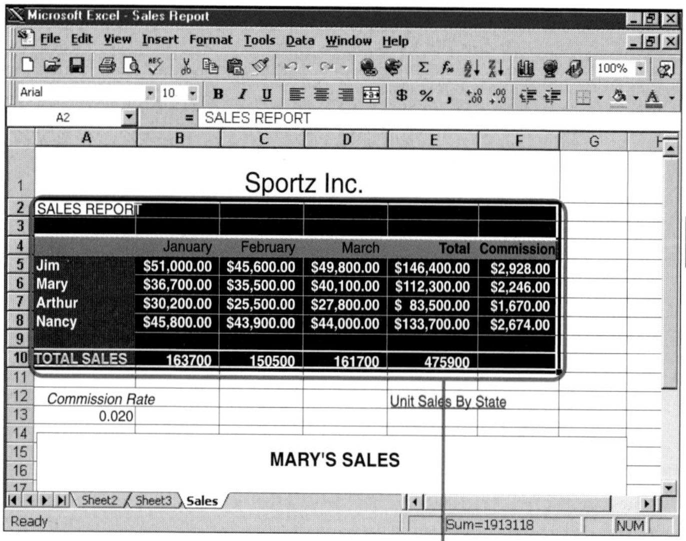

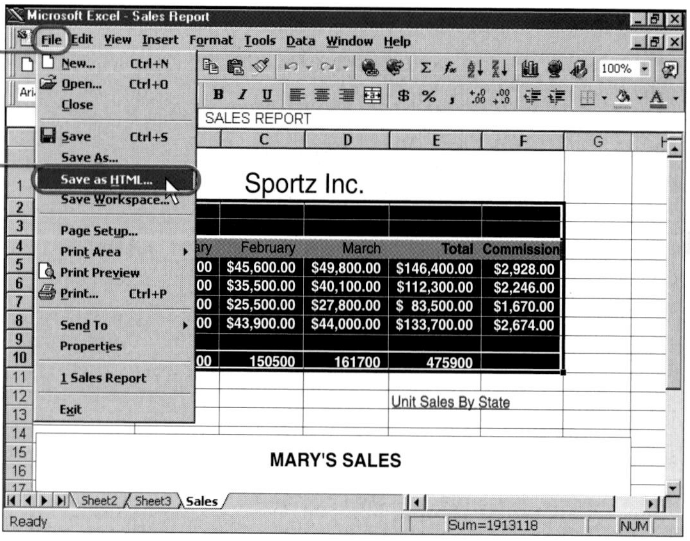

1 Open the workbook containing the information you want to save as a Web page. To open a workbook, refer to page 32.

2 Select the cells containing the information. To select cells, refer to page 16.

3 Move the mouse over **File** and then press the left mouse button.

4 Move the mouse over **Save as HTML** and then press the left mouse button.

Note: If the ***Save as HTML*** *command is not available, you need to add the Web Page Authoring (HTML) component from the Microsoft Excel or Microsoft Office CD-ROM disc.*

■ The **Internet Assistant Wizard** dialog box appears.

What is an intranet?

An intranet is a small version of the Internet inside a corporate office. Companies use intranets to distribute information such as monthly sales figures, phone directories and product listings.

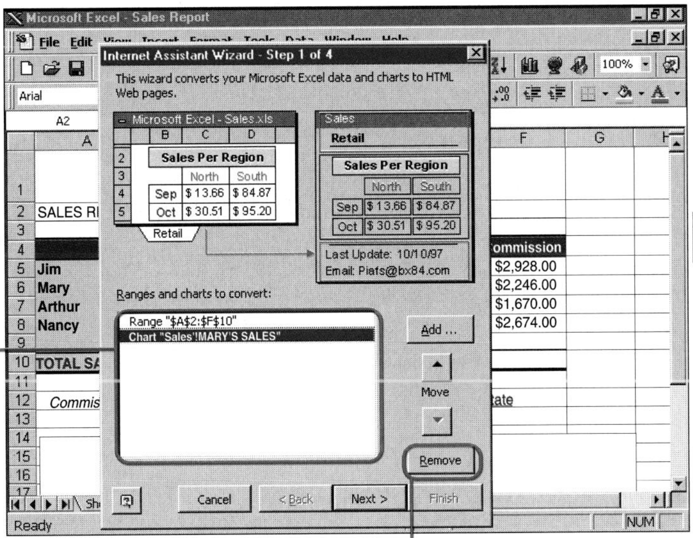

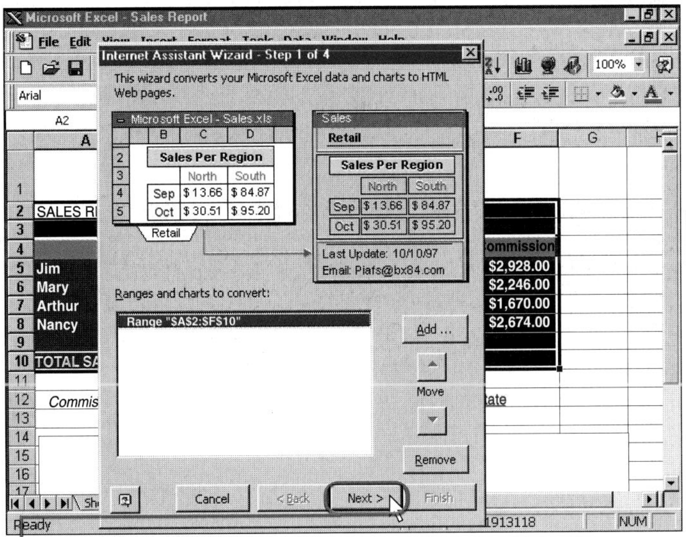

■ This area displays the cells you selected and every chart in your workbook.

5 If you do not want to include a chart on your Web page, move the mouse over the chart and then press the left mouse button.

6 To remove the chart from the list, move the mouse over **Remove** and then press the left mouse button.

7 To continue, move the mouse over **Next** and then press the left mouse button.

CONTINUED

SAVE INFORMATION AS A WEB PAGE

SAVE INFORMATION AS A WEB PAGE (CONTINUED)

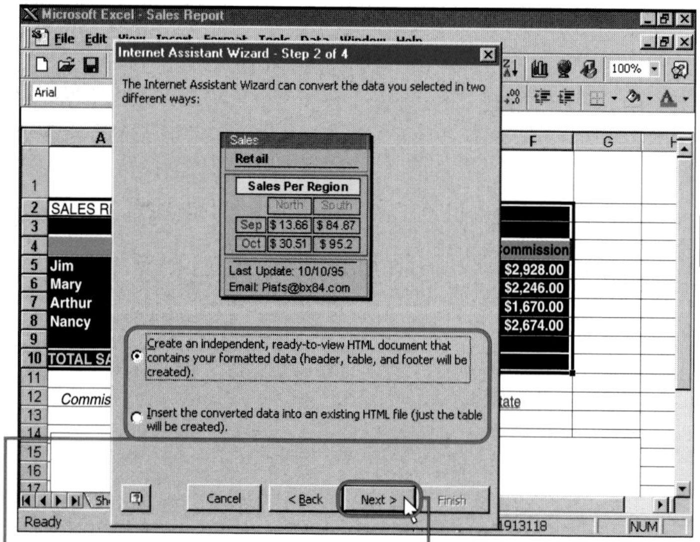

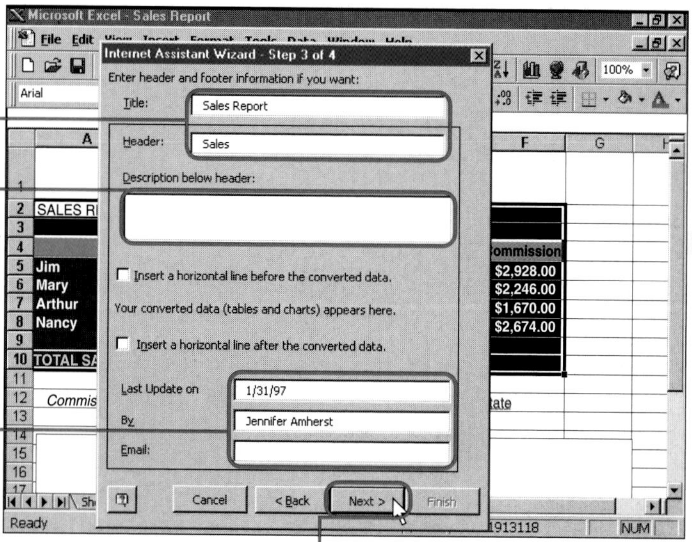

■ Excel asks if you want to create a new Web page or add the information to an existing Web page.

8 Move the mouse over the option you want to use and then press the left mouse button (○ changes to ◉).

9 To continue, move the mouse over **Next** and then press the left mouse button.

■ The information in these areas will appear on your Web page.

10 To enter information into an area, move the mouse I over the area and then press the left mouse button. Then type the information.

Note: If an area contains information you want to delete, move the mouse I over the area and then press the left mouse button. Then press **Backspace** *or* **Delete** *on your keyboard to remove the information.*

11 To continue, move the mouse over **Next** and then press the left mouse button.

How can I view the Web page I created?

You can use a Web browser, such as Internet Explorer, to view a Web page you created.

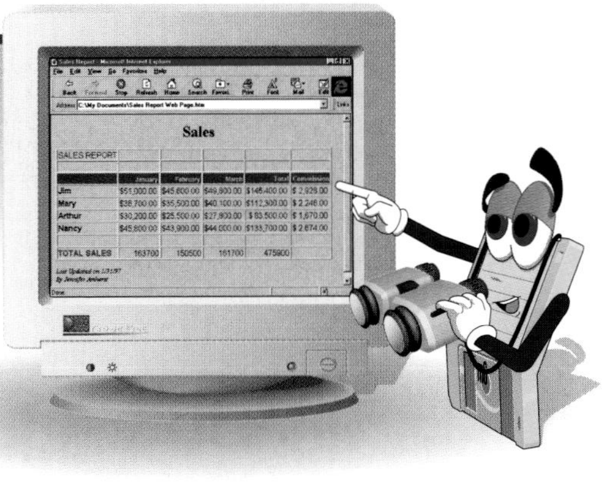

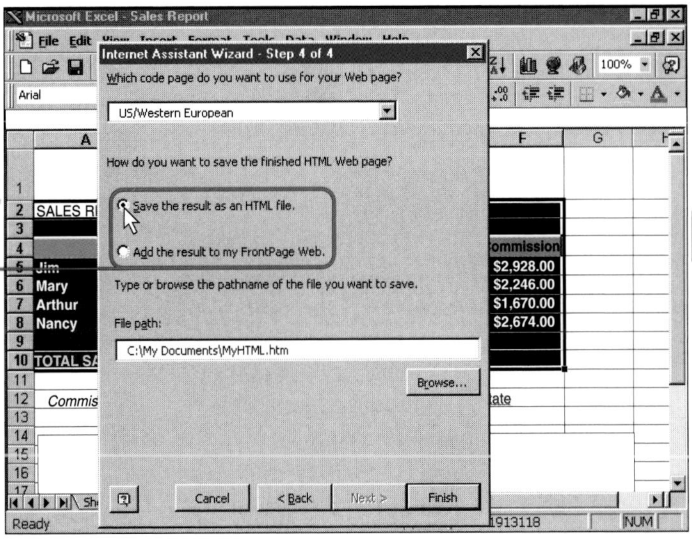

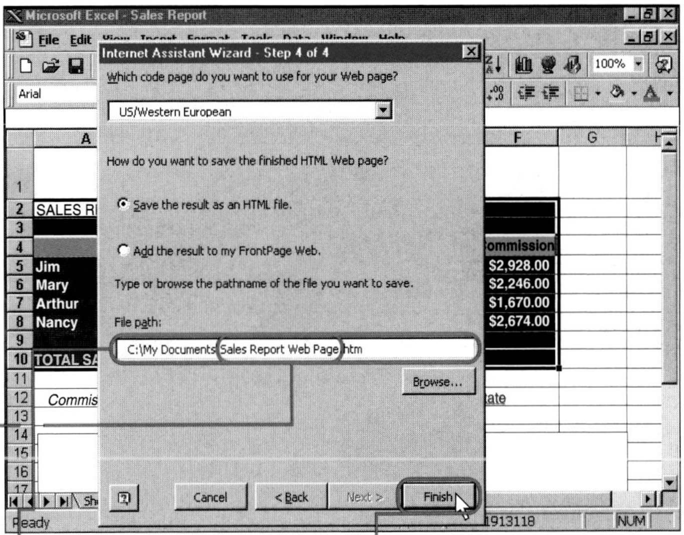

12 Move the mouse over the way you want to save the Web page and then press the left mouse button (O changes to ◉).

Note: If you do not have FrontPage, save the result as an HTML file.

■ This area displays the location and name of the Web page.

13 To change the name of the Web page, move the mouse I over the name and then quickly press the left mouse button twice. Then type a new name.

14 To create the Web page, move the mouse over **Finish** and then press the left mouse button.

INDEX

SALES REPORT
January
February
March
Jim 50000 45600 49800
Mary 36700 35500 40100
Arthur 30200 25500 27800
Nancy 45800 43900 44000
TOTAL SALES

D

E

INDEX

Sportz Inc.
UNIT SALES BY STATE
California 11200
New York 7960
Texas 3049
Utah 2098
24327

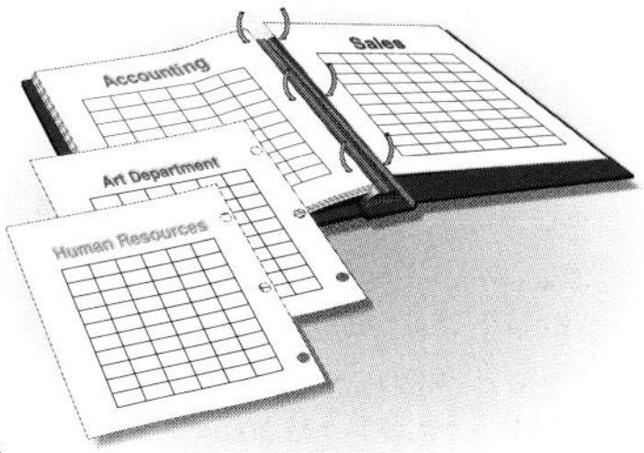

Accounting
Sales
Art Department
Human Resources

maranGraphics
COMPUTER BOOKS

O V E R 3 , 0 0 0 , 0 0 0 S A T I S F I E D U S E R S

OTHER 3-D Visual™ SERIES

SIMPLIFIED SERIES

Windows 95 Simplified
ISBN 1-56884-662-2
$19.99 USA/£18.99 UK

More Windows 95 Simplified
ISBN 1-56884-689-4
$19.99 USA/£18.99 UK

Windows 3.1 Simplified
ISBN 1-56884-654-1
$19.99 USA/£18.99 UK

Word for Windows 95 Simplified
ISBN 1-56884-681-9
$19.99 USA/£18.99 UK

Word 6 For Windows Simplified
ISBN 1-56884-660-6
$19.99 USA/£18.99 UK

Microsoft Office 4.2 For Windows Simplified
ISBN 1-56884-673-8
$27.99 USA/£26.99 UK

Office 97 Simplified
ISBN 0-7645-6009-3
$29.99 USA/£28.99 UK

Creating Web Pages Simplified
ISBN 0-7645-6007-7
$24.99 USA/£23.99 UK

World Wide Web Color Yellow Pages Simplified
ISBN 0-7645-6005-0
$29.99 USA/£28.99 UK

Netscape 2 Simplified
ISBN 0-7645-6000-X
$19.99 USA/£18.99 UK

Computers Simplified, 3rd Edition
ISBN 0-7645-6008-5
$24.99 USA/£23.99 UK

3-D Visual Dictionary of Computing
ISBN 1-56884-678-9
$19.99 USA/£18.99 UK

WordPerfect 6.1 For Windows Simplified
ISBN 1-56884-665-7
$19.99 USA/£18.99 UK

Lotus 1-2-3 R5 For Windows Simplified
ISBN 1-56884-670-3
$19.99 USA/£18.99 UK

SIMPLIFIED BOOKS Also Available

Word 97 Simplified
ISBN 0-7645-6011-5
$24.99 USA/£23.99 UK

FOR CORPORATE ORDERS, PLEASE CALL: 800-469-6616

3-D VISUAL SERIES

from:
maranGraphics™ & IDG BOOKS

Visit our Web site at:
http://www.maran.com

Excel for Windows 95 Simplified
ISBN 1-56884-682-7
$19.99 USA/£18.99 UK

Excel 5 For Windows Simplified
ISBN 1-56884-664-9
$19.99 USA/£18.99 UK

Internet and World Wide Web Simplified
ISBN 1-56884-658-4
$19.99 USA/£18.99 UK

Computers Simplified, 2nd Edition
ISBN 1-56884-676-2
$19.99 USA/£18.99 UK

POCKETGUIDES

The Proven 3-D Visual Approach To Learning Computers In A Handy Pocket Size.

Windows 95 Visual PocketGuide
ISBN 1-56884-661-4
$14.99 USA/£13.99 UK

Word 6 For Windows Visual PocketGuide
ISBN 1-56884-666-5
$14.99 USA/£13.99 UK

ALSO AVAILABLE:

Windows 3.1 Visual PocketGuide
ISBN 1-56884-650-9
$14.99 USA/£13.99 UK

Excel 5 For Windows Visual PocketGuide
ISBN 1-56884-667-3
$14.99 USA/£13.99 UK

WordPerfect 6.1 For Windows Visual PocketGuide
ISBN 1-56884-668-1
$14.99 USA/£13.99 UK

Lotus 1-2-3 R5 For Windows Visual PocketGuide
ISBN 1-56884-671-1
$14.99 USA/£13.99 UK

This is what reviewers are saying about our books...

"We recommend them for any novice 10-90 and for school use, too."
—Franklynn Peterson & Judi K-Turkel, The Business Computer® Syndicated Column

"It's the easiest book on computers I've ever used."
—M.L. Podolsky, BUYLine

"Excellent—Superb!!! Pictures, excellent instructions, easy to understand and to follow. Great for beginners."
—Conley Graves, West Hollywood, California

TEACH YOURSELF BOOKS
ALSO AVAILABLE

Teach Yourself Windows 95 Visually
ISBN 0-7645-6001-8
$29.99 USA
£28.99 UK

Teach Yourself Computers & the Internet Visually
ISBN 0-7645-6002-6
$29.99 USA
£28.99 UK

Teach Yourself Office 97 Visually
ISBN 0-7645-6018-2
$29.99 USA
£28.99 UK

COMING SOON! **Teach Yourself Internet and WWW Visually - ISBN 0-7645-6020-4**

FOR CORPORATE ORDERS, PLEASE CALL: 800-469-6616

The fun & easy way to learn about computers and more!

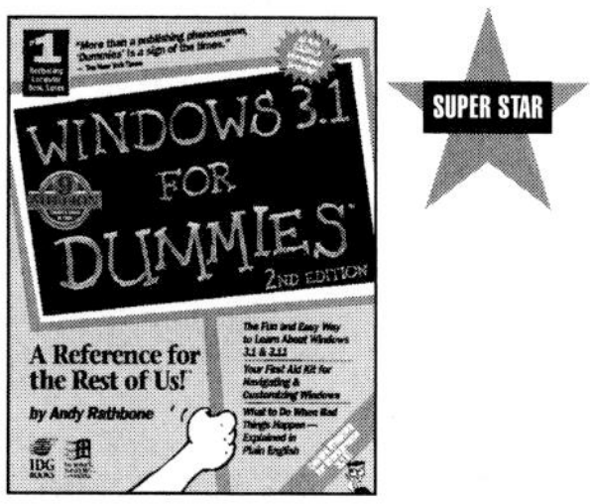

Windows 3.1 For Dummies,™ 2nd Edition
by Andy Rathbone

ISBN: 1-56884-182-5
$16.95 USA/$22.95 Canada

MORE Windows For Dummies™
by Andy Rathbone

ISBN: 1-56884-048-9
$19.95 USA/$26.95 Canada

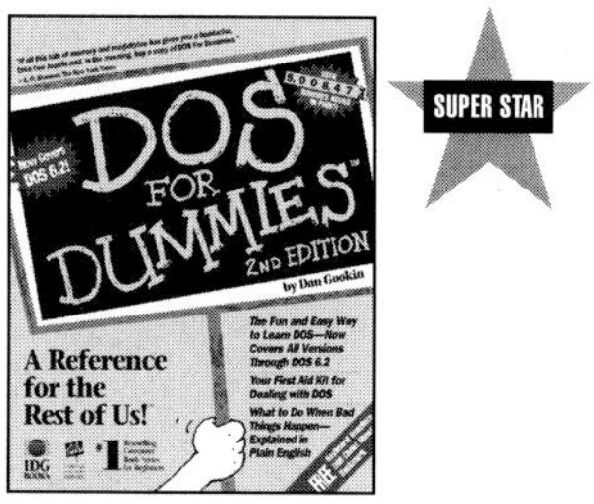

DOS For Dummies,® 2nd Edition
by Dan Gookin

ISBN: 1-878058-75-4
$16.95 USA/$22.95 Canada

The Internet For Dummies™
by John Levine & Carol Baroudi

ISBN: 1-56884-024-1
$19.95 USA/$26.95 Canada

Personal Finance For Dummies™
by Eric Tyson

ISBN: 1-56884-150-7
$16.95 USA/$22.95 Canada

PCs For Dummies,™ 2nd Edition
by Dan Gookin & Andy Rathbone

ISBN: 1-56884-078-0
$16.95 USA/$22.95 Canada

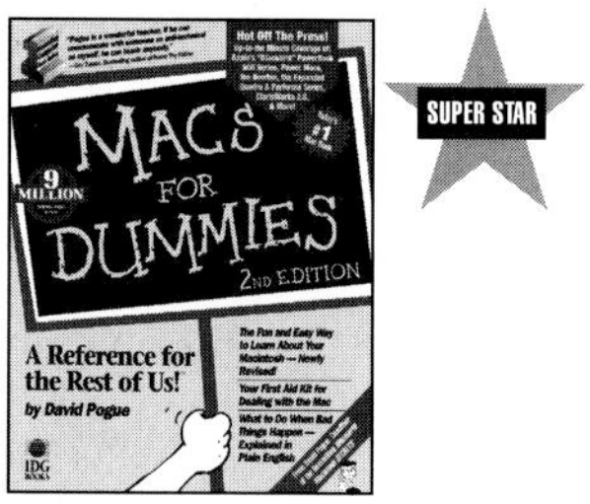

Macs For Dummies,™ 2nd Edition
by David Pogue

ISBN: 1-56884-051-9
$19.95 USA/$26.95 Canada

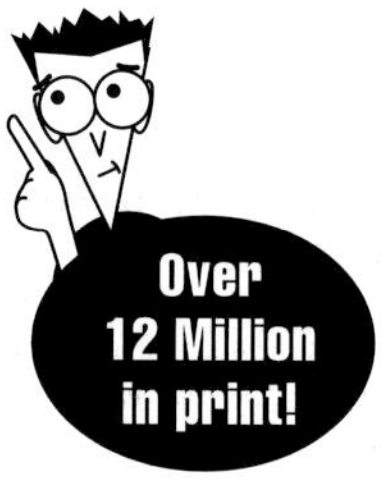

Here's a complete listing of IDG's...For Dummies Titles

Title	Author	ISBN #	Price
DATABASE			
Access 2 For Dummies™	by Scott Palmer	ISBN: 1-56884-090-X	$19.95 USA/$26.95 Canada
Access Programming For Dummies™	by Rob Krumm	ISBN: 1-56884-091-8	$19.95 USA/$26.95 Canada
Approach 3 For Windows For Dummies™	by Doug Lowe	ISBN: 1-56884-233-3	$19.99 USA/$26.99 Canada
dBASE For DOS For Dummies™	by Scott Palmer & Michael Stabler	ISBN: 1-56884-188-4	$19.95 USA/$26.95 Canada
dBASE For Windows For Dummies™	by Scott Palmer	ISBN: 1-56884-179-5	$19.95 USA/$26.95 Canada
dBASE 5 For Windows Programming For Dummies™	by Ted Coombs & Jason Coombs	ISBN: 1-56884-215-5	$19.99 USA/$26.99 Canada
FoxPro 2.6 For Windows For Dummies™	by John Kaufeld	ISBN: 1-56884-187-6	$19.95 USA/$26.95 Canada
Paradox 5 For Windows For Dummies™	by John Kaufeld	ISBN: 1-56884-185-X	$19.95 USA/$26.95 Canada
DESKTOP PUBLISHING/ILLUSTRATION/GRAPHICS			
CorelDRAW! 5 For Dummies™	by Deke McClelland	ISBN: 1-56884-157-4	$19.95 USA/$26.95 Canada
CorelDRAW! For Dummies™	by Deke McClelland	ISBN: 1-56884-042-X	$19.95 USA/$26.95 Canada
Harvard Graphics 2 For Windows For Dummies™	by Roger C. Parker	ISBN: 1-56884-092-6	$19.95 USA/$26.95 Canada
PageMaker 5 For Macs For Dummies™	by Galen Gruman & Deke McClelland	ISBN: 1-56884-178-7	$19.95 USA/$26.95 Canada
PageMaker 5 For Windows For Dummies™	by Deke McClelland & Galen Gruman	ISBN: 1-56884-160-4	$19.95 USA/$26.95 Canada
QuarkXPress 3.3 For Dummies™	by Galen Gruman & Barbara Assadi	ISBN: 1-56884-217-1	$19.99 USA/$26.99 Canada
FINANCE/PERSONAL FINANCE/TEST TAKING REFERENCE			
QuickBooks "X" For Dummies™	by Stephen L. Nelson	ISBN: 1-56884-227-9	$19.99 USA/$26.99 Canada
Quicken "X" For DOS For Dummies™, 2nd Edition	by Stephen L. Nelson	ISBN: 1-56884-210-4	$19.95 USA/$26.95 Canada
Quicken "X" For Macs For Dummies™	by Stephen L. Nelson	ISBN: 1-56884-211-2	$19.95 USA/$26.95 Canada
Quicken "X" For Windows For Dummies™, 2nd Edition	by Stephen L. Nelson	ISBN: 1-56884-209-0	$19.95 USA/$26.95 Canada
The SAT I For Dummies™	by Suzee Vlk	ISBN: 1-56884-213-9	$14.99 USA/$20.99 Canada
TurboTax For Windows For Dummies™	by Gail A. Perry, CPA	ISBN: 1-56884-228-7	$19.99 USA/$26.99 Canada
GROUPWARE/INTEGRATED			
Lotus Notes 3.0/3.1 For Dummies™	by Paul Freeland & Stephen Londergan	ISBN: 1-56884-212-0	$19.95 USA/$26.95 Canada
Microsoft Office 4 For Windows For Dummies™	by Roger C. Parker	ISBN: 1-56884-183-3	$19.95 USA/$26.95 Canada
Microsoft Works For Windows 3 For Dummies™	by David C. Kay	ISBN: 1-56884-214-7	$19.99 USA/$26.99 Canada

Title	Author	ISBN #	Price
INTERNET/COMMUNICATIONS/NETWORKING			
CompuServe For Dummies™	by Wallace Wang	ISBN: 1-56884-181-7	$19.95 USA/$26.95 Canada
Modems For Dummies™, 2nd Edition	by Tina Rathbone	ISBN: 1-56884-223-6	$19.99 USA/$26.99 Canada
Modems For Dummies™	by Tina Rathbone	ISBN: 1-56884-001-2	$19.95 USA/$26.95 Canada
MORE Internet For Dummies™	by John Levine & Margaret Levine Young	ISBN: 1-56884-164-7	$19.95 USA/$26.95 Canada
NetWare For Dummies™	by Ed Tittel & Deni Connor	ISBN: 1-56884-003-9	$19.95 USA/$26.95 Canada
Networking For Dummies™	by Doug Lowe	ISBN: 1-56884-079-9	$19.95 USA/$26.95 Canada
ProComm Plus 2 For Windows For Dummies™	by Wallace Wang	ISBN: 1-56884-219-8	$19.99 USA/$26.99 Canada
The Internet Help Desk For Dummies™	by John Kaufeld	ISBN: 1-56884-238-4	$16.99 USA/$22.99 Canada
The3 Internet For Dummies™, 2nd Edition	by John Levine & Carol Baroudi	ISBN: 1-56884-222-8	$19.99 USA/$26.99 Canada
The Internet For Macs For Dummies™	by Charles Seiter	ISBN: 1-56884-184-1	$19.95 USA/$26.95 Canada
MACINTOSH			
Mac Programming For Dummies™	by Dan Parks Sydow	ISBN: 1-56884-173-6	$19.95 USA/$26.95 Canada
Macintosh System 7.5 For Dummies™	by Bob LeVitus	ISBN: 1-56884-197-3	$19.95 USA/$26.95 Canada
MORE Macs For Dummies™	by David Pogue	ISBN: 1-56884-087-X	$19.95 USA/$26.95 Canada
PageMaker 5 For Macs For Dummies™	by Galen Gruman & Deke McClelland	ISBN: 1-56884-178-7	$19.95 USA/$26.95 Canada
QuarkXPress 3.3 For Dummies™	by Galen Gruman & Barbara Assadi	ISBN: 1-56884-217-1	$19.99 USA/$26.99 Canada
Upgrading and Fixing Macs For Dummies™	by Kearney Rietmann & Frank Higgins	ISBN: 1-56884-189-2	$19.95 USA/$26.95 Canada
MULTIMEDIA			
Multimedia & CD-ROMs For Dummies™, Interactive Multimedia Value Pack	by Andy Rathbone	ISBN: 1-56884-225-2	$29.95 USA/$39.95 Canada
Multimedia & CD-ROMs For Dummies™	by Andy Rathbone	ISBN: 1-56884-089-6	$19.95 USA/$26.95 Canada
OPERATING SYSTEMS/DOS			
MORE DOS For Dummies™	by Dan Gookin	ISBN: 1-56884-046-2	$19.95 USA/$26.95 Canada
S.O.S. For DOS™	by Katherine Murray	ISBN: 1-56884-043-8	$12.95 USA/$16.95 Canada
OS/2 For Dummies™	by Andy Rathbone	ISBN: 1-878058-76-2	$19.95 USA/$26.95 Canada
UNIX			
UNIX For Dummies™	by John Levine & Margaret Levine Young	ISBN: 1-878058-58-4	$19.95 USA/$26.95 Canada
WINDOWS			
S.O.S. For Windows™	by Katherine Murray	ISBN: 1-56884-045-4	$12.95 USA/$16.95 Canada
Windows "X" For Dummies™, 3rd Edition	by Andy Rathbone	ISBN: 1-56884-240-6	$19.99 USA/$26.99 Canada
PCS/HARDWARE			
Illustrated Computer Dictionary For Dummies™	by Dan Gookin, Wally Wang, & Chris Van Buren	ISBN: 1-56884-004-7	$12.95 USA/$16.95 Canada
Upgrading and Fixing PCs For Dummies™	by Andy Rathbone	ISBN: 1-56884-002-0	$19.95 USA/$26.95 Canada
PRESENTATION/AUTOCAD			
AutoCAD For Dummies™	by Bud Smith	ISBN: 1-56884-191-4	$19.95 USA/$26.95 Canada
PowerPoint 4 For Windows For Dummies™	by Doug Lowe	ISBN: 1-56884-161-2	$16.95 USA/$22.95 Canada
PROGRAMMING			
Borland C++ For Dummies™	by Michael Hyman	ISBN: 1-56884-162-0	$19.95 USA/$26.95 Canada
"Borland's New Language Product" For Dummies™	by Neil Rubenking	ISBN: 1-56884-200-7	$19.95 USA/$26.95 Canada
C For Dummies™	by Dan Gookin	ISBN: 1-878058-78-9	$19.95 USA/$26.95 Canada
C++ For Dummies™	by S. Randy Davis	ISBN: 1-56884-163-9	$19.95 USA/$26.95 Canada
Mac Programming For Dummies™	by Dan Parks Sydow	ISBN: 1-56884-173-6	$19.95 USA/$26.95 Canada
QBasic Programming For Dummies™	by Douglas Hergert	ISBN: 1-56884-093-4	$19.95 USA/$26.95 Canada
Visual Basic "X" For Dummies™, 2nd Edition	by Wallace Wang	ISBN: 1-56884-230-9	$19.99 USA/$26.99 Canada
Visual Basic 3 For Dummies™	by Wallace Wang	ISBN: 1-56884-076-4	$19.95 USA/$26.95 Canada
SPREADSHEET			
1-2-3 For Dummies™	by Greg Harvey	ISBN: 1-878058-60-6	$16.95 USA/$22.95 Canada
1-2-3 For Windows 5 For Dummies™, 2nd Edition	by John Walkenbach	ISBN: 1-56884-216-3	$16.95 USA/$22.95 Canada
1-2-3 For Windows For Dummies™	by John Walkenbach	ISBN: 1-56884-052-7	$16.95 USA/$22.95 Canada
Excel 5 For Macs For Dummies™	by Greg Harvey	ISBN: 1-56884-186-8	$19.95 USA/$26.95 Canada
Excel For Dummies™, 2nd Edition	by Greg Harvey	ISBN: 1-56884-050-0	$16.95 USA/$22.95 Canada
MORE Excel 5 For Windows For Dummies™	by Greg Harvey	ISBN: 1-56884-207-4	$19.95 USA/$26.95 Canada
Quattro Pro 6 For Windows For Dummies™	by John Walkenbach	ISBN: 1-56884-174-4	$19.95 USA/$26.95 Canada
Quattro Pro For DOS For Dummies™	by John Walkenbach	ISBN: 1-56884-023-3	$16.95 USA/$22.95 Canada
UTILITIES			
Norton Utilities 8 For Dummies™	by Beth Slick	ISBN: 1-56884-166-3	$19.95 USA/$26.95 Canada
VCRS/CAMCORDERS			
VCRs & Camcorders For Dummies™	by Andy Rathbone & Gordon McComb	ISBN: 1-56884-229-5	$14.99 USA/$20.99 Canada
WORD PROCESSING			
Ami Pro For Dummies™	by Jim Meade	ISBN: 1-56884-049-7	$19.95 USA/$26.95 Canada
More Word For Windows 6 For Dummies™	by Doug Lowe	ISBN: 1-56884-165-5	$19.95 USA/$26.95 Canada
MORE WordPerfect 6 For Windows For Dummies™	by Margaret Levine Young & David C. Kay	ISBN: 1-56884-206-6	$19.95 USA/$26.95 Canada
MORE WordPerfect 6 For DOS For Dummies™	by Wallace Wang, edited by Dan Gookin	ISBN: 1-56884-047-0	$19.95 USA/$26.95 Canada
S.O.S. For WordPerfect™	by Katherine Murray	ISBN: 1-56884-053-5	$12.95 USA/$16.95 Canada
Word 6 For Macs For Dummies™	by Dan Gookin	ISBN: 1-56884-190-6	$19.95 USA/$26.95 Canada
Word For Windows 6 For Dummies™	by Dan Gookin	ISBN: 1-56884-075-6	$16.95 USA/$22.95 Canada
Word For Windows 2 For Dummies™	by Dan Gookin	ISBN: 1-878058-86-X	$16.95 USA/$22.95 Canada
WordPerfect 6 For Dummies™	by Dan Gookin	ISBN: 1-878058-77-0	$16.95 USA/$22.95 Canada
WordPerfect For Dummies™	by Dan Gookin	ISBN: 1-878058-52-5	$16.95 USA/$22.95 Canada
WordPerfect For Windows For Dummies™	by Margaret Levine Young & David C. Kay	ISBN: 1-56884-032-2	$16.95 USA/$22.95 Canada

FOR MORE INFO OR TO ORDER, PLEASE CALL ▸ 800 . 762 . 2974 For volume discounts & special orders please call Tony Real, Special Sales, at 415. 312. 0644

ORDER FORM

TRADE & INDIVIDUAL ORDERS
Phone: **(800) 762-2974**
or **(317) 895-5200**
(8 a.m.–6 p.m., CST, weekdays)
FAX : **(317) 895-5298**

EDUCATIONAL ORDERS & DISCOUNTS
Phone: **(800) 434-2086**
(8:30 a.m.–5:00 p.m., CST, weekdays)
FAX : **(817) 251-8174**

CORPORATE ORDERS FOR 3-D VISUAL™ SERIES
Phone: **(800) 469-6616**
(8 a.m.–5 p.m., EST, weekdays)
FAX : **(905) 890-9434**

Qty	ISBN	Title	Price	Total

Shipping & Handling Charges

	Description	First book	Each add'l. book	Total
Domestic	Normal	$4.50	$1.50	$
	Two Day Air	$8.50	$2.50	$
	Overnight	$18.00	$3.00	$
International	Surface	$8.00	$8.00	$
	Airmail	$16.00	$16.00	$
	DHL Air	$17.00	$17.00	$

Subtotal ______

CA residents add applicable sales tax ______

IN, MA and MD residents add 5% sales tax ______

IL residents add 6.25% sales tax ______

RI residents add 7% sales tax ______

TX residents add 8.25% sales tax ______

Shipping ______

Total ______

Ship to:

Name ______

Address ______

Company ______

City/State/Zip ______

Daytime Phone ______

Payment: □ Check to IDG Books (US Funds Only)
□ Visa □ Mastercard □ American Express

Card # ______ Exp. ______ Signature ______

maranGraphics™